Little River

Little River

An Overview of Cultural Resources for the Rio Antiguo Feasibility Study, Pima County, Arizona

Scott O'Mack, Scott Thompson, and Eric Eugene Klucas
with contributions by Pamela Asbury-Smith, Karry L. Blake,
Rebecca M. Dean, Jeffrey A. Homburg, and Thomas E. Tolley

Prepared for the
Pima County Administrator's Office
Archaeology and Historic Preservation
201 N. Stone Ave., 7th floor
Tucson, AZ 85701-1207

Contract No. 16-04-S-125897-0599, Work Order No. 5RCERT
Contract No. 25-04-S-133807-0104, Work Order No. 5RCERT

Technical Series 82
Statistical Research, Inc.
Tucson, Arizona

Statistical Research Technical Series

Series editor: Jeffrey H. Altschul
Production manager: Toni Tallman
Graphics manager: Cynthia Elsner Hayward
Production assistants: Karen Barber, Peg Robbins

Cover design: Lynne Yamaguchi and Cynthia Elsner Hayward
Front cover photograph courtesy of Special Collections,
University of Arizona Library, Tucson, Ms. 280, box 13, folder 16.

This report was originally published as Technical Report 02-23.

Published by Statistical Research, Inc.
P.O. Box 31865
Tucson, AZ 85751-1865

ISBN 1-879442-81-7

First printing: July 2004
2 4 5 3 1

Typeset and printed in the United States of America.
Printed on acid-free paper.

CONTENTS

LIST OF FIGURES

LIST OF TABLES

ACKNOWLEDGMENTS

The authors extend their thanks to the many people who contributed to the Río Antiguo overview. We would especially like to acknowledge the various contributions of our colleagues at Statistical Research, Inc. Dr. Teresita Majewski, principal investigator for the overview, oversaw the research and writing of the overview and provided frequent and timely encouragement. Dr. Jeffrey Homburg, archaeologist and soil scientist, prepared the discussion of geology and archaeological potential that appears in Chapter 5. Pam Asbury-Smith helped pull together the General Land Office (GLO) information presented in Chapter 4 and also prepared the first draft of the GLO map. Rebecca Dean and Karry Blake carried out the site files research at the Arizona State Museum, and Rebecca wrote the first draft of the site descriptions. Tom Tolley helped edit the tables, the maps, and the references cited section and also tracked down a few hard-to-find sources. Chester Schmidt and Chris Rohe prepared the excellent oversize map included as an appendix with the overview. Cindy Elsner Hayward and Lois Kain made time in their busy schedules to prepare the numerous graphics. Heather Emslie proofread the final report. And the production team of Lynne Yamaguchi and Karen Barber assembled the drafts and final, complex and difficult tasks made even more difficult by the time constraints we placed on them.

For their valuable assistance in researching the history of the Río Antiguo study area, we would also like to thank: Mr. David Faust, director of the Old Fort Lowell Museum; the staff of the research library of the Arizona Historical Society in Tucson; and the staff of Special Collections at the University of Arizona Library in Tucson. Ms. Jeanne Turner of the Old Fort Lowell Neighborhood Association was also very helpful when we contacted her; unfortunately, a shortage of time prevented us from consulting the unpublished research files on the Fort Lowell area maintained by the association.

We would also like to acknowledge the assistance of Nathaniel "K. C." Nash of the Bureau of Land Management (BLM) Public Information Center in Phoenix. Mr. Nash, whose long experience with GLO records has been invaluable to us on several occasions, passed away unexpectedly during preparation of the overview. He was a model of efficiency and courtesy in providing us access to the GLO records maintained by the BLM, and it is sad that he is gone.

Finally, our thanks go to Roger Anyon, Cultural Resources Coordinator for Pima County and our contact for Río Antiguo. Roger, who happens to live in the Río Antiguo study area, has been helpful and understanding throughout the preparation of the overview.

CHAPTER 1

Introduction

In 2001, the Pima County (Arizona) Flood Control District and the U.S. Army Corps of Engineers (COE) initiated a joint project to address ecosystem, recreation, and flood control concerns along a stretch of the Rillito River between Craycroft Road and Campbell Avenue in Tucson. The project, christened El Río Antiguo, began with a feasibility study, including an overview of cultural resources in the vicinity of the project area. This report presents the results of the overview, conducted by Statistical Research, Inc. (SRI), of Tucson under contract to the Pima County Administrator's Office. It is intended as a baseline for the archaeological and historical research that may be prompted by construction for El Río Antiguo.

Project Setting

El Río Antiguo (hereafter, the Río Antiguo project) focuses on a river valley with a long history of human occupation. The Rillito River (sometimes called Rillito Creek; hereafter, simply the Rillito) is the principal stream in one of two major drainages in the Tucson Basin. The water it carries, now only seasonally, comes primarily from the Santa Catalina and Rincon Mountains, which border the basin on the north and east, respectively. The Rillito flows east to west along the southern foot of the Santa Catalinas, eventually draining into the Santa Cruz River about 8 miles northeast of downtown Tucson (Figure 1).

The Santa Cruz is the principal stream of the other major drainage in the Tucson Basin. Its source is in the Patagonia Mountains, just north of the border with Mexico. The Santa Cruz flows south to north along the western edge of the Tucson Basin before draining (seasonally) into the Gila River, some 60 miles from its source, not far from Phoenix. Because Spanish exploration of southern Arizona originated in Mexico and because the Santa Cruz Valley was long the main corridor for travel from Mexico into Arizona, the Santa Cruz River has always been considered the primary river of the Tucson Basin, and the Rillito has been considered its tributary. The much greater length of the Santa Cruz above the confluence of the two rivers supports this distinction and was perhaps the inspiration for the Spanish name for its evident tributary, the Rillito, the "Little River." The name has a certain appropriateness today, given that the Rillito is, much more often than not, completely dry, but the name belies the true character of the river. In his early study of the Rillito Valley, the engineer and geologist George E. P. Smith wrote,

> Only by courtesy can the Rillito be said to empty into the Santa Cruz, for the latter is but a brook compared with the raging floods of the former. At the junction of the two rivers the width of the Santa Cruz is 60 feet while the width of the Rillito . . . is 300 feet, and the river beyond has the appearance of being a continuation of the tributary [1910:118].

After a century of changes wrought by human and natural forces, the contrast between the two rivers at their confluence is not so great today, but even in Smith's day, the Rillito, like the Santa Cruz, was

1

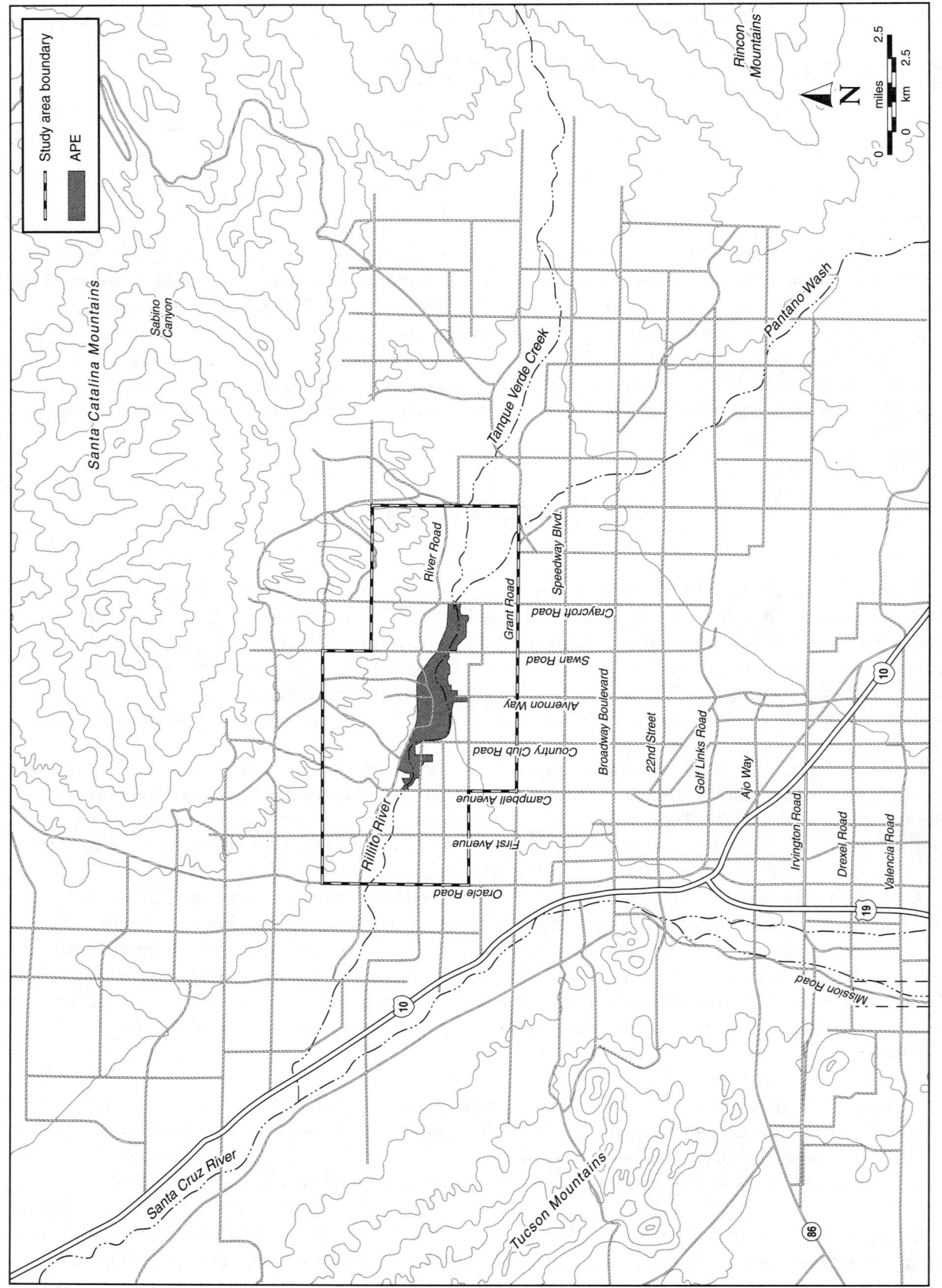

Figure 1. Map of Tucson, Arizona, and vicinity.

more often a "dwindling stream" than an implacable torrent, with a modest flow that rose and sank intermittently along its sandy course. The Rillito is fed by two streams that drain different parts of the Tucson Basin in different ways: Tanque Verde Creek, which has its source at the corner of the basin, where the Santa Catalina and Rincon Mountains meet, and Pantano Wash, which originates (under the name Cienega Creek) many miles south of the Rincons.

Smith was the first to note the differing contributions of the two tributaries. The flow in Tanque Verde Creek depends primarily on the rain and snowmelt of the adjacent mountains, to the degree that, as Smith (1910:120) discovered, the amount of rain falling in the Tucson Basin is generally unrelated to the amount of water flowing in Tanque Verde Creek. What matters instead is how much rain or snow is falling in the Santa Catalinas and Rincons, which are drained by numerous washes that feed into the creek. In general, the flow is greatest during the winter rains of November through March, but the modest year-round flow that once characterized the Rillito was also supplied by Tanque Verde Creek. Pantano Wash, on the other hand, experiences its greatest flow in the summer months, when the heavy rains of the monsoon season (July–September) are funneled down the wash from the eastern portion of the Tucson Basin and a vast area to the south and east. The contrast between the two tributaries is evident in a 1949 aerial photograph of the vicinity of their confluence, undoubtedly taken during the monsoon season (Figure 2). The bed of Tanque Verde Creek is conspicuously dry, but Pantano Wash is visible as a dark ribbon, its flow remaining discrete within the bed of the Rillito even somewhat west of the confluence.

Tanque Verde Creek, as a name for the stream that joins Pantano Wash to form the Rillito, is actually a recent application of a name that in Smith's day referred only to the portion of the creek upstream from its confluence with Agua Caliente Wash. The 5 miles of the creek from Agua Caliente Wash down to Pantano Wash were originally considered the first 5 miles of the Rillito, and descriptions of the Rillito and its tributaries by Smith and others in the nineteenth and early twentieth centuries follow that usage. We follow the modern usage throughout this overview and acknowledge the earlier usage only when necessary to avoid confusion.

Tanque Verde Creek was, in at least one way, more consequential to the history of the Río Antiguo study area than Pantano Wash, although the latter stream contributed more to the devastating floods in the Rillito during the historical period. Tanque Verde Creek, unlike Pantano Wash, originally had a substantial subsurface flow (or "underflow," as it was usually called), which was first tapped by farmers in the late nineteenth century and carried downstream by ditches and flumes to fields along the Rillito. The phenomenon of the underflow was a major focus of Smith's (1910) study of the Rillito Valley, which was intended both as a geological study and a guide to the most efficient agricultural use of water in the valley. In his study, Smith described two locations along Tanque Verde Creek where there was perennial flow: one at Tanque Verde itself, the "green tank," or natural reservoir, that gave the creek its name, located about 3 miles east of the mouth of Agua Caliente Wash, and one at the mouth of Ventana Canyon, about 2 miles upstream from the confluence of Tanque Verde Creek and Pantano Wash, near the point where Sabino Canyon Road now crosses the creek. At the latter location, the underflow of the valley was forced to the surface by the structure of the underlying sediments, then remained at or not far below the surface for about 2 miles, to just below the confluence with the Pantano. Smith called this 2-mile stretch of the creek "the Narrows," because the underflow here behaved in a manner analogous to "that of surface streams at constricted points" (1910:111). It was in the Narrows that farmers in the valley buried the heads of their ditches to take advantage of the underflow when their ditches with conventional heads ceased to carry water, which happened soon after the start of settlement in the valley.

Prior to Euroamerican settlement of the Rillito Valley, which began around 1860, the Rillito supported a lush riparian environment along its banks, just as the Santa Cruz River did during the same period. Smith described how he imagined the Rillito Valley looked four or five decades before his study. His description, which is based on unknown sources and probably somewhat idealized, is the only substantial one we have found of the valley as it was before 1860:

Figure 2. Aerial view of the vicinity of the confluence of
Tanque Verde Creek and Pantano Wash, 1949 (photograph courtesy
of the Arizona Historical Society, Tucson, Accession No. 18237).

The entire valley was at that time an unbroken forest, principally of mesquite, with a good growth of grama and other grasses between the trees. The river course was indefinite—a continuous grove of tall cottonwood, ash, willow, and walnut trees with underbrush and sacaton and galleta grass, and it was further obstructed by beaver dams. The vegetative covering on mountain slopes, on foothills and plains held the rainfall, causing a large proportion of it to be absorbed into the soil. Such portion as found its way to the river channel was retarded and controlled in its flow, and perhaps not oftener than a century did a master flood erode and sweep the river channel [Smith 1910:98].

In Smith's account, this primordial paradise disappeared shortly after the U.S. Army established Fort Lowell in 1873 just south of the confluence of Tanque Verde Creek and Pantano Wash. The settlers that followed the Army to the valley cut down the trees, plowed the floodplain, and let livestock graze the grasses to oblivion. Soon, the erosion of fields and trails led to accelerated runoff, and "[n]ew and un-usual floods cut out a wide channel, washed the cottonwoods away, and exposed the white sand." By the 1890s, "the present deep broad wash" of the Rillito was established (Smith 1910:98).

If the Rillito was well incised and prone to floods by Smith's time, it became only more so in the years that followed. Major floods occurred with disturbing frequency over the next 70 years, culminating in one of the river's largest recorded floods in October 1983. The water table in the Rillito Valley, like that of the Tucson Basin as a whole, dropped steadily, and the once-lush riparian environment of the valley disappeared (see Ciolek-Torrello and Homburg [1990:10–11] for a summary of flood and channel history). The Rillito floodplain continued to be farmed, but by 1930 or so the underflow had sunk out of reach and fields were watered almost exclusively by wells. Today, the agricultural landscape that re-placed the original riparian environment of the Rillito Valley has itself largely disappeared, and the valley has become, in its entirety, a part of greater Tucson.

The Area of Potential Effects and the Study Area

The area of potential effects (APE) for the Río Antiguo project corresponds closely with the Rillito floodplain between Craycroft Road and Campbell Avenue, with the addition of small, immediately adjacent areas of the Santa Catalina foothills (see Figure 1). The study area for the current overview encompasses all of the Río Antiguo APE, plus a much larger area defined by arbitrary distances from the Rillito. The eastern and western limits of the study area are 2 miles from the eastern and western limits of the APE, or at Sabino Canyon and Oracle Roads, respectively. The northern and southern limits of the study area correspond to the section lines that are at least 1 mile but no more than 2 miles from the channel of the Rillito. This places the northern limit of the study area in the lower Santa Catalina foot-hills and the southern limit in the north-central portion of Tucson. The study area boundary was estab-lished primarily to limit the scope of our archaeological site files search and our review of General Land Office (GLO) transactions. We expand our discussion beyond the boundary many times in the overview, as required by the subject matter.

Organization of the Overview

The overview consists of five chapters, including this introduction. Chapter 2 is a brief history of archaeological, historical, and ethnographic research on southern Arizona, outlining a context for future research in the Río Antiguo study area. Chapter 3 is a survey of Native American culture history in southern Arizona, as documented both archaeologically and ethnographically, with an emphasis on the study area. Chapter 4 surveys Euroamerican culture history in the same region, with a similar emphasis on the study area. Chapter 5 presents our summary of information on previously recorded archaeological sites and archaeological survey coverage in the study area, including detailed descriptions of four archaeological sites (two prehistoric, two historical-period). The same chapter also includes a discussion of archaeological potential in the study area based on a consideration of geomorphology.

The overview has two appendixes. Appendix A is an oversize map of GLO transactions in the study area during the period 1880–1939. Appendix B consists of descriptions of previously recorded archaeological sites in the study area (excluding the four major sites described in Chapter 5). All archaeological site numbers appearing in Appendix B or in any other part of the overview are Arizona State Museum (ASM) numbers.

As a final note, we generally avoid the term "Papago" when referring to the Tohono O'odham or any aspect of their culture, out of respect for their own decision, in 1981, to change the name of their tribe from the Papago Indian Tribe to the Tohono O'odham Nation. However, we do use Papago when referring to historical entities such as the Papago Indian Reservation or to the pottery made by the Tohono O'odham in the historical period, for which archaeologists have long used a number of type names that include the word.

History of Research

This chapter outlines the history of research into the prehistory, history, and ethnography of the Río Antiguo study area. Our emphasis is on the place of the study area in the wider research context of southern Arizona culture history. As a part of the Tucson Basin, the Rillito Valley has been a focus of human life in southern Arizona for 10,000 years or more and has experienced most aspects of human use of the wider region. But the Rillito Valley was also essentially unoccupied for at least 150 years of the historical period, from approximately 1700 to 1850, and possibly for a century or more earlier. This hiatus in occupation encompassed the years of early and intensive interaction between the native peoples of the Tucson Basin and the missionaries and other representatives of Spanish culture, a period of major consequence in the history of southern Arizona and a subject of perennial interest to anthropologists and historians. The Río Antiguo study area has contributed only minimally and indirectly to this small but especially significant segment of southern Arizona culture history.

Other aspects of culture and history in the Río Antiguo study area compensate for the early-historical-period gap. During the many millennia of prehistory, the Rillito Valley experienced essentially the same complex sequence of occupation as the Santa Cruz Valley, the other, better-studied major valley in the Tucson Basin. And during the 150 years since historical-period settlement began in the Rillito Valley, it has experienced a uniquely significant set of events and processes, including the building of the only nineteenth-century U.S. military post in the Tucson Basin (Fort Lowell), the establishment of the only independent Mormon community in the basin (Binghampton), and the development of a system of gravity-fed irrigation without a substantial local parallel (the underflow ditches of Tanque Verde Creek).

Our goal in this chapter is to outline the context within which future archaeological, historical, and ethnographic research along the Río Antiguo study area will necessarily take place. We frequently mention individual cultural resources within the Río Antiguo study area, but we reserve discussion of the research carried out at individual sites in the study area for Chapter 5. In the same chapter, we provide an inventory of all previously identified cultural resources in the study area, a summary of previous cultural resource survey coverage, and a discussion of archaeological potential based on a geomorphological characterization of the study area.

The Archaeology of Prehistory

Two large, well-known prehistoric village sites, University Indian Ruin and the Hardy site, fall within the Río Antiguo study area. A variety of other, smaller prehistoric sites have also been recorded there, and it is likely that many more sites of a range of sizes and dates are still preserved on and adjacent to the floodplain of the Rillito. The prehistory of the Rillito Valley has not received the same degree of archaeological attention already paid to the Santa Cruz Valley, but it has the potential to help answer many of the same questions that have guided research along the Santa Cruz over the past several decades. In this section, we consider how the prehistory of the study area has been incorporated into interpretations of southern Arizona prehistory as a whole, and how archaeological research in the study area has influenced, and has been influenced by, archaeological research in the wider region.

Early Reconnaissance and Excavation in the Tucson Area

It did not constitute archaeological research in the strictest sense, but one of the earliest observations of prehistoric ruins in the Tucson Basin was made by Adolph Bandelier when he passed through the area in the 1880s en route to the Sierra Madre of Mexico. Bandelier noted the remains of "a few scattered houses of the detached dwelling type," located 16 miles east of Tucson at "Estanque Verde" (Bandelier 1890: 470–471). This likely refers to Tanque Verde Ruin, located approximately 15 km (9.3 miles) southeast of the study area at the confluence of Pantano Wash and Rincon Creek. He described the associated pottery as typical of southern Arizona. Bandelier also paid a visit to Fort Lowell, the U.S. Army post at the confluence of Pantano Wash and Tanque Verde Creek, and provided the first description of the prehistoric remains later named the Hardy site (AZ BB:9:14) (Gregonis 1997). Bandelier mentioned the presence of what were apparently the remains of a Classic period structure east of the fort. Since subsequent work at the Hardy site revealed no such features, it is likely that he was referring to the nearby University Indian Ruin (AZ BB:9:33), located across Pantano Wash approximately 1.5 km (0.93 mile) to the east (Gregonis 1997:5).

Some 30 years after Bandelier's brief visit, Ellsworth Huntington, an associate of the Carnegie Desert Laboratory at Tumamoc Hill, visited several major sites in the Tucson Basin, including several sites along the Rillito, among them the Hodges site (AZ AA:12:18). His most important contribution during these informal visits was his conclusion that the alluvial deposits along the major drainages were geologically recent. Huntington argued that there was a high likelihood of cultural deposits buried beneath the alluvium and that sites along the course of the major drainages, such as the Santa Cruz River, may not be readily visible on the surface. This hypothesis has been substantiated numerous times, perhaps most dramatically in recent excavations by Desert Archaeology, Inc., of Tucson along the Interstate 10 corridor (Gregory 1999; Mabry 1998; Mabry et al. 1997).

By the mid-1920s, more-formal archaeological investigations within the Tucson Basin were beginning to take place. Much of this early work was directed by Byron Cummings, then-head of the Department of Archaeology at the University of Arizona. In part as a way to provide training for students, Cummings directed excavations at several sites in the Tucson Basin, as well as reconnaissance surveys of the eastern portion of the basin. Sites investigated by Cummings and his students included Tanque Verde Ruin and University Indian Ruin. Work at the latter site continued intermittently into the 1930s under the direction of Emil Haury. More-extensive excavations were carried out in 1940–1941 under the direction of Julian Hayden, with aid from the National Park Service (NPS) and the Civilian Conservation Corps (Hayden 1957).

The Era of Private Research Institutions

The early 1920s saw the establishment of three private research institutions in Arizona that would have a profound impact on the course of archaeological research in the Southwest, including the Tucson Basin, for decades to come. The first was the Museum of Northern Arizona (MNA) in Flagstaff, founded by Harold S. Colton and Mary-Russell Colton in 1928. Established in part as a response to the archaeological activities of eastern institutions, which shipped most of their collections out of state, the MNA was dedicated to the art and science of northern Arizona, with a focus on the interdisciplinary study of human-land relationships. Perhaps the most enduring aspect of the early research of the MNA was the work on ceramic typology conducted by Colton and his colleague Lyndon Hargrave (Colton and

Hargrave 1937). This taxonomy, reflecting Colton's training as a biologist, remains the standard classificatory system for the ceramics of northern Arizona. Colton attempted to create a similar typology for the ceramic wares of southern Arizona, but poor health prevented him from completing this project.

The activities of the second private research institution had a more direct impact on southern Arizona. Gila Pueblo, founded in 1928 by Harold Gladwin and Winifred Macurdy (who later married Gladwin), focused much of its research efforts on the desert regions of the Southwest. Archaeologists from Gila Pueblo, led by E. B. Sayles, were the first to report on the Archaic cultures of southern Arizona. In their pursuit of the spatial boundaries of the "red-on-buff" culture, Gila Pueblo archaeologists scoured the greater Southwest, from Texas to California and from Utah to northern Mexico. In the Tucson Basin, much of this work was carried out by Frank Midvale (originally Mitalsky or Mittvalsky), who first recorded many of the large sites known today. This reconnaissance work by Gila Pueblo, along with pioneering excavations at such sites as Snaketown (Gladwin et al. 1937) and Roosevelt 9:6 (Haury 1932), both directed by Emil Haury, served to define the Hohokam culture.

One of the most important projects directed by Gila Pueblo in the Tucson Basin was the excavation of the Hodges site, located at the confluence of the Santa Cruz and Rillito Rivers. Work at this large village, then referred to as the Gravel Pit Ruin, was begun in 1936 under the direction of Carl Miller (Betancourt 1978a:7). Gila Pueblo began its work at the site in 1937, with Isabel Kelly directing the excavations. During the course of the project, Kelly noted the similarities and dissimilarities in the ceramic collection when compared with contemporaneous materials for the Phoenix Basin and, in response, developed a ceramic typology for the Tucson Basin that is still used today. Unfortunately, Kelly's tenure with Gila Pueblo ended in 1938, delaying the publication of her work. In the 1950s, James Officer, then a graduate student in the Department of Anthropology at the University of Arizona, began the work of compiling Kelly's document for publication, but he did not complete the task. The volume was finally edited by Gayle Hartmann and published as an Anthropological Paper of the University of Arizona in 1978 (Kelly 1978).

The same year that Gladwin and Macurdy established Gila Pueblo, William Shirley Fulton and Rose Hayden Fulton founded the last of the three privately funded institutions in the Southwest. The Amerind Foundation was established in Dragoon, Arizona, with the stated purpose "to increase the world's knowledge of ancient man by excavation and collection, by study and analysis, and to display and publish the resultant artifacts and data for public enlightenment" (Di Peso 1967). Fulton hired Carl Tuthill, then a student at the University of Arizona, to supervise the early field endeavors, including excavations at the Gleeson site (Fulton and Tuthill 1940). This work laid the foundation for the primary research focus of the Amerind Foundation—studying the cultural identity of the prehistoric inhabitants of southeastern Arizona.

The debate over the cultural identity of the prehistoric inhabitants of southeastern Arizona pitted the archaeologists of Gila Pueblo against their counterparts at the Amerind Foundation. The position of Gila Pueblo was that the early inhabitants of southeastern Arizona were Mogollon, a culture defined by Haury in 1936. Fulton, who had earlier proposed the term "Dragoon" to refer to archaeological materials observed in the vicinity of Texas Canyon, saw the prehistoric peoples of southeastern Arizona as "basically Hohokam with little Mogollon influence" (Fulton 1940:63). Later, Charles Di Peso, hired by Fulton to replace Tuthill at the Amerind Foundation, proposed a third alternative. Di Peso argued that rather than being a version of a previously identified archaeological culture, the prehistoric peoples of southeastern Arizona represented a discrete cultural tradition of their own, one he called O'otam. The O'otam, in Di Peso's view, occupied the nonriverine desert regions of southern Arizona. The Hohokam, he argued, were an immigrant group from Mexico that settled along the Salt and Gila Rivers, establishing large villages and extensive irrigation systems. The Hohokam culture "dominated" the O'otam until ca. A.D. 1300, when the Hohokam were forced back into Mexico and the O'otam reemerged during what became known as the Classic period (Di Peso 1956). Far from resolving the issue, Di Peso's proposal simply fueled the debate, with the competing positions becoming further entrenched.

Few excavations were conducted in the Tucson area during the 1940s, when archaeological investigations of the area were largely limited to surface reconnaissance. During this period, Emil Haury and his students surveyed much of the Empire Valley, the results of which were presented by Earl Swanson in a master's thesis (Swanson 1951). In 1941, Edward Danson conducted an archaeological survey along the Santa Cruz River from its headwaters north to the town of Tubac. These data also were presented in a master's thesis (Danson 1946). Nearly a decade later, Paul Frick extended the coverage of the Santa Cruz River valley through his survey of the middle reaches of the river from Tubac north to Sahuarita (Frick 1954).

In the late 1950s, Malcolm Rogers conducted an independent, informal archaeological survey along the terraces along the Rillito River and Pantano Wash. He selected these geologically old surfaces in the hopes of identifying traces of early occupation in the Tucson Basin contemporary with the San Dieguito and Amargosan cultures he defined for the desert regions of California and western Arizona (Rogers 1958). Dealing exclusively with surface finds, Rogers argued that the lithic material he observed was as old as the surface on which they were found. Although few archaeologists today accept the extreme antiquity of the materials identified by Rogers, they represent a clear Archaic period presence along the *bajada* of the Santa Catalina and Rincon Mountains.

The New Archaeology and Cultural Resource Management

The archaeological investigations described above were focused largely on addressing questions of culture history—defining the spatial parameters of archaeological "cultures" and building regional chronologies. This characterized American archaeology until the early 1960s, when, prompted in part by Walter W. Taylor's polemical 1948 publication *A Study of Archaeology,* several scholars began to extend the focus of archaeological research to include investigation of the processes whereby cultures adapted to their physical surroundings and how these adaptations changed through time. Under the general rubric of the "new archaeology," the study of cultural processes came to dominate American archaeology, influencing both the direction of research and the kinds of data that were collected and analyzed. Projects emphasized interdisciplinary research, with environmental data taking a prominent role in archaeological interpretation.

Concurrent with the ascendence of processual archaeology among American archaeologists was an equally important transition in how archaeological projects were selected and funded. Beginning with the Interagency Salvage Program of the NPS and the Reservoir Salvage Act of 1960 (King et al. 1977), federal monies became available for archaeological research. In 1955, the Arizona Highway Salvage program was established at ASM. For the next 26 years, archaeologists surveyed more than 2,000 linear miles of right-of-way (ROW) in advance of road construction and improvement, recording hundreds of cultural properties. Unfortunately, few of these sites were excavated, and reports on even fewer were fully published.

In 1965 and 1966, ASM engaged in salvage excavations at 10 sites in the southern portion of the Tucson Basin for the Arizona Highway Department under the auspices of the Arizona Highway Salvage program (Greenleaf 1975). All but two of these sites were within the San Xavier District of the Tohono O'odham Nation (then the Papago Indian Reservation), a few miles south of Mission San Xavier del Bac. Collectively referred to as Punta de Agua, the sites included both prehistoric and historical-period properties (Greenleaf 1975:11). Of the 10 sites, data recovery operations were conducted at six. Excavations at the prehistoric sites produced data that allowed for the refinement of the Tucson Basin ceramic chronology first proposed by Kelly from her work at the Hodges site (Greenleaf 1975). These data reinforced Kelly's observation of a divergence in ceramic traditions from the sequence established for the Gila Basin beginning with the Colonial period, insofar as the Tucson Basin materials shared characteristics of both the Gila Basin and the Mogollon area (Greenleaf 1975:108; Kelly 1978:3).

With the passage of the National Historic Preservation Act in 1966, the National Environmental Policy Act of 1969, and the Archaeological Resource Protection Act of 1979, the pace of contract archaeology accelerated in the American Southwest, because of both rapid growth and the extent of public lands. In response, cultural resource management (CRM) divisions were established at ASM, Arizona State University, and the MNA. Archaeologists were also added to the staffs of several federal agencies, including the Bureau of Land Management (BLM) and various national forests. With the enactment of CRM laws, archaeology in the United States became largely reactive in nature, with samples often dictated by management needs rather than research agendas. This being said, the increased pace of archaeological data collection and research prompted by the new legislation resulted in significant advances in our understanding of prehistory, especially in the traditionally overlooked areas of the desert Southwest.

The Tucson Basin was one of the areas that benefitted greatly from the expanded attention mandated by the new cultural resource laws. Many of the early CRM projects in the basin were surveys, greatly expanding the inventory of known sites. Beginning in the late 1970s, flood control modifications to several of the major drainages within the Tucson Basin conducted by the COE engendered several archaeological inventory, testing, and data recovery projects along the Rillito and other major drainages in and around Tucson. In the late 1970s, the COE contracted with the Cultural Resource Management Section of ASM to evaluate the impact of proposed flood control measures along eight of the major drainages, including sections of the Santa Cruz River near Marana and Continental, Rodeo Wash, Airport Wash, Cañada del Oro Wash, the Rillito, Pantano Wash, Tanque Verde Creek, and the Agua Caliente Wash (Gregonis and Huckell 1980). For the Rillito portion of the project, designated the Tucson Urban Study, ASM archaeologists investigated the entire reach of the drainage, from the confluence of Pantano Wash and Tanque Verde Creek to the Santa Cruz River. Four person-days were spent on field reconnaissance, which involved the relocation of 20 of the 23 previously identified sites within the project area (Gregonis and Huckell 1980:56). All but seven of the sites were relocated and evaluated; the remaining sites were located on private property and could not be inspected.

The archaeological properties investigated under the auspices of the Tucson Urban Study included 11 prehistoric sherd-and-lithic scatters, 10 Hohokam habitation sites (two of which contained historical-period ranching features), and the Valley of the Moon, a historical-period amusement park (Gregonis and Huckell 1980:62). The prehistoric sites reflected a range of occupation from A.D. 300 to the end of the prehistoric period (ca. A.D. 1450) and included two large village sites: the Sunset Mesa Ruin, a large late pre-Classic period site located at the confluence of the Rillito and the Santa Cruz (Ciolek-Torrello et al. 1999), and the Hardy site, a multicomponent Hohokam village site near the confluence of Tanque Verde Creek and Pantano Wash (Gregonis 1997). Despite decades of development along the investigated drainages, Gregonis and Huckell concluded that there was a high likelihood of intact cultural deposits at many of the sites and that considerable research potential remained.

With ASM's withdrawal from active CRM research in 1990, the burden for federal-, state-, and county-mandated archaeological work in southern Arizona fell largely to private firms. This work was accelerated through the enactment of new legislation at both the federal and state levels. In 1990, the Native American Graves Protection and Repatriation Act (NAGPRA) was enacted, mandating the reburial of human remains held in museum collections and the repatriation of sacred objects to federally recognized Indian tribes. The act also affected the direction of future research on human remains and burial goods, requiring tribal input throughout the process. Although NAGPRA applied only to projects on federal lands or funded with federal monies, similar laws were enacted by the State of Arizona, affecting state lands and state-funded projects. Tribal input in the NAGPRA process was also enhanced by the establishment of CRM programs administered by the tribes themselves.

In 1983, Northland Research, Inc., of Flagstaff contracted with the COE to conduct a Class I cultural resources inventory of the major drainages of the Tucson Basin, overlapping much of the work included in the Tucson Urban Study (Marmaduke 1983). Northland archaeologists reevaluated the sites visited earlier by ASM, concluding that the assessments of Gregonis and Huckell were still relevant.

11

During the summer of 1990, SRI completed a program of cultural resource reconnaissance along the same 10.8-mile segment of the Rillito that defined the Tucson Urban Study and Northland's subsequent resurvey (Ciolek-Torrello and Homburg 1990; Harry and Ciolek-Torrello 1992). As with the earlier investigations, this project was undertaken in preparation for COE-sponsored modifications to the Rillito in response to seasonal flooding. These modifications included both channelization of the floodway and the construction of overbank protection facilities and recreational areas. Unlike the previous studies, however, SRI was directed to engage in subsurface testing at a number of sites within the immediate impact area. The project area encompassed a 600-foot-wide ROW on either side of the existing channel, covering the same areas as the earlier Tucson Urban Study. An initial archival search of the project area identified 21 cultural properties within the ROW, most initially recorded by Frank Midvale in the 1930s. Several of the sites identified by Midvale had since been impacted by development. Eight sites could not be relocated during the survey portion of the project.

Test excavations were conducted at eight sites along the project corridor. Of these, four were recommended as eligible for listing in the National Register of Historic Places (NRHP). These include the Sunset Mesa Ruin (AZ AA:12:10), a large Hohokam habitation site with a later historical-period component near the confluence of the Rillito and the Santa Cruz; the Shannon Ranch site (AZ AA:12:12), a historical-period ranch site with an earlier Hohokam component; AZ BB:9:18, a Colonial period Hohokam habitation site with an associated historical-period trash dump; and Binghampton (AZ BB:9:238), a historical-period Mormon settlement encompassing a dispersed surface scatter of prehistoric artifacts.

The proposed widening of Craycroft Road in 1982 prompted archaeological testing and data recovery at a late Rincon phase habitation site (AZ BB:9:54) immediately north of the Rillito, approximately 0.20 km west of the confluence of Tanque Verde Creek and Pantano Wash (Huntington 1982). This project was conducted by ASM archaeologists for the Pima County Department of Transportation. Prior to ASM's work, an unknown portion of the site had been destroyed by earlier construction on Craycroft Road, construction of a utility access road, and placement of several subsurface utility lines. Fieldwork began with the excavation of a series of backhoe trenches placed perpendicular to the existing roadbed. These trenches exposed four subsurface architectural features in an undisturbed portion of the site (Huntington 1982:95). The architectural features exhibited considerable morphological variation, with two broad types being identified, subrectangular and oval, all constructed in shallow pits. Furthermore, the lower walls of three of the pit structures, including both of oval features, consisted of naturally rounded river cobbles set into a caliche plaster. Although no absolute dates were obtained from the site, the ceramic data suggested that the site was a single-component habitation locus dating to the end of the Rincon phase of the Sedentary period. Substantial trash deposits and the diversity of artifacts encountered indicated that the site was occupied year-round and that most, if not all, domestic and economic activities were represented (Huntington 1982:131).

The decade of the 1990s saw an explosion of archaeological activities in the Tucson Basin. Road improvement and development projects sponsored by the Arizona Department of Transportation (ADOT), Pima County, the COE, and other entities resulted in expanded survey coverage and excavations at a diverse set of archaeological sites, from small, seasonal settlements to large villages. Several areas that had not been intensively explored in the past, such as the heavily alluviated floodplain of the Santa Cruz River, became the focus of extensive investigation. Data generated during these projects have led to lively debate concerning the culture history of the Tucson Basin and the cultural affinity of its prehistoric inhabitants. The following paragraphs summarize the results of a sample of these projects.

One of the most extensive survey projects undertaken in the Tucson Basin was the Northern Tucson Basin Survey (Fish et al. 1992). This survey centered on the area between the Tortolita and Tucson Mountains and encompassed large areas of *bajada,* the floodplain of the Santa Cruz River, and areas around the Picacho and Silverbell Mountains. This project resulted in the delineation of the Marana platform mound community and the investigation of Cerro Prieto, a large *trincheras* site in the Los Robles area (Downum 1993).

Pima County–sponsored improvements along Mission Road required additional excavation at the West Branch site. This work, carried out by SRI, expanded on the previous work by Desert Archaeology, testing its hypothesis that the site was an important locus of pottery manufacture for the Tucson Basin. SRI uncovered evidence of ceramic production and additional data demonstrating the importance of local clay sources in the production process (Altschul et al. 1996). The construction of the Desert Vista Campus of Pima Community College gave Desert Archaeology a similar opportunity to revisit a previously excavated site. This project affected a portion of the Valencia site, previously investigated by Desert Archaeology (Doelle 1985). The Desert Vista project afforded the opportunity to investigate the early ceramic period occupation of the site (Wallace 2003).

Two separate projects, one conducted under the auspices of Pima County and the other sponsored by ADOT, led to archaeological investigations of portions of the Julian Wash site, a large multicomponent village located near the intersection of Interstates 10 and 19. In 1992 and 1993, SRI conducted data recovery operations on a section of the site between 10th Avenue and Interstate 19, along the channelized portion of Julian Wash (Whittlesey 1999). This work was carried out for Pima County and the COE in advance of construction of a park along the wash. A larger section of the site closer to the Santa Cruz River was investigated by Desert Archaeology for ADOT in advance of improvements to Interstate 19. These two projects collected important data on the early Colonial period, a time period that had not been widely studied in the Tucson Basin.

Perhaps the most-extensive excavations conducted during the 1990s in the Tucson Basin were sponsored by ADOT as part of improvements to Interstate 10. This work, carried out by Desert Archaeology, included the excavation of several substantial Archaic period settlements, most notably the Santa Cruz Bend and Los Pozos sites. Prior to this work, the Archaic period was known primarily from seasonal camps and limited-activity sites away from the river (Gregory 1999; Mabry 1998; Mabry et al. 1997). Evidence of maize agriculture and water-control features were found at several Archaic period sites by Desert Archaeology at about the same time that SRI was finding similar evidence at the Costello-King site, an Archaic period site in northwestern Tucson (Ezzo and Deaver 1998). Radiocarbon dates from Costello-King indicated maize production as early as 3,000 years ago, the earliest evidence so far of maize agriculture in the Southwest. These data supported Huckell's argument for an "Early Agricultural period" coterminous with the San Pedro phase of the Late Archaic (Huckell 1995). This proposed shift in terminology for the Late Archaic period is still controversial.

The discovery of evidence for irrigation and maize cultivation at several sites along the middle Santa Cruz River has prompted a reanalysis of the mechanisms whereby agriculture was adopted in the Southwest. Conventional wisdom had irrigation technology being introduced into the area by the Hohokam, replacing a system of farming dependent on rainfall and seasonal flooding. These data indicate the appearance of more-sophisticated techniques much earlier than previously believed, suggesting an indigenous development of the technology.

Projects funded by private developers also contributed to the rapidly expanding archaeological database of the Tucson Basin. In 1993, SWCA, Inc., of Tucson excavated part of the Gibbon Springs site, a Tanque Verde phase village in the northern Tucson Basin. Of special note was the recovery of charred beams of piñon pine that provided the first tree-ring dates from the desert Southwest (Ahlstrom and Slaughter 1996). Although dates were obtained only from a single feature, the data indicated that it may be possible to develop a dendrochronological sequence for the Tucson area, significantly enhancing the precision of local chronologies.

Research on the Historical Period

The historical period in southern Arizona began with the arrival of the first Europeans to the region in 1539. In that year, the Franciscan friar Marcos de Niza and a small Spanish expedition traveled north from Mexico to the pueblo of Zuni, following the San Pedro and Gila Rivers for part of their route. The expedition left no trace of its momentary presence in the region, but it did inaugurate a century and a half of intermittent Spanish exploration of what is now the state of Arizona (see Chapter 4). It was not until the explorations of the Jesuit father Eusebio Francisco Kino at the end of the seventeenth century that the Spanish presence in southern Arizona became substantial enough to produce a significant documentary record, but the impact of the Spanish presence farther south was probably felt along the middle Santa Cruz River long before Kino arrived. We use "historical period" here in the conventional sense of the entire period from first Spanish contact to the end of the twentieth century, with the understanding that the first 150 years or more are sometimes better characterized as the "protohistoric period," a time when European impacts on native ways of life were real but not yet direct.

The historical period can be studied through both written documentation and the archaeological record, which has led to the development of the two independent disciplines of history and historical archaeology in the Southwest, as elsewhere in the United States. The overlap between the two is inevitable and frequent, as much in the Río Antiguo study area as anywhere, but their histories are distinct enough to warrant separate consideration here. As with the prehistoric archaeological sites in the study area, our discussions of the history of work at individual historical-period sites are reserved for Chapter 5.

Documentary Research

The history of southern Arizona, and thus of the Tucson Basin, first became a subject of modern scholarly study in the work of the late-nineteenth-century American historian Hubert Howe Bancroft. In a monumental synthesis of western history that eventually swelled to more than 30 volumes, Bancroft was the first historian to dig systematically into the unpublished sources documenting the history of the Southwest, from the beginnings of Spanish exploration to the acquisition of the region by the United States. A Californian, Bancroft was interested primarily in the broad sweep of events that shaped California history, but he compiled a large amount of primary source material on the greater Southwest and dedicated a full volume of his work to the history of Arizona and New Mexico (Bancroft 1889). His work has the Anglocentric shortcomings of most historical work of his era—Weber (1992:341) called his treatment of the Hispanic *californios* "fictive, condescending . . . and profoundly racist"—but it is the practical predecessor of all subsequent historical work on the Southwest, including the history of the Tucson Basin.

After Bancroft, the next American historian to take the formerly Spanish and Mexican territories of the United States as his particular subject was Herbert Eugene Bolton, professor for most of his career at the University of California at Berkeley. During the first half of the twentieth century, Bolton invented, then dominated historical study of the region he dubbed the "Spanish Borderlands." Technically, the borderlands included a broad band of the United States extending from ocean to ocean, and Bolton's work occasionally addressed the entirety of that region, but his most important work focused on the Southwest, especially on the early years of Spanish exploration and settlement in Arizona, California, and New Mexico. An early essay on the importance of Spanish missions as frontier institutions (Bolton 1964 [1917]) was the start of a focus on Spanish-indigenous interactions that can still be seen today in the study of the Spanish Colonial period in the region. Bolton was particularly fascinated by the experiences of prominent individual explorers. His detailed studies of the Coronado expedition (Bolton 1990 [1949]) and Kino's many accomplishments (Bolton 1984 [1936]) remain standard works on their subjects. Apart from the work of compiling sources and writing syntheses, Bolton's single most important contribution to the field was to shift the emphasis in western history from a perception of the Spanish and Mexican presence as a minor hindrance to westward Anglo expansion to a perception that their presence was fundamental in determining the subsequent character of the region (on Bolton's contributions and those of his many students, see Bannon 1964, 1978; Weber 1988a, 1991).

Bolton had a prominent successor in borderlands history in John Francis Bannon, who in turn dominated the field from the 1950s into the 1970s. Like Bolton before him, Bannon emphasized the Spanish role in the history of the region, partly as a foil to the continuing Anglocentrism of mainstream American history. Also like Bolton, Bannon wrote important syntheses of borderlands history (e.g., Bannon 1955, 1970), trained many doctoral students in the field, and otherwise avidly promoted professional study of the region. One shortcoming of his work, as with the work of Bolton, was a kind of "overcorrection" inherent in its sometimes romanticized Hispanic emphasis. Bannon and Bolton, and many of the students of both historians, brought Spanish involvement in the history of the region to the fore but thus became apologists, if largely unintentional ones, for Spanish misdeeds. Subsequent historical work on the borderlands, including important work on southern Arizona, has helped to counteract this overcorrection, providing a more balanced view of the Spanish presence in the region, a view that does not neglect, for example, the Spanish role in the precipitous decline of native populations (Weber 1988b).

Since the emergence of the borderlands school, the history of southern Arizona has benefited from the work of numerous historians who have addressed the region in studies of the greater Southwest, of the state as a whole, and of specific places within southern Arizona. Because southern Arizona is one of the few regions in the United States with a lengthy Spanish Colonial occupation, an important Mexican period occupation, and a continuing, substantial Mexican-American population, many works dealing with southern Arizona history are devoted to one or another aspect of the Hispanic presence in the region. Weber, in a series of major works on Southwest history (1979, 1982, 1992), included southern Arizona as an important and, in many ways, unique region during the Spanish Colonial and Mexican periods. Officer (1987) provided a detailed synthesis of the Spanish Colonial and Mexican periods in what he called Hispanic Arizona, basically the part of Arizona sold by Mexico to the United States in 1854. Kessell (1970) provided one of the few detailed studies ever made of a single mission in what was once northern New Spain, the Jesuit mission at Guevavi, on the upper Santa Cruz River. Elsewhere, Kessell (1976) redressed the long-standing neglect of the Franciscan presence in southern Arizona, a neglect fostered by an enduring fascination (partly attributable to Bolton) with the earlier Jesuit presence in the region. Sheridan et al. (1991) compiled scattered scholarly articles on the Franciscan period to a similar end. Kessell (1976) is also a fundamental source on other aspects of the later Spanish Colonial and Mexican periods in southern Arizona.

Other important sources on the missions of northern New Spain include Burrus (1971), McCarty (1976, 1981, 1996), and Polzer (1976, 1998). Fontana (1996) assembled and considered widely scattered information on the mission at San Xavier del Bac, carrying the story to the present day. Dobyns (1976), taking Spanish Colonial Tucson as his focus, documented the role of the missions, and the Spanish presence more generally, in the decline of native populations in southern Arizona. The impact of Spanish colonialism on native demography in northern New Spain was also the focus of books by Jackson (1994) and Reff (1990). Dobyns (1959) was also responsible for a large, unpublished compilation of sources and writings on the presidio at Tubac, the center of Hispanic settlement in the region during two decades of the eighteenth century.

The study of the Spanish Colonial and Mexican periods in southern Arizona does not, of course, end at the current international border. Once a part of the vast colony of New Spain and subsequently of the Mexican state of Sonora, southern Arizona must ultimately be understood with reference to the greater history of those political entities. In this regard, it is important to note that a substantial body of relevant historical literature on northern New Spain and Sonora exists only in Spanish, produced primarily by Mexican scholars. An introduction to this literature, and an important resource to all historians of the region, is the six-volume *Historia general de Sonora*, recently released in a second edition (Gobierno del Estado de Sonora 1997).

An important institutional resource for the history of northern New Spain is the Documentary Relations of the Southwest (DRSW) section of ASM. Since the creation of DRSW in the 1970s, its staff has worked to collect, catalog, transcribe, translate, analyze, and publish primary source materials on northern New Spain preserved in Mexican, U.S., and European archives. This ongoing effort has resulted in the publication of major individual documents, collections of documents, and research guides, including works by Barnes et al. (1981), Naylor and Polzer (1986), Polzer (1976), Polzer and Sheridan (1997), and Hadley et al. (1997), as well as the production of indexes to document collections and microform copies of important documents and collections. Of related significance is a detailed study by Gerhard (1993) of territorial and administrative units in northern New Spain, based on a comprehensive review of sources in Mexican and Spanish archives. Gerhard's book is an important guide to the amount and kinds of primary source material available for specific areas in northern New Spain.

Tucson became the social and economic center of southern Arizona during the latter half of the nineteenth century, and historical research on the century following the Gadsden Purchase reflects this status. Two works on the history of Tucson bear particular mention. The first is Sonnichsen's *Tucson: The Life and Times of an American City* (Sonnichsen 1982); the second is Sheridan's *Los Tucsonenses: The Mexican Community in Tucson, 1854–1941* (Sheridan 1986). Together, the two works illustrate the diversity of subject matter presented by Tucson's history and the variety of research emphases that such diversity requires. Sonnichsen's *Tucson* is a highly original and entertaining history of political events and social change in the city, basically since the Gadsden Purchase. Mexican-Americans are an important part of his account, because they have always been a part of the city's population, but their presence is often overshadowed by the dominant roles played by white Tucsonans. Sheridan's *Los Tucsonenses* also begins with the Gadsden Purchase, but his deliberate focus is the "other Tucson," the Mexican-American community that formed the majority of the city's population until the first decade of the twentieth century. The Mexican-American community had deep roots in the pre-U.S. period, enduring connections with the Mexican state of Sonora, and an important but often undervalued role in the political and economic life of the city. Both Sonnichsen's and Sheridan's works are valuable in their own ways, but *Los Tucsonenses* is an important reminder of how much of southern Arizona's history would escape a purely Anglocentric approach.

Histories of the state of Arizona as a whole naturally devote considerable attention to southern Arizona, the portion of the state with the longest continuous historical-period occupation. Important syntheses of Arizona history include works by Farish (1915–1918), Lamar (1966), Wagoner (1970, 1975), and, most recently and most notably, Sheridan (1995). Sheridan's survey of Arizona history has quickly become the standard introduction to the subject and includes useful summaries of events and processes in southern Arizona, especially Tucson and the Santa Cruz Valley. Sheridan is also a contributor to an excellent collection of essays by various authors on the history of Tucson (Southwestern Mission Research Center 1986). The collection includes its own useful summary of works on Tucson history (Southwestern Mission Research Center 1986:149–152).

Use of the term "Borderlands" in Bolton's sense of the term has not died out entirely, but in recent years the historiography of the region has undergone a significant shift in perspective away from an emphasis on the status of the region as an outpost first of Spanish, then Anglo civilization. The shift corresponds with a major shift in Latin American and western history in the last few decades away from an elitist, event-oriented historiography and toward a "history from below" (Radding 1997:xvi), a focus on the broader implications of the often mundane aspects of everyday social and economic life, including the lives of previously neglected groups of people such as ethnic minorities and women. The "new western history" (Limerick 1987; Limerick et al. 1991), for example, eschews an earlier emphasis on the western American frontier as simply an instrument in the inevitable expansion of U.S. agriculture and industry and devotes itself to reconstructing the lives of all people living under, affected by, or simply bypassed by that expansion. Similar emphases are evident in recent Latin American history as a whole, and in borderlands history more particularly. Work by Weber (1992) was a turning point in this regard for the history of the borderlands, a term he generally avoided (on other aspects of the evolving historiography of the borderlands, see the essays in Weber 1988c). A recent book by Cynthia Radding (1997) took up the typical borderlands topic of colonial society in northwestern Mexico, but instead of focusing on the successes and failures of the Spanish empire in the region, the author looked at how the convergence of Spanish and Indian cultures, and of different classes of people within Spanish colonial society, shaped the history and environment of the region. Jackson (1998) gathered essays of a similar bent by several authors dealing with various parts of the borderlands. Another aspect of the shift is a greater emphasis on comparative studies. In a series of essays, a volume edited by Guy and Sheridan (1998) compared the impacts of Spanish colonialism on northern New Spain and northern Argentina, the two most peripheral portions of Spain's American colonies.

Spanish, Mexican, and Anglo-American occupation of the Tucson Basin has centered on the manipulation of the basin's principal streams for agricultural and other purposes. The impact of such manipulation came early to the Santa Cruz Valley, but relatively late to the Rillito Valley, where settlement began only in the second half of the nineteenth century. In both valleys, the impact increased dramatically with the arrival of the Anglo-American industrial economy in 1880, the year the Southern Pacific Railroad reached Tucson. In addition to direct modifications of the rivers themselves, wider processes of environmental change prompted or exacerbated by the spread of ranching, farming, and other landscape-modifying activities led eventually to the transformation of the two rivers from shallow, meandering, perennial streams to deeply entrenched channels that carry water only during heavy rains. The transformation of the Santa Cruz River (and, to a lesser extent, the Rillito) in the decades after the Gadsden Purchase has been treated in several book-length works, some dealing specifically with the Santa Cruz Valley or the Tucson Basin more generally (Betancourt 1990; Kupel 1986), others dealing with the general phenomenon of environmental degradation and arroyo formation in the Southwest (Bahre 1991; Cooke and Reeves 1976; Dobyns 1981; Hastings and Turner 1965; see also Sheridan 2000). The physical and cultural history of the Rillito Valley had an early and influential student in George E. P. Smith (1910), an engineering professor at the University of Arizona whose work we discuss in some detail in Chapter 4.

Historical-Archaeological Research

As elsewhere in the United States, the archaeology of historical-period sites in southern Arizona got its start as a tool of historic preservation. In the early 1900s, as a response to national concern for the loss of major historical sites, a federal program to protect and preserve important ruins was established, and in 1908, the ruins of the Franciscan mission at Tumacácori, on the west bank of the Santa Cruz River about 40 miles south of Tucson, was designated a national monument. By 1920, Tumacácori was the focus of excavations aimed at identifying and reconstructing features that would help to stabilize the crumbling church (Pinkley 1936). Limited excavations of a similar nature in the 1920s and 1930s and then a major excavation in 1934 and 1935 by Paul Beaubien (1937) followed. Beaubien's purpose was to provide a detailed map of the mission by tracing wall lines through excavation. The results of his efforts, which include a detailed map of the 79-plus rooms of the complex, served as a guide to subsequent reconstruction and landscaping at the monument. Unfortunately, his original site records have been lost, and most of the artifacts he recovered were from contexts disturbed by the extensive looting that plagued the site prior to its designation as a monument. Later archaeological work at Tumacácori in the 1950s and 1960s included further efforts at stabilization and reconstruction and also resulted in the identification of the earlier Jesuit mission at the site (see Shenk [1976] for a summary of work at Tumacácori, much of it unpublished).

No other historical-period site in southern Arizona has received the sustained attention paid to Tumacácori, although Tumacácori itself still awaits a comprehensive archaeological study (for summary comments on Spanish Colonial period archaeology in southern Arizona as a whole, see Majewski and Ayres
[1997]). Three other Spanish Colonial period sites on the upper Santa Cruz—Guevavi, Calabazas, and
Tubac, all associated with different parts of Tumacácori's history—did not see professional archaeological work until much later, when stabilization and interpretation were again the motives. The modest ruins
of the mission church at Guevavi, several miles upstream from Tumacácori, were documented as part of
a larger architectural study in 1917 and recorded as an archaeological site by Emil Haury in 1937, but the
site was not formally excavated until 1964 (Robinson 1976). Further excavation took place at Guevavi in
1991 (Burton 1992a), and documentation of surface features at both Guevavi and Calabazas, a nearby
visita (dependent mission settlement), took place in 1992 (Burton 1992b). The only other archaeological
work at Calabazas was an evaluation of the ruins for a stabilization plan (Stone 1979). Fontana (1971)
has looked at the history of Calabazas in detail, from the establishment of the *visita* through the abandonment of the site by later Anglo-American residents in the late nineteenth century. The site of the former
presidio at Tubac, just downstream from Tumacácori, was not formally excavated until the 1970s (Shenk
and Teague 1975). Later excavations at the site have still not been reported in full (Williams 1992). A
number of small-scale excavations have also been carried out recently at Tubac (Barton et al. 1981; Fratt
1981; Huckell and Huckell 1982). To the east of the Santa Cruz River valley, along the San Pedro River,
the ruins of the presidio at Terrenate were excavated in the 1950s by Charles Di Peso (Di Peso 1953),
who assumed that the site also had a significant protohistoric Sobaipuri occupation (this component is in
fact probably of prehistoric age). The Spanish occupation of the presidio lasted only four years (1776–
1780; Williams 1986a), but Di Peso's excavations documented a substantial Spanish Colonial component. More recently, surface remains at the site have been studied by Sugner and Reid (1994) and Waugh
(1995).

Apart from the early work at these Santa Cruz River sites, historical archaeology in southern Arizona
had a relatively late start, especially when compared with the development of the field in the eastern
United States. As elsewhere in the West, the late start was due in large part to a relative scarcity of historical-period sites, at least of the kinds of sites that historical archaeology was initially interested in. In
addition to its early role as a tool of preservation, historical archaeology began as an adjunct to history, a
way of addressing questions posed by traditional historical research. This dual role as preservation tool
and adjunct to history prompted an early emphasis on the major sites of traditional narrative history—
colonial-period missions, townsites, forts, battlefields, and the like—the kinds of sites the East had in
abundance but that were fewer and widely scattered in the West. In southern Arizona, the Spanish Colonial presence was especially ephemeral, limited to a handful of major sites, and two of these—the mission and the presidio at Tucson—were largely destroyed in the nineteenth and early twentieth centuries
by the growth of the region's single urban center.

Mission San Xavier del Bac, the best-preserved Spanish Colonial site in southern Arizona, has been
subject to surprisingly little archaeological work. The first excavations at the site took place in 1958,
when a group of University of Arizona students led by Bernard Fontana and William Robinson dug in
two areas near the extant mission church (Robinson 1963). The most important find was an architectural
complex initially thought to be a series of workshops associated with construction of the 1797 church.
Later excavations by Fontana in the 1970s showed that the architectural remains were in fact part of the
1757 church, which had been subdivided into rooms (Majewski and Ayres 1997:72). Other than later
analyses of animal bone (Olsen 1974) and artifacts (Barnes 1972, 1980; Cheek 1974) recovered from the
site and a few small-scale excavations (e.g., Ayres 1970a; Ciolek-Torrello and Brew 1976), San Xavier
has not seen any further archaeological study. The lack of archaeological research is due in part to the
status of the mission and its grounds as a sacred and actively used part of the San Xavier District of the
Tohono O'odham Nation.

Within the city of Tucson, the first professional recognition that the archaeology of nonindigenous peoples not only was possible but could contribute significantly to the history of the region, came in 1954 (Barnes 1984:213), when Emil Haury and Edward Danson excavated a small area near the presumed northeast corner of the Tucson presidio (Chambers 1955; Olson 1985). The project was prompted by the demolition of a building to make way for a parking lot. In addition to apparent remnants of the presidio wall, Haury and Danson documented the remains of a U.S. period house that stood on the site and, below the level of the presidio, a Hohokam pit house. This brief episode set the pattern for much of the historical archaeology subsequently carried out in Tucson and its vicinity: it has usually been done in association with construction projects, and it has usually been done by archaeologists trained first as prehistorians, not historical archaeologists. To the credit of Haury the prehistorian, he recognized the importance of the presidio find and presented it with as much enthusiasm as he did the pit house (Haury and Fathauer 1974).

Despite its central role in the history of Tucson, the presidio has seen only limited archaeological work since Haury and Danson dug there, the primary reason being that it was largely destroyed or is obscured by modern downtown Tucson. Ayres (1979; see also Barnes 1983) excavated in the Tucson Museum of Art block and the presidial cemetery during the Tucson Urban Renewal Project of 1968–1974. Since then, Thiel (1998a, 1998b; Thiel et al. 1995) has made significant contributions in a series of small-scale projects, tentatively identifying further portions of the presidio wall and excavating associated and overlying features. Thiel also recently led excavations at the northeast corner of the presidio, near the site of Haury and Danson's 1954 excavations, as part of the City of Tucson's Río Nuevo development project.

The remains of Tucson's other major Spanish Colonial site, Mission San Agustín del Tucson, lie across the river from downtown Tucson and at the eastern foot of Sentinel Peak. Like the presidio, Mission San Agustín has been heavily disturbed by later development, and until only recently it had seen even less archaeological work than the presidio. Summaries of the history of the site and of the limited (and unpublished) archaeological investigations there have been provided by Doelle (1997), Hard and Doelle (1978), Smiley et al. (1953), Wasley (1956), and Williams (1986b). In recent years, a series of surveys and test excavations has been carried out in the vicinity of the mission (Diehl 1997; A. Diehl and M. Diehl 1996; M. Diehl and A. Diehl 1996; Elson and Doelle 1987a; Freeman et al. 1996; Mabry and Thiel 1995; Thiel 1995a, 1995b, 1997, 1998c), confirming the generally disturbed nature of the area but also documenting features associated both with the mission and with later periods.

Large-scale excavations of Mission San Agustín were conducted between November 2000 and February 2001 by Desert Archaeology, in another part of the city's Río Nuevo project. The results have not yet been published, but the work has established that much of the site documented by Wasley in the 1950s has since been destroyed, including the foundations of the mission *convento* and church. The site was damaged significantly prior to 1940 by clay mining, then used as a landfill by the city in the late 1950s. The latter use apparently included bulldozing much of the site. Desert Archaeology did discover substantial sections of the stone foundation of the west wall of the mission compound, the stone foundation of the mission granary, a stone-lined canal that may have served as the mill race for nearby Warner's Mill (built after the mission was abandoned), a well used for trash disposal by Chinese gardeners living near the abandoned mission in the late nineteenth century, and numerous pit houses and other features associated with intensive prehistoric use of the same location (Bawaya 2001; Center for Desert Archaeology [CDA] 2001). In other parts of the Río Nuevo project, Desert Archaeology carried out excavations in 2001 in two other locations: first, in an area immediately north of Mission San Agustín and just south of Congress Street, and subsequently, in an area immediately west of the mission, in the vicinity of the mission gardens. The results of both projects will be published soon.

More often than in most places in the United States, historical archaeology in southern Arizona has been practiced by archaeologists trained in prehistoric rather than historical archaeology (see especially Ayres [1991] on this tendency in the Southwest and its associated problems). One reason for this is the nature of the earliest historical-period sites in the region. The missions and presidios of the eighteenth and early nineteenth centuries were never exclusively nonindigenous settlements and, indeed, were intended as the places where the Spanish missionary and military enterprise would strive to incorporate indigenous people into greater Spanish society. Accordingly, prehistorically oriented archaeologists have always viewed Spanish Colonial sites and the documentary records associated with them as important sources of information on indigenous culture. This means that an interest in the most recent version of pre-Hispanic indigenous culture (or the least-adulterated historical-period version of indigenous culture) has been the motivation for a significant amount of historical and historical-archaeological (using historical-archaeological in a strict sense) research in southern Arizona. Much of this research is best characterized as protohistoric in focus (e.g., Di Peso 1948, 1951, 1953, 1956; Doelle 1984; Huckell 1984a; Riley 1975, 1976, 1985, 1987), given that indigenous peoples of limited or no direct experience with Europeans are often the primary subjects of interest, but the accompanying historical reconstructions of the earliest Hispanic presence and the nonindigenous material culture recovered at protohistoric sites can be important sources of information regarding the history and archaeology of unequivocally historical times.

In the 1960s, two changes affecting the professional archaeological community brought about both a great expansion in the amount of historical archaeology carried out in southern Arizona and a shift in the kinds of sites studied by historical archaeologists. The first change was a sudden expansion of historic preservation law at the federal, state, and local levels, as already noted in our consideration of the development of prehistoric archaeology. The second change was the growing influence of the loosely defined "history from below" paradigm discussed above. The impact of the new historic preservation laws was to set as the focus of archaeological research whatever site happens to be physically in the way of a development project. Working with a very liberal definition of historical significance (any site at least 50 years old is potentially significant), contract archaeologists since the 1960s have been busy recording and evaluating everything from urban outhouses to abandoned mine shafts to farmstead artifact scatters. Prompting further interest in these mundane historical-period sites was the growing perception that it is precisely such sites that can contribute to a fuller understanding of the social, cultural, and economic life of a period and place—in other words, historical archaeology from below (for example, see Berge [1968:2], who characterizes historical archaeology's proper focus as "the way of life of common, ordinary people of which the world is comprised in far greater numbers than the famous heroes of history").

The increasing recognition in historical archaeology that small, peripheral, nonelite, or rural sites were potentially important sources of historical or anthropological information was also partly the result of the rise of processual archaeology in the 1960s, an approach that, in the simplest terms, led archaeologists to consider not simply what their data told them about a specific time and place but what the broader implications were for other times and places—what the general anthropological implications of their data were. Processual archaeology never became the force in historical archaeology that it became (and remains) in prehistoric archaeology, but aspects of the processual approach made their way into the practice of historical archaeology throughout the United States at about the same time that a whole variety of previously ignored historical-period sites were being recorded by contract archaeologists. Historical archaeologists continued to search for and excavate the sites prominent in traditional historical narratives, but their research even at these sites became structured around processual concerns.

In southern Arizona, the first time that historic preservation law and the processual variety of historical archaeology converged in a significant way was in the excavations carried out in the Tucson Urban Renewal Project, which began in 1968 and continued intermittently until 1974 (Ayres 1968, 1970b). The project included historical research, architectural inventories, and archaeological excavations in anticipation of the complete razing of a large area in downtown Tucson. Although it was hindered by inconsistent funding and has never been completely reported, the project yielded a number of interesting studies of the Spanish Colonial, Mexican, and U.S. period occupations in downtown Tucson, most showing the influence of the processual concerns newly current in archaeology (Anderson 1968, 1970; Ayres 1969,

1971, 1978, 1979, 1980; Clonts 1983; Lister and Lister 1989; Olsen 1978, 1983; Renk 1969; Roubicek 1969). There have been numerous subsequent compliance-driven excavations of historical-period sites in downtown Tucson, with a continued emphasis on processual interpretations, but none has addressed as large an area as the Tucson Urban Renewal Project. The largest of subsequent projects have been devoted to individual city blocks or portions of blocks (Ayres 1990; Ciolek-Torrello and Swanson 1997; Eppley and Mabry 1991; Mabry 1991; Mabry et al. 1994; Thiel 1993, 1995c; Thiel et al. 1993, 1995). Smaller projects have addressed individual or multiple small parcels and linear utility corridors (Dutt and Thiel 1999; Fortier 1980; Gilman 1997; Gilman and Swartz 1998; Levi 1996; Mazany 1981; Noll and Euler 1996; Thiel 1995d, 1996, 1998b, 1998d; Thiel and Desruisseaux 1993).

Contract archaeology in southern Arizona during the past several decades has seen a similar explosion in the number of projects recording, testing, and excavating historical-period archaeological sites. In most cases, historical archaeology has been only a part (and often a small part) of the overall focus of such projects, in which prehistoric archaeology continues to be the chief concern. Nonetheless, there is a growing body of information on the historical archaeology of the Tucson Basin, in large part because of the efforts of contract archaeologists. Because many of these projects have been outside of the historical urban core of Tucson, most of the historical-archaeological sites they have recorded have been rural in nature, such as ranches, homesteads, mines, and dumps. The projects have ranged in size from relatively large survey projects (e.g., Ayres 1984a; Ayres and Stone 1983; Betancourt 1978a, 1978b; Dart 1989; Fontana 1965; Gregonis and Huckell 1979; Jones and Dart 1997; Seymour et al. 1997; Simpson and Wells 1983, 1984; Stein 1993; Wellman 1994; Wells and Reutter 1997) to a variety of smaller survey, testing, and excavation projects (e.g., Baar 1996; Chavarria 1996; Diehl et al. 1996; Doak et al. 1995; Faught 1995; Harry and Ciolek-Torrello 1992; Jones 1995a, 1995b, 1996, 1997, 1999; Kaldahl 1999; Mabry 1998; Slaughter et al. 1993; Slawson et al. 1987; Sterner 1996, 1999; Tucker 1997; Vanderpot et al. 1993; Wallace 1996, 1998; Yoder, Holloway, Myers, and Slaughter 1996; Yoder, Myers, and Slaughter 1996).

Individual ranch sites in the Tucson area that have been subject to significant archaeological study include two nineteenth-century ranches: Rancho Punta de Agua, an early Anglo-American (and later Mexican-American) ranch located a few miles south of San Xavier del Bac (McGuire 1979, 1983), and Romero Ranch, an early Mexican-American ranch forming part of the Romero Ruin archaeological site at Catalina State Park (Elson and Doelle 1987b; Roubicek et al. 1973; Swartz 1991, 1993). The first post-1900 homestead to be intensively studied in the Tucson area (and one of the few post-1900 sites of any kind to be studied intensively) is the Lewis-Weber Homestead, located on the site of the NPS's Western Archeological and Conservation Center in Tucson (Curriden 1981). Another notable ranch site that has recently received archaeological attention is Agua Caliente Ranch, located in the northeastern corner of the Tucson Basin, about 8 miles east of the Río Antiguo study area (Slaughter et al. 1995; Wellman and Slaughter 2001). Elsewhere in the northern Tucson Basin, a number of ranch and homestead sites were the focus of historical research and archaeological survey by Stein (1993), and another nineteenth-century Mexican homestead, the Bojórquez Ranch, was recently excavated by Jones (2001). East of the Tucson Basin, at Fort Huachuca in Cochise County, Sterner and Majewski (1998) conducted historical-archaeological investigations of the Slash Z Ranch and three other early-twentieth-century sites. Not far from Fort Huachuca, along the San Pedro River in Santa Cruz County, an early Anglo-American ranch that eventually was home to Mexican- and Chinese-Americans has been intensively studied by Fontana and Greenleaf (1962).

Historical-archaeological studies of mining in southern Arizona include Ayres's survey of sites in the Rosemont area (1984a), Teague's study of mines on Tohono O'odham lands (Teague 1980), and surveys of other parts of the region by Slawson and Ayres (1992, 1993, 1994). Kentucky Camp, a small, early-twentieth-century gold-mining camp in the Santa Rita Mountains south of Tucson, has been the focus of historical investigations and an ongoing restoration project by the U.S. Forest Service. The project has included limited excavations associated with the restoration efforts (Farrell 1993, 1995).

Within the Río Antiguo study area, historical-archaeological sites have been routinely recorded along with prehistoric sites during the major surveys of the Rillito Valley (see above), but there has yet to be an intensive study of a historical-archaeological site in the study area. Fort Lowell (AZ BB:9:40), the single U.S. fort in the Tucson Basin, saw limited archaeological work 40 years ago (Johnson 1960) and occasional limited work since then, but no substantial excavation or systematic survey of the environs. The Mormon community of Binghampton (AZ BB:9:238), established on the north bank of the Rillito around 1898 and now occupied largely by non-Mormons, was first recorded as an archaeological site in a COE-sponsored survey by SRI (Ciolek-Torrello and Homburg 1990). The site has since seen limited additional survey (Parkhurst et al. 2001), but no excavation. We discuss both Fort Lowell and Binghampton as cultural resource sites in more detail in Chapter 5.

Irrigation was an indispensable part of agriculture in the study area in the late nineteenth and early twentieth centuries, and a number of archaeological studies have looked at irrigation features from that period. The most interesting of these studies has been SRI's discovery and excavation of a portion of a wooden box flume passing under the bed of the Rillito just west of Craycroft Road (Sterner 1996). The flume was one of several such structures originating upstream in Tanque Verde Creek and designed to tap the underflow in the valley for use on fields along one or both banks of the Rillito. We discuss this find and its relationship to similar features in the study area in Chapter 4.

Ethnographic Research

The history of ethnographic research in southern Arizona is short and uncomplicated, at least in comparison to other parts of the Southwest, where some Native American groups—the Hopi, the Navajo, and the Zuni, most notably—have seen the seemingly continuous presence of professional ethnographers for the last 75 years or more. The relative lack of ethnographic research in southern Arizona is not because of any lack of Native Americans in the region, or any lack of Native Americans still living on their traditional lands. The largest Native American community in southern Arizona, the Tohono O'odham Nation (prior to 1981, known as the Papago Indian Tribe), is the fourteenth-largest federally recognized tribe in terms of population (the Cherokee and the Navajo are the largest and second largest, respectively) and occupies the second-largest reservation in the country (about 3,000,000 acres; the Navajo reservation, in northeastern Arizona, northwestern New Mexico, and southeastern Utah is larger). The Tohono O'odham today also occupy much the same territory used by their ancestors since long before the arrival of Europeans in the region. The relative lack of research is also not the result of any failure of traditional culture to survive intact to the era of modern ethnography. By the end of the nineteenth century, Tohono O'odham culture was changing rapidly and dramatically, and many traditional practices disappeared entirely in the first half of the twentieth century, but the ethnography that has been carried out among the Tohono O'odham indicates that there has never been a shortage of traditional culture to study, regardless of the kinds of changes it might be undergoing.

The principal reason for the limited ethnographic record in southern Arizona is ultimately environmental: the severity of the climate in the region long discouraged Euroamerican settlement outside of a few well-watered riparian strips. This meant that the Native Americans of the region, in particular the Tohono O'odham living in the vast desert region west of the Santa Cruz River, had only limited contact with Spanish, Mexican, and Anglo-American settlers. This in turn meant there were relatively few conflicts between Tohono O'odham and Euroamericans over land and other resources and a corresponding lack of Euroamerican interest in the nature of Tohono O'odham social and economic organization. This eventually translated into a relative lack of anthropological interest on the part of Anglo-American anthropologists, whose access to Native American subjects was typically made possible by the reduction of a once-recalcitrant tribe's range to a small reservation. The Tohono O'odham adaptation to their extreme environment, which demanded a simple material culture and an intermittently nomadic way of life, also contributed to this lack of interest, at a time when many anthropologists were attracted to the highly developed craft traditions or ceremonial complexities of southwestern communities like those of the Hopi and Zuni.

Nonetheless, a significant amount of ethnography exists for the Tohono O'odham, as it also does for the closely related Akimel O'odham (or Pima) of the Gila River and for the Yaqui, who first settled in southern Arizona in the late nineteenth century to escape persecution in Mexico. The Apache, long the nemesis of Spaniards, Mexicans, Anglos, and O'odham in southern Arizona, also have been frequent subjects of formal ethnography, and their presence in the region, generally viewed by non-Apaches as predatory and destructive, has been an important one. Here we consider briefly the history of the ethnography of each of these Native American groups. As we discuss in Chapter 3, there is little evidence for the physical presence of any of these groups in the Río Antiguo study area during the historical period. Nonetheless, the status of the Rillito Valley prior to 1850 as a place people used but did not live in was determined by the relationships that prevailed among the Native American groups living in the immediate vicinity, and by the separate responses of the O'odham and Apache to the European presence after 1700.

O'odham

Formal ethnographic research in southern Arizona began in the late nineteenth century with the work of W. J. McGee, an anthropologist with the Bureau of American Ethnology (BAE). McGee made an ethnographic foray into Mexico through Nogales in 1894, eventually preparing a monograph on the Seri but leaving unpublished his notes on the Tohono O'odham, especially those living south of the international border (Fontana 1989:86–89). McGee was among the first anthropologists to note the great *trincheras* constructions of Sonora and Arizona. Frank Russell, another BAE anthropologist, spent a year with the Akimel O'odham (or Pima) of the Gila River in 1901–1902, a period when Akimel O'odham culture and economy were rapidly succumbing to Anglo-American impacts. His monograph on the Akimel O'odham (Russell 1975 [1908]) remains the primary source on Akimel O'odham culture.

Ruth Underhill, a student of pioneer anthropologist Franz Boas at Columbia University, conducted fieldwork among the Tohono O'odham from 1931 to 1935. Boas's students had already worked among most of the other major tribes of the Southwest prior to Underhill, and her work represented one of the last extensions of the Boasian program into the region. Her many subsequent publications on the Tohono O'odham (then still called the Papago), particularly two monographs (Underhill 1939, 1946), form the heart of the ethnographic record for the tribe. Underhill also collaborated with biologist Edward Castetter of the University of New Mexico on important ethnobiological work among the Tohono O'odham (Castetter and Underhill 1935). Castetter did additional ethnobiological work among the Tohono O'odham independent of Underhill (Castetter and Bell 1942). More recently, Rea (1997, 1998) has carried out major studies of O'odham ethnobotany and ethnozoology.

Not surprisingly, anthropologists at the University of Arizona in Tucson have been responsible for the bulk of the ethnographic work carried out among the Tohono O'odham since Underhill. When Emil Haury began his Papaguería project in 1938, he included ethnographic investigations as a complement to his studies of the archaeology and physical anthropology of the region, and soon other University of Arizona anthropologists took interest. Graduate students in the Department of Anthropology began turning out theses and dissertations on a variety of Tohono O'odham topics. Bernard Fontana, generally recognized as the leading authority on Tohono O'odham culture and history, completed a dissertation on cultural change among the Tohono O'odham in 1960 (Fontana 1960). This work was preceded by an important monograph on the modern Tohono O'odham pottery tradition by Fontana and other University of

Arizona students (Fontana et al. 1962), prepared just before the tradition almost completely disappeared. Fontana has since published a wide variety of articles and monographs on the Tohono O'odham, including the only book-length survey of the Tohono O'odham since Underhill's monographs (Fontana 1989) and valuable essays on Tohono O'odham culture and history in the *Handbook of North American Indians* (Fontana 1983a, 1983b). Fontana, who has lived adjacent to the San Xavier District of the Tohono O'odham reservation since the 1950s, has also been actively involved in the extensive preservation work recently undertaken at Mission San Xavier del Bac (Fontana 1997). His history of the mission, originally published in 1961 but recently revised (Fontana 1996), remains a standard reference.

Because Tohono O'odham culture changed dramatically before the era of formal ethnography, students of the modern Tohono O'odham have almost always combined ethnographic observations with ethnohistorical research to reconstruct at least some aspects of the culture as it was prior to the major impacts of the twentieth century. In fact, it is safe to say that Tohono O'odham ethnography has always been at least as ethnohistorical as it has been ethnographic. Examples of such work are studies carried out under the auspices of the University of Arizona's Bureau of Ethnic Research (later the Bureau of Applied Research in Anthropology) as part of a Tohono O'odham federal land claims case (e.g., Hackenberg 1974). Many other projects by University of Arizona–trained anthropologists have had an applied-anthropology focus (e.g., Van Willigen 1971).

The form and function of the many small, O'odham-built Catholic churches on the Tohono O'odham reservation were the subject of another University of Arizona anthropology dissertation (Griffith 1973). This study initiated the career of the well-known University of Arizona folklorist, James "Big Jim" Griffith, whose many subsequent interests have included the "spiritual geography" of the Tohono O'odham, a subject he considered from various angles in a collection of essays (Griffith 1992). Another student at the University of Arizona, Gary Nabhan (1983), wrote a dissertation on Tohono O'odham agriculture, the first of several notable studies of Tohono O'odham ethnobotany by him (e.g., Nabhan 1982, 1985).

Outside the University of Arizona, Harvard-trained anthropologist Donald Bahr of Arizona State University has published several books and numerous articles on Tohono O'odham language and culture, based on his own ethnographic fieldwork and reanalysis of O'odham texts gathered by earlier investigators (Bahr 1975; Bahr et al. 1974, 1997). In addition, he has looked closely at the evidence for Hohokam-O'odham cultural continuity in O'odham oral tradition (Bahr 1971; Bahr et al. 1994). His student David Kozak also has worked closely with O'odham oral tradition (Kozak and Lopez 1999). All of this work recognizes the central role of oral tradition in Tohono O'odham culture, a role emphasized earlier by Underhill (1938; Underhill et al. 1979). The work of Bahr is notable also for its inclusion of individual Tohono O'odham in the process of gathering and analyzing texts and its explicit acknowledgment of their participation.

Also worth noting here is a valuable synthesis of Tohono O'odham culture and history by Erickson (1994), prepared on behalf of the Tohono O'odham Nation as a textbook for Tohono O'odham schools.

Apache

In 1793, the commander of the Spanish presidio at Tucson established a settlement for pacified Apaches (*apaches mansos*) on the east bank of the Santa Cruz River, immediately adjacent to the presidio. This settlement, never large but always important as an example of how the Apache of southern Arizona might be convinced to live in peace, endured until at least the 1870s. It is probably the only time prior to the twentieth century that Apaches ever stayed in the Tucson Basin for longer than it took to raid an O'odham or Spanish village. But despite their usual absence from the valley, the Apache had a profound impact on its history through their persistent raids, beginning at least as early as the seventeenth century and continuing well into the second half of the nineteenth century. This was particularly true of the

Rillito Valley, over which the Apache had de facto control for more than a century and a half, even if their presence there was limited to occasional visits.

Of the seven generally recognized Apachean-speaking groups, two lived in relative proximity to the Tucson Basin and had a role in its history: the Chiricahua Apache and the Western Apache. The Chiricahua occupied a large area in southeastern Arizona and southwestern New Mexico, and the Western Apache—actually five distinct bands lumped together for convenience by anthropologists—occupied a comparably large area in eastern and central Arizona. The often violent interaction of both major groups with Euroamericans, especially Anglo-Americans in the second half of the nineteenth century, has been documented in countless histories (Spicer [1962:229–261] provides a concise history of Apache-Euroamerican interaction), but purely ethnographic research has been limited. For the Chiricahua Apache, Opler (1937, 1941, 1942, 1983) has produced the most substantial works. For the Western Apache, important works are by Goodwin (1939, 1969), Kaut (1957), and Basso (1969, 1970, 1983, 1996).

Yaqui

For most of their history, the Yaqui lived exclusively in a region centered on the Río Yaqui in what is now southern Sonora, Mexico. Only in the late nineteenth century did groups of Yaqui come to settle in southern Arizona, forced to emigrate by a Mexican government eager to turn over their communal lands to large private landholders, or *hacendados*. In the Tucson area, small groups of Yaqui settled principally in two locations: Pascua Village on the near north side of Tucson and a smaller satellite community in Marana, northwest of Tucson.

The foremost ethnographic works on the Yaqui, in both Mexico and Arizona, are those of Spicer (1940, 1954, 1983), a professor of anthropology at the University of Arizona for most of his career (now deceased). He was also author of a detailed overview of Yaqui culture and history (Spicer 1980). Other important ethnographic works dealing with the Yaqui, primarily in Mexico, are by Beals (1943, 1945). An autobiographical account by a Yaqui has also been published (Moisés et al. 1971). Painter (1986) has described religious beliefs and ceremonies at Pascua Village.

CHAPTER 3

Native American Culture History

This chapter surveys Native American culture history in the Río Antiguo study area, from the earliest occupation some 10,000 years ago to the present day. The discussion has two main sections: the first discusses the prehistoric era prior to the arrival of Europeans, and the second looks at Native American groups that have lived in or near the study area since European contact. The focus in both sections is, of necessity, wider than the Río Antiguo study area. Because Native Americans are not known to have had permanent settlements in the Rillito Valley for at least a century and a half after European contact, the second section of the chapter is particularly dependent on information from outside the study area, especially from the nearby Santa Cruz Valley. We do make direct connections to locations within the study area throughout the chapter as appropriate.

Prehistory

The prehistory of the Rillito Valley is part of the prehistory of the Tucson Basin as a whole, and the following paragraphs attempt to show how the Río Antiguo study area fits within the larger research domain of Tucson Basin prehistory. The discussion outlines the sequence of prehistoric occupation in the study area and includes comments on relevant major and minor prehistoric sites.

Paleoindian Period

The earliest human occupation of the Americas is generally associated with the Paleoindian period. Paleoindian culture was characterized by a hunting-and-gathering economy and small, highly mobile bands adapted to a climate that was cooler and wetter than today. Paleoindian sites are often associated with the remains of extinct species such as mammoths, camels, and giant ground sloths, leading many archaeologists to consider big-game hunting the focus of the Paleoindian economy.

Despite a considerable number of buried Paleoindian sites in southeastern Arizona, most notably along the San Pedro River (Haury 1953; Haury et al. 1959), very little evidence of a Paleoindian presence in the Tucson Basin has been found. The sparse remains that do exist consist of isolated surface finds of Clovis projectile points (Huckell 1982). These isolates include points from the Avra Valley, the Valencia site (AZ BB:13:15) (Doelle 1985:181), the San Xavier District of the Tohono O'odham Nation, and the Tucson Mountains (Huckell 1982). The absence of buried Paleoindian sites in the Tucson Basin has been variously attributed to a lack of deep excavations in the heavily aggraded floodplains of the major streams (Huckell 1982), a massive erosional event that removed these deposits (Haynes and Huckell 1986; Waters 1988), and sporadic, low-intensity use of the Tucson Basin by Paleoindians, resulting in an inherently sparse archaeological presence (Whittlesey et al. 1994:109).

Post-Clovis Paleoindian materials are all but nonexistent in the Tucson Basin. Huckell (1982) described two points from two sites just outside the Tucson Basin that resembled Plainview points. One point came from the Tortolita Mountains and the other from the lower San Pedro River valley.

Archaic Period

The Archaic period is relatively better known in southern Arizona than the preceding Paleoindian period. This is especially true of the later portion of the period and is largely the result of recent explosion in contract archaeology related to development in and around the Santa Cruz River floodplain, especially in the vicinity of the confluence of the Santa Cruz with the Rillito. Similar to the Paleoindian period, the Archaic period was characterized by an economy based on the gathering of wild plant and animal resources. The Archaic period differs from the Paleoindian period, however, in the greater diversity of plant and animal species that were exploited. This more diverse subsistence base undoubtedly lessened the need for a highly mobile way of life.

The Archaic period has traditionally been divided into three periods: the Early Archaic period (10,500–6800 B.P.), the Middle Archaic period (6800–3500 B.P.), and the Late Archaic period (3500–1650 B.P.) (Huckell 1984b:138). Whittlesey (1997:46) has discussed the recent confusion in terminology related to the expanding Archaic database and the terminological dilemmas resulting from the recognition that agriculture is considerably older in the southern Southwest than once believed.

Early Archaic Period

The Early Archaic period is poorly known in southern Arizona and is especially underrepresented in the archaeological record of the Tucson Basin. In fact, as Huckell (1984b:137) has reported, the Tucson Basin has yielded no direct evidence for an Early Archaic occupation, with the possible exception of Rogers's claim of early materials on the *bajada* of the Santa Catalina and Rincon Mountains (Rogers 1958). Once again, it is probably an investigative bias rather than a lack of occupation in the region that has created this gap in our knowledge. At present, the Early Archaic period is known in detail only at sites in the Sulphur Springs Valley of southeastern Arizona. There, Sayles defined the Sulphur Spring and Cazador stages of the Cochise culture based on the presence or absence of projectile points at sites along Whitewater Draw (Sayles 1983, based on work published originally as Sayles and Antevs 1941). These Early Archaic deposits are characterized by frequent milling stones and flaked stone tools, excluding projectile points in the Sulphur Spring stage but including a variety of point types in the Cazador stage. More recently, Whalen (1971) challenged the validity of the Cazador stage, suggesting that it and the Sulphur Spring stage are simply variant expressions of the same cultural phenomenon.

Middle Archaic Period

In contrast to the Paleoindian and Early Archaic periods, the Middle Archaic period is relatively well known in southern Arizona and the Tucson Basin. In southern Arizona, the Middle Archaic period includes the Chiricahua stage of the Cochise culture, known from sites in the San Pedro River valley and Sulphur Springs Valley (Sayles and Antevs 1941), and the Amargosan I and II stages of the Amargosan tradition, known from sites in the Papaguería and the lower Colorado River valley (Rogers 1939).

The economy of the Middle Archaic period was based on the exploitation of a number of environmental zones. Small base camps and limited-activity sites associated with resource procurement and processing are common in upland and *bajada* environments (Huckell 1984b:139–140). The data are sparse, but Middle Archaic peoples probably practiced a seasonally organized procurement strategy that emphasized upland environments in the fall and lowland areas during the rest of the year (Whittlesey 1997:48). In contrast to the preceding Early Archaic period, projectile points are common at Middle Archaic sites, but the large floodplain villages of the Late Archaic period have not been documented for the Middle Archaic (Huckell 1984b:139), and only recently have excavations of a Middle Archaic site been undertaken on the Santa Cruz River floodplain (Gregory 1999).

Excavation of the Middle Archaic component at Los Pozos, a site on the Santa Cruz River floodplain about 9 miles west of the Río Antiguo study area, has produced a single direct radiocarbon date on maize of 4050 B.P. (Gregory 1999:118). This date helps to push back the timing of the introduction of maize in the Southwest and is consistent with other material recovered from sites along the Santa Cruz River, suggesting that maize agriculture and irrigation had a long history of codevelopment in this environment (see also Ezzo and Deaver 1998). Although no irrigation features were recorded in the Middle Archaic component at Los Pozos, the presence of maize in an area of such intensive use of the floodplain suggests that the stage was set early on for the development of subsequent agricultural strategies.

Recently completed excavations by Desert Archaeology for the Río Nuevo project have recovered possible evidence for Middle Archaic houses arranged in a courtyardlike group at AZ BB:13:6, just west of downtown Tucson. Analysis of radiocarbon dates and artifacts from these excavations will be necessary to verify this interpretation.

Late Archaic (Early Agricultural) Period

The beginning of the Late Archaic period, or the beginning of what is now often called the Early Agricultural period, is marked by an apparent intensification of human occupation of southern Arizona, including the Tucson Basin. Settlements became larger, and a movement toward dependence on agriculture is evident. Because of important recent discoveries along the Santa Cruz River (Ezzo and Deaver 1998; Mabry 1998) and in the Cienega Valley (Huckell 1995), we now know substantially more about this period than we did 10 years ago (see Huckell 1984b).

The Late Archaic period is now generally subdivided into two phases. The San Pedro phase, first defined by Sayles (1941), is estimated to date from 1500 to 500 B.C. and is characterized by large side- or corner-notched projectile points, shallow oval to egg-shaped structures with basin floor plans and often a single large bell-shaped pit, a ground stone assemblage reflecting seed milling, a limited assemblage of shell artifacts, and some anthropomorphic figurines of fired clay (Huckell 1995:118–119). The succeeding Cienega phase dates roughly from 500 B.C. to A.D. 200 and ends with the appearance of pottery. Houses of the Cienega phase are typically round in plan with vertical pit walls and level floors. Many houses contain postholes (Huckell 1995; Mabry 1998), and at the Santa Cruz Bend site, many houses had numerous bell-shaped and cylindrical pits, suggesting an increased concern with storage. The Cienega projectile point is a hallmark of the Cienega phase. Unlike San Pedro projectile points, Cienega points have a distinctive corner notch and are often manufactured from siliceous materials. There is also an elaboration of ground stone manufacture in the Cienega phase.

In general, the Late Archaic period was a time of decreasing mobility in which people came to rely more and more on agriculture. This is not to say that previous patterns of land use were abandoned entirely. There continues to be evidence for the use of seasonal camps in upland areas. These camps likely complemented the more intensively focused settlements of the Santa Cruz River floodplain at sites like Santa Cruz Bend and Stone Pipe, where hundreds of habitation structures have been uncovered (Mabry 1998). This duality of settlement is consistent with a seasonally based system in which upland areas were used in fall and winter for gathering wild resources, and large settlements like the Santa Cruz Bend site were used during the summer, when agriculture on the floodplain and the alluvial fans was most productive (Whittlesey 1997).

Other sites along the Santa Cruz River have evidence of Late Archaic or Early Formative period occupations, and it is likely that many sites with documented later components contain as-yet-unrecognized components of Late Archaic or Early Formative age. This is especially true for sites located on or near the floodplain of the Santa Cruz, and the same probably holds for sites along the Rillito. During investigations at the San Xavier Bridge site (AZ BB:13:14), located adjacent to the Santa Cruz about 8 miles south of Tucson, radiocarbon samples obtained from a hearth exposed by the river returned a date of 820 ± 400 B.C. (Ravesloot 1987a:65). This feature, cut into the basal clays, probably represents the earliest preserved occupation of the site. Excavations by ASM on Tumamoc Hill, just west of Tucson, have produced evidence of not only a Late Archaic period occupation but early maize cultivation as well (Fish et al. 1986). Radiocarbon dates from maize kernels recovered in levels below the better-known Classic period component returned dates with range midpoints of 520 B.C., A.D. 320, and A.D. 620 (Fish et al. 1986:569). Recent explorations by Desert Archaeology in Locus 2 of the Valencia site (AZ BB:13:15), about 5 miles south of Tucson, exposed several Cienega phase houses arranged in a roughly circular pattern around an area devoid of architectural features. Immediately west of Tucson, Desert Archaeology exposed a Cienega phase component at the Clearwater site, the name given to the prehistoric component of AZ BB:13:6. Here, Cienega phase canals and several Early Formative period houses were investigated (CDA 2001). In addition to these newly acquired data, several houses at nearby AZ BB:13:74 have recently been reinterpreted as Cienega phase in age (Mabry 1998).

Formative Period

For the purposes of discussing Tucson Basin chronology, the Formative period is usefully divided into five discrete periods: the Early Formative period, the Pioneer period, the Colonial period, the Sedentary period, and the Classic period.

Early Formative Period

As with the Late Archaic period, our knowledge of the earliest portion of the Formative period in the Tucson Basin has been greatly enhanced by recent excavations. The Early Formative period began with the adoption of ceramic container technology, an extension of the growing dependence on agriculture noted in the Late Archaic period. Although some very early, crude ceramics were recovered from the Coffee Camp site dating from 200 B.C. to A.D. 1 (Halbirt and Henderson 1993), the earliest developed ceramic industry did not appear until around A.D. 200 (Whittlesey 1997). Recently, Deaver and Ciolek-Torrello (1995) developed a chronology for the Early Formative period that they saw as pansouthwestern in application. The chronology is based on subdivision into several broad horizons based on changes in material culture as a whole but named for changes in ceramic technology.

The earliest period is the Plain Ware horizon, which extended from A.D. 1 to 425. In the Tucson Basin, the Plain Ware horizon equates with the Agua Caliente phase and is characterized by a thin-walled, sand-tempered, coiled brown plain ware; an expedient lithic technology with remnant Archaic period biface technology; a Late Archaic period milling assemblage; and architectural forms similar to Early Pithouse period Mogollon houses (Ciolek-Torrello 1995, 1998). In addition, subsistence seems to have been a mix of agriculture and hunting and gathering, with a continued emphasis on upland resources. Several recently discovered archaeological sites have been assigned to the Agua Caliente phase, including the Houghton Road site (Ciolek-Torrello 1995, 1998), El Arbolito (Huckell 1987), and the Square Hearth site (Mabry and Clark 1994; Mabry et al. 1997).

The Plain Ware horizon was followed by the Red Ware horizon, which Deaver and Ciolek-Torrello (1995:512) have dated to A.D. 425–650. In the Tucson Basin, this horizon is expressed by the Tortolita phase. In the Tortolita phase, red-slipped pottery was added to the ceramic assemblage, and various changes in vessel forms occurred, including the introduction of flare-rimmed bowls. This vessel form may have its source in the Phoenix Basin (Whittlesey 1997), whereas other aspects of the Red Ware horizon technology appear more closely tied to San Francisco Red ware of the Mogollon ceramic tradition (Whittlesey 1995). The flaked stone assemblage continued to be generalized, and the Archaic period biface component disappeared from the tool kit (Deaver and Ciolek-Torrello 1995). Changes in architecture during this phase included a general increase in house size and the formality of construction, but both large communal structures and small residential houses continued to be constructed. Representative sites of this period include the Houghton Road site (Ciolek-Torrello 1995, 1998), Rabid Ruin (Slawson 1990), El Arbolito, and the Valencia Road site, Locus 2 (Huckell 1993).

The Early Broadline horizon began around A.D. 650 with the introduction of painted ceramics and lasted until around A.D. 700, when what is traditionally called the Snaketown phase of the Hohokam culture first appeared (Deaver and Ciolek-Torrello 1995:512). This horizon is poorly represented in the Tucson Basin, and no local phase has been associated with it. The similarity between traditional Mogollon ceramics like Dos Cabezas Red-on-brown and Hohokam Estrella Red-on-gray is the impetus for defining this period as a widespread cultural horizon (Whittlesey 1997:54). The only excavated site in the Tucson Basin to be associated with this horizon is the Dairy site (Altschul and Huber 1995).

Pioneer Period

The beginning of the Pioneer period in the Tucson Basin, dating to around A.D. 700, is signaled by the appearance of a widespread material culture thought to be intrusive from northern Mexico. According to Deaver and Ciolek-Torrello (1995), Snaketown ceramics are the horizon marker of this period. It is in this period that traditional Hohokam culture emerged throughout much of southern Arizona. Occupation of the Tucson Basin appears to have been fairly extensive, but few sites have been excavated that can contribute information on the Snaketown phase. In general, changes in technology suggest the complete adoption of a sedentary, agricultural way of life. The Pioneer period in the Tucson Basin ended around A.D. 800 with the adoption of a new ceramic tradition and with the construction of ball courts at large primary villages.

Colonial Period

In the Colonial period (A.D. 800–900), the initial Cañada del Oro phase was characterized by the appearance of ball courts as public ritual structures and possibly courtyard groups. Dual occupation of the uplands and lowlands continued as the dominant settlement pattern. It was during the Cañada del Oro phase that a distinct tradition of Tucson Basin ceramics first emerged (Kelly 1978; Whittlesey et al. 1994:142).

There was an increase in the number of sites recorded for the succeeding Rillito phase (A.D. 900–1000), which some have interpreted as a population expansion (Whittlesey et al. 1994:144). The intensity of use of alluvial fans and floodplain environments increased, but upland areas continued to be important for settlement. With the expansion came a new emphasis on large primary villages, which functioned as community centers fulfilling political and social requirements in highly localized social systems. Primary villages were large, exhibited a high diversity and density of associated material culture, and often had one or more public features, namely ball courts. The settlement system focused around the primary village often consisted of one or more hamlets and any number of small farmsteads or other temporary camps associated with resource procurement (Doelle et al. 1987:77).

Sedentary Period

The beginning of the Sedentary period, which in the Tucson Basin is equivalent to the Rincon phase (A.D. 1000–1150), saw the maximum expansion of population in the Tucson Basin. Primary villages continued to be important, but settlements were often located along secondary drainages, and a diversity of settlement types and uses of different environmental zones became the settlement norm. Although Rincon Red-on-brown ceramics were the hallmark, there was an apparent florescence of ceramic color schemes that began in the middle portion of the Sedentary period (Deaver 1989:80–81). This florescence was associated with a major settlement shift, which occurred throughout the Tucson Basin. Several large primary villages appear to have been abandoned at this time, and settlement generally became more dispersed (Craig and Wallace 1987; Doelle and Wallace 1986; Elson 1986). The causes for this sudden settlement shift are not entirely clear, and both environmental and social factors have been implicated. The diversification of settlement types in the middle and late Rincon phase, however, reflected a new emphasis on resource-procurement and -processing sites as part of the overall adaptation to the Tucson Basin. Despite the shift in settlement patterns, elaboration of village structure continued, and courtyard groups remained an important organizational form at many communities. At the same time, several Rincon phase sites exhibited a less formal site structure, with some communities lacking courtyard groups altogether (Whittlesey 1997:61).

Classic Period

The Classic period in the Tucson Basin is divided into two phases, which have traditionally been defined on the basis of associated ceramics. Adequate, independent chronological control for this time period is lacking. The Tanque Verde phase (A.D. 1150–1300) was characterized by the presence of Tanque Verde Red-on-brown ceramics (Greenleaf 1975; Kelley 1978). In the subsequent Tucson phase, Gila Polychrome was added to Tanque Verde Red-on-brown (Whittlesey 1997). This latter phase has been dated A.D. 1300–1450. In addition to the appearance of Tanque Verde Red-on-brown ceramics, the onset of the Classic period has traditionally been defined by widespread changes in material culture, settlement organization, and public architecture. With the Classic period came a new architectural style: rectangular, semisubterranean, adobe-walled rooms became the preferred house form, although pit houses continued to be used. As in preceding periods, dwellings were often stand-alone structures (Whittlesey et al. 1994: 155), although during the Classic period, many were constructed in contiguous groups sharing walled compound spaces (Fish et al. 1992:20). Platform mounds replaced ball courts as public structures in the Classic period, and there was a marked shift in burial practices from cremation to inhumation.

Initially, the Classic period was thought to have been brought about by the movement of Salado populations into the Phoenix Basin and points south (Haury 1945). More recently, several investigators have posited that these changes were a result of in situ cultural change with little external influence (Sires 1987). As with the rest of the Hohokam area, the situation in the Tucson Basin is not entirely clear. Evidence for a gradual, in situ shift was found at some sites, such as at Punta de Agua, where Greenleaf interpreted the transition between late Rincon and early Tanque Verde Red-on-brown ceramics as a continuum in which changes in vessel shapes and design elements represent a transformation of Rincon Red-on-brown into a new ceramic type (Greenleaf 1975:52). Architectural evidence suggests a similar type of experimentation at several communities. Several instances of houses-in-pits existing contemporaneously with aboveground or semisubterranean adobe-walled structures have been documented (Jones 1998; Slaughter 1996). By contrast, the sudden appearance of large settlements like the Marana Community in the northern Tucson Basin is more in accord with population movement into the region (Fish et al. 1992). Clearly, further research that targets migration and the material correlates of ethnicity is necessary before the question can be put to rest. Unfortunately, the level of temporal control available for most sites in southern Arizona will seriously limit our ability to resolve such questions.

Native Americans of the Historical Period

Sometime before Kino's first entry into southern Arizona, the Rillito Valley apparently ceased to be the regular home of any Native American group. For the sedentary people living along the Santa Cruz River, the valley probably continued to serve as a place to hunt and gather food, and perhaps even to farm, but the threat of Apache raids from the north and east, beginning at least as early as 1700, was enough to discourage permanent settlements. The Apache themselves probably also used the valley periodically for hunting and gathering, but the most substantial evidence of their intermittent presence there is the nearly complete lack of evidence for the presence of any other native group.

In this section, we discuss the Native American cultures of southern Arizona after the arrival of Europeans to the region. First, we consider the difficulties of defining the end of prehistory and the beginning of history in southern Arizona and the usual solution of referring to a protohistoric period. Then, we provide brief overviews of the three major historical-period Native American cultures that have lived near, if never permanently in, the Río Antiguo study area: O'odham, Apache, and Yaqui.

Protohistory

Southern Arizona was the northernmost frontier of New Spain for nearly three centuries, from 1539 to the independence of Mexico in 1821, or for most of the Spanish colonial presence in the New World. The remoteness of the region from the center of New Spain meant that the period between initial exploration and actual settlement by Spaniards was unusually long, more than a century and a half (see Chapter 4). The conventional definition of the beginning of the historical period as the moment when Europeans first arrived applies less to southern Arizona than perhaps to any other part of New Spain, because the first substantial European presence, and thus the first substantial descriptions of the region and its inhabitants, did not come until the late 1600s. That is when the Jesuits, most notably Eusebio Francisco Kino, began a program of exploration and missionization in what are now Sonora and southern Arizona—the Pimería Alta, or the upper (i.e., northern) region of the Pima.

The protohistoric period in southern Arizona, linking the end of true prehistory and the beginning of tangible history, is inconsistently defined and poorly understood. Nonetheless, it is a convenient way of referring to Native American cultural developments during a time when European influences—crops and livestock, material culture, and especially disease—were undoubtedly present but largely unaccompanied by Europeans. The first Spanish explorers to cross the Southwest, and presumably Arizona, were Fray Marcos de Niza in 1539 and Francisco Vásquez de Coronado in 1540. Both journeys were poorly documented, the actual routes they followed are uncertain, and neither prompted any further exploration of southern Arizona. The region continued essentially unvisited by Spaniards for the next century and a half. The documentary gap spanning the period between 1539 and the beginning of sustained contact with the Spanish, from approximately 1700, defines the protohistoric period for most archaeologists, although some extend the end date to the establishment of presidios in southern Arizona, beginning in the 1750s (Majewski and Ayres 1997; Ravesloot and Whittlesey 1987; Whittlesey et al. 1994).

There were two major groups of indigenous peoples living in the Pimería Alta at the earliest Spanish contact, distinguished by language and lifestyle. One group was the O'odham, Piman-speaking peoples who were agricultural to a greater or lesser degree, depending on the local environment. Several discrete groups of O'odham can be distinguished on the basis of linguistic and cultural differences. The O'odham as a whole were sometimes referred to by the Spanish as *pimas altos*, the upper Pima, and were recognized as the linguistic brethren of the *pimas bajos*, Piman speakers of the lower Pimería, living farther south in Sonora. The other major group was the Apache, Athapaskan speakers who were primarily hunter-gatherer-raiders living a highly mobile way of life and farming very little. The Apache lived primarily in the regions bordering the Pimería on the north and east, making frequent forays into the Pimería to raid. South of the Pimería Alta and living adjacent to *pimas bajos* were the Opata of the Sonora River valley and the nearby Sierra Madre. Still farther south were the Yaqui, centered on the Yaqui River valley. Sometimes traveling through the Pimería Alta, either to reach sacred places or to trade, were the Zuni, who lived on the high, arid Colorado Plateau of present-day New Mexico. There were also two areas adjacent to the Pimería Alta that were apparently uninhabited, described as *despoblados* in the records of the Coronado expedition. One extended north from the headwaters of the Río Sonora to the headwaters of the San Pedro River, and a second lay north of the Gila River, encompassing much of the central mountains of Arizona (Di Peso 1953; Reid and Whittlesey 1997). Whether these areas were truly uninhabited or their occupants were simply never seen by early Spanish observers is unknown.

Spicer (1962:119) estimated there were as many as 30,000 Piman speakers living in the Pimería Alta in the late 1600s. According to Spicer, the Spanish seemed to think of the O'odham in terms of four major subdivisions. The people they called Pimas, without any qualifying adjectives, lived in the southeastern part of the region, as far south as the upper Ríos San Miguel and Sonora of modern Sonora. In the southwestern area were the Soba, so called because of their leader's name. The Soba were among the earliest O'odham encountered by the Spanish and lived along the Altar River, a place later regarded by Tohono O'odham as the source of their culture (Underhill et al. 1979). As disease and encroachment took their toll, the surviving Soba joined other O'odham groups (Erickson 1994). In the eastern and northeastern Pimería Alta were the Sobaipuri, who lived along the San Pedro River (then called the Río Quiburi or the Río de San Joseph de Terrenate) and the Santa Cruz River (then called the Río de Santa María), as far north as the Gila River and for some distance along it. They too lost their distinct ethnic identity in the 1700s, as they were relocated among other peoples and devastated by disease. Occupying the desert areas in the western and northwestern portions of the Pimería Alta were the Papago, or Papabota, now known as the Tohono O'odham.

The northern limit of Kino's explorations and missionary efforts was the Gila River. Traveling as far north as the Casa Grande—Kino was probably the first European to see it—Kino referred to the people living along the Gila simply as "Pimas" (Bolton 1948). They were subsequently known as the Gileño or Gila Pima and today are known by their own name for themselves, Akimel O'odham. Kino also noted that there were people speaking a different language living to the west of the Pima, as far as the Colorado River. These people, who were on friendly terms with the Pima, he called Opa and Cocomaricopa (Bolton 1948). They were undoubtedly the Yuman-speaking Maricopa.

Apache raids and the Spanish policy of *reducción*, or gathering dispersed *ranchería* populations into missionary centers, combined to move O'odham populations away from their traditional territories and to blur ethnic distinctions. The Sobaipuri in particular were devastated by disease and relocation. By the late eighteenth century, they had ceased to exist except as scattered anonymous elements of other O'odham populations. At the same time, many of the desert-dwelling Tohono O'odham relocated to the Santa Cruz River valley, encouraged by Spanish missionaries who hoped to find replacements for the disappearing Sobaipuri.

By the time professional ethnographers came to record their ways of life, the O'odham people themselves recognized three major divisions based largely on economy and residential patterns, which may approximate much more closely the subdivisions of the protohistoric period than the labels applied to them by the Spanish. These were the Hia C'ed O'odham, or Sand People, the most mobile and least agricultural of the O'odham, living in the western deserts as far south as the Gulf of California; the

Tohono O'odham, or Desert People (the Papago to the Spanish, although this term was sometimes also used for the Hia C'ed O'odham), who shifted between summer farming villages and winter hunting-gathering encampments; and the Akimel O'odham, or River People, who stayed year-round in permanent villages along the Gila River. In the terminology of Fontana (1983b), these groups are, respectively, the No Villagers, the Two Villagers, and the One Villagers. O'odham lifeways are discussed in more detail below.

The Apache also were given many different labels by the Spanish. Unfortunately, the tendency was to call any nomadic people "Apache" whether they were Athapaskan speakers or not. The Jocome and Suma occupied what was later Chiricahua Apache territory in southeastern Arizona and southwestern New Mexico (Spicer 1962:237). Farther to the east were the Jano, Manso, and Jumano, who occupied Chihuahua as far east as the Río Grande. Although the Jocome were probably Apache, Spicer did not think that the Suma were Athapaskan speakers. They more likely were related to the Jumano, semisedentary people who ranged into the Great Plains. Spicer suggested that the Jano were a band of Chiricahua or Mimbreño Apache. Schroeder (1974a, 1974b) thought that the Jano and Jocome were not Apache and that no Apache peoples occupied the region south of the Gila River before the 1680s. Almost nothing is known of the Manso, because they were missionized in the vicinity of El Paso in the 1700s and abandoned their former nonagricultural way of life (Spicer 1962:231).

To the north of the Pimería Alta, beyond the Gila River, were simply the "Apache." Apachería was the term Kino applied to the land lying between the lands of the Pima and those of the Hopi and Zuni to the north (Opler 1983:402). Basso (1983:465) believed the people living in this area later became the Western Apache, who by 1700 had successfully claimed an extensive territory that stretched south from the Mogollon Rim across the Natanes Plateau to the Gila River—essentially the country called *despoblado* by a chronicler of the Coronado expedition.

Other Spanish names for Apache were Querecho, applied to the nomadic people encountered by Coronado and later applied to Apache groups living near Acoma in New Mexico, and Apaches de Gila (or Xila), a vague term for Apache living in southeastern Arizona and southwestern New Mexico. Opler (1983:402) thought that some of the Querechos might have belonged to the Eastern Chiricahua Apache band.

It is difficult to identify protohistoric archaeological sites in southern Arizona, for a number of reasons. First, the documentary sources provide little information about lifeways and material culture. The best descriptions of O'odham culture were written after it had been dramatically transformed by European contact. Similarly, the misinterpretation of some early historical-period sites has created confusion about the material remains that might correspond to actual protohistoric settlements. Second, it is difficult to date protohistoric sites. No archaeomagnetic chronology has been developed for this period, and radiocarbon dates are typically returned with ranges too wide to be useful. Third, the way of life of at least one of the peoples to occupy the region, the Apache, was not likely to leave easily recognizable remains.

We do know that the Akimel O'odham (Gila Pima) and Sobaipuri at the time of European contact were agricultural and lived in brush houses covered with mats, similar to Hohokam pit houses. Juan Mateo Manje, Kino's military escort on many of his travels, provided the following description of San Agustín de Oiaur, one of the largest settlements in the vicinity of modern Tucson:

> Here the river runs a full flow of water, though the horses forded it without difficulty.
> There are good pasture and agricultural lands with a canal for irrigation. The Indians
> harvest corn, beans, and cotton from which they make cloth to dress themselves. Squash,
> melons and watermelons were also raised. We counted 800 souls in 186 houses [Manje
> 1954:92].

It is difficult to reconcile this view of early Sobaipuri life with the picture painted by archaeology. Sites that have been attributed to the Sobaipuri in southern Arizona are ephemeral, with little refuse deposition and few artifacts, indicating short-term occupation. They are characterized by oval or subrectangular houses marked by single courses of cobbles presumably used to foot or brace the brush superstructure. Moreover, virtually nothing is known of the lifeways of early Apache peoples in southern Arizona, and no unequivocal early Apache sites have been located.

O'odham

The O'odham were the most populous group of Native Americans living in southern Arizona at the time of European contact. As already noted, the Spanish made a variety of distinctions among groups of O'odham, but these distinctions probably reflect the circumstances of Spanish encounters with the O'odham as much as any distinctions recognized by the O'odham themselves. The most enduring distinctions are those of Akimel, Tohono, and Hia C'ed O'odham, which are based on differing economic emphases and degrees of residential mobility. Here, we discuss these three groups individually, plus two others that had disappeared by the late eighteenth century, the Kohatk and the Sobaipuri. The first three groups have survived into the twenty-first century and are known through a combination of historical and ethnographic documentation. The last two groups are known only through Spanish documentary sources.

Akimel O'odham

Kino first encountered the Akimel O'odham when he reached Casa Grande in 1694. He returned several times over the next eight years, but following his death in 1711, the Akimel O'odham had little if any contact with Europeans until 1736, when another Jesuit, Ignacio Javier Keller, visited the Gila River. By this time, the *rancherías* that Kino had encountered had dispersed. From the mid-eighteenth century to the 1840s, contact with Europeans remained limited, with only sporadic trading by Akimel O'odham at the presidio in Tucson and occasional visits by Spanish traders traveling to the Gila River (Russell 1908).

In the 1840s, most notably during the California gold rush of 1849, the Akimel O'odham proved to be friendly and helpful to Anglo-Americans and others traveling along the Gila Trail, a major route to California. The Akimel O'odham became an invaluable source of supplies, feed for stock, and even protection. Following the Gadsden Purchase, the U.S. Army also found the Akimel O'odham to be helpful, both as a source of supplies and as scouts against the Apache. In the early 1860s, Mormon towns were established at Tempe and Lehi by settlers from Utah. Often at the mercy of the Apache, the Mormons requested assistance from the Akimel O'odham and Maricopa, some of whom moved to Lehi to provide security for the settlers. Later in the nineteenth century, European settlement began to displace the Akimel O'odham, just as it had other peoples in the Pimería Alta. By the start of the twentieth century, the Akimel O'odham were reduced to eight villages along the Gila, most on the south bank (Russell 1908). It is ironic that the Akimel O'odham villages, which for several decades served as the breadbasket of southern Arizona, were deprived of water and reduced to poverty as non-Indian farmers in the Phoenix area diverted the water of the Gila River to their own fields (DeJong 1992).

Prior to Spanish contact, the Akimel O'odham lived in villages or smaller settlements called *rancherías* by the Spanish. Their pole-and-thatch houses were positioned generally within sight but not sound of each other. They raised corn, beans, melons, squash, cotton, and gourds. Whether they practiced irrigated agriculture before the eighteenth century, diverting water from the Gila River by means of ditches, is a topic of controversy. There is no mention of irrigation in the accounts of Kino and Manje, who did mention the use of irrigation by the Sobaipuri; the first mention occurs in Spanish accounts of the mid-1700s.

It does seem likely that the Akimel O'odham used the Gila River as a source of water for their crops (see the discussion in Whittlesey [1998]).

Akimel O'odham men cleared, planted, and irrigated the fields that were harvested later by the women. The diet was mixed but predominantly plant based, with saguaro fruit and mesquite pods being the most abundant and available native foods. During water shortages, the Akimel O'odham were forced to rely more on wild foods, even seeking plants and animals in Apache territory. Around the turn of the nineteenth century, floods occasionally would destroy the irrigation canals and crops, forcing the Akimel O'odham to rely entirely on wild resources (Rea 1997; Russell 1908).

Russell (1908) identified 65 native food plants that provided edible stems, leaves, flowers, seeds, roots, bulbs, nuts, fruits, and berries. Food plants included saltbush, cottonwood, agave, ironwood, mesquite mistletoe, pumpkin, tree cholla, saguaro, mesquite, palo verde, screwbean, watermelon, prickly pear, catclaw, beans, wild onion, muskmelon, cotton, squash, pepper, and acorns. The Akimel O'odham also used many of these food plants—particularly several shrubs, trees, and gourds—for medicinal needs, and used willow shoots, cattails, and devil's claw for basket weaving (see also Rea 1997).

The Akimel O'odham used many wildlife species from the *bajada*, river, and mountains to supplement their plant diet. Animals hunted, fished, and trapped included fish, peccary, badger, antelope, mountain lion, ground squirrel, deer, a variety of birds, rabbit, mountain sheep, and raccoon. Eagles and hawks were kept for their feathers, which were used by the medicine men. The villagers caught lizards and other small animals to feed these birds (Russell 1908; see also Rea 1998). As did other indigenous groups, the Akimel O'odham adopted many plants and animals introduced by the Spanish. Wheat and sorghum were added to their indigenous crops. Winter wheat enabled them to grow two crops in a single season. Cattle, horses, burros, mules, and poultry greatly increased their domestic animal population, which had previously been limited to dogs (Russell 1908).

Tohono O'odham

The Tohono O'odham occupied a large area in the north-central Pimería Alta, also known as the Papaguería to the Spanish, after the Spanish name for the Tohono O'odham, *papagos*. Their intermittently transhumant way of life, a combination of agriculture, hunting, and gathering, was an adaptation to the seasonal extremes of their desert environment. They spent the hot summers in lowland villages, farming the alluvial fans extending from the bases of the mountains, and the mild winters at camps near wells or springs in the mountains, hunting and gathering. This is the typical "Two Villager" way of life discussed by Fontana (1983b). Tohono O'odham farming was most often of the *ak chin* variety, which involved placing brush dams across washes to better distribute mountain runoff across the cultivated portions of alluvial fans (Nabhan 1983).

Castetter and Bell (1942:57) estimated that collected plant foods and game constituted 75 percent of the Tohono O'odham diet. Saguaro, mesquite, prickly pear, and cholla were the most important plants. Each spring, the Tohono O'odham set up cactus camps to gather saguaro fruit, from which they made a variety of dried foods and wine. The saguaro wine ceremony was performed each year to ensure the arrival of the summer rains. Old men who knew the traditional procedures fermented syrup from the saguaro fruit while villagers gathered nightly to dance and sing. When it was ready, the wine was served as a symbol of renewal of life, and participants would drink to the point of intoxication (Underhill et al. 1979).

The Tohono O'odham lived in pole-and-brush houses, slept on grass mats, and carried out many of their daily activities outdoors under *ramadas*. The house, or *ki*, was a dome-shaped structure similar to Hohokam pit houses. Although best known for their beautifully detailed baskets made of devil's claw and grass, the Tohono O'odham were also excellent potters. In the late nineteenth and early twentieth centuries, their manure-tempered ollas were used in virtually every household in Tucson, regardless of ethnicity. Several painted pottery types were made, including red-on-brown, white-on-red, and black-on-red (Fontana et al. 1962; Whittlesey 1986). Saguaro syrup in narrow-necked jars was consistently traded to the Akimel O'odham in exchange for wheat and other goods (Russell 1908).

Tohono O'odham villages consisted of extended patrilineal families. Marriages were arranged with people from other villages, and the wife would usually move into her husband's home, helping her mother-in-law with daily tasks (Underhill 1939). Sometimes the husband would move in with the wife's family, however, if they needed help. Although polygamy was allowed, close relatives could not marry (Erickson 1994). When villages became too large, daughter settlements would split off, retaining close social and ceremonial ties to the mother village.

Although the Tohono O'odham were not aggressive, they were accomplished warriors and generally successful at defending themselves from Apache and other attacks. The Tohono O'odham maintained amicable relations with most of their neighbors, including the Seri to the south, the Lower Pima and Opata to the southeast, the Akimel O'odham to the north, and the Cocopa and Yuma peoples living along the lower Gila and Colorado Rivers to the west. The Tohono O'odham traded with most of their neighbors, exchanging food items, hides, sleeping mats, pottery, and baskets. Songs, ceremonies, and labor also were traded on occasion for food and goods (Erickson 1994).

Because the Tohono O'odham were closely related to the Akimel O'odham in language, culture, and economy, there was much trading, sharing, and intermarriage between the two groups, and especially between the northern Tohono O'odham villages and the Akimel O'odham. The Akimel O'odham, distinguished by permanent houses and large, irrigated fields, were wealthy in comparison to the Tohono O'odham. Tohono O'odham sometimes worked in Akimel O'odham fields during times of shortage, and food was often shared freely between the two groups.

The history of contact between other O'odham groups and Europeans was repeated with the Tohono O'odham. Kino greatly influenced religious and subsistence changes among the Tohono O'odham, just as he had among the Sobaipuri and Akimel O'odham, although the raising of cattle and rituals regarded as curing techniques spread more rapidly than formal Christianity (Spicer 1962). Kino's mission program took approximately 50 years to spread from Sonora to San Xavier del Bac. Following the Gadsden Purchase, the Tohono O'odham developed strong relationships with Mexican- and Anglo-Americans based on their shared need to defend against raiding Apache. The raids were frequent and fierce into the 1860s but decreased significantly following a tragic episode at Camp Grant in 1871, discussed below in the section on the Apache.

In 1874, a reservation was established by executive order for the Tohono O'odham, consisting of 69,200 acres centered on the Franciscan mission at San Xavier del Bac. Eight years later, a second, much smaller reservation was established at Gila Bend for Tohono O'odham who had resettled on the Gila River to the west of the Akimel O'odham villages. Only about 10 percent of the Tohono O'odham population lived on the two reservations in the early years, but the formal designation of reservations eventually provided the Tohono O'odham, particularly those living at San Xavier, with a certain amount of political clout. Squatting on reservation lands by non–Tohono O'odham, especially Mexican-Americans, was at first common near San Xavier, and the lack of a government agency on the reservation (it was at first administered from Sacaton on the Gila River) meant squatting could happen freely. But by 1882, with the help of their federal Indian agent, the Tohono O'odham managed to expel all squatters from the reservation (Erickson 1994:78, 87). A single Mexican-American, José María Martínez, retained his pre-Gadsden Mexican land grant near the mission, under special circumstances.

The late nineteenth century brought another important Anglo-American-imposed change to the Tohono O'odham living at San Xavier. The Dawes Severalty Act of 1887 provided for the allotment of small parcels of reservation land, typically 160 acres, to individual O'odham. The purpose of the act was to encourage O'odham to abandon their previously communal approach to land use, in which families used whatever land they needed, and fixed ownership was unknown. After 25 years, allotted land could be sold like any privately held land, and any reservation land not yet allotted to individual O'odham would be made available to non-O'odham settlers. The federal government considered individual land ownership a necessary step in making reservations throughout the West less dependent on federal aid and administration, but the concept of private ownership was alien to the O'odham, as it was to many other Native Americans, and they adapted slowly to the new system. The act ultimately did have the effect of converting many traditional O'odham into organized growers, commercial stock raisers, and even individual wage earners, and it pushed the O'odham toward a cash-based economy (Erickson 1994:91–94).

In 1916, the federal government granted the Tohono O'odham a much larger reservation to the west of San Xavier, extending from the Baboquivari Mountains westward almost to Ajo and from the border with Mexico northward almost to Gila Bend, encompassing some 2.75 million acres. With a number of minor additions and subtractions during its early years, this huge area has survived largely intact as the current Tohono O'odham reservation. In 1934, the federal Indian Reorganization Act, intended as an impetus to Indian self-government, led to the establishment of a centralized Tohono O'odham tribal government and 11 constituent districts. Each district elected a council, two members of which served as representatives on the tribal council, which itself was headed by a chairman, vice chairman, secretary, and treasurer. The districts also elected their own officers to head the district councils. The U.S. Constitution was the model for the tribal constitution, but the tribal bylaws also reflected O'odham traditions, which encouraged the communal use of land. The tribal council continued the practice of going to villages to discuss problems and issues before they made decisions (Blaine 1981; Erickson 1994:104–107).

Hia C'ed O'odham

The traditional lands of the Hia C'ed O'odham extended from the Gila and Colorado Rivers in the north through the Sierra Pinacate region of Sonora to the Gulf of California and southward to Seri country. The Hia C'ed O'odham have also been called Sand Papago, Areneros, Areneños, and Pinacateños. Other O'odham have called them *Hiá Tatk Kuá'adam,* sand-root eaters, and *Otomkal Kuá'adam*, desert iguana eaters. Although this O'odham group was declared extinct in the early 1900s and consequently denied rights to their traditional lands, approximately 1,300 individuals today identify themselves as Hia C'ed O'odham (Rea 1998).

The Hia C'ed O'odham were divided into northern and southern groups, the latter sharing land and cultural similarities with the Seri in Mexico. The northern group interacted with Yuman-speaking peoples and shared similarities with them. The Hia C'ed O'odham were the most linguistically distinct among the O'odham, speaking faster and having exclusive terms, but were still easily understood by all other O'odham (Erickson 1994).

The Hia C'ed O'odham lands were the driest and hottest of the Pimería Alta and the least densely settled. With only a few places suitable for farming, which they carried out using the *ak chin* system (Rea 1998), most of the Hia C'ed O'odham lived as hunters and gatherers ranging over a large area in small family groups. The Hia C'ed O'odham were distinctive for their heavy use of native fish that could be harvested from tidal pools along the Gulf of California. As a consequence of the lack of arable lands and sparse settlement, the Hia C'ed O'odham remained generally isolated from the influences of Spanish culture, as other areas were explored for ranching, farming, and mining. These same characteristics also kept Apache raiding to a minimum (Erickson 1994).

The Hia C'ed O'odham suffered greatly during the 1850s and 1860s when disease devastated the population. Miners at Ajo and ranchers at Quitobaquito encroached on some of their most desirable lands during this time, but the people managed to survive and found employment constructing the railroad through the Gila River basin. Today, they remain scattered. Most live among Tohono O'odham but have never completely assimilated into the main body of O'odham people. In Mexico, the southern Hia C'ed O'odham met a similar fate, having been relocated by the government from the western end of O'odham lands to Quitovac and other inland areas. They too have merged with other O'odham people (Erickson 1994).

Another detrimental impact to the Hia C'ed O'odham of Arizona came when what is now known as the Barry M. Goldwater Air Force Range was established in the 1940s. The Hia C'ed O'odham were prohibited from using that enormous part of their traditional area. The establishment of Organ Pipe Cactus National Monument and the Cabeza Prieta Game Range left virtually no traditional lands in the United States for Hia C'ed O'odham use (Erickson 1994).

Kohatk

The Kohatk, also spelled Koahadk and Kwahatdk, were distinguished among Tohono O'odham as a dialect group (Erickson 1994), although they were closely related to the Akimel O'odham through intermarriage and trade (Erickson 1994; Rea 1998). Kohatk settlements extended as far south as a line extending between modern Santa Rosa and Tucson (Erickson 1994). They lived mostly in villages located between the Picacho Mountains and the Gila River villages of the Akimel O'odham, in an area today known as the Santa Cruz Flats. Important villages were Kohatk, near the Slate Mountains; Ak Chin, near Picacho; and Santa Ana de Cuiquiburitac, east of the Santa Rosa Mountains (Fontana 1987; Russell 1908; Whittlesey et al. 1994:250). The Kohatk moved between *ak chin* fields on the lower Santa Cruz River and adjacent washes to fields along the Gila River as opportunities allowed (Dobyns 1974; Rea 1998). They seem to have been neither "desert people" nor "river people," but O'odham who regularly moved between and used both environments (Whittlesey et al. 1994:252).

The documentary history of the Kohatk is confusing, including references to village locations (Whittlesey et al. 1994:249–251). What little is known of their cultural ecology parallels the practices of the other O'odham groups (Rea 1998), although they were noted for bringing cattle to the area in the 1820s (Ezell 1961; Rea 1998; Russell 1908; Whittemore 1893). Some desert settlements were sustained by artificial reservoirs, and Dobyns (1974:325) has pointed out that the Kohatk also dug ditches as necessary to water their fields. Their ethnobiology, however, remains speculative. Little is known about Kohatk social organization. If, as documentary sources suggest, the Kohatk were intermediate between Akimel and Tohono O'odham in economic organization and settlement practices, it may be appropriate to view them as socially intermediate as well (Whittlesey et al. 1994:255).

Kohatk material culture was generally similar to that of other O'odham. Historically, they were known as excellent potters (Russell 1908:124). The Akimel O'odham obtained many painted vessels from the Kohatk in exchange for Pima wheat and other foodstuffs. Apparently, Kohatk pottery was highly polished and more often decorated than other O'odham pottery (Fontana et al. 1962:107–109).

The Kohatk experienced little influence from the Spanish, although there were early attempts at missionization (Fontana 1987). Increased pressure from Apache raiding after Mexican independence forced the Kohatk to abandon their villages along the lower Santa Cruz River and take refuge among the villages of neighboring O'odham. Fontana (1987) has indicated that the remaining Kohatk people settled across the Gila River from the Sacaton community, a village that eventually became known as Santan. Other members moved to the Salt River reservation. By the early 1900s, the Kohatk had lost identity as an independent group and had been assimilated into Akimel O'odham and Tohono O'odham communities (Rea 1998).

Sobaipuri

Unfortunately, we know little about the Sobaipuri, who were once the most populous O'odham group in the vicinity of the Santa Cruz River. Although it was the Sobaipuri who were described in Kino and

Manje's accounts of the late 1600s, there is little if any overlap between the documentary and archaeological evidence for the Sobaipuri occupation of southern Arizona. There are several reasons for this. Most important, the Sobaipuri intermixed early on with Tohono O'odham and other Piman-speaking peoples, such that by the 1800s, they had lost their social and ethnic identity. The documentary evidence itself is difficult to interpret and understand. Sobaipuri *rancherías* were easily moved, and because the Spanish names for villages, including saints' appellations, moved along with the villages, maps made at different times may show several places with the same names. It is difficult, therefore, to match an archaeological site with the location of a named Sobaipuri village.

With this caution, what we know of the Sobaipuri is that they once lived in the well-watered valleys of the Santa Cruz and San Pedro Rivers, farming and producing "plentiful crops" of "calabashes, frijoles, maize, and cotton" (Bolton 1948:I:170–171). Chroniclers of the Coronado expedition noted the Sobaipuri's use of turquoise and body painting or tattooing of their faces and bodies. They came to be known, consequently, as Rsársavinâ, meaning "spotted." The Sobaipuri had few interactions with the Spanish until the latter part of the seventeenth century. They maintained trade relations, however, with the Spanish in the Río Grande Valley and presumably also with the Spanish of the Pimería Baja. In the early eighteenth century, the Spanish enlisted the Sobaipuri for military purposes; they provided an armed buffer against raiding Apache (Di Peso 1953). The Sobaipuri were fierce warriors, aggressive and accustomed to war because of their proximity to and frequent encounters with the Apache (Erickson 1994).

From the late 1600s to approximately 1762, the landscape of the Santa Cruz and San Pedro River valleys was characterized by *rancherías,* larger villages, irrigation canals, wells, and cultivated fields (Griffith 1992). Sobaipuri villages appear to have been occupied briefly, and settlement locations shifted rapidly. Seymour (1989:215) has suggested that the suitability of the floodplain for farming was the major determinant in locating villages. Inferred Sobaipuri sites in the San Pedro River valley are located on ridges and terraces above the river. There were at least 14 *rancherías* along the San Pedro River when Kino and Manje visited there in the late 1600s (Whittlesey et al. 1994:237). Approximately 100–500 people lived in each of these villages. South of Santa Cruz de Gaybanipitea (Di Peso 1953), more than 2,000 people lived in numerous small villages. Although villages had existed between the *rancherías* of Quiburi and Cusac, they were abandoned by the 1700s.

The Tucson Basin was densely settled, apparently because of intensive agriculture (Doelle 1984). The stretch of the Santa Cruz River between San Xavier del Bac and San Clemente (thought to be located near Point of the Mountain, at the northern end of the Tucson Mountains) was the center of Upper Pima culture at the time of Spanish contact, with an estimated 2,000 residents (Doelle 1984:207). Other important villages were San Agustín de Oaiur (also spelled Oyaur and Oyaut), San Cosme del Tucson, and Valle de Correa in the north, and Guevavi, Tumacácori, and Calabazas in the south (Whittlesey et al. 1994:234–236).

Sobaipuri lifeways and material culture were evidently similar to those of other O'odham groups in southern Arizona. They lived in oval or round structures built of brush, poles, and mats. Whether they built adobe structures as suggested in some documents (Burrus 1971; Pfefferkorn 1989) is controversial. Some authors (e.g., Masse 1981) think this was the product of Spanish influence. It is probable that the earliest Sobaipuri pottery was the thin, wiped brown ware called Whetstone Plain. Whetstone Plain is very different from known historical-period ceramics of O'odham manufacture, which are thick, well polished, and often red slipped, and which often have black cores resulting from the use of manure temper. Sobaipuri pottery is puzzling for other reasons. Whetstone Plain pottery exhibits similarities to other protohistoric and early-historical-period pottery over a vast region, including Patayan or Yuman ceramics, Apache pottery, Yavapai pottery, and the pottery made by Numic-speaking people, such as Shoshone and Paiute (Ravesloot and Whittlesey 1987). Differentiating among native peoples on the basis of their ceramics is a time-honored practice in archaeology but is notoriously difficult for the early historical period.

A particular type of projectile point with a deeply concave, indented base and serrated edges is attributed to the Sobaipuri (Masse 1981; Ravesloot and Whittlesey 1987). Points like this have also been attributed to the Yavapai (Pilles 1981). Other stone artifacts were relatively undiagnostic, although the raw materials are typically thought to be of better quality than those used in Hohokam stone tools (Brew and Huckell 1987:171).

Little is known of Sobaipuri farming techniques. Documentary evidence suggests use of simple, gravity-fed irrigation channels to divert water from rivers and swampy areas to fields, but no archaeological evidence of these has yet been found. The archaeological data indicate a low frequency of ground stone tools, plant remains, storage facilities, and other materials usually associated with an intensive reliance on agriculture. We do not know whether this reflects factors of preservation or other factors. Prior to Spanish contact, the Sobaipuri raised maize, beans, squash, cotton, melons, and three kinds of gourds. Cotton was spun and woven into clothing. Following the arrival of the Spanish, they added wheat, barley, chili, sugar cane, sweet potatoes, and watermelons to their fields. The Sobaipuri used a wide variety of native wild plants for food, construction purposes, and medicine. Mescal, or agave, was used for food and drink and in crafts; mesquite wood was used for construction, and mesquite beans were eaten; and the fruit of cacti such as prickly pear and saguaro was used for food. Many plants provided treatments for a variety of ailments (Di Peso 1953). The Sobaipuri also added stock raising to their subsistence activities when the Spanish introduced cattle, sheep, goats, horses, donkeys, and mules. The introduction of these new foods brought changes to the allocation of labor and the value system, in addition to changes in subsistence.

Interactions among the Sobaipuri and their neighbors ran the gamut from hostilities to intermarriage. Spanish sources from the late 1600s indicate that, although Apache peoples lived east of the San Pedro River and along the banks of the Gila River, they had been raiding O'odham settlements for many years. Language was a common bond among the natives of the Pimería Alta, and the Sobaipuri maintained frequent communications with the Akimel O'odham and the Tohono O'odham. Their relations with the Akimel O'odham in particular included frequent trade and intermarriage. During the 1600s, the Sobaipuri evidently maintained friendly communication and commerce with their Hopi and Zuni neighbors to the north. Although Wyllys (1931, cited in Di Peso 1953) characterized the Sobaipuri as haughty and arrogant, they were looked up to by the other natives of the Pimería Alta, presumably because of their lack of malice. Citing Bolton (1948), Di Peso (1953) wrote that Kino also noted these temperament differences, adding that the Sobaipuri were generous in their poverty, sharing necessities with visitors as they were able. Opposition and rivalry between the Sobaipuri and other indigenous groups was expressed through fighting, and later in races and contests.

Sobaipuri living along the Santa Cruz and San Pedro Rivers had a long history of intermarriage and cooperative action when the need arose. When Kino arrived, the Apache were already pushing hard against the eastern boundary of Pimería Alta. Recognizing the warlike reputation of the Sobaipuri, the Spanish sought to organize the villages of the San Pedro Valley into a military alliance to defend the northern frontier of New Spain. This attempted militarization eventually had disastrous consequences (Fontana 1983a:137). The *reducción* policy and missionization actually increased Apache raiding, as the concentrated livestock, weapons, and stored food provided an additional lure (Ezell 1983:149).

Problems with Apache raiding became so great that in 1762 the San Pedro Sobaipuri joined the Santa Cruz Sobaipuri at Santa María de Suamca, San Xavier del Bac, and San Agustín del Tucson, significantly changing the ethnic composition of the valley. This also left the San Pedro Valley—once a Sobaipuri barrier against the Apache—essentially defenseless and unprotected. There is controversy over the reasons that the Sobaipuri abandoned the San Pedro River valley. Some authors think that the Sobaipuri simply fled in the face of the hostile Apache (Kessell 1976), whereas others believe that Sobaipuri resettlement was by order of Spanish *reducción* policy and carried out by military officers (Dobyns 1976). Both processes were probably at work.

The densely settled villages of the Santa Cruz River valley quickly succumbed to epidemics against which the residents had little inherited resistance. By 1773, the population of San Xavier del Bac was greatly reduced as a result of both epidemics and Apache raids. Tohono O'odham, encouraged to settle at the mission beginning around 1800 to replace the Sobaipuri population lost to disease and war, inter-married with the remaining Sobaipuri, and the loss of Sobaipuri ethnic identity was inevitable. In 1776, the Tubac presidio was relocated to Tucson. Within the next quarter century, the Spanish population increased as ranchers and miners moved into the Santa Cruz Valley, contact between Spanish and O'odham peoples increased, and the native population decreased (Bronitsky and Merritt 1986; Erickson 1994; Ezell 1983; Whittlesey at al. 1994). No Sobaipuri remain today.

Major sites that have been attributed to Sobaipuri occupation include England Ranch Ruin, located along the Santa Cruz River south of Tucson (Doyel 1977); Santa Cruz de Gaybanipitea, excavated by Di Peso (1953); three sites in the Santa Rita Mountains excavated during the ANAMAX-Rosemont project (Huckell 1984c); and Alder Wash Ruin, on the San Pedro River (Masse 1985). Some of these sites have objects of European manufacture, such as glass beads and metal tools, but others do not. There are other isolated finds and components at sites that have been attributed to the Sobaipuri, including a late occupation at the San Xavier Bridge site (see review in Ravesloot and Whittlesey [1987]). Several flexed inhumations with Sobaipuri-style projectile points and unusual accompaniments, including a shell trumpet, a golden eagle skeleton, and arrow-making kits, were found at the site (Ravesloot 1987b). Excavated sites that Di Peso attributed to the Sobaipuri—the supposed village of Quiburi in the San Pedro Valley (Di Peso 1953) and San Cayetano in the Santa Cruz Valley (Di Peso 1956)—probably were not the native Sobaipuri settlements their excavator claimed them to be. The former is the site of the Spanish presidio of Santa Cruz de Terrenate, and although some Sobaipuri may have lived at or near the presidio, the structures that Di Peso excavated and attributed to them probably were not Sobaipuri but Spanish (Masse 1981; Seymour 1989; Whittlesey 1994; Whittlesey et al. 1994:239–241); the latter is a Classic period Hohokam site with evidence for some later (probably middle or late 1800s) O'odham occupation (Whittlesey 1994; Whittlesey et al. 1994:241; Wilcox 1987). It is unfortunate that, although there have been excavations at the locations of several Sobaipuri villages in the Santa Cruz Valley, including San Xavier del Bac, Guevavi, and Tumacácori, few traces of the late-1600s to early-1700s occupation have been found.

Apache

In sharp contrast to sedentary farmers such as the Akimel O'odham, the Apache were the most mobile of southwestern peoples. Instead of defining their lives with reference to a particular river valley, the Apache centered their lives on the mountains of southern and central Arizona. The mountains defined their traditional territories, provided them with food and shelter, and embodied their sacred places. In times of conflict, the mountains were their refuge. Because of their uniquely close familiarity with the mountains, the Apache were able to pursue their way of life long after many other Native Americans had resigned themselves to reservations.

The Apache were relatively recent migrants to the Southwest, although the timing of their entry has been widely debated. Most scholars agree that the Apache, who are classified linguistically as Southern Athapaskan speakers, moved southward from an original home in Alaska or southern Canada sometime around A.D. 1500, if not earlier. Their language, culture, and lifeways reflect this distinctive origin and comparatively recent history. All Apache peoples were highly mobile and made their living by a combination of hunting, collecting wild plant foods, raiding, and some farming. This way of life brought them into frequent and often violent contact with sedentary, farming Native Americans and the Euroamericans who came later.

Ethnographers subdivide the Apache into several hierarchical groupings on the basis of territorial, linguistic, and cultural differences. The largest grouping was the tribe or division, traditionally subdivided into smaller groups and bands. Two groupings whose traditional territories overlapped are most important in southern Arizona history. These are the Aravaipa band, part of the San Carlos group of the Western Apache, and the Central Chiricahua band of the Chiricahua Apache.

The Aravaipa band was called *tcéjìné* ("dark rocks people") for a region in the Galiuro Mountains near to where they lived. As their name suggests, the Aravaipa band made Aravaipa Canyon their home base. Their territory included the lower San Pedro River valley as far north as the Gila River and the mountains bordering the valley—the Santa Catalina, Rincon, Santa Teresa, and Galiuro Mountains. Their seasonal round followed the cycle of the year and the ripening of wild crops. Family groups separated from the main band in search of wild foods, usually bringing back the prepared crop for consumption and storage. In late spring, they planted corn at Aravaipa Canyon. In summer, they lived in the mountains overlooking Tucson and the Santa Cruz River valley. The fruit of the saguaro brought them to the San Pedro Valley in July, and they gathered acorns near Oracle in the fall. Fall was harvest time, and after the crop was brought in, they lived in secure winter camps located in the Galiuro and Santa Teresa Mountains, from which their men mounted raids into Mexico. One of the most important traditional foods was mescal, or agave. The hearts of the plants were roasted in huge pits near the sites where they grew, and the prepared mescal was brought back to camp. In addition to food, mescal provided a fermented drink, fibers for sewing, and a fibrous stalk for lance shafts and musical instruments.

Bands were composed of 3–12 local groups, which were the fundamental unit of Western Apache and Chiricahua Apache society. Chiricahua bands were smaller, consisting of 3–5 local groups, and the local group was named after some prominent natural landmark in its range or labeled by the name of its chief. Each local group consisted of 2–10 family clusters, or *gota,* usually totaling 10–30 households, who returned each year to the group's farming site. Clans, or large kinship groupings, were nonterritorial and served to regulate marriage, extend kinship beyond the family, and provide economic and social support. Cutting across group and other boundaries, clans served to create an expansive web of kinship bonds. The minimal residential unit was the *gowa,* or camp, a term referring to the house, its occupants, and the camp itself. Dwellings were dome-shaped or conical pole-and-brush structures often referred to as wickiups. The largest and most permanent structures were called *nesdango'wa* (ripe fruits wickiup) and were located at the farm sites. Archaeologically, a *gowa* can often be recognized only by the rock rings that once formed the wickiup foundation. The Chiricahua Apache occasionally built tepees or hide-covered structures.

The Central Chiricahua band ranged around the present-day towns of Duncan, Willcox, Benson, and Elgin in southern Arizona, and they held mountain strongholds in the Dos Cabezas, Chiricahua, Dragoon, Mule, and Huachuca Mountains. Each local group had a "chief" or "leader" who gained prominence because of his bravery, wisdom, eloquence, and ceremonial knowledge. The local group was important in regulating social and economic institutions, including marriage, raiding parties, and ceremonial events. The Chiricahua depended more heavily on wild plant foods, hunting, and raiding, and less on farming, than the Western Apache, who probably were the most farming-dependent of the Apache tribes. Mescal was also the Chiricahua band's most important food plant. The tender stalk was roasted and the crown was dug up, trimmed, and baked in an underground pit oven. The baked mescal was sun dried and stored, supplying food for many months.

Apache ceremonialism was based on the acquisition and manipulation of supernatural power and complicated rituals for curing and protecting against illness, success in hunting and warfare, and marking life-cycle events. The most important of the latter were puberty ceremonies for girls, which lasted four days and involved ritual songs and dances, dancing by masked impersonators of the mountain spirits, social dancing, and food redistribution.

Raiding was an integral part of Apache culture and was considered lawful and just. The principal ethnographer of the Western Apache wrote that "The size of the territory in Sonora over which the

Western Apache raided is extraordinary. The Apache knew it like their own country, and every mountain, town, or spring of consequence had its Apache name" (Goodwin 1969:93). Raiding parties ventured as far as the Gulf of California. Raids brought the Apache horses, mules, cattle, hides, blankets, clothing, metal to fashion knives and arrow points, saddles and bridles, and firearms. O'odham, Mexican, and American farms in southern Arizona and northern Sonora, with their livestock and rich stores of grain, were frequent targets of Apache raids. Horses and mules were often killed and eaten during raids, providing a highly transportable food source as well as transportation and enabling the Apache to extend their raiding activities across considerable distances—as far as the Seri country along the Gulf of California.

As would be expected for such a mobile people, basketry, wood, and fiber products were used for most containers and most domestic purposes, and pottery was little emphasized. Pitch-coated baskets served as water containers. Cradleboards were made of wood, and these lightweight carriers enabled infants to accompany their mothers on resource-collecting parties. Beautifully fashioned carrying baskets were used in the harvest. Ceramics were typically dark gray or brown pots with conical bases, often with wiped surfaces and incised or finger-indented rims. During the historical period, bottle glass was often flaked to fashion arrow points, although metal was preferred. The Western Apache in particular were inveterate collectors and recyclers, often reusing grinding stones and other items collected from prehistoric sites (Whittlesey and Benaron 1998). This propensity, combined with the emphasis on perishable material culture, makes Apache sites difficult to identify archaeologically.

When the Spanish first arrived in Arizona, Apache predations on the O'odham were well established. Apache raiding crippled Spanish attempts to establish missions in Pimería Alta in the 1700s and was one reason for the abandonment of the San Pedro River valley by the Sobaipuri (Kessell 1976). The Spanish presidio of Santa Cruz de Terrenate along the San Pedro River was occupied for only four eventful years, beginning in 1775, before Apache raiding forced its abandonment (Sugnet and Reid 1994; Williams 1986c). The presidio at Tubac was relocated to Tucson in 1776, and as the Spanish population began to grow, the pace of Apache raiding accelerated. Following an unprecedented Apache attack on the presidio in 1782, commander Don Pedro Allande began a vigorous campaign against them. Four years later, the Spanish viceroy Bernardo de Gálvez instituted a pacification policy combined with aggressive military action. A key point of this policy was the resettlement of friendly Apache, called *apaches mansos* or *apaches de paz* (Dobyns 1976; Officer 1987), at the royal presidios. A contingent of more than 100 Apaches, primarily Western Apache of the Aravaipa band, was settled at Tucson in 1793 (Dobyns 1976: 98). Members of the Pinal band settled there in 1819 (Dobyns 1976:102). Few if any traces of this occupation remain today.

As Anglo-American miners and settlers spread into Arizona, the Apache found it increasingly difficult to live by their traditional, mobile ways. No reservations had been established for them, and conflict was rampant. Soldiers and settlers kept the Aravaipa band on the move for many years, destroying their farms and camps. Beginning in 1866, several stations were set up to provide the Apache with rations, clothing, and protection from lawless settlers in exchange for their promise of peaceful behavior. Camp Grant was one such site, and the locale of one of the most shameful chapters in the history of Apache-American relations. The camp was established on the San Pedro River at its junction with Aravaipa Creek in the late 1850s and abandoned and reopened in response to federal policy after the Civil War. In 1871, the Aravaipa band under the leadership of Eskiminzin and a number of Pinal band members settled near Camp Grant, then commanded by Lt. Royal Whitman.

Mistakenly believing that the Aravaipa Apache at Camp Grant were responsible for raids on Tucson, Tubac, and Sonoita, and angered by what they perceived as the government's slow response to their requests for help and Whitman's supposed coddling of the "murderers," the people of Tucson decided to punish the Aravaipa on their own. In April 1871, 6 Anglos, 48 Mexicans, and 94 Tohono O'odham from San Xavier attacked the Aravaipa and Pinal Apache at Camp Grant, mutilating and killing more than 100, mostly women and children, and capturing 27 children. "It was slaughter pure and simple," Sheridan (1995:80) has written, "because most of the Apache men were off hunting in the mountains or carrying out surreptitious raids." President Grant insisted that the perpetrators be brought to trial. The sham deliberation lasted 19 minutes and ended with acquittal. Whitman was court-martialed three times after the massacre.

The Camp Grant massacre left all Apache people wary of Anglo-American claims of peace. It was also a stunning indictment of federal Indian policy. Following the massacre, Gen. George Crook was installed as the head of the Department of Arizona. His campaign against the Apache and Yavapai was based on a sweeping offensive assisted by Indian scouts, coupled with destruction of winter food supplies. Relationships between Western and Chiricahua Apache were always somewhat strained, and they worsened after some of the Western Apache allied with the U.S. Army in its campaign against the Chiricahua.

Starvation and weakness took their toll, and by 1872, Crook's campaign began to succeed. The remaining Apache leaders were ready to discuss peace. Many Apache were forced to move to a newly established reservation at San Carlos in 1875. After several unsuccessful attempts to relocate the Chiricahua, including a particularly sad sojourn at San Carlos and a failed attempt to establish a reservation for them in southeastern Arizona, the Chiricahua continued to raid in Arizona, New Mexico, and Sonora. Peace was not established until Geronimo surrendered in Skeleton Canyon in southeastern Arizona in 1886, and the Chiricahua were deported to Florida (Faulk 1969; Schmitt 1960; Sonnichsen 1986; Thrapp 1967).

Four Apache reservations were hurriedly established between 1871 and 1872 as part of the federal government's "peace policy" (Basso 1983:480). The White Mountain Reservation was established in 1871, and an executive order in 1872 added the San Carlos Division to the reservation (Kelly 1953:23). The White Mountain and San Carlos Apache Reservations were formally partitioned in 1897 (Majewski 1998:323). Many Aravaipa Apache also settled at Bylas on the Gila River in the late 1800s. The exiled Chiricahua Apache in Florida were transferred to a reservation at Fort Sill, Oklahoma, in 1894. In 1913, they were given full freedom, and some moved to New Mexico to share a reservation with the Mescalero Apache (Opler 1983:409). Today, most Western Apache in Arizona live on the White Mountain and San Carlos Apache Reservations; the Chiricahua Apache have intermarried and relocated, dispersing the once distinct band.

The Apache had a significant impact on the history of the Río Antiguo study area in two ways. First, they effectively prevented settlement in the Rillito Valley by either Native Americans or Europeans beginning at least as early as 1700 and continuing until at least 1850. In 1873, the year Fort Lowell was established at the confluence of Tanque Verde Creek and Pantano Wash, only a handful of settlers were living in the Rillito Valley. Second, the war waged against the Apache in southern Arizona as a whole was the primary reason for the establishment of the fort, which provided escorts for overland wagon trains and served as a supply depot during the Apache campaign. The building of the fort encouraged settlement along the Rillito in the 1870s and 1880s, both because it eliminated the threat of Apache raids in the valley and because of the market it represented for the products of farming and ranching (see Chapter 4).

Attacks against the Apache were also sometimes mounted from Fort Lowell during the same period. Given the importance of Apache scouts to the Army campaign in Arizona (Vanderpot and Majewski 1998), it seems likely that Apache scouts occasionally stayed at Fort Lowell, but we have not found any references to their presence there. On the other hand, it is certain that Apache prisoners were sometimes housed temporarily at the fort. The Arizona Historical Society preserves a haunting photograph of two Apache prisoners at Fort Lowell in the 1880s (Figure 3). The young men are handcuffed together, and each wears shackles on his legs. Each man also has what is probably a reservation tag hanging around his neck.

**Figure 3. Apache prisoners at Fort Lowell, ca. 1883–1884
(photograph courtesy of the Arizona Historical Society, Tucson,
Accession No. B94656).**

Yaqui

The Yaqui are members of the diverse Uto-Aztecan language family, which includes, at some remove from the Yaqui, the various Piman-speaking O'odham peoples. The Yaqui speak a dialect of Cahita, a language once spoken in a large area in what are now the Mexican states of Sonora and Sinaloa. The traditional home of the Yaqui is in Sonora, along both banks of the Yaqui River and in the portions of the Sierra Madre drained by its tributaries. Because of persecution by the Mexican government in the late nineteenth century, groups of Yaqui abandoned their traditional territory for locations elsewhere in northern Mexico and southern Arizona. In the Tucson area, the Yaqui eventually settled in two primary locations: Pascua Village on the near north side and a smaller satellite community in Marana, northwest of Tucson. There were small enclaves established earlier in Barrio Anita, just north of downtown, and at Mezquital, south of Tucson (Spicer 1940:21, 1983:237).

Traditional Yaqui territory included rich agricultural lands in the Yaqui River valley and equally important gathering areas in the adjacent Sierra Madre. The lower elevations of the Yaqui Valley were vegetated with subtropical, thorn-thicket vegetation and dense cane brakes. The valley's upper reaches, and the lands bordering the lower valley on the north, had typical Sonoran Desert vegetation: mesquite varyingly interspersed with cacti, cottonwood, palo verde, and other trees and shrubs (Moisés et al. 1971). At Spanish contact, the Yaqui were primarily horticulturalists and lived in scattered *rancherías* in the Yaqui River valley. Initial contact came in 1533, but the interaction was brief and of little consequence to the Yaqui. The conquest of Sonora did not begin in earnest until the early seventeenth century, when Diego Martínez de Hurdaide headed three campaigns against the Yaqui. Although the Yaqui were successful in fending off all three attempts at conquest, Jesuits soon entered Yaqui territory and introduced the Yaqui to Christianity (Moisés et al. 1971).

The Yaqui had a social and political system that combined bilateral kinship with a strong sense of community. They lacked clans and had little in the way of hierarchical social structure. Family groups lived in scattered clearings along perennial watercourses, the typical *ranchería* settlement pattern noted by the Spanish in much of northern New Spain. The clearings were surrounded by tall, dense vegetation that gave a distinctly nonurban appearance to Yaqui settlements (Spicer 1980). Yaqui agriculture was tied to the natural flooding cycle of the river. The Yaqui hunted various wildlife species, with a special emphasis on deer. Deer also had a particular religious significance. Wild plants, including cane and native trees such as mesquite, supplied foods and construction materials (Moisés et al. 1971; Spicer 1980).

When Jesuits came to Yaqui country in the seventeenth century, they established churches in eight locations and, in typical Spanish fashion, consolidated the scattered *rancherías* around the missions (Moisés et al. 1971). Relations between the Jesuits and the Yaqui were generally good, and many Yaquis were quickly converted, at least nominally, to Christianity. Although most converts relocated near the missions, they insisted on retaining their scattered *ranchería* style of settlement, refusing to accept the Spanish grid as a village plan. With a new focus on the missions as the center of their communities, the Yaqui developed highly productive and successful agricultural villages, as they continued to work and farm for community benefit. Their acceptance of Christianity resulted in a blending of traditional culture with a belief in Christ, the Virgin Mary, the saints, and the efficacy of Catholic ritual, particularly the rituals of Lent and Easter (Spicer 1980).

The Yaqui were incorporated into the Spanish colonial economy when they began using the lands at the missions to produce crops for market. They were soon engaged in wage labor for mining and ranching interests that took them away from their home bases. Generally recognized as hard workers and skilled miners, most Yaqui never abandoned their traditional way of life, even when pressured to do so by Spanish colonial policies that threatened their traditional livelihood. Following the expulsion of the Jesuits from New Spain in 1767, encroaching Spanish settlement served only to strengthen the resolve of the Yaqui to protect their land and identity. Their intimate knowledge of the Sierra Madre and their ability to exploit a variety of environments made it difficult for the Spanish colonial government to impose its will on the Yaqui (Spicer 1980).

The Franciscans who replaced the Jesuits were not as successful with the Yaqui as their predecessors, and relations between the Yaqui and the Spanish became strained. Things grew worse following Mexican independence in 1821. In 1825, the Mexican government tried to collect taxes from the Yaqui, but joining forces with the Mayo, Lower Pima, and Opata, the Yaqui ran the Mexican government out of the region. The show of force, as in earlier events, was not sustained beyond that particular confrontation, and Mexican forces gradually returned. In 1853, a period of intermittent warfare began that would continue into the twentieth century (Moisés et al. 1971; Spicer 1980).

As the struggle for control over land and resources continued, factionalism developed among the Yaqui. Some fought against the Mexicans; others fought for them. By the late 1800s, decades of violence and the devastation of smallpox epidemics had taken their toll. The population of the Yaqui living under Mexican control in the eight Yaqui mission villages was approximately 4,000, although many more lived outside the Yaqui Valley. The skirmishes continued, but peace treaties and settlement programs gradually brought more and more Yaqui under Mexican control (Moisés et al. 1971; Spicer 1980).

Massacres of the Yaqui by the Mexican army at the turn of the nineteenth century led to the emigration of many survivors, including to Arizona. Political turmoil continued into the 1920s, when another wave of Yaqui refugees fled to Arizona. Since 1927, the Yaqui have continued their struggle to hold on to their lands in Sonora, mostly without success, although a reservation of a sort was established by the Mexican government that included land north of the Yaqui River and the Bacatete Mountains (Moisés et al. 1971). The Yaqui who sought refuge in southern Arizona brought with them a strong sense of community, many elements of their traditional culture, and their folk Catholicism. They also maintained ties to and communications with the Sonoran Yaqui (Griffith 1992; Moisés et al. 1971; Spicer 1980).

The Yaqui of southern Arizona, best exemplified by the residents of Pascua, retain many traditional cultural features, but they have undergone much social change in Arizona. In Arizona, they are not the dominant indigenous group they were in their Sonoran homeland, and they do not retain the cohesiveness of their Sonoran kin. They have an unstructured village authority, weak social control, and an economy based on wage labor and welfare. Their ceremonial lives are more individually based and are not coordinated with work as they are in Sonora. In spite of these changes, such traditional Yaqui institutions as ritual coparenthood *(compadrazgo)* and ceremonial societies *(cofradías)* are still important in Pascua life (Spicer 1940). As a group, the Yaqui are deeply religious. Modern Yaqui religion is a fusion of aboriginal beliefs with Spanish and Mexican Catholicism. The annual religious cycle functions through the *cofradías,* of which five are men's and two are women's. Although ceremonial cycles, feast days, and local patron saints differ from village to village, Easter is the major religious holiday for the Yaqui. The rituals and ceremonial events surrounding this religious season are complex (Moisés et al. 1971).

For the Arizona Yaqui, ethnic status takes precedence over nationality, entitling them to build a house, to farm, or to graze cattle on Yaqui territory, and to use the natural resources found in Yaqui territory, whether in Arizona or Sonora. They are also able to participate in Yaqui farming and fishing societies and cattle cooperatives. McGuire (1986) pointed to four characteristics of Yaqui polity and ethnicity that support the persistence of the ethnic Yaqui: (1) the Yaqui are a corporate ethnic group rather than an ethnic population; (2) recognition of being Yaqui is ascribed through genealogy rather than achieved; (3) ethnic identity is understated; and (4) the three dimensions of status—wealth, power, and prestige—are not connected. Today, the Pascua Yaqui number more than 9,000 people. Many live in Pascua Village, which was annexed by the City of Tucson in 1952. Others reside on the more recently established New Pascua reservation southwest of Tucson. Following a long and difficult battle, the Pascua Yaqui gained federal recognition from the U.S. government in 1982 and ratified their first constitution in 1988.

The Yaqui have an interesting but poorly documented connection to the Río Antiguo study area as early members of the agricultural labor force. Spicer (1940:20) noted that the development of irrigated agriculture in southern Arizona in the period 1900–1912 encouraged a steady flow of Yaquis into the region to work as farm laborers, leading to the establishment of Yaqui settlements near Tucson, Phoenix, and Yuma. By the time of Spicer's ethnographic work at Pascua, almost all of the people in the village (men, women, and children) picked cotton seasonally on the large farms along the Santa Cruz River, particularly near Marana. The rest of the year, most of the men worked at one of three jobs: building and cleaning irrigation ditches, making adobes, or serving on railroad section gangs (Spicer 1940:30). There is limited evidence that Yaqui men worked on farms along the Rillito. Gursky (1994:16) has noted that in the early 1900s, Nephi Bingham, founder of the Mormon community at Binghampton (near the approximate center of the study area; see Chapter 4), hired 60 men, "half of whom were Yaqui Indians," to help build the irrigation system used by the community.

For the first two decades of its existence, the village of Pascua relied for water on a large irrigation ditch running nearby (Spicer 1940:28, 1980:240). This ditch was undoubtedly the main canal routing water from the Santa Cruz River near Sentinel Peak to the Flowing Wells Ranch, which was established around the turn of the century by Frank and Warren Allison and later owned, in turn, by Levi Manning and the Tucson Farms Company (see O'Mack and Klucas 2001). The Flowing Wells Ranch occupied a large tract just north of Pascua and not far west of the Río Antiguo study area, and Yaquis were apparently a part of the labor force there. In 1907, George E. P. Smith, an engineering professor at the University of Arizona who was making a detailed study of irrigation in the Rillito Valley at the time (see Chapter 4), published a paper on the advantages of cement pipe over open ditches for irrigation. In his article, he included a photograph of Yaqui men making cement pipe at Flowing Wells Ranch (Figure 4).

Figure 4. Yaqui men making sections of 15-inch cement pipe at
Flowing Wells Ranch, ca. 1907. See Smith (1918:100) for a description
of the scene (photograph courtesy of Special Collections,
University of Arizona Library, Tucson, Ms. 280, box 14, folder 7).

CHAPTER 4

Euroamerican Culture History

The first arrival of Europeans in what is now southern Arizona took place around 1539, which, in the strictest sense, can be taken as the start of the historical period in the region. As an indication of the beginning of Euroamerican influence on the region, however, 1539 is both too late and too early: too late, because it is likely that certain Spanish introductions, especially Old World diseases, preceded Spaniards in the region by a decade or more; too early, because apart from a few mostly uneventful Spanish probes in the first half of the sixteenth century, there was no real Spanish presence in the region until the very end of the seventeenth century. The year 1539 seems especially early when considering the Rillito Valley, which went unsettled and largely unvisited by Spaniards and their Mexican and Anglo-American successors in the region until the second half of the nineteenth century. Euroamerican culture history in southern Arizona began unequivocally by 1700, but the Río Antiguo study area did not have a tangible place in that history until a century and a half later.

The discussion that follows is organized by broadly defined themes that have influenced the history of the Río Antiguo study area: Native American–Spanish interaction; the decline of the colonial system after Mexican independence; mining, farming, and ranching; settlement and land tenure; and transportation. Rather than a strictly chronological discussion, we consider change through time as it relates to each theme, although we make regular links to the three major periods of southern Arizona history: the Spanish Colonial period (1539–1821), the Mexican period (1821–1854), and the U.S. period (1854–present). The Rillito Valley essentially lacked permanent residents in the first two periods, during which both Euroamerican and Native American activities in the Tucson Basin were restricted largely to the nearby Santa Cruz River valley. Thus, our discussion of Native American–Spanish interaction and the decline of the colonial system serves as backdrop to eventual developments in the study area rather than as an account of anything that took place there. Not long after the start of the U.S. period, the study area became a part of the wider economic and social sphere of southern Arizona; we pay particular attention to the ways this happened during the first 75 years of the U.S. period.

Native American–Spanish Interaction

For its first 280 years, southern Arizona history was largely defined by the interaction that took place between the Native Americans living in the region and the Spanish explorers, missionaries, and settlers who entered it and sometimes stayed. This is not to say that Native American lives were defined by this interaction—Native Americans had their own worlds of interest and significance and did not sit waiting for the Spanish to initiate things—but what we know of the nearly three centuries of Spanish presence in the region originates in documents produced by the Spanish in their efforts to understand and control what they found in the region, especially its native inhabitants. The history of the Spanish presence in southern Arizona is the history of how two ways of life confronted each other and responded to the demands imposed by the confrontation.

Early Spanish Exploration

The Spanish conquest of southern Arizona began as it had begun in so many other places in the New World following the arrival of Columbus—with exploratory journeys, or *entradas,* into the region by small groups of Spanish adventurers accompanied by Native American guides (Figure 5). The earliest *entradas* into southern Arizona had little or no immediate impact on the region—no settlements were established, no resources were extracted, and interactions with the indigenous peoples were fleeting— but these journeys of exploration were nonetheless of great consequence to the subsequent history of the region. The information, accurate or otherwise, that was gathered in each *entrada* was inevitably the impetus for further *entradas,* then for religious missions, and eventually for attempts at settlement. Just as important, each successful *entrada* confirmed the feasibility and validity of the Spanish colonial enterprise and the greater purposes of spreading the Catholic faith, expanding the wealth of the crown, and bringing Spanish civilization to uncivilized places. An understanding of the Spanish presence in southern Arizona begins with an appreciation of this remarkable impulse to explore and expand, an impulse pursued at a scale with few precedents in human history. The sources consulted for the following discussion are summaries of the early period of Spanish exploration by Fontana (1994:19–31), Hartmann (1989: 16–35), Officer 1987:25–28), Sheridan (1995:24–28), Weber (1992:35–49), and Whittlesey et al. (1994: 228–230).

The first directly documented Spanish *entrada* into what would become southern Arizona came in 1539, when a Franciscan friar named Marcos de Niza led a small expedition northward from the town of Culiacán, in what was then northernmost New Spain, to the vicinity of the pueblo of Zuni, in what is now western New Mexico. It is uncertain whether Niza himself made it as far north as Zuni, but he likely did pass through southeastern Arizona, traveling along a stretch of the San Pedro River and reaching the Gila River before returning to Culiacán. His only non–Native American companion for most of the northward journey was a North African called Esteban. Esteban did reach Zuni, where he was shot full of arrows by suspicious Zuni.

Niza's expedition was commissioned by the newly appointed viceroy of New Spain, Antonio de Mendoza, in an effort to gather knowledge of the northwestern frontier of the colony. Mendoza was especially interested in confirming reports that somewhere to the north lay the Seven Cities of Antilia, legendary places of high culture and fabulous wealth believed to rival Tenochtitlan, the Aztec capital in central Mexico conquered by Fernando Cortés in 1521. Interest in the Seven Cities had recently been piqued by the arrival at Culiacán of Alvar Núñez Cabeza de Vaca and his companions, who had spent the preceding eight years wandering the northern deserts after being shipwrecked on the coast of Texas. The doomed Esteban had been among Cabeza de Vaca's party, which might have passed through southern Arizona at some point, although their route is impossible to reconstruct precisely. Esteban was chosen for Niza's expedition based on his knowledge of the northern deserts and his presumed skills in dealing with the indigenous peoples, skills that failed him in the end.

The most important product of the first *entrada* into Arizona was Niza's subsequent report to Antonio de Mendoza, which, for many people, confirmed the existence of the Seven Cities (thenceforth the Seven Cities of Cíbola, the name for Zuni heard by Niza). Because of Niza's glowing descriptions of Cíbola, in 1540, Mendoza commissioned a much more substantial *entrada,* led by Francisco Vásquez de Coronado and consisting of some 300 Spaniards, 1,000 Native American guides and porters, and 1,500 head of cattle, horses, and mules. Niza, one of five friars who accompanied Coronado, served as Coronado's principal guide as far as Cíbola, where the hopes of Coronado and his companions were bitterly disappointed. Much of Coronado's route, which eventually led him as far as the Great Plains, is difficult to reconstruct, but he, too, passed through southeastern Arizona, probably also traveling along a portion of the San Pedro River. Over the next two years, Coronado's lieutenants made numerous exploratory side trips, including at least a dozen into Arizona, but none of these trips included further exploration of the southern portion of the state.

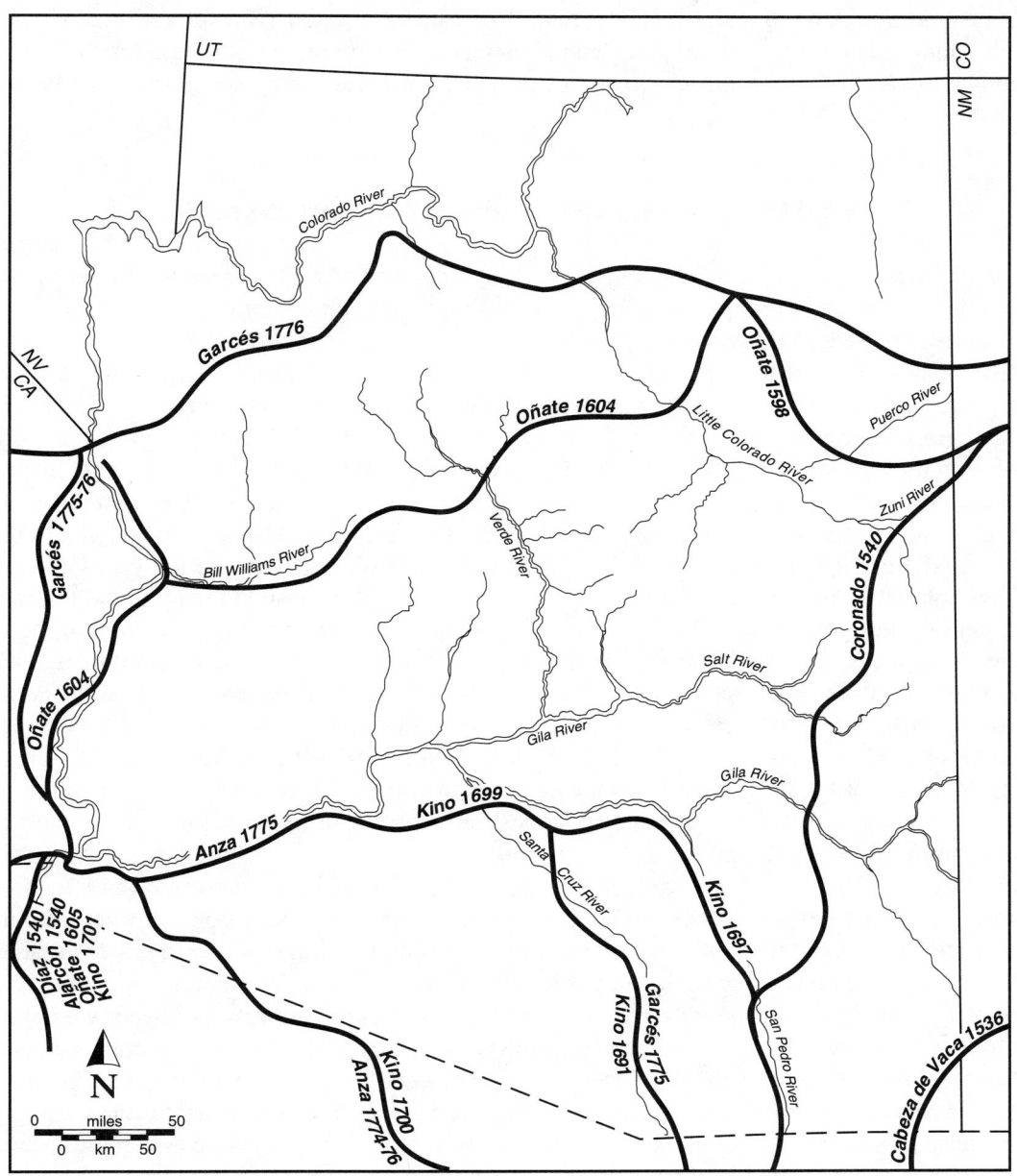

Figure 5. Routes of early Spanish explorers in southern Arizona.

55

Despite the Coronado expedition's success in exploring a vast area and collecting a great deal of potentially useful information, its failure to find anything remotely like the legendary Seven Cities led to a near hiatus in exploration of Arizona for the next century and a half. During this period, the occasional Spanish expedition did enter Arizona from northern New Mexico, where a permanent Spanish settlement was founded at Santa Fe by 1610. These expeditions gathered information and made contacts with indigenous peoples in various parts of the state, but the only one to go south of the Gila River was Juan de Oñate's expedition to the mouth of the Colorado River in 1604. Intensive exploration of southern Arizona did not begin until late in the seventeenth century, corresponding with the efforts of Eusebio Francisco Kino to extend the Jesuit missionary effort northward from established bases in what is now Sonora.

New Plants, New Animals, New Diseases

If the most obvious impacts of the Spanish exploration of southern Arizona were not on the peoples and places encountered by explorers but on other Spaniards thus enticed to enter the region, a more subtle process initiated by the earliest *entradas* was ultimately of even greater significance. This was the process of biological and technological exchange that began the moment Europeans first arrived in the New World, a process that likely affected the native peoples of southern Arizona even before Spaniards set foot in the region. Sheridan (1995:23) has characterized the earliest *entradas* into Arizona as "little more than ripples on the surface of a deep dark lake," as compared with events of less immediate historical interest but much greater long-term impact, such as "the exchange of seeds, the theft of a horse herd, the introduction of an iron plow." The introduction of the plow to southern Arizona probably had to wait until Jesuits actually carried one there and showed the locals how to use it, but Spanish crops and domestic animals were already a part of Native American lives when Kino first visited the region at the end of the seventeenth century. For example, Kino's military escort, Capt. Juan Mateo Manje, reported that watermelons and muskmelons were being grown by the Sobaipuri along the Santa Cruz River in 1697. Both crops were Spanish introductions to the New World, but they had evidently entered the area well in advance of Spanish expeditions (Ezell 1961:32). In a more dramatic fashion, the Apache had long since incorporated the horse into their nomadic, raiding way of life. Ironically, Spaniards first brought horses to the New World to aid in its conquest, but the early acquisition of horses by the Apache, either by theft or by happenstance, soon turned the previously pedestrian Apache into a formidable and enduring threat to Spanish control of the northern frontier.

The Sobaipuri of the Santa Cruz River valley were long-accomplished farmers when Kino first entered the region, but they also depended heavily on the resources that they could extract from the surrounding desert. They lived lives of variable sedentism, settling in villages along the river to farm for part of the year, then dispersing to scattered parts of the surrounding region to hunt and gather a wide variety of animals and plants. One important reason the Sobaipuri did not rely exclusively on agriculture for their food was climatic: the elevation of the Santa Cruz Valley meant that for several months each winter, the possibility of frost made planting a winter crop an unacceptable gamble. Corn, beans, and squash, the three major native cultivars, all lacked the tolerance to frost necessary to survive a typical winter. Because of this vacant niche in the agricultural cycle, the Sobaipuri were especially receptive to the introduction of the principal Spanish cultivar, wheat, which was highly frost tolerant and made living and farming year-round on the Santa Cruz feasible. The increased yields from agriculture that resulted from adding wheat to the cycle also made larger settlements possible, which became a defensive consideration as Apache raiding intensified in conjunction with the influx of Spaniards into the region. Wheat was first introduced to the Santa Cruz Valley by Kino in the 1690s, but it probably did not become a major part of the Sobaipuri diet until the 1730s, when permanent missions were finally established at Guevavi and San Xavier del Bac. Nonetheless, by the middle of the eighteenth century, wheat was a major crop for the Sobaipuri along the Santa Cruz, and by the 1770s, it had become a major crop even for the Akimel O'odham along the Gila River, beyond the sphere of direct missionary influence (Sheridan 1988).

As much as any other factor, it was the Sobaipuri's own recognition of the potential role of wheat in their diet that led to its enthusiastic adoption, but the increased sedentism that growing wheat allowed for played perfectly into the Jesuits' plans to transform the Sobaipuri way of life from one of "pagan intransigence" (Sheridan 1988:156) to one of Christian stability. The Jesuits viewed the flexibility in the settlement pattern that the Sobaipuri required in their seasonal reliance on hunting and gathering as a major obstacle to be overcome by the missions, and the introduction of European crops was a logical first step in making a sedentary lifestyle both feasible and desirable. At least in this one aspect of the missionizing process, the motivations of the Sobaipuri and the Jesuits seem to have to coincided. In addition to wheat, the Sobaipuri benefitted from the introduction of a vast array of Spanish cultivars, including legumes such as garbanzos and lentils; vegetables such as cabbage, onions, garlic, and leeks; herbs such as mustard, mint, anise, and pepper; and fruits such as grapes, apples, peaches, quinces, plums, pomegranates, apricots, and figs. As Sheridan (1988:157) put it, "Thousands of years of Old World experience and experimentation were suddenly placed in Piman hands." Of course, by the time the Jesuits arrived in southern Arizona, Europe as a whole was already benefitting from thousands of years of New World agricultural experimentation, as the many cultivars native to the Americas (most notably, corn and potatoes) had quickly become integral parts of many Old World diets and economies.

In southern Arizona, the Apache were the native people perhaps most transformed by the introduction of a Spanish domestic animal, but Spanish livestock had a significant impact on the Sobaipuri as well. In 1699, Captain Manje reported that horses were being kept by the Sobaipuri of the San Pedro Valley, and by the early 1700s, herds of horses, cattle, sheep, and goats had been started by the Jesuits at a number of other Sobaipuri settlements (Sheridan 1988:159–160). Horses were the first introduction to play a significant role among the Sobaipuri, serving both as beasts of burden and as weapons in their perpetual struggles with the Apache. Cattle, goats, and sheep spread more slowly and generally under missionary supervision, but their impact on the Sobaipuri economy was greater. Sheridan (1988:161) noted that these three domestics were especially important because they "converted grasses and other plants which humans could not eat into meat, cheese, and milk" and so provided a reliable source of animal protein. If the Sobaipuri were obliged by the adoption of year-round agriculture to give up much of their earlier hunting-and-gathering use of the desert, they partially recovered such use indirectly through the adoption of animal grazing.

Whatever benefits the native peoples of southern Arizona enjoyed as a result of the introduction of Old World plants and animals were greatly overshadowed by the effects of another, largely one-sided, biological exchange that spread deadly Old World diseases throughout the Americas beginning with Columbus's first landing in 1492. Prior to that first landing, the native peoples of the Americas had developed for at least 12,000 years in isolation from Old World diseases such as measles, influenza, and smallpox. Consequently, the rates of resistance to these diseases were extremely low among Native Americans at the time of contact, and the effects of the many epidemics that soon raced through the Spanish colonies, especially the epidemics of smallpox, were devastating. Native American populations throughout the hemisphere declined by 66–95 percent during the Spanish Colonial period, and entire societies simply disintegrated under the pressures of depopulation (Crosby 1972; Sheridan 1995:23–24).

There has been considerable debate about the effects and timing of epidemics among the native peoples of southern Arizona. Certainly, the first effects were felt before permanent Spanish settlements arose in the region, and at least a few archaeologists speculate that the demise of the prehistoric Hohokam people is attributable to the arrival of European diseases. The usual end date given for the Hohokam occupation of southern Arizona is A.D. 1450, but the archaeological chronology has enough room for error to make a close correspondence between the end of the Hohokam and the arrival of European diseases a possibility worth considering. Reff (1990:279–280) attempted to reconstruct the origin and course of epidemics in northwestern New Spain during the early colonial period and concluded that the region experienced the same rapid and devastating depopulations in the sixteenth century as the core areas of the Spanish colony—namely, central Mexico and Peru—had. Reff stopped short of attributing the Hohokam collapse primarily to the effects of disease, but he did see processes of change that began in late prehistoric times as likely exacerbated by epidemics during the first century or more of the colonial era.

Perhaps more significant is Reff's conclusion that what enabled the early missionizing efforts of the Jesuits in northwestern New Spain to succeed was the demoralization of Native American communities caused by epidemics and severe depopulation. Having suffered repeatedly from the effects of epidemics, the Native Americans of the region often responded favorably to Jesuit programs of conversion, resettlement, and agricultural change, because they were desperate for a solution to what they themselves perceived to be disintegrating social, cultural, and economic systems (Reff 1990:277–278, 1998). But Jesuit (and, later, Franciscan) attempts to restructure Native American society in northwestern New Spain ultimately failed, because Native American populations never stopped declining. And if an acceptance of social change was at first a response to increased mortality, increased mortality itself was soon the price of that acceptance. Jackson (1994) has stressed that epidemic disease, although a major factor in Native American population decline, was never the sole factor. The missionary institutions that were brought to the frontier and imposed on the local people, ostensibly for their benefit, were themselves devastating to Native American ways of life, often intentionally so. The physical and psychological stresses suffered by Native Americans under the missionary system contributed substantially, if not always measurably, to the decline of Native American populations throughout New Spain, and the Piman-speaking peoples of what is now southern Arizona were not exempt from these effects.

The Jesuit Expansion into Southern Arizona

The Spanish missionary effort in northwestern New Spain began in 1591, when two Jesuit fathers were sent from Mexico City to a small Spanish settlement along the Río Sinaloa, in what is now the Mexican state of the same name, to begin the conversion of the indigenous people of the region. From this modest start, the Jesuit order soon expanded northward, founding missions in the succession of river valleys that drain the western slopes of the Sierra Madre. Occasionally, the people they encountered staunchly resisted their efforts to introduce Catholicism and a Spanish way of life, but more often, the presence of the Jesuits was accepted or at least tolerated. By the 1620s, Jesuit missions extended well into the Pimería Baja, the "lower," or southern, portion of the territory belonging to the Piman-speaking peoples, in what is now northern Sinaloa and southern Sonora. The proselytization of the Pimería Baja would occupy the Jesuits for the next 65 years, after which the Jesuit order finally expanded into the northern portion of Piman-speaking territory, the Pimería Alta, an expansion made possible largely by the efforts of Kino (Bannon 1955; Ortega Noriega 1985a).

Born and educated in northern Italy, Kino arrived in Mexico as a Jesuit in 1681. His first assignment was to accompany a military expedition to Baja California, where he served both as cartographer and as minister to the Native Americans subdued by the expedition. The attempt to establish a Spanish settlement in Baja California was ultimately unsuccessful, and Kino was eventually selected to direct the expansion of the mainland Jesuit frontier into the Pimería Alta. He began by establishing a series of missions that extended up the principal rivers of the region—most notably, Mission Nuestra Señora de los Dolores at the headwaters of the Río San Miguel, near the present-day city of Magdalena, Sonora. Founded in 1687, Mission Nuestra Señora de los Dolores served for the next 24 years as Kino's base of operations, the starting point of his famous expeditions into the northern Pimería Alta that led to the founding of missions along the Santa Cruz River (Ortega Noriega 1985b).

Kino's first entry into what is now Arizona was in 1691, when he reached the Sobaipuri settlement at Tumacácori on the Santa Cruz River. Over the next 10 years, he made numerous trips up the same river—which he called Santa María—as far north as the ruins of Casa Grande, and he eventually traveled down the Gila River to its confluence with the Colorado. Kino was interested in finding both new territory to missionize, which he found in abundance in the Sobaipuri villages along the fertile Santa Cruz, and a land route to Baja California, which would ease the transport of supplies and livestock to fledgling missions there. After a series of arduous trips into the deserts south of the Gila, Kino eventually convinced himself that there was a land route to Baja California, but his claimed discovery was viewed with skepticism until years after his death in 1711. It was the opening of a vast new area to Jesuit missionizing and his subsequent direction of that missionizing effort that became Kino's most enduring contributions (Bolton 1984; Hartmann 1989:36–56; Ortega Noriega 1985b).

In 1731, 20 years after Kino's death, the first permanent Jesuit missions were established at the Sobaipuri villages of Guevavi and Bac along the Santa Cruz (Figure 6). Each of the two missions was intended to be a *misión cabecera,* a primary mission with a resident Jesuit priest who would minister to the natives both at the *cabecera* and at two or three nearby dependent *visitas,* smaller settlements without resident priests. Earlier attempts to establish missions at both Guevavi and Bac during Kino's lifetime had failed, but now the Jesuits succeeded in instituting essentially the same missionary program that was already in place at the many Jesuit missions to the south. The basic goal of the Jesuit mission was the conversion of the natives to Catholicism, but the pursuit of that goal along the Santa Cruz River, like its earlier pursuit elsewhere in northwestern New Spain, involved fundamentally changing the lives of the natives, convincing them not only to abandon their religious beliefs but to alter the nature of their association with the landscape around them.

The keystone of the Jesuit effort to convert Native Americans was the *reducción,* literally "reduction," the gathering of Native Americans into permanent communities "for more efficient and effective administration, both spiritual and temporal" (Polzer 1976:7). In the communities formed by *reducción,* Native Americans were instructed in the faith, encouraged to abandon practices incompatible with Catholicism, monitored as to their genuine acceptance of Catholic doctrine, and put to work in projects for the communal good—most notably, the construction and maintenance of irrigation systems. The success the Jesuits had in convincing the natives of northwestern New Spain to participate in *reducción* varied widely, from violent rejection to peaceful acquiescence, but the Sobaipuri of the Santa Cruz Valley were generally amenable to the process. The precise reasons for their apparent acceptance of this most basic of Jesuit demands were complicated. The constant threat of Apache raids undoubtedly made the Jesuits and their Spanish military escorts appealing as potential allies. The agricultural regime introduced to the region by the Jesuits, with its livestock, wide variety of cultivars, and dependable winter crops, also must have appealed to people living in a demanding and inconsistently productive environment. And there is the real possibility, already noted, that the Sobaipuri way of life at the end of the seventeenth century was already so devastated by the impact of European diseases that the Sobaipuri would accept any change that would bring stability to their lives.

Whatever factors influenced the original decisions of the Sobaipuri, the Jesuit mission settlements at Guevavi and San Xavier del Bac became permanent homes for many of them for much of the remainder of the eighteenth century. They were baptized there, participated in the religious life of the mission (to the degree that the resident Jesuit saw fit), and farmed mission lands using both indigenous and Spanish crops and methods. But beyond the adoption of Spanish agriculture and the rudiments of Catholicism, it is impossible to say how much their new lives actually reflected a conversion to a Spanish way of life, and this is even more the case for the Sobaipuri settled in or near dependent *visitas* such as Tucson and Arivaca. In addition, almost nothing is known about the impact of the missions on the Sobaipuri's use of areas away from the main rivers, the areas once frequented in the Sobaipuri seasonal round. The enthusiasm with which the Sobaipuri adopted wheat farming and livestock raising at the missions suggests that they quickly abandoned the nomadic dimension of their way of life, but Sobaipuri culture consisted of

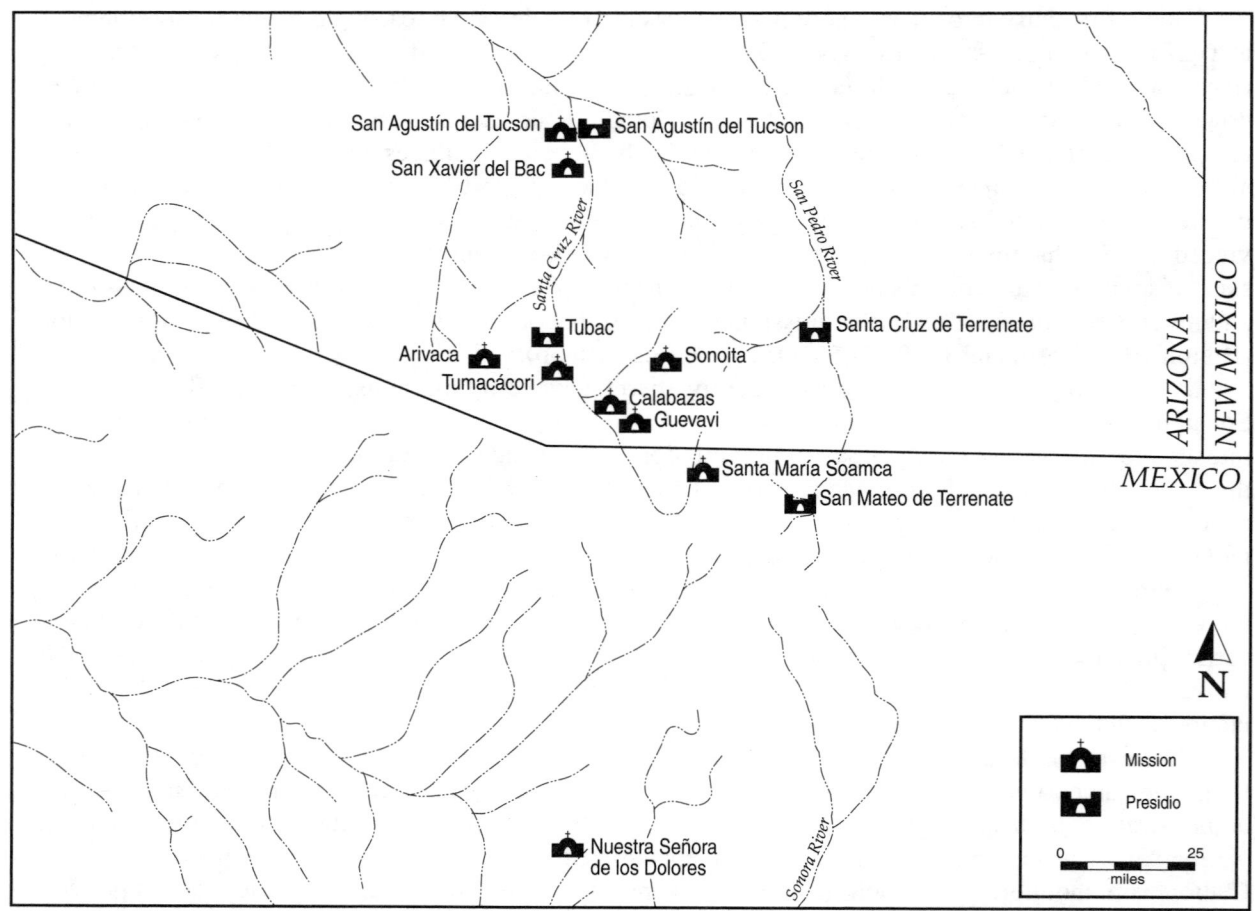

Figure 6. Selected Spanish Colonial sites in the Pimería Alta.

more than the routines of subsistence. According to Reff (1990:268–271), native acceptance of Jesuit teachings—religious, social, and economic—throughout northwestern New Spain was at best superficial, and even a century or more after initial contact, Jesuits would complain about the continuing difficulties in transforming native lives. In the northernmost Pimería Alta, where the Jesuit presence was more tenuous than anywhere else in the northern borderlands, the veneer of Catholicism and Hispanicism must have been especially thin.

The Jesuit missionary effort in northwestern New Spain differed in a number of significant ways from earlier missionary efforts by other orders elsewhere in the colony, and these differences had their effects in the northern Pimería Alta. One major difference can be found in the character of the Jesuit order itself. Founded in 1536, the Society of Jesus was the youngest of the major orders to proselytize in New Spain, and it had attracted an especially devoted and well-educated group of young men to its ranks. Jesuit devotion included a genuine concern for the well-being of the native people placed in their charge, which frequently led them to shield the natives from the abuses of ordinary Spaniards eager to exploit their labor. "The Jesuits," wrote Reff (1990:7), "largely were free of the vices that characterized their countrymen." A basically humane approach to their dealings with the natives (there were exceptions, of course), combined with an emphasis on learning native languages and understanding native customs, was an important factor in the success of the Jesuits in expanding their missions over such a vast area in a relatively short period of time.

Another important difference between the Jesuit enterprise and earlier missionary efforts was the nearly exclusive access to native populations that the Jesuits enjoyed, especially in the northern reaches of the Pimería Alta. In central Mexico, by contrast, the first Spanish institution that many native people were exposed to was the *encomienda,* which placed the Native American population of a given region at the disposal of a private Spaniard (usually a former conquistador). In theory, the Native Americans would simply pay tribute to the Spaniard, but in practice, the tribute took the form of labor in the Spaniard's mining or agricultural ventures. The *encomienda* was responsible for the early deaths of tens of thousands of Native Americans in central Mexico and elsewhere in the New World and had largely ceased to be royal policy by the time the Jesuits began their efforts in northwestern New Spain (Weber 1992:124–125). Elsewhere in New Spain, including much of northern Mexico, missionization occurred simultaneously with the expansion of secular Spanish enterprises, most notably mining. Missionary orders such as the Franciscans often had to recruit natives in competition with mining operations and to negotiate for the rights to native labor. But in the Pimería Alta, the Jesuits were almost always the vanguard of Spanish exploration and settlement. Private Spanish interests would eventually arrive to compete with a Jesuit mission for land and labor but usually after the mission had chosen lands for itself, established relations with the local Native Americans, and generally made itself the principal Spanish presence in the region (Atondo Rodríguez and Ortega Soto 1985).

Following the expulsion of the Jesuits from all Spanish colonies in 1767, the Franciscan order inherited the Jesuit system of missions in the Pimería Alta and pursued largely the same policies of *reducción* and conversion, except that severely dwindling native populations forced the Franciscans to look elsewhere for new converts. The Franciscans working at the Santa Cruz River missions found them primarily among the Tohono O'odham, the Piman speakers of the vast desert region to the west of the river. Coaxed into becoming sedentary river farmers, the Tohono O'odham became the largest component of the native populations at Guevavi and Bac beginning in the late eighteenth century. Life at the Franciscan missions was relatively benign for them, especially compared with the fate of Native Americans living in the Franciscan missions soon established in Alta California. Jackson (1998:78) noted how the Franciscans placed much heavier demands for labor on the natives in the Alta California missions than they ever placed on the natives in southern Arizona, and the California natives suffered accordingly. The difference in the Santa Cruz Valley was the result of less ambitious Franciscan architectural projects, a more intermittent Franciscan presence at the missions, and less reliance on mission production by the local Spanish military.

Presidios and *Gente de Razón* in Southern Arizona

In addition to the task of converting the Sobaipuri to Catholicism, the Jesuits in the Santa Cruz Valley, like their brethren elsewhere in the Pimería Alta, were charged with transforming the local way of life into a Spanish one, based in permanent, year-round villages and the raising of Spanish crops and livestock. As discussed above, their efforts met with only limited success. However, from the perspective of ordinary Spanish people on the northern frontier—*gente de razón,* as they called themselves, "people of reason"—the presence of the missions and the military protection afforded them suddenly made settlement of the region seem feasible. Spanish settlers in search of irrigable fields, grazing lands, and minerals began to drift into the region, often establishing operations near the missions. In the vicinity of the Santa Cruz Valley, this pattern of settlement received a boost in 1736 when silver was discovered a few miles southwest of modern Nogales, at a place called Arizonac (the place-name, slightly modified, now refers to an American state). By the end of the 1730s, a fair number of Spanish families had settled in the immediate vicinity of Guevavi and Tubac, and there were likely other Spanish families farther north along the Santa Cruz (Kessell 1970:51–52; Officer 1987:32).

The discovery at Arizonac quickly played out, but the modest influx in Spanish population prompted by the discovery created an increased demand for Spanish military protection of the region. It was clear even prior to the Arizonac discovery that the most persistent and vexing problem faced by the Jesuit missions, by the Sobaipuri settled at the Santa Cruz missions, and by the few Spaniards bold enough to settle along the far northern frontier was unrelenting harassment by the Apache, who roamed unrestricted over a vast area to the north and east of the Pimería Alta. Each new Spanish arrival in the Santa Cruz Valley and its vicinity represented another tempting target for Apache raids. The Spanish military responded in 1741 by establishing a presidio at San Mateo de Terrenate on the headwaters of the San Pedro River, at what was presumed to be the front line of the Apache problem, although still some 50 miles southeast of Guevavi (Kessell 1970:76–78; Officer 1987:33). The new presidio did extend the Spanish military presence to the north and west of the presidio at Fronteras, but the Santa Cruz River missions remained isolated and poorly protected from Apache depredations. Nonetheless, the number of Spanish settlers in the vicinity of the missions gradually increased.

As Spanish settlement of the Pimería Alta slowly expanded northward, the Upper Pima were increasingly obliged to share or relinquish entirely the limited arable lands available along the region's major rivers. By the middle of the eighteenth century, following a variety of abuses by both settlers and Jesuits around the Pimería Alta, the Upper Pima, including the Sobaipuri of the Santa Cruz Valley, had had enough. In 1751, under the direction of an Upper Pima leader who had earlier assisted the Spanish military in pacifying the Seri, they revolted, killing more than 100 settlers and badly damaging missions throughout the region, including those at Guevavi and San Xavier del Bac, and their outlying *visitas*. The Spanish settlers living along the Santa Cruz retreated as a group to the presidio at Terrenate, abandoning their fields, herds, and belongings to the enraged Sobaipuri. The wider uprising, now known as the Pima revolt, was quelled within four months of the initial violence, but sporadic attacks by groups of disaffected Sobaipuri continued to occur for several years afterward.

In 1752, as a direct response to the Pima revolt, the Spanish military established a presidio at Tubac, about halfway between Guevavi and Bac, in an effort to better protect the Santa Cruz missions. San Ignacio del Tubac thus became the first permanent, officially sanctioned Spanish settlement in what is now Arizona. By 1760, Juan Bautista de Anza's (the younger) first year as *comandante* of Tubac, the problems with the Sobaipuri had largely subsided, partly because of Anza's charismatic presence but also in great part because of a steady decline in the Sobaipuri population caused by disease, relocation to avoid the missions, and flight from Apache depredations (Dobyns 1976:10–17; Ewing 1945; Kessell 1970:102–109, 154–156; Officer 1987:35–39).

The Apache threat grew steadily from 1760 onward, abetted early on by the Spanish military in two unintentional ways. In 1762, in an effort to repopulate the dwindling Santa Cruz missions, the colonial government ordered the military to relocate the entire Sobaipuri population of the San Pedro Valley to the settlements of their congeners along the Santa Cruz River. This action removed the last buffer between the Santa Cruz missions and the Apache, whose nearest targets for raids were simply moved one more valley to the west. Also in the 1760s, the attentions of the military force garrisoned at Tubac were diverted from the Santa Cruz missions by several extended expeditions to the south to help fight the resurgent Seri. With a weakened military force at Tubac, raids by Apaches in the Santa Cruz Valley escalated in frequency and ferocity (Dobyns 1976:19–23; Kessell 1970:161–162; Officer 1987:44–45).

The Jesuit tenure in southern Arizona came to an abrupt end in 1767, when the Jesuit order in its entirety was expelled from all Spanish territories by royal decree. Control of the northern missions transferred to the Franciscans, who soon sent friars to the Pimería Alta, that "unsolicited inheritance from the Jesuits" (Kessell 1976:3). The Franciscan order, founded in 1226, was much older than the Society of Jesus (founded in 1534) and also preceded the Jesuits in the New World by 67 years. The Franciscans were the first and most active order in the missionization of central Mexico, beginning their work in 1524, just three years after the fall of the Aztec capital of Tenochtitlan. The Franciscan friars assigned to the existing missions of the Pimería Alta would build on the work of conversion and resettlement begun by the Jesuits, but they would also bring with them two and a half centuries of experience missionizing elsewhere in Mexico. They would leave their own distinctive mark on the people and places of the northern frontier, a mark they would eventually leave on the many Franciscan missions of Alta California (McCarty 1996).

The expulsion of the Jesuits brought chaos to the already unstable missions along the Santa Cruz River. In the interim year preceding the arrival of the Franciscans, the chaos deepened as the mission Sobaipuri, recently decimated by disease, abandoned many of the river homes and fields they had maintained under the Jesuits. When the Franciscans arrived, only a few dozen Sobaipuri were still in residence at Guevavi and Bac, and the *visitas* were in comparable decline. Almost all of the Spanish living in the region, a total of around 500 people, were settled at the Tubac presidio, largely as a defense against continuing Apache raids. Shortly after the first Franciscan friar settled at San Xavier, the mission suffered a devastating Apache attack, the first of countless Apache raids witnessed by the Franciscans during the 70-odd years of their presence along the Santa Cruz (Kessell 1976:11–25; Officer 1987:45–48).

Apache aggression made all lives difficult in the later eighteenth century and was the chief influence on the pattern of native as well as Spanish settlement in the Santa Cruz Valley. In 1768, the *misión cabecera* at Soamca was completely destroyed in an Apache attack, never to be reoccupied. In 1770, the Sobaipuri who had resettled at Tucson were threatening to abandon the area for the Gila River because of Apache attacks. Fearing that their departure would mean a badly weakened Spanish presence on the middle Santa Cruz, Anza persuaded them to stay by promising them help in building fortifications and a church. A large earthen breastwork and a church, presumably of adobe and soon dedicated to San Agustín, were completed by 1771, marking the first Spanish attempts at architecture in the immediate vicinity of Tucson (Kessell 1976:56; McCarty 1976:16–18; Officer 1987:48).

Around the same time, farther up the Santa Cruz River, the Franciscans installed at Guevavi decided that life at the original *misión cabecera* had become too dangerous. Prompted by devastating Apache attacks on the *visitas* of Calabazas and Sonoita, the Franciscans transferred the *cabecera* downstream to Tumacácori, which was considerably closer to the presidio at Tubac (Kessell 1976:57). The Franciscans at Tumacácori and San Xavier, the two remaining *cabeceras* on the Santa Cruz, spent the next few years suffering further Apache raids, watching their already badly thinned Sobaipuri population continue to dwindle from disease and desertion, and making largely unsuccessful attempts to coax the Tohono O'odham into converting and settling along the river (Kessell 1976:78–80; Officer 1987:48–50).

In 1775, the military organization of the entire northern frontier of New Spain underwent a transformation at the hands of Hugo O'Conor, an Irish expatriate and officer in the Spanish army who had been assigned the task of modernizing and improving the presidial system of frontier defense, from the gulf coast of Texas to the Pimería Alta (Moorhead 1975:47–74). For the presidio at Tubac, this meant transfer downstream to a site just across the river from the Sobaipuri *ranchería* at Tucson, a site marked out by O'Conor on August 20, 1775. Like the Native American village that became a *visita,* the new presidio was christened San Agustín del Tucson. By 1776, the garrison formerly stationed at Tubac was in residence at Tucson, and in 1777, the first fortification of the new site was erected: a wooden palisade with a surrounding ditch. The palisade was eventually replaced by a massive wall of adobe that stood 10–12 feet high, measured 3 feet wide at the base, and enclosed 300 square yards. The layout of the fortification followed (at least loosely) the specifications of a royal order for presidio construction (Dobyns 1976:56–61; Officer 1987:50–51; Williams 1988). Also in 1775, just a few days after O'Conor chose the site for the Tucson presidio, he chose a new site for the presidio at San Mateo de Terrenate, a location farther down the San Pedro River, not far from modern Tombstone. This second new presidio, named Santa Cruz de Terrenate, suffered unrelenting Apache attacks and crippling problems with supplies for a little more than four years before being abandoned in early 1780 in favor of its previous location (Whittlesey et al. 1994; Williams 1986c).

From the establishment of the presidio to the early 1790s, the Spanish garrison at Tucson devoted almost all of its time and energy to fighting the Apache. The other Tucson, the *visita* and Sobaipuri village across the river, quickly became socially and economically linked with the presidio settlement and, of course, relied on it for its own defense from Apache attacks. A change in policy following the presidial reforms led the Spanish army to attempt to pacify the Apache through a combination of continuous military harassment and enticements to settle and live peacefully in the vicinity of the presidios. By 1793, the strategy had paid off, and pacified bands of Apaches *(apaches mansos)* began to settle just downstream from the presidio, ostensibly to take up the settled Spanish way of life. But the Apache never became the agriculturists that the Sobaipuri villagers across the river were, and their primary associations were always with the presidio. They depended heavily on the rations of grain, beef, and tobacco that the garrison supplied to them, provisions that, in the garrison's view, were well spent. The Spanish army continued its policy of alternating harassment and enticement of hostile Apache until the end of the colonial era (Dobyns 1976:82–105).

The period of relative peace that followed Apache pacification saw a continued decline in the Sobaipuri population, the intermittent settling of Tohono O'odham in Akimel O'odham villages, and a modest but steady influx of *gente de razón* into the region. By the start of the nineteenth century, the Sobaipuri who had been the original impetus for Spanish missionizing in the Santa Cruz Valley had become scarce, largely supplanted by Tohono O'odham. The mission settlements at Tumacácori and San Xavier del Bac remained predominantly Native American, but the Spanish were now a conspicuous presence at Tumacácori, the Tucson presidio, and Tubac, which in 1787 had once again become a presidio. The total Spanish population was nonetheless very low: an official census taken of the Tucson presidio and the surrounding area (including San Xavier) in 1804 counted 1,015 *gente de razón*. The same census listed 88 soldiers and their families, plus 8 civilian households, at Tubac and 88 *gente de razón* at Tumacácori (Dobyns 1976:133–141; Kessell 1976:245–246; Officer 1987:77–82). With the gradual increase in the Spanish population and the relative security afforded by Apache pacification, the occasional Spanish family attempted farming, ranching, or mining in outlying areas such as Arivaca and the San Pedro Valley, but most Spaniards continued to congregate in or near the three Santa Cruz Valley settlements (Officer 1987:82–83; Sheridan 1995:37–38).

Late in the Spanish Colonial period, despite the decline of the Sobaipuri population and a consequently tenuous labor force, the Franciscan missions at Tumacácori and San Xavier del Bac managed to replace their modest old churches with new ones. Recent Tohono O'odham converts contributed much of the labor. Construction of the church at San Xavier, the same church that survives today, began around 1781 and was completed by 1797. At Tumacácori, a new church was begun in 1802, but because of financial difficulties and a shortage of labor, it was not completed until 1828, and only then in a much reduced version of the original plan. The remains of the church are now the primary attraction at Tumacacori National Monument (Schuetz-Miller and Fontana 1996:86–88, 90–94). Apart from these two architectural accomplishments—of which the church at San Xavier was by far the most striking—the centers of the Spanish presence in southern Arizona at the end of the colonial era were visually unimpressive. Tucson and Tubac were little more than "flat-roofed adobe buildings clustered beside a ragged patchwork of fields" (Sheridan 1995:38). But whatever its appearance, a Spanish way of life, albeit a way of life adapted to the harsh conditions of the Santa Cruz Valley—isolation, Apache predation, and limited water—was now well established on the northern frontier.

Decline of the Colonial System under Mexico

The Spanish Colonial period ended in 1821, when Mexico won its independence from Spain. The impact of independence on the far northern frontier was not immediate—the presidios accepted the transfer of power to the new Mexican government largely without issue—but it was decisive in determining the future of the region. Because of the inability of the Mexican government to continue providing support, financial or otherwise, to the northern frontier, independence from Spain brought with it the collapse of "just about every institution that had held the Spanish frontier together" (Sheridan 1995:45). The presidio at Tucson, soon weakened by lack of supplies, arms, and reinforcements, saw its most important weapon for Apache pacification—rations for the *apaches mansos*—withdrawn because of a lack of funds. Apache raiding throughout southern Arizona once again became a major threat and continued unabated throughout the Mexican era.

The missions, although they escaped the secularization mandated for the rest of Mexico shortly after independence, were dealt a serious blow when all Spaniards were officially expelled from Mexico in 1828. The Spanish-born Franciscans at San Xavier and Tumacácori were ordered to leave, and no priest was ever again in residence at either mission during the Mexican era. Officially, the missions remained intact and were generally viewed as useful to the government's purpose of securing the frontier, but through a combination of official neglect and local coveting of mission property, the influence of the missions in the Santa Cruz Valley steadily declined. As the missions declined and Hispanics put more pressure on mission lands, the Tohono O'odham who had come to depend on those lands suddenly became a problem themselves, although never to the same degree as the Apache (Kessell 1976:275–319; Officer 1987:100–104, 130–133; Sheridan 1995:44–47; Weber 1982:50–53).

During the turbulent decades of the Mexican period, the Hispanic population of southern Arizona actually declined somewhat. Despite the decline, the period saw a great increase in the number of land grants petitioned for and granted to Hispanic settlers in the region (the earliest large land grants were actually petitioned for under the Spanish government and eventually granted under Mexican law). Major land grants along the Santa Cruz River and in adjacent areas included San Ignacio de la Canoa (along the Santa Cruz, north of Tubac), San Rafael de la Zanja (along the headwaters of the Santa Cruz), Tumacácori and Calabazas (former lands of the Tumacácori mission), San Ignacio del Babocómari (in the San Pedro Valley), and San José de Sonoita (along Sonoita Creek, a tributary of the upper Santa Cruz) (Figure 7). In some cases, these grants included lands "abandoned" by the missions (the official status of such lands was often not clear) and still farmed by Tohono O'odham associated with the missions. The granting of land to a Hispanic rancher usually meant an end to its use by mission dependents; this was an important source of unrest among the Tohono O'odham. Although the land grants consisted of many thousands of acres, the constant threat of Apache raids meant that they often did not actually get used for ranching. Sheridan (1995:49) has called them "little more than adobe islands in a desert sea—isolated, vulnerable, easily destroyed." By the end of the Mexican era, most either had been abandoned or were barely hanging on. The most substantial impact of the granting of these large tracts of land occurred after the tracts were bought by Anglo-American interests later in the century (Mattison 1946; Officer 1987: 106–110; Sheridan 1995:127–129; Wagoner 1975:159–239).

The settlements along the Santa Cruz River saw little direct evidence of the war waged between the United States and Mexico from 1846 to 1848. The sole visit to the Santa Cruz Valley by U.S. troops was a brief stop in December 1846 by the Mormon Battalion, which was en route to the Pacific coast. The battalion entered Tucson unopposed by the presidio troops, who had withdrawn to San Xavier to avoid a battle. The loss of a huge portion of Mexican territory in 1848 due to the Treaty of Guadalupe also had no immediate impact on the people living along the Santa Cruz, whose status as the northernmost outpost of Sonora remained unchanged and whose hard lives fighting the Apache and farming the desert continued as before. The only substantial change in the last years of the Mexican era was the increasing number of Anglo-Americans passing through the area, most notably the sudden wave of Anglo-Americans headed to California during the 1849 gold rush. Even after the Gadsden Purchase was ratified in 1854, making all of what is now Arizona south of the Gila River a part of the United States, it was two years before the presidio at Tucson was abandoned by its Mexican garrison (Officer 1987:262–283; Sheridan 1995:49–57; Wagoner 1975:259–297).

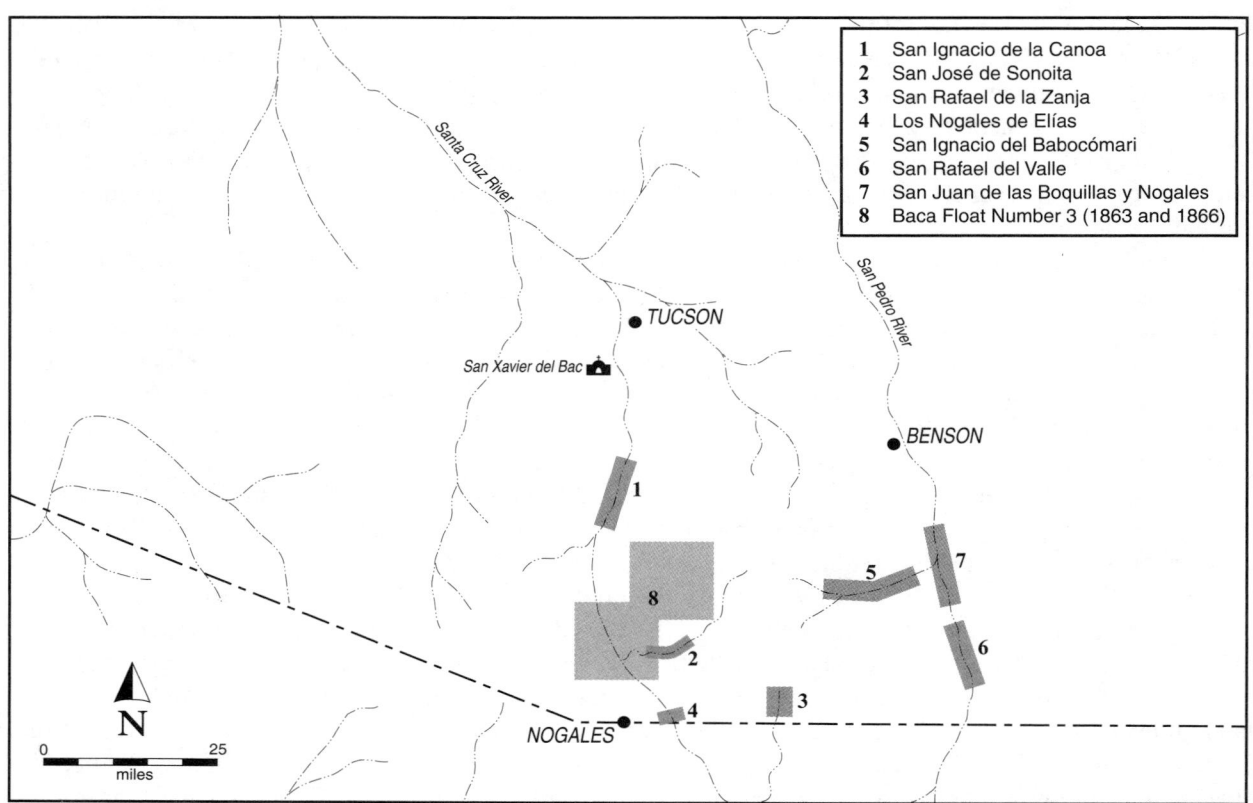

Figure 7. Selected Mexican land grants in southern Arizona.

Following the incorporation of southern Arizona into the United States, the Mexican presence in the region became increasingly centered in Tucson, at the same time that the city was becoming the hub of Anglo-American settlement and enterprise. The most significant aspect of the Mexican presence after the Gadsden Purchase was its essential continuity with pre-Gadsden days. Most of the families who had established themselves along the Santa Cruz River and in outlying areas chose to remain there, and even many of the presidio troops, after first abandoning Tucson and Tubac for Sonora, came back to lead civilian lives in U.S. territory. For most Mexicans, Tucson remained an extension of Sonoran culture and society. The Anglo-American population grew slowly but steadily in the first few decades after the Gadsden Purchase, knitting itself, to a degree, into the existing Mexican social structure (intermarriage among Mexicans and Anglo-Americans was fairly common) and sharing the dangers of life in a region still under Apache threat. But despite their minority status, the Anglo-Americans quickly dominated the regional economy, in large part because of the capital they brought with them into an area that, prior to their arrival, had been decidedly poor. Although the culture of the city remained predominantly Mexican, as did its population, Anglo-American traditions grew steadily stronger as Anglo-American money entered the region. In 1880, the year the railroad arrived, Anglo-Americans truly began to dominate life in Tucson, politically, economically, and culturally. Nonetheless, people of Mexican descent and culture remained in the majority in Tucson until shortly after the turn of the century. Mexicans, or more properly, Mexican-Americans, remain a viable and distinctive presence in Tucson today, despite a century and a half of imposed secondary status.

Mining, Farming, and Ranching

Of the three major economic pursuits that characterized southern Arizona through much of the historical period—mining, farming, and ranching—only ranching was introduced by Europeans. The Native Americans of the region, using their own repertoire of crops and techniques, had farmed competently for many centuries before Europeans arrived, and the extraction of precious metals from the earth, although never pursued on a large scale, had a similarly long history in the Americas. Native American farming in the Pimería Alta was transformed by the introduction of Spanish crops in the seventeenth and eighteenth centuries (see above). Native Americans also were among the freelance prospectors at placer deposits in early Spanish mining camps on the northern frontier, although many more Native Americans ended up laboring in Spanish vein-mining operations, often against their will, particularly in the major mining settlements of what are now Sonora and Chihuahua (Radding 1997:32–40). As for ranching, the people of the Pimería Alta began raising cattle, sheep, and goats shortly after Jesuits introduced the practice in the late seventeenth century, and small-scale ranching remains a part of rural Native American life in the region today.

Spanish mining, farming, and ranching in the Pimería Alta also benefited from the encounter with Native Americans, but far more from the land and labor that the encounter yielded than from any exchange of knowledge and technology. Spanish settlers spread through the Pimería Alta on the heels of the Jesuits with little interest in the subsistence strategies of Native Americans—the New World crops that Spaniards used had been adopted many years earlier—and every interest in establishing Spanish-style mining operations, farms, and herds. On the northernmost frontier of New Spain, where isolation and Apache raids limited Spanish settlement largely to the Santa Cruz Valley, the scope of these three pursuits never approached that of other parts of the Pimería Alta, much less that of the wealthiest places in New Spain. Nonetheless, it was the attempt to recreate a traditionally Spanish economy on the far northern frontier that caused the first major transformation of the southern Arizona landscape.

The second major transformation came in the late nineteenth century, following the arrival to the region of the "industrializing world economy" (Sheridan 1992:168). Anglo-Americans began settling in southern Arizona immediately after the Gadsden Purchase of 1854, bringing with them their own interest in mines, farms, and ranches, and both the technology they used and the scale of their operations were at first similar to those of their Hispanic counterparts. Not until 1880, the year the railroad reached southern Arizona, did mining, farming, and ranching become large, heavily capitalized businesses, closely linked to the greater financial world of the United States. Almost overnight, the three mainstays of the southern Arizona economy saw sweeping changes in scale and complexity, and the landscape that supported them was altered forever.

The following paragraphs outline the history of mining, farming, and ranching in southern Arizona and discuss how each mode of production was pursued in and near the Río Antiguo study area.

Mining

The first Spanish settlements along the Santa Cruz River might have been the Jesuit missions at Guevavi and San Xavier del Bac, but the search for gold and silver was as responsible for bringing Spaniards to the region as a desire to spread Catholicism. The very name *Arizona* derives from a place called Arizonac, just southwest of modern Nogales, where silver was discovered in 1736. The discovery occurred just five years after the Santa Cruz missions were officially established, and the strike led to the first wave of Spanish prospectors to the region, many of whom stayed after the strike at Arizonac petered out (Officer 1987:4). Sheridan (1992:160), noting the central role of mining camps in opening new areas to settlement in northern New Spain, has called the Spanish mining frontier "the cutting edge of empire,"

67

where ordinary Spaniards first mingled regularly with Native Americans and where Native Americans were first exposed to the novelties of Spanish economy and society. In southern Arizona, mining never played the dominant economic role that it did in the major mining centers of Sonora and Chihuahua, but the hope that it might kept a steady flow of Spaniards coming to the region throughout the colonial period.

Officer (1991), sifting through a variety of confusing and ambiguous documentary data regarding Spanish mines in southern Arizona, concluded that the actual extent of mining in the region during the Spanish Colonial and Mexican periods was very limited. Locations where mining likely did take place were limited to silver deposits in the Santa Rita Mountains, in the Arivaca area, and at the south end of the Huachuca Mountains, and gold deposits in the Sierrita Mountains, in the Arivaca area, and on Mount Benedict, west of Guevavi. The precise locations where most of this mining took place are unknown. Despite a great number of optimistic legends to the contrary, there is no good evidence that Spanish and Mexican mining ever took place in the Tucson Mountains, the Patagonia Mountains, the Ajo region, or a variety of other places that would later claim the interest of Anglo-American miners. Factors that limited every Spanish enterprise in southern Arizona—remoteness from Mexico City and the constant threat of Apache raids—were especially limiting to mining. The remoteness of southern Arizona from Mexico City made the procurement of tools and supplies (such as mercury for processing silver) prohibitively expensive, and the limited range of presidio protection made miners who worked the isolated deposits easy targets for the Apache. "Even in the most favorable locations," Officer (1991:8) wrote, "Arizona mining could not have amounted to much in Hispanic times."

Two features of Hispanic mining in southern Arizona survived the Gadsden Purchase to become incorporated into the Anglo-American approach to mining. The first was an acceptance of the mythical abundance of Arizona's mineral resources, an abundance first postulated by Spaniards at Arizonac, accepted hopefully by Hispanic miners for the next 120 years, and seized on enthusiastically by Anglo-Americans from the 1850s onward. Polzer (1968) suggested that much of the mythology of Arizona's buried wealth was in fact Anglo-American in origin, either the optimistic yearnings of small-time prospectors or the propaganda of commercial mining interests looking for financial backing, but as Officer (1991) noted, there were plenty of Hispanic antecedents for the Anglo-Americans to build on.

The second feature of Hispanic mining that Anglo-Americans borrowed was its technology. Hispanic miners exploited the two basic varieties of deposit—placer and vein (or lode). Placer deposits (literally, "pleasure" deposits), the most common source of gold, consisted of gold-bearing gravels exposed on the ground surface, often in or adjacent to a streambed. The typical method used to isolate gold from a placer deposit was panning, using a *batea,* a large, conical-bottomed vessel of hardwood or sheet metal. This method was supplemented by dry washing, or winnowing the ore from heavier gravels by throwing the ore-bearing gravel in the air over a blanket, and by amalgamation, the use of mercury to draw small particles of gold together in the *batea.* Anglo-Americans entering the Spanish frontier adopted these simple methods early on (Coggin 1987; Fansett 1952; Sheridan 1995:147–148; Wilson 1952).

Silver was more commonly mined from veins than from placer deposits. Silver was also much more abundant than gold in northern New Spain, and the Spaniards entering southern Arizona brought with them a variety of methods for extracting and processing silver ore. Nonetheless, the technology was still relatively simple, and the more-involved processes used in the major mining centers of Mexico were generally not used on the northern frontier. Mining along a vein usually began with shallow, open-pit diggings, then progressed to vertical shafts 2–4 m deep, sometimes augmented with small horizontal drifts. Deeper shafts might prompt measures to control flooding and the use of wooden beams as reinforcements, but given the limited nature of mining in southern Arizona, it is doubtful that even these simple steps were commonly taken. An important tool for processing silver ore, also adopted by early Anglo-American miners, was the *arrastre,* a large, circular, stone-floored depression, with a central post and a horizontal beam suspending two large boulders. The boulders were dragged by mules in a circle around the post, pulverizing the coarse ore dumped on the stone floor (Keane and Rogge 1992:26;

Sheridan 1995:147–148; West 1993:50–53). Officer (1987:16–17) noted that knowledge of these and other methods, first developed in the Spanish Colonial period, was brought by Mexican immigrants to Tubac after 1856, as mines abandoned many years earlier because of the Apache threat were reopened. "From this point on," he wrote, "Hispanic miners would play an indispensable role in the development of Arizona's mineral industry."

Although a great deal of placer and vein mining (including the beginnings of mechanized hard-rock mining) took place elsewhere in Arizona during the 1860s and 1870s, the first major strike in southern Arizona did not come until after the Apache threat in the region had been significantly curtailed by the U.S. Army. In 1878, silver was discovered in the hills near Tombstone in Cochise County, and by 1880, the discovery had created a town of 10,000 people or more where two years earlier there had been none. Mining at Tombstone during its short boom—the mines were largely abandoned by the end of the 1880s—underwent all of the changes seen in mining throughout the West during the same period. Powerful business interests bought up the major claims, the extraction and processing of ore became increasingly large scale and mechanized, and hired workers replaced individual prospectors in performing the manual labor of mining (Schillingberg 1999; Sheridan 1995:152–160). The railroad, which crossed southern Arizona two years after the Tombstone discovery, was a major factor in the early development of industrial mining in the region, linking the mines to the markets and technological innovations of the East. By the 1880s, large mining interests in Arizona were buying and building their own railroads to service their mining operations (Irvin 1987; Sheridan 1995:167–168).

Anglo-Americans began entering southern Arizona in search of mining opportunities immediately after the Gadsden Purchase. Although the number of miners in the region grew slowly, by the 1860s, the competition for claims, combined with a lack of clarity about how U.S. mining laws should apply in the newly acquired region, led to the establishment of mining districts modeled after those formed by groups of independent miners in California and Nevada. A mining district corresponded to a recognized mining area, such as a valley or group of hills. Its official boundaries and a set of regulations to govern mining within the district were established by agreement among the miners who were active there. The regulations addressed matters such as how claims must be filed, what the limits of individual claims were, and how disputes would be settled. Every district had its own set of regulations, but the regulations were generally very similar from district to district. Even after federal laws governing mining were passed in the late 1860s, mining districts continued to be an important regulatory mechanism at the local level, and districts continue to serve a regulatory function today (Lacy 1987:7–9).

The first mining district established in the vicinity of the Santa Cruz River was the Cerro Colorado District near Arivaca, the regulations of which were published in 1864 (Lacy 1987:9). Other districts soon followed, and by the 1970s, there were more than 30 recognized districts in Pima County (Keith 1974). The names and delimitations of districts have changed often since the 1860s, but the areas occupied by the districts have remained the same; most are situated in the islandlike clusters of mountains scattered around the county, typical locations of major mineral outcrops (Wilson 1995). Many of these districts have seen repeated episodes of mining since the nineteenth century, particularly copper mining, which began as early as 1865 in the Silver Bell District west of Tucson (Tuck 1963:31). In some districts, communities sprang up near ongoing mining operations. In the Rosemont District, another copper-producing area in the Santa Rita Mountains southeast of Tucson, for example, the town of Rosemont had two different incarnations, 1894–1910 and 1915–1921 (Ayres 1984a). In the Greaterville District, located on the eastern slopes of the Santa Ritas, the discovery of gold placers in 1874 gave rise to the community of Greaterville in the late 1870s, although the town was already dwindling by the early 1880s. Kentucky Camp, a complex of buildings erected as headquarters for a hydraulic mining operation at the Greaterville deposit in the early twentieth century, has since become a National Register Historic District (McDonald et al. 1995; Orrell 1998).

Copper became the focus of the mining industry in southern Arizona not long after the collapse of the silver market in the late 1880s, a collapse largely responsible for the demise of Tombstone. The most important copper-mining operation in the region, by far, was centered at Bisbee in southeastern Arizona. By the end of the century, the Copper Queen mine at Bisbee had a large, modern smelter; many miles of underground rail; and a huge labor force. It was also one of the richest copper mines in the world (Graeme 1987; Sheridan 1995:165). Improved metal prices in the late 1890s also led to an increase in production in the Helvetia, Rosemont, Silver Bell, Twin Buttes, and Mineral Hill Districts of Pima County, districts that subsequently enjoyed a heyday during World War I, when the demand for copper rose sharply in response to weapons manufacturing. The Ajo District, about 110 miles west of Tucson, also began large-scale copper production at the start of the war. In all of these districts, production declined after the end of World War I, nearly disappeared during the Great Depression, and then rose again during World War II (Wilson 1949:5–6).

The most recent stage in the development of mining in southern Arizona has been the nearly complete conversion from underground mining to large, open-pit extraction, a change implemented throughout the industry after World War II. The conversion has involved a great increase in mechanization, which has in turn allowed both for increased exploitation of lower-grade ores and much less reliance on human labor. Yet despite the increased production created by open-pit extraction, the general trend for copper throughout the United States since World War II has been one of decline, largely because of the expansion of copper-mining operations overseas (Hyde 1998:189–190). Nonetheless, the copper industry continues to be a major force in the southern Arizona economy, and the enormous open excavations and mountains of tailings and slag left on the landscape by copper mining since World War II are inescapable reminders of the industry's importance.

Because the Río Antiguo study area consists largely of floodplain, it has never been affected directly by mineral mining. The Santa Catalina Mountains, immediately north of the study area, constitute the nearest focus of mining in any period, and it was only at the fairly distant north slopes of the range that mining ever became a large-scale pursuit. Copper deposits in the Marble Peak mining district near the town of Oracle were first developed intensively around the start of World War I and have produced, intermittently, many tons of copper ore since then (Wilson 1949:15–16). Our search of GLO records at the state office of the BLM in Phoenix (see the discussion in the Settlement and Land Tenure section below) yielded information on just one mining claim in the immediate vicinity of the study area. In 1929, the Texas Arizona Copper Company received a mineral patent on the 115-acre Young America claim in Sections 2 and 3 of Township 13 South, Range 14 East, about 4 miles north of the Rillito on the lower slope of the Santa Catalinas. We have found little information on the history of this copper-producing claim, but it was apparently first owned and mined some 20 years before by W. R. Ramsdell, who named it the Pontatoc Mine. Ramsdell also built Pontatoc Road, which runs north from River Road, at a point just east of Alvernon Way, to the mine. He also built a camp to house 65 Mexican miners and their families while they worked the mine from 1917 until the end of World War I. After the war, the price of copper dropped and the mine closed, never to be reopened (Leavengood 1999). We have not found anything on the fate of the patent granted to the Texas Arizona Copper Company in 1929.

Farming

The Spanish settlers of southern Arizona practiced agriculture largely for the sake of subsistence, much like the Native Americans who preceded them in the region. Somewhat ironically, the largest producers of both native and introduced crops in southern Arizona throughout the Spanish Colonial and Mexican periods were not the Spanish, who had made so many additions to the Sobaipuri way of farming, but the Sobaipuri themselves and, later, the Tohono O'odham (Officer 1987:15). On the mission lands along the Santa Cruz River, Sobaipuri and Tohono O'odham farming never yielded the kinds of surplus that would make the trading of produce a major enterprise, but by the end of the Mexican period, the Akimel O'od-ham living along the Gila River had become prolific wheat farmers with abundant surpluses. When the

California gold rush of the late 1840s started funneling people across Arizona along the Gila Trail, the Akimel O'odham became "the first agricultural entrepreneurs in Arizona" (Sheridan 1995:97), trading surplus wheat to supply-seeking travelers. By 1870, they were producing and selling a surplus of more than three million pounds of wheat per year. Unfortunately, the Akimel O'odham soon lost the key to their agricultural success when Anglo-American farmers upstream began diverting the water of the Gila for their own irrigation projects (Sheridan 1995:97–98).

Two major factors limited the scale of Hispanic agricultural endeavors in southern Arizona. The first was the constant problem of distance: the Santa Cruz Valley was too far from central Mexico either to make the export of agricultural produce profitable or to encourage enough settlement to create a local market. Officer (1987:15) wrote, "The isolation of the Pimería Alta and its limited population provided little inspiration for major agricultural development." The second limiting factor was the obvious environmental one: in a region of generally high aridity, the land suited to agriculture was restricted to narrow swaths of the major river valleys, and for virtually the entire Hispanic era, the only valley sufficiently protected from the Apache by the presidios was the Santa Cruz. For Hispanic farming, as for Sobaipuri farming, irrigation was the key to maximizing productivity in an arid, circumscribed environment.

Irrigation had been used by Native Americans in southern Arizona for many centuries before Spaniards arrived in the region, but the Spaniards were also heirs to an ancient tradition of irrigation—one that ultimately had Roman and Arabic antecedents—that they brought with them from Europe (Meyer 1996). On the northern frontier of New Spain, where labor was scarce and engineers were nonexistent, only the simplest techniques of the tradition came into common use; this made the physical side of Hispanic irrigation not substantially different from its Native American counterpart. The basic element was the acequia (canal), a hand-excavated earthen ditch, leading from a simple diversion point in a stream to an agricultural plot. Acequias typically ranged in depth from 2 to 9 feet and in width from 1 foot to 7 feet. Depending on topographical circumstances, they might be straight or winding, single or multiple (Meyer 1996:41–42; Sheridan 1995:189).

The social side of Spanish irrigation was as important to the success of the system as the physical side. The amount of water available for farming along the Santa Cruz was limited and unpredictable, and even the small Spanish population living there had to be conservative in its use of the resource. The traditional Spanish institutions that helped ensure equitable distribution of irrigation water during times of scarcity were the *común de agua* (water users' association) and the *juez de agua* (water judge) or *zanjero* (canal overseer). The *juez de agua,* elected by the *común de agua,* was assisted by a *mayordomo* (ditch boss), who helped him implement a strict rotation of water usage when a shortage occurred. Indian settlements under Spanish control also were supposed to have *jueces de agua* or functionaries serving a similar role (Meyer 1996:64–66; Sheridan 1986:14–15, 1995:189). There is direct evidence of these institutions in the Mexican-American settlement along the Santa Cruz River as late as the 1880s (Sheridan 1986:64–65), and their pervasiveness throughout the northern frontier in the Spanish Colonial period makes it likely that they existed in southern Arizona from the start of Spanish settlement.

Despite the burdens of isolation and aridity, Spanish farming was largely a success along the Santa Cruz. Clustered at the Tubac and Tucson presidios, Hispanic farmers planted corn, wheat, barley, garbanzos, lentils, and a variety of vegetables, as well as fruit trees and grapevines. The most important crop was wheat, not entirely because of a Spanish preference for wheat over corn but because wheat, which was frost tolerant and matured in winter, could take advantage of the most dependable irrigation season. The occasional surplus raised by Hispanic settlers would be sold to the commander of the presidio. Soldiers at the presidio also sometimes cultivated gardens, and in the latter part of the Mexican period, they were expected to plant crops to feed their horses and other livestock. At different times during both the Spanish and Mexican periods, settlers from Tucson visited the San Pedro Valley to plant and harvest crops, protected from Apache attack by escorts of presidio soldiers (Jones 1979:194; Officer 1987:15; Sheridan 1986:15).

The essential characteristics of Hispanic agriculture along the Santa Cruz were, according to Sheridan (1986:15), "scarcity and cooperation," and the successful balancing of the two by Hispanic farmers continued well into the U.S. period. Officer (1987:290) noted that by 1862, eight years after the Gadsden Purchase, Anglo-American immigrants to Tucson had already acquired considerable property in and around the town, but they found it difficult to purchase agricultural lands along the river. This situation changed soon enough, as both Anglo-Americans and newly arrived Mexicans began to acquire land both by purchase and by claims made under the Homestead Act. The newcomers were often more interested in acquiring land for speculative purposes than for agriculture and, in either case, were altogether uninterested in conforming to the traditional Hispanic practice of irrigation conservation. Disputes soon arose along the Santa Cruz between new landholders who wanted to divert the flow of the Santa Cruz to some private purpose, such as to power a flour mill, and traditionalists who were thereby denied access to the flow they had long depended on (Sheridan 1986:63–65).

Historical-period agriculture had a later start in the Rillito Valley, but it shared a number of characteristics with its counterpart in the Santa Cruz Valley. As along the Santa Cruz, Mexican farmers preceded Anglo-American farmers along the Rillito, even though settlement along the Rillito did not begin until after the Gadsden Purchase. As along the Santa Cruz, the earliest methods of farming undoubtedly included a combination of Native American and Spanish crops and techniques. And as along the Santa Cruz, the *sine qua non* of farming in the valley was irrigation, diverting water from the river onto nearby fields. The development of irrigation along the Rillito during the second half of the nineteenth century and the early twentieth century also shared certain characteristics with its development in the Santa Cruz Valley, although minor distinctions in the physiography of the two valleys made irrigation along the Rillito a special adaptation in many ways, as we discuss in the next section.

The possibilities of irrigated agriculture made the Rillito Valley attractive to a wide variety of people in the second half of the nineteenth century. In addition to Mexican and mainstream Anglo-American farmers, the valley eventually supported a substantial Mormon farming community (see below) and even a small number of Chinese farmers who originally settled in Tucson after 1880, when their jobs building the Southern Pacific Railroad ended (Lister and Lister 1989:3). The increasing population of Tucson in the last two decades of the nineteenth century brought a rise in demand for crops such as alfalfa (for livestock forage) and vegetables. Vegetable gardens, many of which were operated by Chinese farmers, sprang up on the west bank of the Santa Cruz River near downtown. Chinese gardening operations were generally small, but the Chinese were successful at both growing and marketing their crops and were an established part of the Tucson community for several decades (Sheridan 1986:65–66; Xia 2001:84–93). Their presence in the Río Antiguo study area is poorly documented, but, like all of the people who chose to farm along the Rillito, they undoubtedly recognized that Tucson would long require a reliable supply of food. In 1910, George E. P. Smith described a situation that would drive farming along the Rillito for decades to come:

> The Rillito Valley possesses one advantage that is rarely held by a new agricultural
> district. The advantage consists of a large and waiting market for its production in the
> city of Tucson. The present population is about twenty thousand. There is practically no
> direct production of wealth in the city; it is a city of consumers [Smith 1910:101].

Irrigation in the Rillito Valley

Irrigated agriculture along the Rillito may have had its start in prehistoric times, but if so, archaeologists have yet to find evidence of prehistoric canals or other water-control features in the valley (see Chapter 3). Given its early presence in the Santa Cruz Valley, and the fundamental similarities of culture history and environment along the two rivers, it is unlikely that irrigation was not practiced along the

Rillito in prehistoric times, especially considering the success of simple, gravity-flow irrigation there during the historical period. As long as archaeological projects continue to be carried out along the Rillito, in advance of development projects or otherwise, the eventual discovery of prehistoric irrigation features seems inevitable.

During the historical period, by contrast, irrigated agriculture in the Rillito Valley is easily studied, although primarily with documentary rather than archaeological evidence. For about 70 years, or roughly 1860 to 1930, farming with gravity-flow irrigation was the essential business of life along the Rillito. This was especially true in the eastern portion of the study area, close to the points of diversion for most of the water used by farmers, but it was also true for large areas downstream that were watered by extensions of the same ditches. Irrigation along the Rillito never matched the scale or technological sophistication of systems eventually seen along the Santa Cruz River near Tucson, and it lacked the model once provided along the Santa Cruz by earlier O'odham systems, but the Rillito presented its own special challenges to water diversion, and the ways the challenges were met prior to the advent of intensive groundwater pumping constitute a unique and interesting history.

George E. P. Smith and the Rillito

The history of irrigation along the Rillito in the late nineteenth and early twentieth centuries is known largely through the work of George Edson Philip Smith, an engineering professor at the University of Arizona from 1900 to 1955. There are sources pertinent to the subject that were not produced by Smith (see below), but the major source, and the one that makes interpretation of most of the others possible, is Smith's *Groundwater Supply and Irrigation in the Rillito Valley* (1910). Published as a bulletin by the University of Arizona Agricultural Experiment Station, the book documents Smith's investigation of the geology and irrigation potential of the Rillito Valley during the years 1905–1909. It was well received and widely distributed on publication and helped establish an international reputation for Smith as an expert on irrigation and water supply in the desert Southwest (Downs 1937:1279; Haney 1985:44, 54, 56). Its local impact was also considerable. Smith (n.d.) later claimed that the book "led indirectly" to the Tucson Farms Company's decision to focus on the Santa Cruz Valley, because of his conclusions about the difficulties of capturing the subsurface flow of the Rillito (see O'Mack and Klucas [2001] and Logan [2002:165–170] on the large and complex irrigation works of the Tucson Farms Company, built on the Santa Cruz River in 1912). In addition to its original importance as a geological study and a statement of how irrigation along the Rillito should develop, Smith's book remains valuable for its descriptions and accurate maps of irrigation systems in use at the time it was written, as well as for its comments on the history, virtues, and defects of those systems.

Smith conducted a variety of field studies during the course of his investigation and became intimately familiar with the Rillito Valley and its inhabitants, in particular the farmers who were building and maintaining irrigation systems along the river (Figure 8). An important part of Smith's investigation was his measurement of the subsurface flow in the valley using his own version of a recently devised electrical method. The method involved driving 2-inch-diameter pipes into the bed of the river to various depths, with sets of pipes at upstream and downstream locations. An electrode was inserted into each pipe, and a salt solution was injected into the upstream pipes. The rate of downstream diffusion of the salt solution was measured by changes in an electrical current created and registered by the electrodes (Smith 1910:128–130; see also Smith 1964:6–7). Smith conducted the tests along two cross sections of the river, designed to measure what turned out to be the remarkably rapid underflow passing through what he called the Narrows (see Chapter 1): one cross section was placed at the mouth of the Narrows, or about 500 feet downstream from the Fort Lane (i.e., Craycroft Road) crossing, and one was placed in Tanque Verde Creek, directly opposite the Montijo house, at about the midpoint of the Narrows (Figure 9). As discussed later, the Montijos were early settlers and homestead patentees living just north of Fort Lowell, on the point of land between Tanque Verde Creek and Pantano Wash.

Figure 8. A man operates a homemade pumping plant for irrigation in the Rillito Valley, ca. 1906. See Smith (1910:99) for a description of the scene (photograph courtesy of Special Collections, University of Arizona Library, Tucson, Ms. 280, box 13, folder 16).

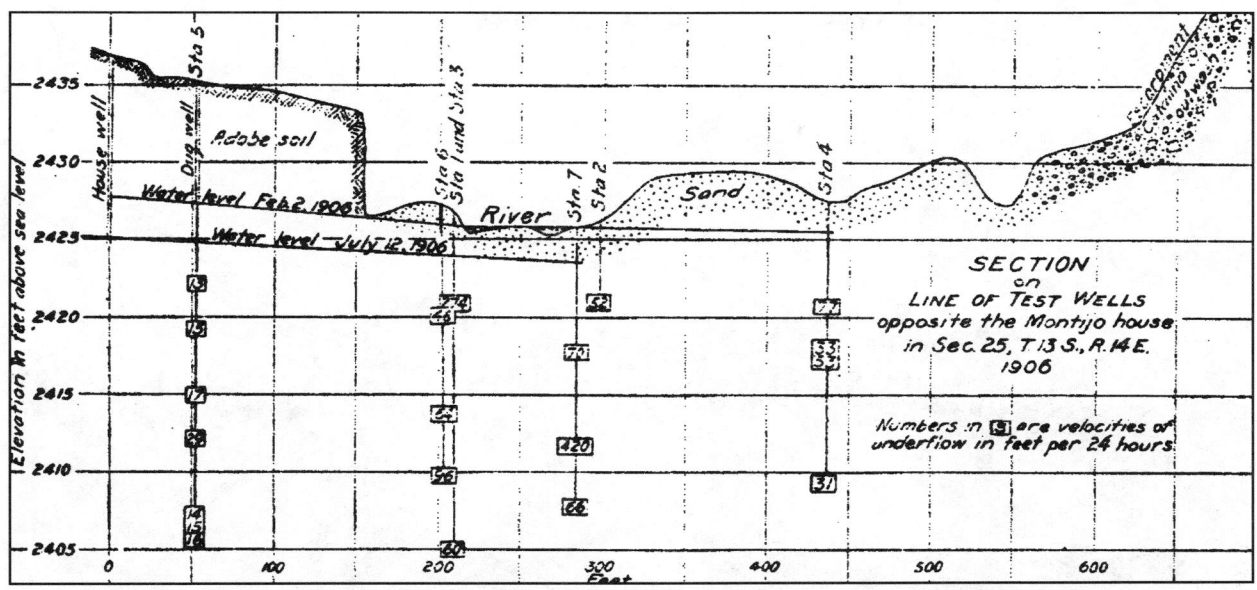

Figure 9. Cross section of the bed of Tanque Verde Creek opposite the Montijo house, prepared by Smith (1910:Figure 16).

The heavy pine maul used to drive the test pipes prompted Smith to enlist the help of some local farmers, as a photograph reproduced in his book indicates (Figure 10). The original print of the photograph, kept among Smith's papers at the University of Arizona Library, has written on its back, in Smith's hand, the names of the three men wielding the maul: E. Bingham, Anton[io] Salazar, and B[ernardino?] Díaz. "E. Bingham" was probably Erastus Bingham, the father of Nephi Bingham, the original settler of the Mormon community taking shape about 3 miles downstream from the site of the testing. At the time of the testing, the Binghams were actively maintaining a ditch with its head in the immediate vicinity of the Montijo cross section (see below). We have not found any further information about Antonio Salazar, but he was presumably part of the El Fuerte community already established nearby around the ruins of Fort Lowell. Bernardino Díaz was probably a member of the Díaz family known to have lived and farmed in the immediate vicinity of the cross section (see the discussion of El Fuerte below). He was undoubtedly the same man who built the Díaz ditch, apparently the first underflow ditch in Tanque Verde Creek, with its head about a mile upstream from the test site (see below). The note on the back of the photograph includes a reminder of certain social attitudes that prevailed at the time of Smith's work: below the three men's names is written, "One white man = 2 Mexicans."

Smith later conducted similar tests at several other locations in the valley, including locations at some distance from the Rillito. These tests required the use of more elaborate, mule-powered drilling rigs, and Smith again turned to local men for assistance. Among the unpublished photographs from his work in 1906 is one labeled simply "Well-driller and family" (Figure 11). The identity of the well driller is uncertain, but it may be Carl Monthan, the only well driller mentioned by name in Smith's book (1910:156). In addition to drilling his own test wells, Smith also collected data on stratigraphy and groundwater levels from existing wells across the portion of the Tucson Basin lying between the Rillito and the Santa Cruz River, in an effort to characterize the water table. The map of the water table he prepared based on these data was the first detailed map of groundwater in the basin (Figure 12).

Smith was an established expert on irrigation and hydrology before his study of the Rillito, and he spent most of the rest of his long life (he died in 1975 at 101) closely involved in water-supply issues

Figure 10. Three local men use a heavy maul of Oregon pine to drive a test pipe into the bed of Tanque Verde Creek, part of G. E. P. Smith's study of subsurface flow in the Rillito Valley, August 3, 1906 (photograph courtesy of Special Collections, University of Arizona Library, Tucson, Ms. 280, box 13, folder 16).

Figure 11. A well driller and his family, photographed by G. E. P. Smith during his work along the Rillito in 1906 (photograph courtesy of Special Collections, University of Arizona Library, Tucson, Ms. 280, box 13, folder 16).

affecting Tucson, the state of Arizona, and the Southwest more generally (Haney 1985:44). A list of his publications, most of which deal with some aspect of irrigation or water supply, has more than 100 items (Smith 1955). Since he frequently relied on his Rillito experience when working on later projects, including many projects elsewhere in the Tucson Basin, his subsequent publications also occasionally provide information on irrigation along the Rillito. His collected papers, now archived at the University of Arizona Library (Ms. 280, Special Collections), have been of particular value to the Río Antiguo overview. The papers include most of his published work, many unpublished items, some of the original photographs used in his publications, and other, unpublished photographs.

Early Irrigation Efforts

Even in the wettest years, and before any lowering of the water table or changes in the way the surrounding terrain absorbed and repelled rain, the Rillito never flowed year-round, which meant that the simplest method of irrigation—extending ditches from the river's edge to nearby fields—had only seasonal success in the study area. According to Smith, there were more than thirty small, conventional ditches diverting water from the Rillito at the time of his study, but, "The flood seasons . . . are too short to mature ordinary crops, often only one or two irrigations are possible, and only on years of exceptional river flow are such ditches profitable" (Smith 1910:99). The earliest attempts to irrigate land along the Rillito, presumably made by the earliest settlers in the valley, were probably limited to diverting the river's

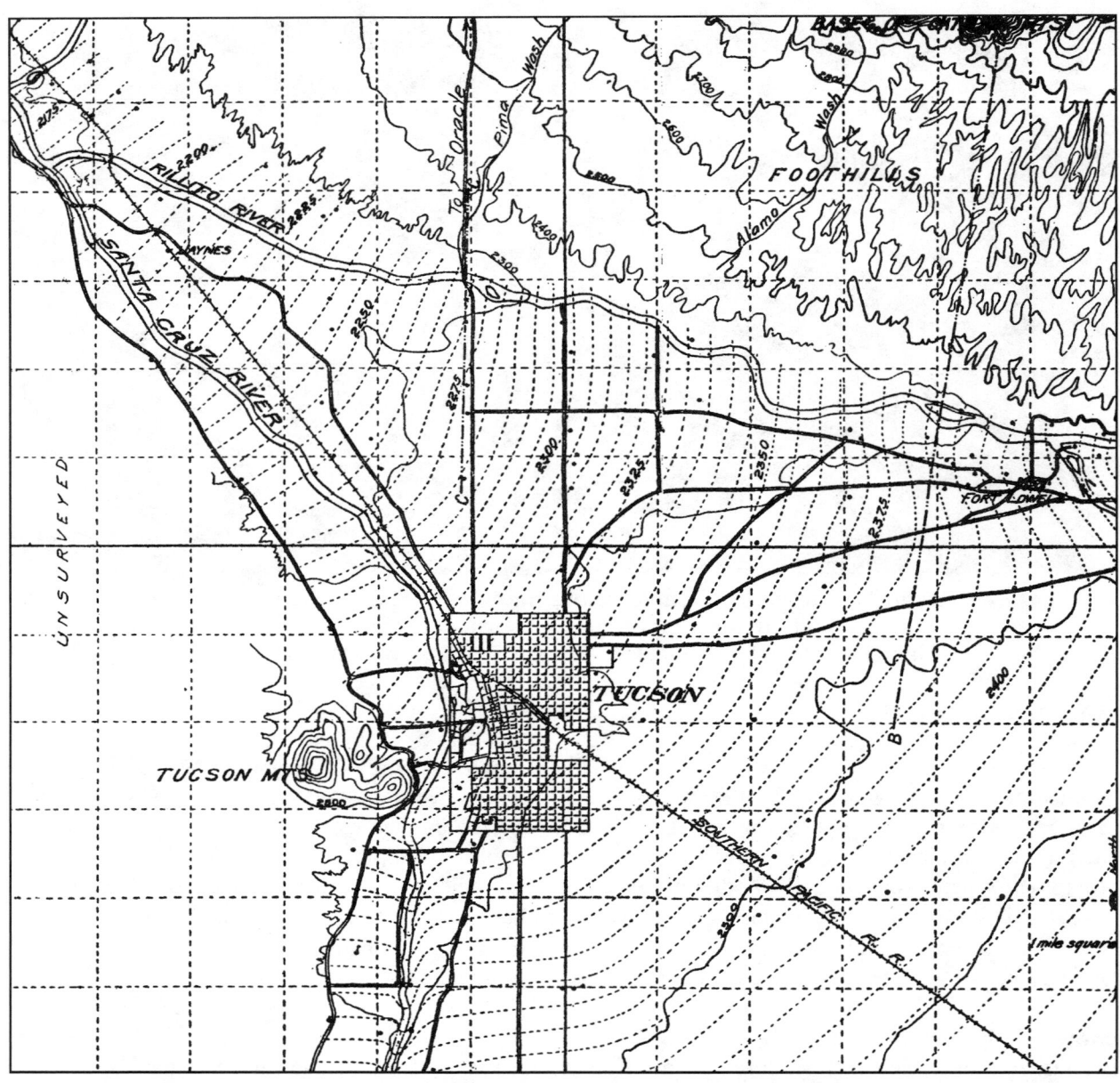

Figure 12. Water contour map of the Rillito and Santa Cruz Valleys in the vicinity of Tucson for May 15, 1908 (from Smith 1910:Figure 49).

unreliable surface flow, but an alternative method, which involved sinking the head of a ditch below the bed of the river to capture the water flowing more reliably through the sand, soon had the most success.

In a later discussion, Smith (1911a) suggested that the first attempts to tap the "underflow" of the Rillito amounted to no more than digging ordinary diversion ditches deeper, "a custom which was known to the 'padres' and which is quite common in many sections of old Mexico to this day." Whatever the antiquity of the method, Smith goes on to imply that at least some of the many underflow ditches along the Rillito at the time of his study were originally just that, ordinary ditches made deeper. Since we have little specific information on any ditch prior to Smith's study—we know that one or two ditches diverted water from Tanque Verde Creek for use at Fort Lowell as early as 1872 (see below), but not much else—the set of ditches he documented in 1910 may be the best approximation possible of the ditches that existed in the area 20 or 30 years earlier.

Actually, the first documented attempt to tap the underflow in the Rillito was much more than the deepening of an existing ditch, but the fact that it was proposed and executed at all suggests that some-one had already established the reliability of the underflow in less ambitious projects. In 1886–1888, the Santa Catalina Ditch and Irrigation Company built a system fed by a large ditch heading in the bed of the river, in Section 28 of Township 13 South, Range 14 East. This is the immediate vicinity of the river's big bend and adjacent to where the Mormon community of Binghampton was later established. Years later, Smith described the project, a substantial piece of engineering in its day:

> Instead of a headgate there was a heavy concrete infiltration gallery one-quarter mile long buried in the river bed. . . . The cross-section of the gallery was four feet in width and four and a half feet high inside with an arched top. It was built on a grade of two feet per mile and at the upstream end the floor was eleven feet below the river bed. The dis-charge was taken out on the north bank but a fourth of a mile below it was passed under the river in a stavepipe inverted siphon five feet in diameter. A wide canal was built for two miles below the siphon covering several thousand acres of land [Smith 1910:99].

The project was the subject of considerable interest around Tucson, and photographs survive of the wooden "stavepipe" siphon under construction (Figures 13 and 14). The siphon was of the same basic design as other buried redwood pipes of the era (for example, a 26-inch buried water main built in 1892 by the Yuma Light and Water Company; Kwiatkowski 1996:Figures 6.23 and 6.24), although larger than most. During construction, the system as a whole was touted by the *Arizona Daily Star* as an example of innovative solutions to the shortage of irrigation water in the desert:

> This project is the first that has been attempted in Arizona to bring the underflow of water to the surface, but it is the project that will prove the initial step of a system for irrigation that will revolutionize irrigation in Arizona and will make many thousands of acres capable [of] reclamation, which under the old system of depending entirely upon surface water, could not be utilized. The STAR is free to say that it believes that every acre of land in the Rillito valley can and will be reclaimed to agricultural purposes through the new system of irrigation [*ADS*, 9 June 1887].

But the system was never put into service, at least not in its original design. According to Smith (1910:100), on September 13, 1887, a flood filled the nearly completed canal with sand. It was sub-sequently cleared, but then the completed siphon also filled with sand, and the project was abandoned. Smith does not indicate why the project was not considered redeemable, but Alexander Davidson, the man hired to build the system, later recalled that the wooden siphon had fallen apart:

**Figure 13. Construction of a redwood flume in the bed of the Rillito by the
Santa Catalina Ditch and Irrigation Company, ca. 1887
(photograph courtesy of the Arizona Historical Society, Tucson, Accession No. 4075).**

Of all fool ideas for an irrigation project perhaps that of Fair of New Rochelle and Bullock of Cleveland [presumably, the proprietors of the Santa Catalina Ditch and Irrigation Company] was the most foolish. I was to have charge of the work and George Doe to do the carpentry. . . .

[Fair and Bullock] proposed to tap the Rillito at a point about five miles N.E. of Tucson, just below Ft. Lowell, near where the Binghams now live, run the water down the south [*sic* for north?] side of the river to opposite Hancock's tract of land then under the river onto Hancock[']s and other land.

I wanted to go further up where we could get more water, but they declared that if we would drive an open cut upstream for a short way we would have plenty. Then I suggested an open cement lined ditch and an iron pipe under the river but their idea was a huge five foot in diameter redwood pipe. Large enough to water the whole country. . . . Well, when we got pretty far along there was a big flood and we turned the water in to see what would happen. It happened all right, the frail two inch thick wood gave way and our irrigation project was ended [Davidson 1930–1936:25–26].

**Figure 14. Recently completed redwood flume built by the Santa Catalina
Ditch and Irrigation Company in the bed of the Rillito, ca. 1887
(photograph courtesy of the Arizona Historical Society, Tucson, Accession No. 4073).**

Davidson was an early settler of the Rillito Valley, as was his carpenter for the project, George Doe; both men later developed their own underflow ditches farther up the Rillito (see below). Davidson's reference to "Hancock's land" is undoubtedly to the 160-acre homestead patented in 1892 by James F. Hancock in the NE ¼ of Section 29 (Township 13 South, Range 14 East), immediately west of and across the river from where Nephi Bingham later settled (see below). Bingham, the founder and name-sake of Binghampton, reportedly bought his original 60-acre parcel from Davidson, who must have settled in the area by the early 1890s. A house presumed to have been built by Davidson around 1895 still stands on the former Bingham parcel (Parkhurst 2001:section 8, p. 2), in the SW ¼, NE ¼ of Section 28 (Township 13 South, Range 14 East). Davidson was not the original homesteader of this parcel, which was part of a 160-acre homestead patented by William Edwin Rowland in 1890 (see below). The Rowland homestead straddled the river, and although we have not found anything to confirm it, David-son seems to have bought property from Rowland on both sides of the river (perhaps the entire 160-acre homestead) shortly after the patent was granted. The 1893 Roskruge map of Pima County (Figure 15) shows Davidson as a landowner in the SE ¼ of Section 28, on the south bank of the river; it was ap-parently this land, or a portion of it, that Davidson donated to the community of Binghampton in the early 1900s to build a school (Gursky 1994:27).

Davidson's decision to settle along the Rillito was presumably connected with his work on the failed Santa Catalina project, but the land he eventually bought was not patented by Rowland until 1890, three

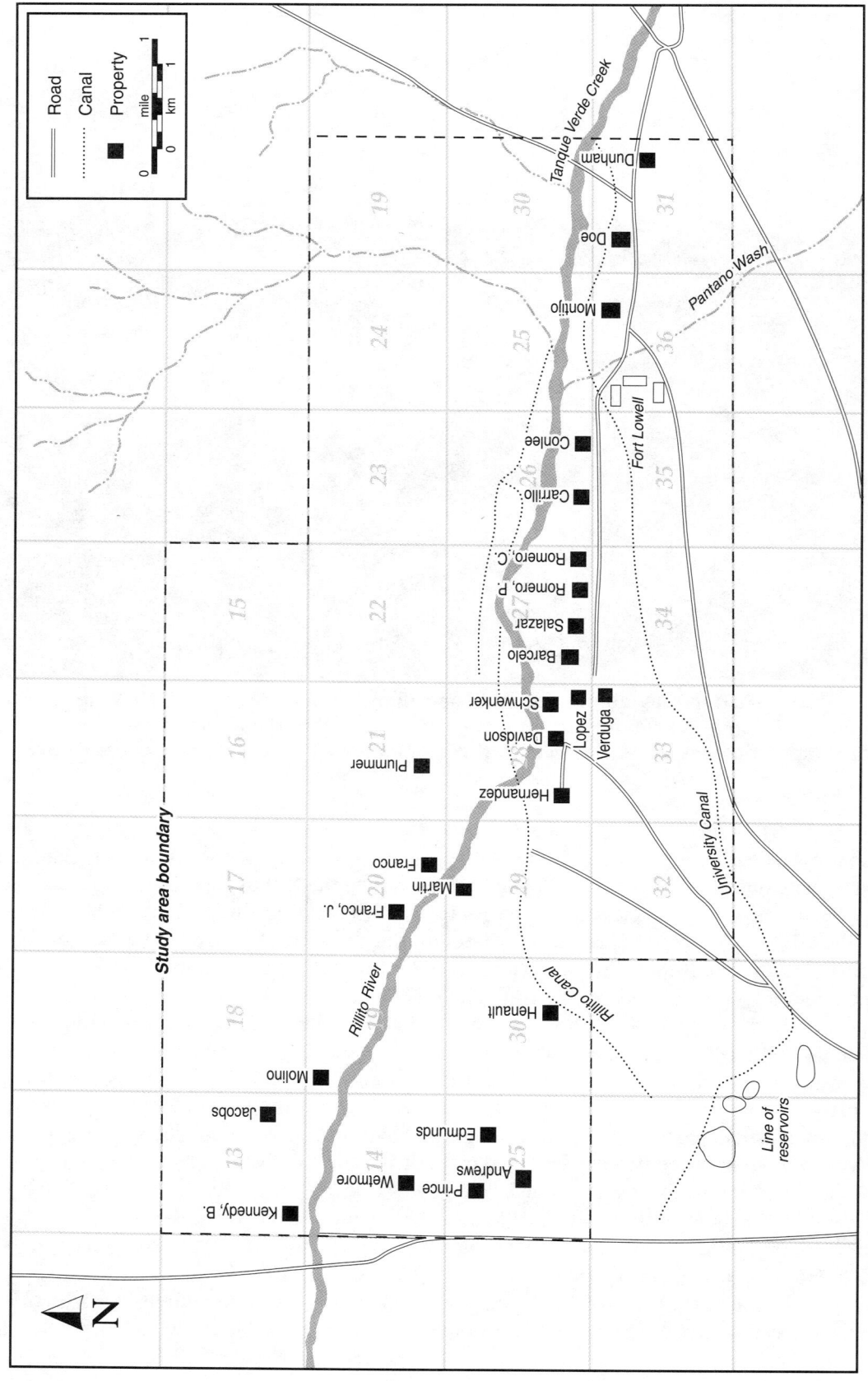

Figure 15. Map of cultural features within the study area depicted on 1893 map of Pima County (based on Roskruge 1893).

82

years after the project's demise. Davidson's own underflow ditch, in use at the time of Smith's study, may have been a later, partial reuse of the main Santa Catalina ditch, since the latter ditch probably crossed his property. There is some indication that the Santa Catalina system was being finished or rebuilt by 1891 (Stolbrand 1891:11). As discussed later in this section, Davidson's association with one of the proprietors of the Santa Catalina Ditch and Irrigation Company lasted until at least 1909; presumably, he did not voice his opinion of their failed project until later.

Ironically, a few years after the Santa Catalina project failed, Davidson was at work on another underflow project centered on the confluence of the Rillito with the Santa Cruz River, about 9 miles downstream from the Santa Catalina project. In 1894, the supporters of the project formed the La Junta Canal Company, with plans to bring more than 50,000 acres of land under cultivation along the Santa Cruz. Despite the misgivings Davidson later claimed to have had about using a redwood siphon in the Santa Catalina project, the La Junta project would also rely on "a large redwood pipe" (*ADC*, 20 March 1894).

Underflow Ditches in the Early Twentieth Century

When Smith carried out his study of the Rillito, there were nine ditches with buried heads in the Narrows, plus three other ditches originating farther up Tanque Verde Creek. All 12 ditches appear on Smith's map of water contours in the Fort Lowell vicinity (Figure 16), which is the principal (sometimes the only) record of the location of each ditch. The last three ditches—the Campbell, the Daily, and the Romero—were not of primary interest to Smith and did not extend into the Río Antiguo study area, so we do not discuss them here. Smith prepared a slightly more detailed map for the area immediately north and west of Fort Lowell (Figure 17); it allows a closer look at a few ditch characteristics not evident in the larger map. Turner (1990:44) includes a map of irrigation ditches in the Fort Lowell vicinity that is clearly based on Smith's maps with a few added details, apparently derived from her own research or that of her collaborators, Edward and Rosamond Spicer. We did not have an opportunity to consult the research files of Turner and the Spicers (the files are kept by the Old Fort Lowell Neighborhood Association) to determine the sources for their map, but we do cite the map here when it depicts something not provided on Smith's maps. An earlier, unpublished paper by Turner (1981) discusses the ditches in the Fort Lowell area in more detail, but it is largely lacking in references. This paper does provide some helpful clues as to the origin of the first ditches in the study area.

In addition to Smith's (1910) discussion and depictions of the nine underflow ditches, other information useful for understanding the history of the ditches derives from a lawsuit filed in 1911 by Andrew R. Swan against Charles H. Bayless, Nephi Bingham, J. Knox Corbett, and the Rillito Farms Company. The plaintiff farmed land in Sections 26 and 35 of Township 13 South, Range 14 East, just east of Fort Lane and south of the Rillito, using a ditch and water rights he had purchased from the Cole brothers. According to Swan, the defendants in the suit had misappropriated water to which he had prior rights by moving and deepening their ditch heads in Tanque Verde Creek (see the discussion below). The formal complaint filed by Swan (Canal Company Records 1911) provides numerous details about the history of the ditches covered by the suit. Smith was eventually asked by the parties to the case, and by W. H. Sawtelle, the Pima County judge hearing the case, for his expert opinion on the matter. His report to the parties in the case (1911a) and a letter he wrote to the judge (1911b) provide further interesting details; the former item includes what is apparently a draft of Smith's formal testimony in the case. Smith also published comments on the case and his participation in it (1911c:570–572; 1936:90–91). We used these sources, supplemented occasionally by information from other sources, for the following individual ditch histories. Further research would undoubtedly yield other relevant sources, especially if the complete files of the lawsuit initiated by Swan were consulted, and some of the conclusions we reach here would undoubtedly have to be modified.

By way of introduction, it is useful to cite Smith's (1911a) definition of an underflow ditch: "One whose bed is situated below the natural groundwater level so that groundwater seeps into the ditch and flows away by gravity. It may be an open excavated ditch, or a covered, but not watertight, conduit."

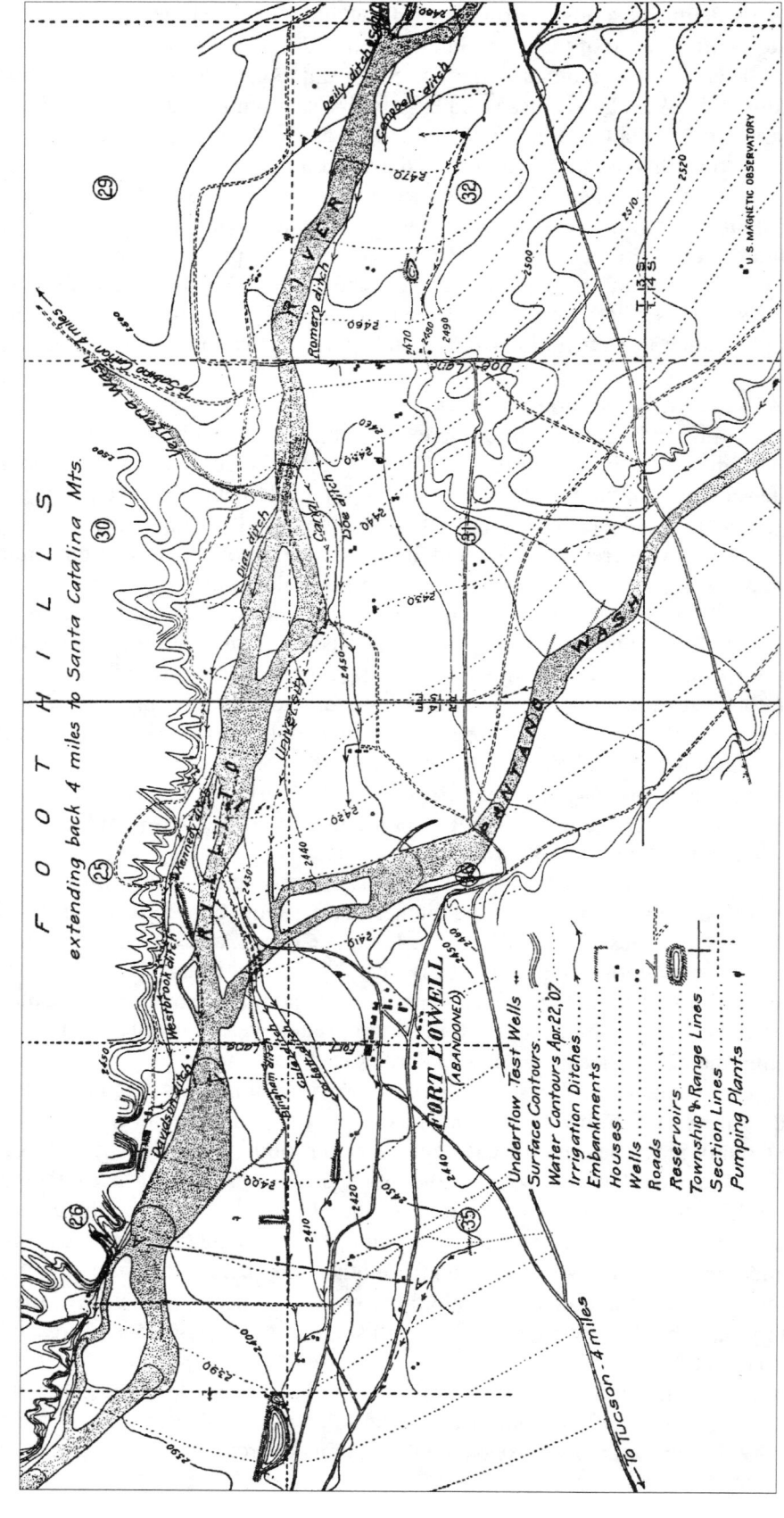

Figure 16. Water contour map of the Rillito Valley in the vicinity of Fort Lowell for April 22, 1907 (from Smith 1910:Figure 50).

84

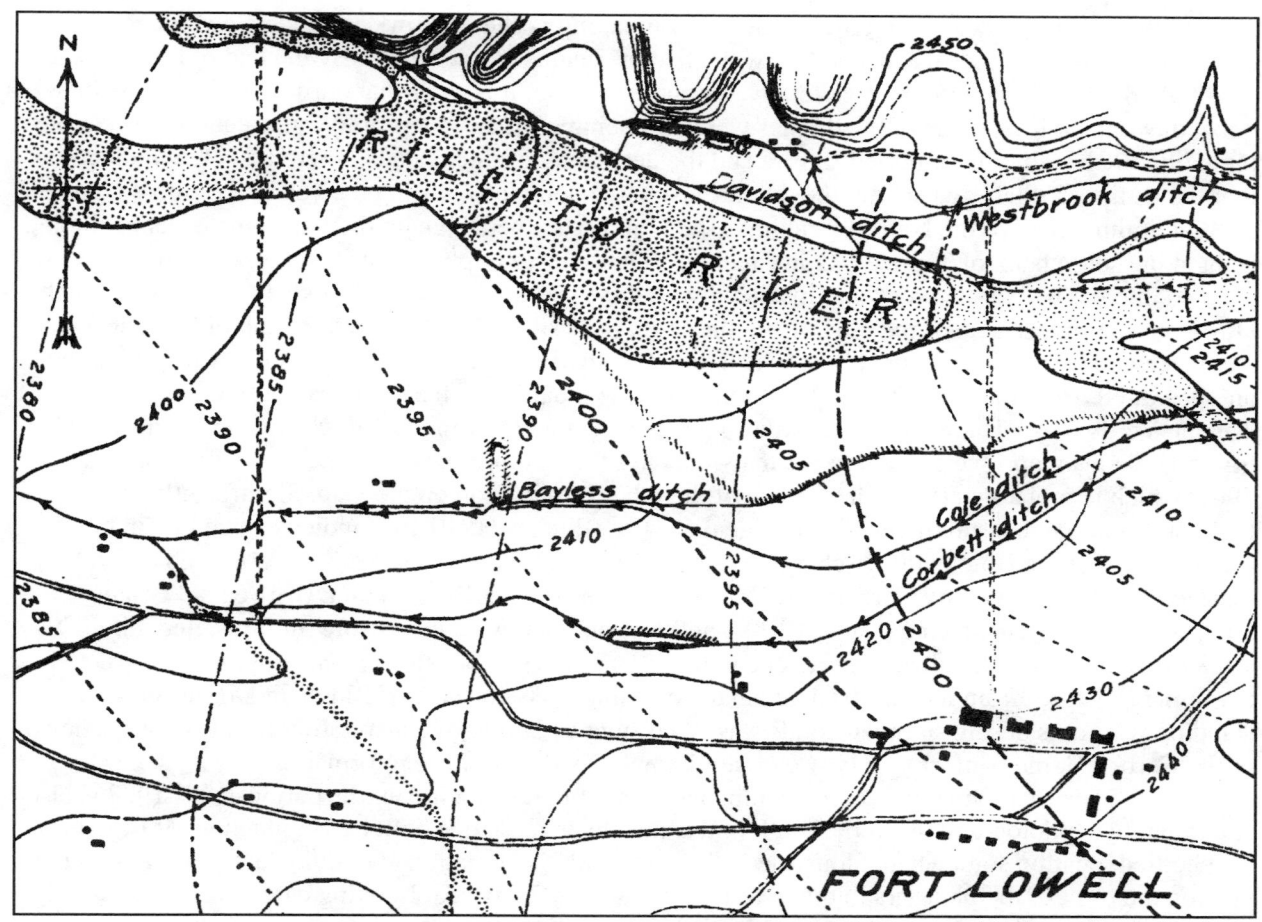

Figure 17. Water contour map of the immediate vicinity of Fort Lowell showing different contours after a flood season (November 1, 1906; the dash-and-dot lines) and during a dry season (February 1, 1907; the dotted lines) (from Smith 1910:Figure 56).

Redwood box flumes became the usual covered conduit in the study area. The box flume served both to convey water from the head of the ditch and to allow infiltration of water between the planks of the box, or at least the planks forming the cover of the box; we have not found a good description of exactly how a box flume worked. A number of the ditches discussed below also began at a "head box," which was basically a segment of box flume built perpendicular to the primary flume and to the flow of water in the river. Smith (1907:182–183) was an early advocate of using reinforced concrete pipe instead of redwood boxes for the buried flumes of underflow ditches, but we did not find any evidence that his advice was followed by the builders of the nine ditches discussed here.

Bingham (or Bayless). The Bingham ditch was built by Nephi Bingham, who by the time of Smith's work had expanded his farming efforts to the south side of the Rillito just west of Fort Lowell. Smith also refers to this ditch as the Bayless ditch, in reference to Charles Bayless, Bingham's frequent business associate and part owner of the University ditch, which by 1910 fed into the Bingham ditch. Also by the same year, the Bingham ditch was watering land owned by Bayless, either exclusively Bayless land or in addition to land owned by Bingham.

Smith (1910:196) described all nine ditches originating in the Narrows as "underflow ditches," in other words, having heads excavated below the bed of Tanque Verde Creek. By the end of his fieldwork in 1909, all nine ditches apparently did have buried heads, but it is clear that during the five years he was collecting data at least some of the ditches were still being built or undergoing significant modifications, including the installation of buried flumes and the deepening of ditch heads. There are a few indications that the Bingham ditch was among the ditches just being completed during the years of Smith's study.

On Smith's map of the Narrows vicinity (see Figure 16), the Bingham ditch is depicted as beginning right at the south bank of Tanque Verde Creek, which seems to imply that its head was not, in fact, excavated into the bed of the creek and instead diverted the creek's surface flow like a conventional ditch. However, the first stretch of the ditch, from the south bank of the creek to the far bank of Pantano Wash, is represented by a double dashed line, which undoubtedly indicates a buried pipe or box flume and not an open ditch. How the flume would have functioned without being fed by a head buried directly in Tanque Verde Creek is not clear, but it may simply mean that the Bingham ditch was not complete when Smith made his map. The caption to the map indicates that it represents water contours for April 22, 1907, which is probably also the latest date of the other information on the map. Significantly, Smith's table of discharge measurements for the nine underflow ditches (1910:197) indicates that his first measurement of the Bingham's discharge was not made until January 31, 1908, even though several measurements of the nearby Corbett and Cole ditches were made the preceding two years. Perhaps the Bingham was not yet carrying water in 1907, and was put in service just before Smith started taking his 1908 measurements. This does contradict a note by Turner (1990:44) that Nephi Bingham constructed his flume in 1903, "from its head to the Pantano crossing." The success of Bingham's flume at withstanding washouts during summer floods was, according to Turner, the inspiration for the construction of the Corbett flume. Unfortunately, we do not know the sources of her information.

That the Bingham ditch was being completed or modified sometime in the period 1907–1908 is also suggested by a photograph taken by Smith of a water-diversion fence built by Bingham in 1907 at an unspecified location somewhere along the Rillito. The only information about this feature comes from a note on the back of the photograph that reads "Bingham 1907 stocada. Looking east Jan. 12, 1908" (Figure 18). The "stocada" (the word is an anglicized version of Spanish *estacada*, or stockade) consisted of a line of stakes driven into the stream bed along the inside of one bank, then densely interwoven with brush. A ditch ran adjacent to this feature, excavated into the sandy stream bed. The "stocada" must have served either to divert water into the ditch or to prevent the erosion of the river bank, or both. Smith did not comment anywhere on the relationship of the ditch and "stocada" to the Bingham ditch, but the two features may have constituted parts of the Bingham ditch head, excavated into the bed of Tanque Verde Creek. Their absence from Smith's map suggests that they were built in the latter half of 1907, between the date of the map and the date of the photograph. Elsewhere, Smith (1911a) refers in passing to the "Bayless head box," which implies that the Bingham ditch head, once constructed, consisted of a lumber infiltration box similar to the one on the Corbett ditch, which is better documented (see below). How the "stocada" and accompanying ditch functioned in relation to the buried head box is unclear.

We have found no other information about the buried flume of the Bingham ditch, except for notes by Smith (1911a) that its head was 3 feet higher than the head of the Cole ditch, and that its total fall was only 0.73 feet. Smith recommended, as part of a solution to the lawsuit filed by Swan, that the Corbett flume be deepened and extended down Tanque Verde Creek to join the Bingham flume, which would have eliminated the segment of the Corbett ditch running across the point of land between the Tanque Verde and Pantano Wash. Apparently this never happened, since the Corbett continued to flow independently until only recently. As discussed below, Smith reported in 1910 that the University ditch emptied into the Bingham, which became the case only after Smith prepared his map in 1907. The University was extended along the east bank of Pantano Wash to a point directly over the buried Bingham flume, into which it discharged via a concrete drop box.

Figure 18. "Stocada" (or *estacada*) built in 1907 by Nephi Bingham somewhere along the south bank of the Rillito or Tanque Verde Creek, January 12, 1908, view to the east (photograph courtesy of Special Collections, University of Arizona Library, Tucson, Ms. 280, box 14, folder 18).

After becoming an open ditch on the south side of Pantano Wash, the Bingham flowed generally westward, roughly along the line between Sections 26 and 35 (Township 13 South, Range 14 East), passing a small excavated reservoir (which it presumably fed) on the line between the SE ¼ and SW ¼ of Section 26. On Smith's smaller map (see Figure 17), the Bingham is labeled the Bayless and is depicted as crossing the Cole at the south end of the small reservoir before continuing westward. The Bingham/Bayless eventually joined with the Corbett ditch in the northwest corner of Section 35, then emptied as a single ditch into a large excavated reservoir at the southeasternmost corner of Section 27. This reservoir is probably "the Bingham tank near Fort Lowell, designed to store river water" mentioned by Smith (1910:122). The association among ditch owners Bingham, Bayless, and Corbett, suggested here in the merging of ditches and ditch names, is confirmed in their association as defendants in the suit filed by Swan in 1911, and in later irrigation ventures along the Rillito (see below).

The Bingham ditch depicted on Smith's map was not the first or necessarily the most important of Nephi Bingham's irrigation projects. As discussed earlier in the chapter, Nephi Bingham and his extended family first settled and farmed on the north bank of the Rillito, another mile and half west of the apparent end of the Bingham ditch. The farmland there was watered by the Davidson ditch, which, since it is labeled as such on the Smith map, was probably still owned by Davidson in 1907. Bingham bought his first land from Davidson, but Davidson apparently remained the owner of the principal ditch watering the original Binghampton settlement on the north bank of the river. Bingham undoubtedly expanded and modified Davidson's system within the immediate vicinity of Binghampton. For example, he apparently built the large earthen reservoir still visible near his original house (the reservoir is now a playground for the Montessori school that occupies the old Bingham property) and a series of small distribution ditches fed by the reservoir (Ciolek-Torrello and Homburg 1990:63–64).

Cole. The head of the Cole ditch, depicted on the Smith map as originating in the middle of Tanque Verde Creek, was very close to the head of the Bingham ditch, and like the Bingham ditch, it ran from Tanque Verde Creek to the far side of Pantano Wash via a buried flume (see Figure 16). The complaint filed by Swan in 1911 (Canal Company Records 1911) states that the head of the Cole was on the property of Petronilo Provencio, in the SE ¼, SW ¼ of Section 25 (Township 13 South, Range 14 East). We know that Provencio received patent on a 40-acre homestead there in 1912 (see below). The complaint also describes the Cole head and ditch in fairly specific terms:

> [T]he head of the said Cole ditch is sunk in the sands of the bed of said Rillito River [i.e., Tanque Verde Creek] to a depth of approximately ten feet, and . . . from this head the water is flumed underground for a long distance down the bed of said River, and thence carried in a Southwesterly direction, and out of the bed of said River, and into the open ditch . . . [Canal Company Records 1911:9].

The complaint does not indicate that the Cole ran all the way to the other side of Pantano Wash via a buried flume, but Smith's map makes this clear. West of Pantano Wash, the Cole ran westward not far south of the Bingham, eventually running immediately adjacent to it, then ending about a quarter-mile short of the reservoir fed by the Bingham and the Corbett.

According to Swan, the Cole ditch was first constructed in 1898 by William and Robert Cole, to water the separate lands of the two brothers in Sections 26 and 35, just east of the Narrows and south of the Rillito. By 1911, Swan had bought Robert Cole's one-half interest in the ditch, as well as the water rights and the associated land, and the Rillito Farms Company and Nephi Bingham had bought William Cole's one-half interest in same. Part of Swan's complaint centered on the extension of the Corbett ditch upstream from its original location by its owner, J. Knox Corbett. The extension took place in 1906 or 1907, and Swan attributed the subsequent lack of water in the Cole ditch to the new location of the Corbett ditch head, which was collecting water that the Cole ditch previously collected, water to which Swan had prior rights. Swan was prohibited from lowering the head of his ditch by the gradient of the Cole flume and the elevation of the fields watered by the ditch, a situation discussed by Smith (1911a) in his comment on the suit.

A segment of the Cole ditch is apparently still visible in the field, just west of Craycroft Road. This segment appears on the 1992 Tucson North 7.5-minute USGS quadrangle map as the northern of two parallel ditches in the NE ¼ of the NE ¼ of Section 35 (Township 13 South, Range 14 West).

Corbett (or Jordan). The Corbett ditch received its name from J. Knox Corbett, a South Carolinian who came to Tucson in the 1880s and had his initial business success as the founder of a large lumber and hardware business. Corbett is best known today as the original owner of the J. Knox Corbett House, an early-twentieth-century landmark in downtown Tucson. Several of Corbett's siblings also settled in Tucson in the nineteenth century, including an older half-brother, William Corbett, who was paymaster at Fort Lowell for a time (Lyons 1981). Turner (1990:44) notes that the Corbett ditch was named "after the Franklin Corbett family who ran a small dairy near Swan Road." We have not found any other information regarding this dairy. William Corbett did have a son named Franklin (Lyons 1981:10), but we have not researched his life. If the Corbett ditch had an association with Franklin Corbett, it was secondary to its original association with his uncle, J. Knox Corbett.

According to Swan's 1911 complaint, Corbett became owner of his ditch around 1906, but it was "originally constructed by parties unknown to this plaintiff some thirty years since" (Canal Company

Records 1911:6). This would place the original construction of the ditch around 1881, during the period that the area was part of the Fort Lowell military reservation. Turner (1990:44) states that the Corbett ditch likely predated Fort Lowell by about five years, "and was made by ranchers and farmers who settled here in the 1860s," but she does not indicate a source for this information. Swan noted, without further comment, that the ditch was formerly known as the Company No. 4 ditch, a name we have not seen in any other source (Turner indicated this alternative name on her map, but her source may have been Swan's complaint). A possible referent for the "Company" of the earlier name is the Pima Land and Water Company, which was granted a ROW for an irrigation ditch across this portion of the Fort Lowell military reservation by an act of Congress in 1889 (Pima Land and Water Company 1888). It is not entirely clear that the company (which was apparently a predecessor of some kind to the Tucson Farms Company; see O'Mack and Klucas 2001) ever exercised its ROW or built a canal near the fort. As we discuss below, the University ditch owned by Bayless and the Rillito Farms Company in 1911 was apparently a reuse and modification of the upper portion of the University Canal depicted on the 1893 Roskruge map, a feature built, we suspect, by the Pima Land and Water Company (see below). Perhaps the portion of the Corbett ditch west of Pantano Wash was originally part of that ditch, which led to the name, "Company No. 4."

Also according to Swan, the Corbett ditch as originally built did not extend up the bed of the Rillito (i.e., Tanque Verde Creek) as it did in 1911. Instead, he claimed that it "had its head or source at a distance of some five or six hundred feet down said river and westerly from the present head or source of said ditch, and that the head of said ditch . . . was not sunk in the water bearing sands of the said Rillito River but was constructed on the surface of said stream" (Canal Company Records 1911:6). It was Corbett, in collaboration with Frank Jordan, co-owner at the time of both the ditch and the lands it watered, who reconstructed and deepened the ditch and extended its head up the Tanque Verde to a point where it captured water rightfully belonging to Swan. Swan also indicated that by the date of his complaint, Corbett had purchased Jordan's portion of the ditch and water rights, but that the Rillito Farms Company was now involved in the ownership of same.

Whatever the validity of Swan's complaint, it is clear that Corbett and Jordan were building a new, sunken head for their ditch in Tanque Verde Creek at the time of Smith's study. In the table of discharge measurements included in his book, Smith (1910:197) indicated that the measurement of the Corbett taken on June 19, 1907, came just after the "buried flume and new head" of the Corbett were completed. He also included two photographs of the project, along with a few statistics: the length of the flume buried in the streambed was 1,520 feet, and the head box, the top of which was 6 feet below the natural river bed, measured 38 feet long by 4 feet wide by 3.3 feet deep (1910:198–199). Smith's photographs of the head box (Figures 19 and 20), which ran perpendicular to the flume at its upper end, show that it was built in much the same way as the Davidson flume, portions of which were documented archaeologically by SRI in 1996 (see below). The sides of the box consisted of heavy planks set on edge, with a top of smaller planks laid across them; the bottom was presumably also of smaller planks laid crosswise to the sides. Smith's photographs show only the head box, not the flume itself, but the method of construction, judging from the Davidson flume, was probably identical, except that the flume may have had smaller dimensions in cross section. The primary purpose of the flume was to carry water, whereas the head box served to collect water through infiltration; the latter purpose may have required a wider and deeper box than the flume. The head box may also have been of a looser construction than the flume, to allow water to enter it. Unfortunately, we have not found a description of exactly how such a head box worked. It is conceivable that the flume itself, in addition to its conveyance function, also allowed infiltration, if only through its top.

Consistent with the depiction on his 1907 map, Smith (1911a) noted that the outlet or lower end of the Corbett-Jordan flume was in Petronilo Provencio's field, or just south of Tanque Verde Creek. From Provencio's land, the Corbett continued as an open ditch across the point of land between Tanque Verde Creek and Pantano Wash, crossed under the Pantano via a buried flume, then entered an open ditch on

89

Figure 19. Head box of the Corbett-Jordan flume during construction, around 1907, view presumably to the north. A Mexican laborer stands on the flume leading away from the head box (photograph courtesy of Special Collections, University of Arizona Library, Tucson, Ms. 280, box 13, folder 16).

Figure 20. Head box of the Corbett-Jordan flume during construction, around 1907 (photograph courtesy of Special Collections, University of Arizona Library, Tucson, Ms. 280, box 13, folder 16).

the south side of the Pantano. From there, the ditch continued westward roughly parallel to the Bingham and Cole ditches, fed a small, linear reservoir in the NW $^{1}/_{4}$ of the NE $^{1}/_{4}$ of Section 35 (Township 13 South, Range 14 East), and eventually joined the ditch formed by the merging of the Bingham and Cole, in the NW $^{1}/_{4}$ of the NW $^{1}/_{4}$ of the same section (see Figure 16). Before Jordan sold out to Corbett, the two men used the water from the ditch on fields in Sections 26 and 35, and the same fields were still watered by the ditch under the later ownership of Corbett and the Rillito Farms Company (Canal Company Records 1911:6).

According to unpublished notes by Frank Jordan (1959), he and J. Knox Corbett went into partnership in 1907, buying a farm along the Rillito near Fort Lowell. This was undoubtedly the land watered by the Corbett ditch and referred to in Swan's complaint. Jordan sold his interest in the farm in 1911, presumably to the Rillito Farms Company, Corbett's new partner. At the time Jordan made his notes (1959), the land belonged to Lewis Douglas, the well-known U.S. congressman and ambassador to England.

Jordan's association with the Rillito Valley was a long one. He moved to Tucson from Yuma in 1904 to serve as superintendent of the Flowing Wells Ranch, just west of the Río Antiguo study area, where Levi Manning was cultivating 2,000 acres, using water routed from—ironically, considering the proximity of the ranch to the Rillito—the Santa Cruz River at Sentinel Peak (*ADS*, 21 April 1957; see O'Mack and Klucas [2001] on the Manning irrigation works near Sentinel Peak). After his association with Corbett ended, Jordan lived in the Tucson area intermittently but maintained a farm along the Rillito. In the 1920s, he served for several years as president of the Pima County Farm Bureau (*ADS*, 19 March 1926; 35 August 1928).

We have not researched the later ownership of the Corbett ditch, but Turner implied that Lewis Douglas (whose last name appears on her map as an alternative name for the ditch) and perhaps other owners used the ditch for many years after Corbett's ownership ended. The ditch ran through the Mexican-American community of El Fuerte that grew up around the fort after its abandonment, which meant that it occasionally served as a source of water for the community (Figure 21). According to Turner, the Corbett ditch "even now runs six to eight months out of the year" (1990:44). A segment of the ditch was recently recorded by Stephen (1998) as part of AZ BB:9:325. The same segment also appears on the 1992 Tucson North 7.5-minute USGS quadrangle map as the southern of two parallel ditches in the NE $\frac{1}{4}$ of the NE $\frac{1}{4}$ of Section 35 (Township 13 South, Range 14 West). The Corbett ditch continues to be one of the stops along the walking tour of the old Fort Lowell neighborhood during the annual Reunión de El Fuerte.

Davidson. As discussed above, Alexander Davidson settled in the vicinity of the Rillito's big bend shortly after his participation in the failed project of the Santa Catalina Ditch and Irrigation Company. It is likely that the Davidson ditch depicted on Smith's map of the Narrows was a reuse of the main ditch of the Santa Catalina project, but Smith's map does not extend to the big bend, where the failed redwood flume of the Santa Catalina project was located.

Smith's map (see Figure 16) shows the Davidson ditch originating along the north bank of Tanque Verde Creek about a quarter mile east of Fort Lane. It runs down the bed of Tanque Verde Creek to a point just west of Fort Lane, then onto the north bank of the Rillito where it runs to the west edge of the map. The portion of the ditch in the bed of Tanque Verde Creek is depicted with a single dashed line, which probably indicates that it was not being used or maintained in 1907, the date of Smith's map. In 1906, Smith took photographs of the ditch where it ran in the bed of the creek. On the back of one of the photographs, Smith wrote, "An illustration of how not to build an irrigation canal. The ditch shown lies in the coarse sand of the riverbed, and the loss by seepage is very fast. . . . Six days after this picture was taken a sudden flood entirely destroyed this ditch for ¼ mile" (Figure 22). Smith's table of discharge measurements (1910:197) lacks readings for the Davidson in 1907, and the table includes a note on the Davidson for 1908, "Buried flume nearly completed." Smith did not indicate the location of Davidson's flume project on his map, but he did take a photograph of the project in 1908 (Figure 23). It is clear that after the flood of 1906, Davidson decided to improve his system by installing a buried wooden flume.

The location of the portion of the Davidson flume shown in Figure 23 is uncertain—it is not clear where a "bend in the line" would be required for a flume that would presumably have run directly up Tanque Verde Creek from the north bank of the Rillito—but the location of other portions of the flume were established in excavations by SRI in 1996 (Sterner 1996). Two segments of the flume were discovered under the bed of the Rillito, one near the north bank, the other near the south bank, both just west of Craycroft Road (Fort Lane). Together the two segments mark a roughly southeast-northwest line across the modern channel of the Rillito (Sterner 1996:18), but it is difficult to tell how this line would have related to the course of the river when the flume was built. A comparison of Smith's 1907 map and the 1992 Tucson North 7.5-minute USGS quadrangle indicates that the south bank of the Rillito just west of Craycroft Road is now about 400 feet north of where it was in 1907.

The portions of the Davidson flume uncovered by SRI in 1996 were remarkably well preserved (Figure 24). The segment near the north bank of the Rillito led to a poured concrete well of uncertain date, built to tap the flume through its top. The location of the well, called Schroeder's Well after its current owner, probably corresponds to the original head of the open Davidson ditch that ran down the north bank of the Rillito, as depicted on Smith's 1907 map.

Figure 21. Soledad Olivas of the El Fuerte community washes clothes in Corbett ditch, ca. 1920s (photograph courtesy of the Arizona Historical Society, Tucson, Accession No. 66080).

Figure 22. Davidson ditch, 1906 (photograph courtesy of Special Collections, University of Arizona Library, Tucson, Ms. 280, box 13, folder 16).

Díaz. The Díaz ditch apparently belonged to Bernardino Díaz, who was probably a member of the Díaz family mentioned by Turner (1990:26) that farmed land "directly north of the fort, on the other side of the Rillito." According to Turner, the family immigrated from Sonora when the fort was still in service. On the Smith map, the Díaz ditch originates in Tanque Verde Creek at the mouth of Ventana Canyon, apparently from a buried head. It soon runs onto the north bank of the creek and ends after about a half-mile, perhaps at fields cultivated by Díaz. The head of the Díaz seems to be in the same spot as the head of the Buckalew ditch (later called the Westbrook), which was first dug by Díaz and Mercedes Tapia (see below). Either the Díaz or the Buckalew is probably the "old Mexican ditch" referred to by Smith (1911a) and implied to be the earliest underflow ditch in the Narrows. As noted above, Bernardino Díaz is apparently one of the men in a photograph taken by Smith in 1906 (see Figure 10).

On Turner's map, "Montijo" is given as an alternative name for the Díaz ditch. The source for the alternative name is not given, but it presumably refers to the Montijo family, two members of which, Jesús and Jesús, Jr., patented 160-acre homesteads in the immediate vicinity in 1900 and 1903, respectively (see below). The Díaz ditch as depicted on the Smith map crossed the homestead of Jesús, Jr., but we do not know if Montijo was still the owner of that parcel in 1907.

94

Figure 23. Construction of the Davidson flume at a bend in the line, May 22, 1908 (photograph courtesy of Special Collections, University of Arizona Library, Tucson, Ms. 280, box 13, folder 16).

Doe. George Doe was one of the early settlers of the Fort Lowell area and patented a 160-acre claim along the south bank of Tanque Verde Creek in 1897 (see below). His ownership of this parcel gave him access to the bed of the creek at the upper end of the Narrows, immediately opposite the mouth of Ventana Canyon. This is where the Doe ditch on Smith's map originates, although it is not clear from Smith's map that the ditch used a buried flume. Smith (1910:197) started taking discharge measurements on the Doe ditch in 1908, but the ditch may have been dug long before that. In 1883, Doe offered to sell the Army the rights to irrigation ditches he had dug near Fort Lowell (see below), but there is no way of knowing if one of these ditches was the Doe ditch depicted on Smith's map. The ditch on the map does end just east of the ruins of the fort, without crossing Pantano Wash.

In 1906, Smith took a photograph of a dike of willow trees built by Doe, presumably at the head of his ditch and at the south bank of the Tanque Verde (Figure 25). By the time of the photograph, the willows in the dike had taken root and become substantial trees, suggesting that the irrigation features in use by Doe in 1906 had been built many years earlier.

Kennedy. On Smith's map, the Kennedy ditch originates at the north bank of Tanque Verde Creek, near the center of the Narrows and close to the heads of the Bingham, Cole, and Corbett ditches. It is not clear from the map if the Kennedy head included a buried flume, and we have not found any other source of information on the ditch. Smith (1910:197) took discharge measurements from the Kennedy beginning in

**Figure 24. Section of the Davidson flume excavated by SRI in 1996,
view to the southeast.**

Figure 25. George Doe's willow tree dike, 1906 (photograph courtesy of Special Collections, University of Arizona Library, Tucson, Ms. 280, box 14, folder 18).

1905, but he does not comment specifically on the ditch. On his map, the Kennedy runs along the north bank of the Tanque Verde for about three-fourths of a mile before ending just east of Fort Lane.

University. The origin of the name of this ditch (or canal, as it is labeled on Smith's map) is uncertain, but its earliest appearance is on the 1893 Roskruge map, which shows it beginning in the upper reaches of the Narrows, running west across Pantano Wash near the ruins of the fort, then generally west for more than 5 miles to a series of reservoirs not far north of Tucson. We have found nothing specific about the date of construction or original ownership of the ditch or the reservoirs. Smith (1910:197), in a note to his discharge measurement of the ditch in January 1908, stated, "This ditch [has been] reopened after being idle some years. It discharges into the Bingham ditch." The note came one year after the preparation of his map, which shows the University originating at the south bank of Tanque Verde Creek, just opposite the mouth of Ventana Canyon, then running west for about a mile near the south bank of the creek before emptying into the north bank of Pantano Wash. The entire course of the ditch is represented with a dashed line, confirming that it was not being used when Smith made his map. It was somewhere along this stretch, after the University was once again in use, that Smith built a simple wooden weir to measure the flow in the ditch (Figure 26). Smith was an early advocate of accurate flow measurements to avoid wasting irrigation water; he published recommendations for weirs based in part on his experiments on the underflow ditches (Smith 1913).

Figure 26. A simple wooden weir on the University ditch, probably built by George E. P. Smith, November 18, 1908 (photograph courtesy of Special Collections, University of Arizona Library, Tucson, Ms. 280, box 14, folder 20).

There is no indication on Smith's map of the University's original route west of Pantano Wash, although, as suggested above, the Corbett ditch may have occupied part or all of it. The University canal depicted on Roskruge's map may have been built by the Pima Land and Water Company, which was granted a ROW across the Fort Lowell military reservation in 1889 that apparently corresponded to the route of the University (Pima Land and Water Company 1888). We have not found any other information about this company. By 1911, the year of Swan's complaint, the portion of the University east of Pantano Wash was owned by Charles Bayless and the Rillito Farms Company, undoubtedly the parties responsible for renovating the ditch and routing it into the Bingham. According to Swan, Bayless became the owner in 1908 and lowered the head of the ditch that year to capture more water, then lowered it twice again in 1910. The University head was 200 feet downstream from the head of the Buckalew (the Westbrook ditch on Smith's map), but Swan claimed that by lowering the head of the University, Bayless was using water rightfully belonging to the Buckalew, in which Swan had a partial interest (Canal Company Records 1911). Swan could not lower the head of the Buckalew to compensate, because he would not then have the necessary grade for gravity flow to his distribution ditches.

In her map of ditches in the Fort Lowell area, Turner (1990) indicated that the University drained into the Bingham via a drop box located on the north bank of Pantano Wash. The drop box would have led down to the buried flume of the Bingham, which then continued west under Pantano Wash. Turner does not indicate a source for this information, but her depiction is probably accurate. In 2000, SRI

Figure 27. Concrete drop box that once connected the University ditch to the buried flume of the Bingham ditch (from Homburg and Kurota 2000:9).

conducted a small archaeological survey for Pima County along the north bank of Pantano Wash and discovered the drop box that Turner apparently depicts on her map (Figure 27) (Homburg and Kurota 2000). SRI later discovered that the route of the University ditch to the drop box is still plainly evident in the field and corresponds to the ditch still depicted on the 1992 Sabino Canyon 7.5-minute USGS quadrangle running parallel to the south bank of Tanque Verde Creek (O'Mack and Riggs 2001).

Westbrook (or Buckalew). The original name of the Westbrook ditch depicted on Smith's map was apparently the Buckalew (see the map of Turner, 1990), although we have not discovered when a change in ownership of the ditch prompted the name change, and we have found nothing on owners named either Westbrook or Buckalew. The Buckalew ditch is discussed in Swan's complaint (Canal Company Records 1911). Its head was in Tanque Verde Creek, "at a point approximately 200 feet north of the section line between sections 30 and 31 of [Township 13 South, Range 15 East], and at a point approximately 300 feet Northwesterly from the northwest corner of the NE $\frac{1}{4}$ of the NE $\frac{1}{4}$ of said section 31." This places the head within a 160-acre parcel purchased from the GLO in 1911 by Jesse Worley (see below) and just north of George Doe's homestead, at the mouth of Ventana Canyon. Swan makes no reference to Worley in his complaint, which suggests Worley bought the parcel after the complaint was filed.

According to Swan, the Buckalew was originally dug by Mercedes Tapia and Bernardino Díaz in March 1894. Either this ditch or the Díaz ditch is probably the "old Mexican ditch" implied by Smith (1911a) to be the oldest of the underflow ditches in the Narrows. When the Díaz was first built, Tapia had a four-sevenths interest in the ditch and Díaz a three-sevenths interest. In 1899, Díaz sold his interest to the Cole brothers, each of whom then owned three-fourteenths of the ditch and water right, which they apparently used to water the same lands watered by the Cole ditch. By 1911, Swan was owner of Robert

99

Cole's three-fourteenths interest, and Rillito Farms and Nephi Bingham owned the three-fourteenths of William Cole. Charles Bayless had also purchased the other four-sevenths from Tapia, and Rillito Farms apparently had some partial interest in this four-sevenths. An understanding of what this tangled web of ownership meant for the complaint filed by Swan is perhaps a goal for future research.

On Smith's 1907 map, the Westbrook ran along the north bank of Tanque Verde Creek to a point about 500 yards west of Fort Lane, where it apparently ended, but by the time of Swan's complaint, the Buckalew joined the Cole at its head in Tanque Verde Creek. The change presumably took place when Swan became part owner of the Buckalew and chose to route his portion of the flow into the Cole ditch, of which he was also part owner. Turner's map depicts a diversion ditch coming off the south side of the Buckalew, ending at a drop box apparently connected to the head of the Cole. The source for this depiction is unknown, but it may simply be a reconstruction based on the information in Swan's complaint.

Early Corporate Irrigation

We discussed above the ambitious project of the Santa Catalina Ditch and Irrigation Company in the vicinity of the Rillito's big bend. We have not found any additional specific information about this company or the ultimate fate of its project, but the association of at least one of its principals with Alexander Davidson, the man who built the failed redwood flume, apparently lasted for many years. Around 1900, John M. Fair, mentioned by Davidson as one of the owners of the Santa Catalina project, formed the Rillito Canal Company, with himself as principal owner and Davidson as his agent. The Rillito Canal Company and its holdings went through a number of corporate incarnations between 1900 and 1923, an evolution partially documented in company records preserved at the Arizona Historical Society in Tucson (Ms. 1129, folders 4–6). The following discussion is based largely on information in those records, with a few references to other sources as indicated.

The 1893 Roskruge map (see Figure 15) depicts the route of the Rillito canal, which originates in the Narrows near the mouth of Ventana Canyon, then runs west along the north bank of Tanque Verde Creek and the Rillito to the river's big bend. It crosses the Rillito near where the Santa Catalina ditch must have passed under the river to water the Hancock land (see above), then continues west and southwest for a few miles, ending just north of the reservoirs mentioned earlier in our discussion of the University ditch. Given its name, it seems likely that the Rillito canal was associated in some way with the Rillito Canal Company of John Fair, but the depiction on the Roskruge map apparently predates the formation of the company by several years. Since the route of the Rillito canal seems to have incorporated at least a part of the Santa Catalina project's alignment, the depiction on the Roskruge map must represent a continuation of ownership or planning by Fair and his associates from the years of the failed Santa Catalina project until the formation of the Rillito Canal Company around 1900.

We do not know if the Rillito Canal Company built or used any irrigation features after its formation, but the association with Davidson continued for another decade, during which Davidson was busy building his own irrigation system (see above). In company documents from 1908–1910, Davidson and his wife, Sarah, are indicated as Vice President and Secretary, respectively, of the company. In 1910, the Rillito Canal Company apparently sold its property and water rights to the Rillito Farms Company, which at its formation included five stockholders: John Mets, Nephi Bingham, H. E. Farr, Frank Webb, and J. Knox Corbett (who was also the chairman). This was probably the beginning of the association between Bingham and Corbett that led to the lawsuit by Swan in 1911. Bingham, whose property in the big bend area of the river was probably crossed by the Santa Catalina project, thus became part owner of the apparent successor to the Santa Catalina which presumably still had ditches crossing Bingham's property.

The Rillito Farms Company apparently spent the next several years borrowing money, buying land and water rights, and attempting to dominate the business of irrigated agriculture in the study area. In 1918, for unclear reasons, the company decided to sell its irrigation system—its ditches, flumes, wells, and pumping equipment, but apparently not its land—to the Rillito Water Company. The ownership and purpose of the latter company are not clear, but it held its purchase for only five years, then sold out to the Rillito Irrigation District in 1923.

The Rillito Irrigation District apparently had its genesis some 14 years earlier, when George E. P. Smith and four other Tucsonans (including Charles Bayless, the owner of one of the underflow ditches and a prominent banker, and W. H. Sawtelle, the judge who heard Swan's complaint) proposed the organization of the Rillito Irrigation Project (Rillito Irrigation Project 1909). The idea for the project grew out of Smith's recognition that the underflow ditches along the Rillito would never provide enough water to allow for a significant expansion of agriculture in the valley, since the ditches could only tap the uppermost portion of the underflow. Wells, pumps, and a larger distribution network were needed, as well as a cooperative organization that would oversee distribution and negotiate disputes among individual water users (see Smith 1910:196, 225–226). It is not clear by what steps the Rillito Irrigation Project proposed in 1909 became the Rillito Irrigation District of 1923, but the latter was soon in operation, apparently using some of the features originally built by the Santa Catalina Ditch and Irrigation Company. A map of ditches and other features in the Rillito Farms Irrigation District was prepared by the engineer J. Moss Ruthrauff sometime in the 1920s (Ruthrauff n.d.; the map is too large to reproduce here). The location of the head of the main ditch, as well as the route of the ditch, are approximately the same as those of the Davidson ditch as depicted on Smith's 1907 map. When the main ditch reaches the big bend area on the north bank of the river, it fed into the reservoir on Nephi Bingham's property, which distributed water to a series of lesser ditches, including one that continued west and passed under the Rillito, presumably at the same location as the original Santa Catalina ditch. In 1989, SRI recorded the main ditch, the reservoir, and three lesser ditches as a part of the archaeological site of Binghampton, the remains of the Mormon community founded by Nephi Bingham at the end of the nineteenth century (Ciolek-Torrello and Homburg 1990) (Figure 28).

It is not clear how successful the Rillito Irrigation District was, either as a commercial enterprise or a cooperative water-users' organization. In 1933, Smith prepared an assessment of the financial condition of irrigation districts around Arizona, in response to the obvious effects of the Depression on most of them. His only notes on the Rillito Irrigation District were that it was currently inactive and "should be dissolved" (Smith 1933:table following page 134). By 1930, the water table in the Rillito Valley had dropped below the reach of underflow ditches, and farmers using wells for irrigation were apparently uninterested in cooperative arrangements.

Ranching

Farming was only one-half of the traditional Spanish economy that the earliest settlers brought to southern Arizona. The other half, which came to have a much larger impact on the regional landscape later in the historical period, was stock raising. Sheridan (1986:14) has characterized the traditional Hispanic way of life in southern Arizona as "agropastoralist," relying on a mixed economy of farming and stock raising, much like the rest of northern New Spain during the colonial period, and deriving ultimately from a way of life common throughout rural Europe. Hispanic agropastoralism in southern Arizona continued largely unchanged during the Mexican period and well into the U.S. period, when it was also adopted by the earliest Anglo-American settlers in the region.

The first livestock brought to the northern frontier of New Spain were the small herds of cattle and horses distributed by Father Kino in the 1690s to Pima villages scattered around the region (Sheridan 1988:160). This was the beginning of Pima stock raising, which was soon successful in its own right in supplementing the Pima diet, although Hispanic ranching did not become a significant presence in southern Arizona until after the Jesuit missions at Guevavi and Bac were staffed with resident priests in 1731. The Spaniards drawn north by the discovery of silver at Arizonac in 1736 were soon settling along the upper reaches of the Santa Cruz River, grazing cattle on the lush grasslands of the valley, just as

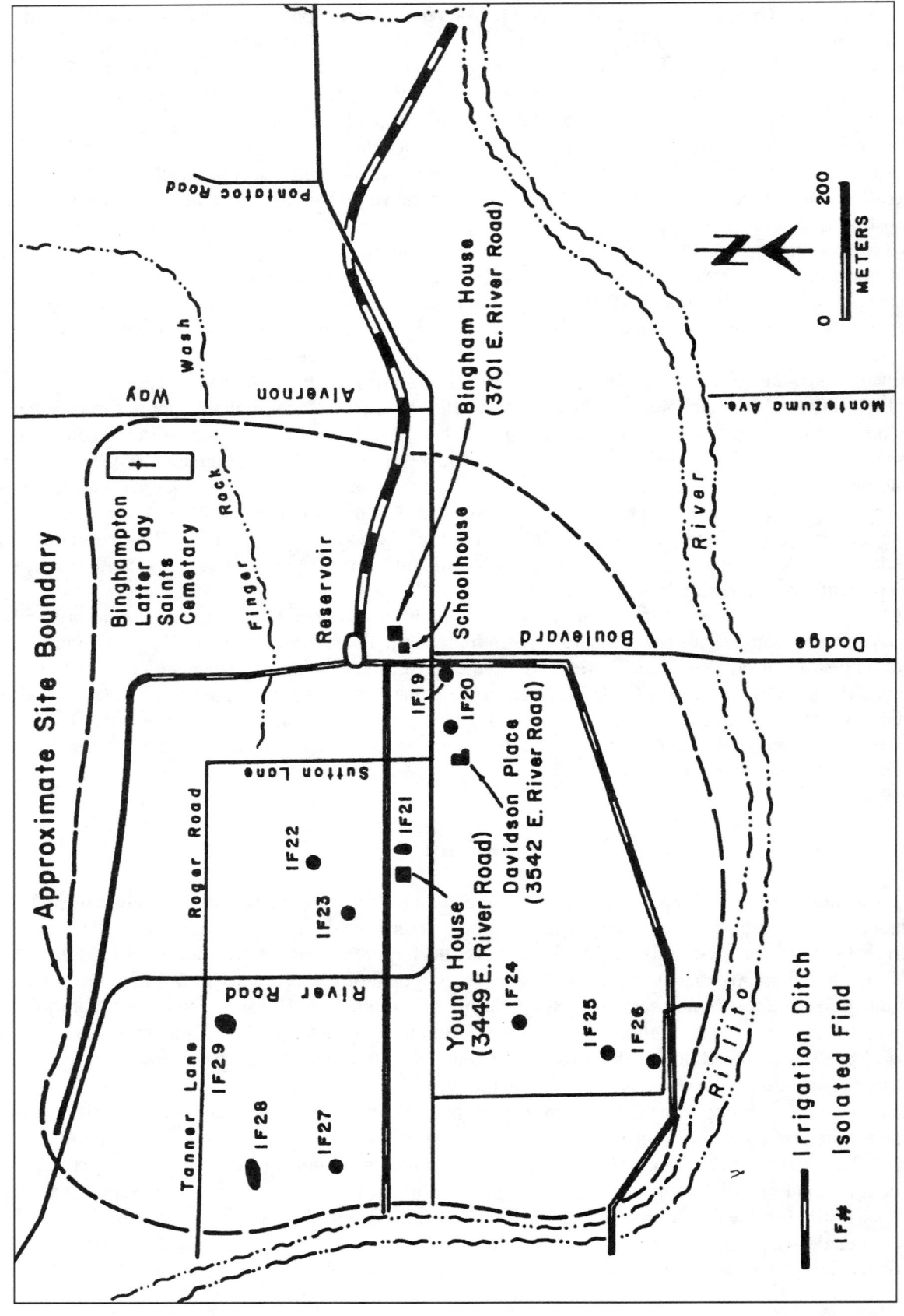

Figure 28. Map of the archaeological site of Binghampton, AZ BB:9:238 (ASM), showing irrigation features associated with the Rillito Irrigation District (from Ciolek-Torrello and Homburg 1990:65).

Spaniards had so often done farther south in New Spain during the previous two centuries. By 1752, when the presidio at Tubac was established in response to the Pima revolt of 1751, Spaniards were grazing cattle along much of the Santa Cruz south of Tucson and had expanded westward into the Arivaca region. By the end of the Spanish Colonial period, the numbers of cattle in the region reflected a successful but circumscribed enterprise. In 1804, 3,500 head of cattle were reported for the Tucson vicinity, with another 1,000 around Tubac; in 1818, the mission at Tumacácori reportedly had 5,000 cattle, and San Xavier, around 8,800 (Dobyns 1976:51; Officer 1987:15, 31; Sheridan 1995:127–129).

Except for the limited activity in the Arivaca region, stock raising in southern Arizona during the Spanish Colonial period was generally confined to the Santa Cruz Valley, for the perennial reason that the risk of Apache raid was too high at any distance from the presidios at Tucson and Tubac. Following Mexican independence, the effectiveness of the Santa Cruz presidios declined as the connections to central Mexico became even more tenuous, but despite the decline, Hispanic ranchers were determined to take advantage of the large grasslands that lay well outside of presidio control, such as along the San Pedro River. The result of their determination was the era of large land grants discussed above, when individual Hispanic settlers petitioned for and received vast tracts of land from the Mexican government. These grants soon supported large herds of cattle, but by the 1830s, the Apache had killed or chased away most of the ranch owners and run off their cattle (Wagoner 1952:24–36). These cattle were apparently the origin of the large herds of wild cattle reported by the earliest Anglo-American visitors to southern Arizona, although the numbers of cattle in the region, both before and after the ranches were abandoned, have often been exaggerated. Sheridan (1995:129) has suggested that the total population of cattle in southern Arizona during the Mexican era never exceeded 20,000–30,000 animals, because, in addition to the predations of Apache, ranching in the region before the 1840s was limited by the lack of a dependable market for beef.

The problems with the Apache continued for another 40 years, and by the time Anglo-Americans started passing through southern Arizona on their way to California in the late 1840s, Hispanic ranching in the region was a shadow of its earlier self. During the years following the gold rush, large herds of cattle were driven by Anglo-American ranchers across southern Arizona from Texas to be sold as beef in the mining communities of California (a pattern that actually continued until about 1870), but not until the Gadsden Purchase in 1854 did Anglo-Americans make some initial attempts to raise cattle in the region. Their successes were limited by the same factors that plagued Hispanic ranching: Apache raids and distance from markets. One of the first Anglo-Americans to run cattle in the Tucson area was Bill Kirkland, who in 1857 brought 200 head of cattle to the San Ignacio de la Canoa Ranch, located along both banks of the Santa Cruz south of Tucson. By 1860, the cattle had been stolen and Kirkland had moved on to a different location (Wagoner 1952:33). Also along the Santa Cruz south of Tucson, a German immigrant named Fritz Contzen started Rancho Punta de Agua in 1855 with about 500 head of cattle. He, too, suffered repeated Apache raids and had given up on ranching by the 1860s (McGuire 1979). Other ranchers in the Tucson Basin during the same period suffered similar fates. For example, in 1844, Francisco Romero established a ranch near the Cañada del Oro on the western slopes of the Santa Catalina Mountains north of Tucson. In 1870, after two and a half decades of intermittent Apache violence, the hardy Romero and his family were finally driven from the ranch for good (Mabry 1991: 62–69).

The Civil War, which made southern Arizona an area of Union-Confederate contention for a brief time, put a stop to Anglo-American ranching at the start of the 1860s. The Apache extended the hiatus for another decade and a half. In 1870, the year Gen. George Crook arrived in southern Arizona to begin his long campaign to subdue the Apache, the territorial census reported only 1,800 cattle in all of Pima County, which at that time encompassed almost all of Arizona south of the Gila River (Wagoner 1952: 36). The situation changed rapidly as the Apache frontier was pushed eastward from the Tucson Basin during the 1870s. By 1873, both Mexican- and Anglo-American ranchers had successful small operations along the Santa Cruz River, and similar operations were soon springing up in the Arivaca region to the west of the Santa Cruz, along Sonoita Creek to the east of the river, and along the Cañada del Oro. There were also a number of successful Mexican ranches along Tanque Verde Creek, east of the Río Antiguo study area (Mabry 1991; Wagoner 1952:39–41). The spread of ranches along the principal streams of the region was soon accompanied by the gobbling up of all available sources of water, including streams and springs, by ranchers claiming parcels under the Homestead Act and the Desert Land Act. By patenting a claim on a parcel with a water source, ranchers could have de facto control over surrounding parcels without water, and some ranchers built major land holdings by having other people (such as employees) file claims that the rancher would then buy up cheaply when they were patented (Mayro 1999:40).

The arrival of the railroad in 1880 was a major boost to the cattle industry in southern Arizona, which from then on was dominated by large business interests. An important example of the shift was the 1883 purchase of the San Rafael land grant along the headwaters of the Santa Cruz River by a consortium of eastern investors organized by Colin Cameron, who was not a cattleman by training or inclination, but a businessman. By combining shrewd legal maneuvering with ruthlessness, Cameron developed the San Rafael into a major enterprise. For years, he vigorously contested the original 17,000-acre allotment of the grant, claiming that it should have been 152,000 acres, and although he never won a larger allotment, he was able to graze a large herd on many times the official acreage for the remainder of the century. He was also one of the few large ranchers in the region to recognize and act against the problems of overgrazing that soon plagued the industry. In 1903, well after the boom of the 1880s was over and most of southern Arizona had been grazed to destruction, he was still able to sell the San Rafael for $1,500,000 (Hadley and Sheridan 1995:97–107; Sheridan 1995:125–126).

Most ranchers in the 1880s, however, kept grazing as many cattle as they could, both on their own acreage and on the abundant acreage still in the public domain. By the start of the 1890s, it was apparent to many ranchers that overgrazing had quickly become a serious problem. To compound the problem, the early 1890s saw several years of severe drought. The grass soon disappeared, having been pulled from the ground by its roots by starving cattle. "It was a disaster of biblical proportions," Sheridan (1995:141) wrote, "one in which nature and greed conspired to magnify their individual effects." From 50 to 75 percent of all of the cattle in southern Arizona died, most surviving animals were shipped out of the region to avoid complete losses, and numerous ranching operations of every size folded (Sheridan 1995:140–141; Wagoner 1952:53–54).

A key to the disaster of the 1890s was the nature of ownership and control over the range lands of southern Arizona. Cattle-raising operations were almost always based on private land holdings, but use of the large surrounding tracts of public lands for grazing was unavoidable, both from the standpoint of the acreage required to support a herd of profitable size and because the federal government could never practically prevent cattlemen from using the land. Since the 1890s, cattlemen and the federal agencies responsible for public lands have struggled, sometimes in cooperation, sometimes in conflict, to adapt the raising of cattle to the limitations of the southern Arizona environment and to address the dilemma posed by an industry that both requires access to large areas of public land to be profitable and constitutes a threat to the health of those public lands when multiple individuals use it for the same purpose. Mayro (1999:47–55) has reviewed the history of federal policies regarding the access to federal lands allowed to private ranchers. These policies have included grazing districts, leases, and fees administered by federal agencies such as the Forest Service and the BLM (see also Collins 2001). Although ranching in southern Arizona during the twentieth century saw periods of relative success and decline, it has survived into the twenty-first century as a viable industry in large part because of the conservation of public lands made possible by the combination of federal management and the responsible practices of many private ranchers.

By the time of the 1890s disaster, a dozen or more ranches had been established a few miles east of the Río Antiguo study area along Tanque Verde Creek, clustering near its confluence with Agua Caliente Wash (see Figure 15). The primary attraction of the area was the perennial presence of water in portions of both streams, and a few of these ranches survived as successful operations into the twentieth century (Wellman and Slaughter 2001). Within the study area itself, cattle ranching was probably practiced at a small scale by most early settlers from at least as early as the 1870s, as suggested by the complaints of the commanding officer at Fort Lowell that the local residents regularly allowed their cattle to graze and wander at will on the military reservation (see below).

There were apparently no major cattle operations based in the study area, which may be attributed in part to the importance placed on farming the Rillito floodplain. Nonetheless, at least some farmers also raised beef cattle, dairy cattle, or both. We discuss dairy farms briefly below, but one reference to raising beef cattle along the Rillito is worth mentioning. Bartley Cardon, a retired professor of agriculture at the University of Arizona who was born into the Mormon community of Binghampton in 1913, has spoken of his father's dairy and ranching operation along the Rillito in the 1920s (Cardon 1993). According to Cardon, his father farmed on the north side of the river, in the vicinity of the original Binghampton settlement (at the river's big bend; see below), and fed both dairy and beef cattle on the south side of the river, just north of the present-day intersection of Country Club and Prince Roads. The beef cattle also grazed on a vast area north of the river: "Literally, the range ran from the Oracle Road to the Redington Road and from Rillito Creek up to and on the mountain" (Cardon 1993:2). Cardon was unsure of the arrangement that allowed his father to use such a large area, but it is doubtful that the family had exclusive rights to even a fraction of it. His comment does suggest that the foothills north of the Rillito had long been used by residents of the study area for grazing cattle.

Dairying along the Rillito

Dairy cattle were at least as important as beef cattle to the success of historical-period farming in the Rillito Valley, although the largest dairies in the Tucson area were located outside the Río Antiguo study area, farther down the Rillito near its confluence with the Santa Cruz River, and along the Santa Cruz itself (Davis 1959:93–95; Cunningham 1937:29). The most successful dairy farmers in the study area were undoubtedly the Mormons of the Binghampton community, much of whose agricultural effort went to producing feed for dairy cattle (Turner 1990:47). The typical feed was chopped green corn, sometimes mixed with sunflower seeds, which was stored in large concrete silos, allowing it to ferment before use (Cardon 1993). The silos were a distinctive element of the Mormon landscape in the Binghampton area and a number of examples still survive (Parkhurst 2001; see the photograph in Turner 1990:47). In the same oral-historical interview cited above, Bartley Cardon told of how he helped build his father's two silos, one of which, located just east of the Prince–Country Club intersection, survives today and has been converted into an apartment. Cardon visited the apartment shortly after the conversion and was carried back to the days he helped fill it:

> About 1918, I remember it was before the end of World War I, my Dad built two silos . . . [One has] now been converted into an apartment, and the architect, when he converted it, called me and said, "I understand you know something about this silo, would you like to come out and look at the apartments?" and without describing them, I walked in the silo, took a deep breath and could still smell the silage (laughs) that we used to put in the damn thing because my job was to climb in the silo and tromp down the silage and pack it so that the air was pressed out so that it wouldn't sour but would ferment well anaerobically. . . . I remember the chopper and the blower they mounted in a pipe up the side of the silo, over the top, and the bottom of that was about ten feet underneath and it was perhaps thirty feet high, as I recall, above ground and so that was a forty foot fall and some of those big trucks would come down with corn, ears that were chopped, and

hit you on the head and you got pretty spry moving around so that they didn't clobber you to death as they chop[ped] the silage [Cardon 1993].

Campbell Avenue Farm

Dairy farmers in the study area got a vote of confidence (and perhaps some useful advice) in 1909 when the University of Arizona established its Campbell Avenue Farm on an 80-acre plot just south of the Rillito, on the west side of Campbell Avenue. The farm was designed and built as a model dairy for instruction and research (Haney 1985:50; Martin 1960:96). By 1912, the University Farm Dairy was producing enough milk to supply its own retail milk route, and in 1914, it became the first milk distributor in Tucson to use a self-propelled vehicle (a Model T Ford) for deliveries (Davis 1959:93–94). In 1953, the Ewing Farm, a small, private dairy located on the opposite side of Campbell, was purchased; the 40-acre farm had operated independently since 1929 (Haney 1985:181, 192). Once the Ewing Farm was purchased, the University's dairy operation moved to the east side of Campbell, and the west side facilities were converted to use for nutrition and meats research. The Campbell Avenue Farm is now called the University of Arizona Campus Agricultural Center and is still involved in dairy-related and other agricultural research (Figure 29).

Settlement and Land Tenure

Because of the constant threat of Apache raids, the earliest non–Native American settlement of the Rillito Valley did not take place until at least a few years after the Gadsden Purchase, and substantial numbers of non–Native Americans did not settle in the valley until after 1873, the year Fort Lowell was established. Less than 10 miles from the presidio at Tucson, the Río Antiguo study area was too dangerous for permanent settlement throughout the Spanish Colonial and Mexican periods, and it remained too dangerous for ordinary citizens until the U.S. Army saw fit to build a fort on the south bank of the Rillito. Thus, the history of settlement and land tenure in the study area is a short one, especially compared to the same history in the Santa Cruz Valley, where Euroamerican settlement began.

In this section, we look briefly at the history of settlement and land tenure in the Santa Cruz Valley during the Spanish Colonial and Mexican periods, then more closely at settlement in the Rillito Valley after the Gadsden Purchase. The emphasis is on settlement prior to World War II, but we also touch on recent residential and related development.

Spanish and Mexican Land Grants

The legal authority under which initial Spanish settlement along the Santa Cruz River took place is poorly understood. Spanish concepts of land tenure were, of course, meaningless to the Sobaipuri living in the area, but Spanish law, at least in theory, required that occupation of any part of the Spanish empire (or of any region not yet claimed by the empire) by a Spanish subject first be authorized by the crown (Radding 1997:175–182). The settlement of Spaniards along the Santa Cruz should have been preceded by some form of legal sanction, but in the first half of the eighteenth century and in this most remote portion of the empire, such was rarely the case. Even the Jesuit establishment of missions and the assumption of jurisdiction over surrounding areas was authorized only in the vaguest terms. When Spanish "civilians" began arriving in the area, they generally settled on mission lands, usually near the mission proper but occasionally well removed from it, with the informal permission of the mission priest. Elsewhere in the northern territories, Jesuits and civilians were already at odds over rights to lands and settlement, but in

Figure 29. Aerial photograph of the Campbell Avenue Farm area, view to the north-northeast, ca. 1950. The farm is located on both sides of Campbell Avenue, which crosses the Rillito near the center of the photo (photograph courtesy of the Arizona Historical Society, Tucson, Magee Photograph Collection, Accession No. 448).

the Santa Cruz Valley, as Kessell (1970:99) put it, "Common defense and isolation drew Padre and settlers together."

Gradually, the Spanish occupation of lands near the missions and in outlying areas was regularized, often with legal sanctions adapted to local circumstances or official rewards for the continued efforts of Spaniards to colonize the region. For example, when the presidio at Tubac was reestablished in 1787, the new commander hoped to encourage Spanish settlement at the presidio by invoking a provision of the Royal Regulations of 1772, "whereby those who wished to engage in agriculture could receive title to presidio lands in return for keeping arms and horses available for defense of the country" (Officer 1987: 66). Such grants were made within the bounds of the four square leagues designated for each presidio (Jones 1979:194; Mattison 1946:281–282). Along the Santa Cruz River, these grants frequently conflicted with earlier assignments of mission lands to Native Americans. Under Spanish law, Native American communities also were legal holders of land, although Native American lands were considered to be held in common by a group and the right to ownership was based on historical association with a given parcel. Although Native Americans could and did resort to the colonial legal system to protect their Spanish-given rights, they were invariably at a disadvantage when tangling with private Spanish interests (Radding 1997:171–207). The remoteness of southern Arizona, which generally limited the Native Americans' recourse to either the mission priest or the presidio commander, only exacerbated that disadvantage.

The largest of the land grants to Hispanic settlers, and the ones that became significant as the bases of major Anglo-American cattle-raising operations in the late nineteenth and early twentieth centuries, were distributed at the start of the Mexican period, as mentioned earlier in this chapter. The grants were made, much like the grants of the Spanish Colonial era, to encourage permanent settlement in an area that the central government knew was only a tenuous part of its territory. Almost all of the petitions for large grants were submitted in the 1820s: by the 1830s, most of southern Arizona that was outside of the immediate area of the presidios was too plagued by Apache raids to allow for further settlement. The grants petitioned for were often vast (see Figure 7). San Ignacio de la Canoa, the earliest grant (approved in 1821), was typical in size, covering four *sitios* (four square leagues, or about 17,000 acres) along a prime segment of the Santa Cruz River, from the presidio at Tubac to modern Sahuarita (about 15 miles south of San Xavier). Other grants were as small as 5,100 acres, the final confirmed size of San José de Sonoita, which extended along Sonoita Creek, just west of modern Patagonia. The largest confirmed grant of the era falling wholly within Arizona was San Ignacio del Babocomari, which extended over some 35,000 acres along Babocomari Creek, a tributary of the San Pedro River (Mattison 1946; Officer 1987:106–110; Sheridan 1995:127–129; Wagoner 1975:159–241).

Another major land grant in the Santa Cruz Valley deserves particular mention, because of its unique origin and late confirmation date. This was the Luis María Baca Float No. 3, one of five vast parcels granted to the Baca family as compensation for an enormous grant they had won but were forced to abandon in New Mexico. The original grant was made in 1821 by the Spanish crown, but the Baca family did not win a settlement of the grant until 1860, after New Mexico had become part of the United States. The U.S. government, obliged to honor Spanish and Mexican land grants by the conditions of the treaty signed with Mexico at the end of the Mexican War, compensated the Baca family by allowing them to chose five 100,000-acre "floats" on any nonmineral lands within New Mexico Territory, which at the time included what is now Arizona. Luis María Baca Float No. 3 was first laid out in 1863 directly over the richest portion of the Santa Cruz River valley but was soon moved north and east to center on the Santa Rita Mountains. The validity and location of the grant were the focus of extended litigation that continued until 1908, when the original location was finally confirmed in federal court. Since the 1920s, the lands of the original grant have been subdivided and sold numerous times (Wagoner 1975:200–208).

Settlement along the Rillito after the Gadsden Purchase

If settlement of the Santa Cruz Valley during the Spanish Colonial and Mexican periods was severely limited by the threat of Apache raids, settlement along the Rillito in the same period was virtually non-existent. The occasional Mexican farmer or rancher may have been brave enough to attempt permanent residence at a such a remove from the Tucson presidio—a small ranch was established by Francisco Romero along the Cañada del Oro, even farther from the presidio, in 1844, and was somehow maintained until 1870 before succumbing to the Apache (Mabry 1991:62–64)—but we have found no specific reference to Mexican settlement anywhere along the Rillito prior to the Gadsden Purchase.

U.S. acquisition of southern Arizona in 1854 did not, of course, lead to an immediate increase in safety in the Tucson hinterlands. For the remainder of the 1850s and into the 1870s, Euroamerican settlement north of Tucson was largely restricted to a few stops or watering places along the road to the Akimel O'odham villages on the Gila River. The stop closest to the Río Antiguo study area was at Nine Mile Water Hole, 9 miles north of Tucson on the Santa Cruz River, just upstream from its confluence with the Rillito. By 1869, a settlement known as Laguna had grown up around the watering place, consisting of 80–90 people farming some 500 acres. Eight miles downstream from Laguna at Point of the

Mountain, where the Santa Cruz skirts the northern end of the Tucson Mountains, the Butterfield Overland Mail established a stage station in 1858 (see the Transportation section below). The Butterfield abandoned its southern line in 1861, but other interests operated the Point of the Mountain station intermittently for another 20 years, until it was made obsolete by the arrival of the Southern Pacific Railroad. The station and its water source had attracted a handful of ranchers to the vicinity, and its role as a minor focus of settlement was assumed by the Southern Pacific's Rillito Station, built in 1880 about a mile to the north (Stein 1993:93–100).

According to Smith (1910:98), "The oldest known effort at settlement in the Rillito Valley was that of an Arkansas pioneer who cleared a small area of bottomland just east of Fort Lowell in 1858" (Fort Lowell did not yet exist in 1858, but in Smith's day its location was a convenient reference point). Unfortunately, Smith did not cite a source for this information, and we have not found it anywhere else. In an extract from the proceedings of a Board of Officers meeting at Fort Lowell in 1883, mention is made of a squatter, Robert Rolette, who, in 1859, settled upstream from the fort's eventual location (Hughes 1885). Because there are few other candidates for earliest settler along the Rillito, it is possible that Rolette was the Arkansas pioneer mentioned by Smith (as Turner [1990:6] evidently assumed).

It is not clear whether Smith was considering Mexican settlers when he specified "the oldest known effort at settlement in the Rillito Valley." There are hints that at least a few Mexicans were settled along the Rillito as early as the pioneer from Arkansas. David Dunham, an eventual owner of Robert Rolette's property, first came to Tucson around 1867. Asked in 1928 about his first impressions of Arizona, he noted that when he arrived, "[T]here were two Mexican families in what is now Fort Lowell" (*Tucson Citizen* [*TC*] 1928). The remark may not mean much, because Dunham begins his reply with "There was no Arizona. I was Arizona," which suggests he had a somewhat selective memory. Nonetheless, it is hard to imagine that Mexicans were not among the earliest settlers along the Rillito, especially given their established presence there by the 1870s (see below). The 1873 GLO survey plat of Township 13 South, Range 14 East (Figure 30), apart from its depiction of the recently erected Commanding Officer's Quarters at Fort Lowell, shows only two houses along the Rillito, both with Mexican owners: Leopoldo Carrillo and Pedro Romero (see below). Perhaps these men were the heads of the "two Mexican families" recalled by Dunham. The same map also shows "corn fields" on the south bank of Tanque Verde Creek in the north half of Section 36. This area was part of a 160-acre homestead patent by the Montijo family in 1900; the corn fields may represent the early efforts of the Montijos at that location (see also below).

The U.S. Military Presence along the Rillito

In 1854, the United States extended its territory south from the Gila River to the present international border, but Mexico maintained a military presence in Tucson until March 10, 1856, when Maj. Enoch Steen and a troop of the First Dragoons finally replaced the Mexican soldiers at the Tucson presidio. Steen and his men camped briefly in Tucson before moving south to Calabasas. Within a few months, they relocated once again, this time to the Sonoita Valley where they established Fort Buchanan. In 1860, the Army established Fort Breckinridge (later Camp Grant) at the confluence of the San Pedro River and Aravaipa Creek, in an effort to contain the Apache and to provide safe passage for those traveling along the Southern Emigrant Trail.

The U.S. military presence had a profound effect on Tucson's economic and population growth. Many Euroamericans settled in the area to supply the military contingent, opening mercantile shops in town or operating ranches or farms in the surrounding areas. Tucson quickly became the center of trade with Sonora and the Southwest, an important stop on the Butterfield Overland route to California, and the source of goods and protection for local mining and ranching interests. With the coming of the Civil War, federal troops stationed at Forts Buchanan and Breckinridge received orders to abandon their posts

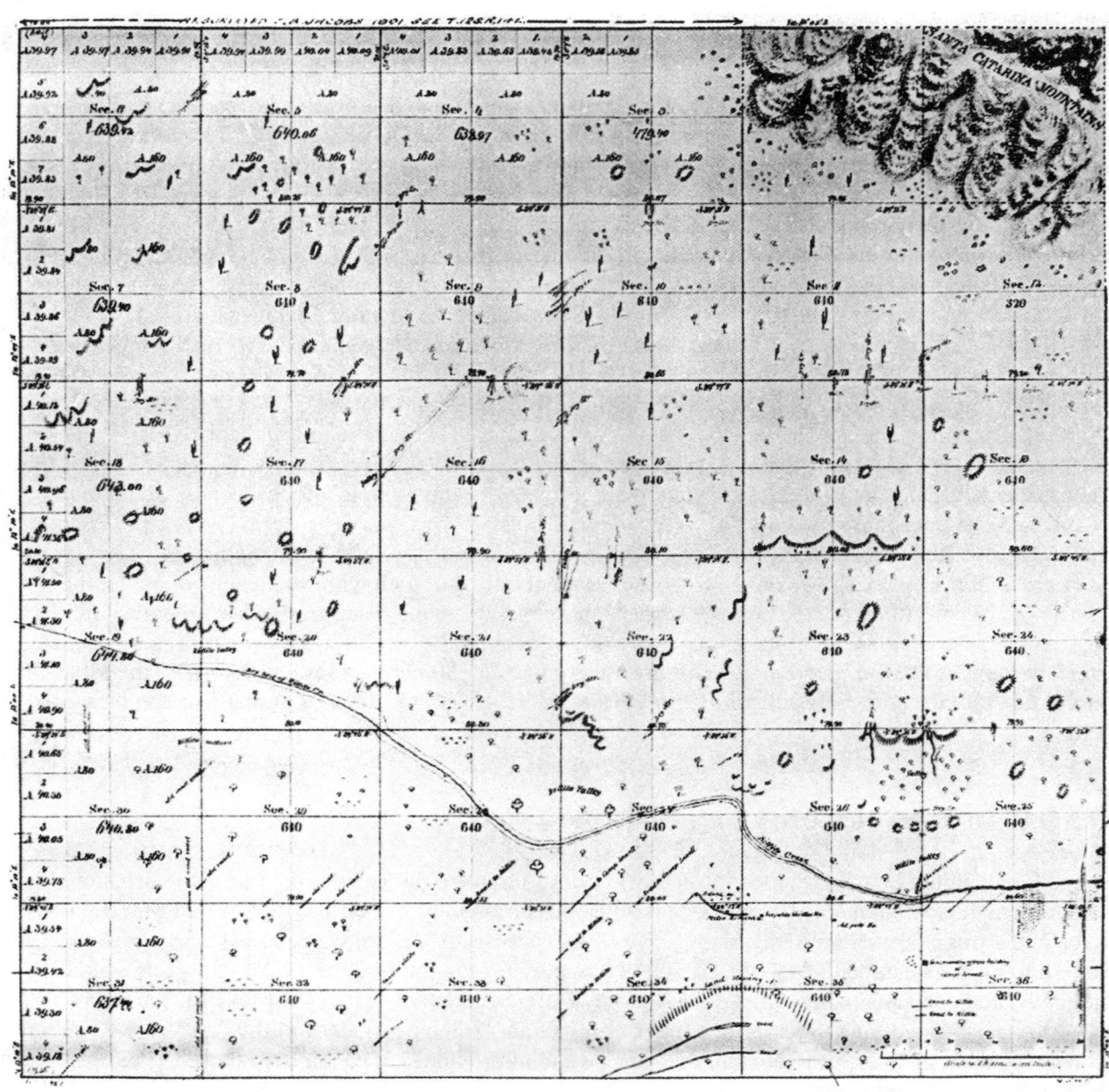

Figure 30. 1873 GLO survey plat of Township 14 South, Range 13 East.

and burn all supplies, lest they fall into the hands of the secessionist troops. Once the soldiers had departed, the Apache began a campaign of plunder and murder that forced most of the Euroamerican miners and ranchers out of the region (Wagoner 1970:6–7).

In February 1862, a Confederate cavalry troop, commanded by Col. Sherod Hunter, occupied Tucson. That spring, the Union organized the California Volunteers, generally known as the California Column, under the command of Col. (later General) James H. Carleton, to respond to the Confederate incursion in southern Arizona. The Confederates lived off the countryside, confiscating food, livestock, and other property of Union loyalists (Whittlesey et al. 1994:300). After exacting oaths of allegiance to the Confederacy and running off those who refused, Hunter and his troops left Tucson to intercept the California Column marching from the west. The two forces engaged in a brief skirmish at Stanwix Station, 80 miles east of Yuma, before Hunter and his men retreated. Several weeks later, small contingents of Union and Confederate forces skirmished at Picacho Pass northwest of Tucson. Hunter subsequently relinquished Tucson to join the larger fight east of the Mississippi. In June, Carleton and the California Column entered Tucson, placed the area under martial law, and seized the property of Confederate sympathizers (Wagoner 1975:447, 452–456; Whittlesey et al. 1994:301). Carleton's troops created a supply depot in Tucson to maintain the California Column as it moved east in pursuit of the Confederates (Peterson 1963:3). In the wake of the Confederate withdrawal, Congress separated Arizona and New Mexico along a north-south line, thereby organizing the Territory of Arizona in 1863.

With the Confederates no longer a threat to Arizona, the U.S. military was able to focus on the Apache problem. The effort began with General Carleton launching a bloody but ineffective war of extermination, but by the end of the Civil War, the numerous forays against the Apache had failed to subdue them (Wagoner 1975:465–467). During the 1870s and 1880s, the Army abandoned Carleton's approach in favor of appeasement. In February 1871, a large group of Aravaipa Apache surrendered to the soldiers at Camp Grant. Hungry and tired of running from the cavalry, they wanted to settle in their ancestral home in Aravaipa Canyon, a branch of the San Pedro Valley. With their promise to give up raiding, the Aravaipa Apache were allowed to settle near the post, given rations, and paid for gathering hay for the soldiers (Wagoner 1970:127; Thrapp 1967:83–84). This policy of appeasement enraged residents of the Santa Cruz Valley who continued to be targets of Apache raiding and murder. According to John Wasson, editor of the *Arizona Citizen*, the only solution seemed to lie in "the slaying of every Apache man, woman and child" (quoted in Sonnichsen 1982:81). The prevalence of this attitude is what soon led to the Camp Grant massacre of April 30, 1871 (see Chapter 3).

Fort Lowell

In 1862, Gen. James H. Carleton established the Tucson Supply Depot to provide a lifeline of food and supplies to his California Volunteers as they pursued the retreating Confederate forces. Carleton ordered Maj. David Fergusson, Chief Commissary Officer, to organize and stock the depot. Fergusson's men quickly constructed warehouses for storage and began shuttling supplies by wagon from Fort Yuma to Tucson. Fergusson contracted with local merchants to supply fresh vegetables and grain. Situated in an area just east of the old Spanish presidio, the depot operated until the fall of 1864 when the troops were transferred north to Prescott, the newly created territorial capitol. Tucson leaders criticized the decision as the removal of troops left them vulnerable to Indian attack. Recognizing the need to protect the settlers from Apache depredations, Gen. John S. Mason, Commander of the District of Arizona, re-established the supply depot in May 1865, and in August 1866, the post became permanent. The post was renamed Camp Lowell after Brig. Gen. Charles R. Lowell, Jr., who died in 1864 at the battle of Cedar Creek, Virginia during the Civil War (Peterson 1963:3–4).

Seven years later, on March 19, 1873, Camp Lowell became Fort Lowell when the commanding officer, Lt. Col. Eugene Asa Carr, moved the post about 7 miles northeast of Tucson to the head of the Rillito River (Figure 31). The Army chose the location for its proximity to what was perceived as a reliable water supply and its distance from the social temptations of Tucson. The fort came to rely on

Figure 31. Watercolor painting of an 1875 sketch of Fort Lowell by Col. J. B. Girard, Post Surgeon (photograph courtesy of the Arizona Historical Society, Tucson, Accession No. 5275).

wells for most of its water, but ditches were initially dug to carry water from Tanque Verde Creek to the post corrals, and to water lawns and cottonwood trees near the officers' quarters. On October 26, 1875, President Ulysses S. Grant ordered 49,920 acres set aside as the Fort Lowell Military Reservation. Eleven years later, 1,711 acres encompassing the lower section of Sabino Canyon were added to the reservation as an additional source of water for the post (Figure 32). Securing a water supply was a constant concern throughout the existence of the fort. By the mid-1880s, water was in short supply, a result of the diversion of water upstream by settlers along Tanque Verde Creek and a consequent lowering of the water table. There were plans to construct a dam in Sabino Canyon and pipe water down to the fort, but the project never materialized. Deep wells with steam pumps eventually solved the water problem on the post.

As discussed, there was a handful of people settled near the site of the fort prior to its construction, and more settled nearby as soon as the fort was built. The settlers were ambivalent about the military presence in the valley. Initially, they welcomed the protection against Apache raids, but the establishment of the reservation in 1875 prompted orders from Lieutenant Colonel Carr to give up their claims in order to assure sufficient supplies of water, grass, and fuel for the fort. Most of the settlers refused, and for the remainder of the fort's existence there was constant bickering between the fort and its civilian neighbors. Concerning the conflict, Carr wrote in 1880:

> Since I took command here, I have found, not only that the annoyances of long standing from the [settlers], were continuing, but that they were increasing. These annoyances consist of cutting off the needed water for the Post, washing clothing etc., in the streams, natural and artificial above us, thus tainting the water we use; using up the grazing to the deprivation of public animals, cutting fuel on the reservation; occupying land and

112

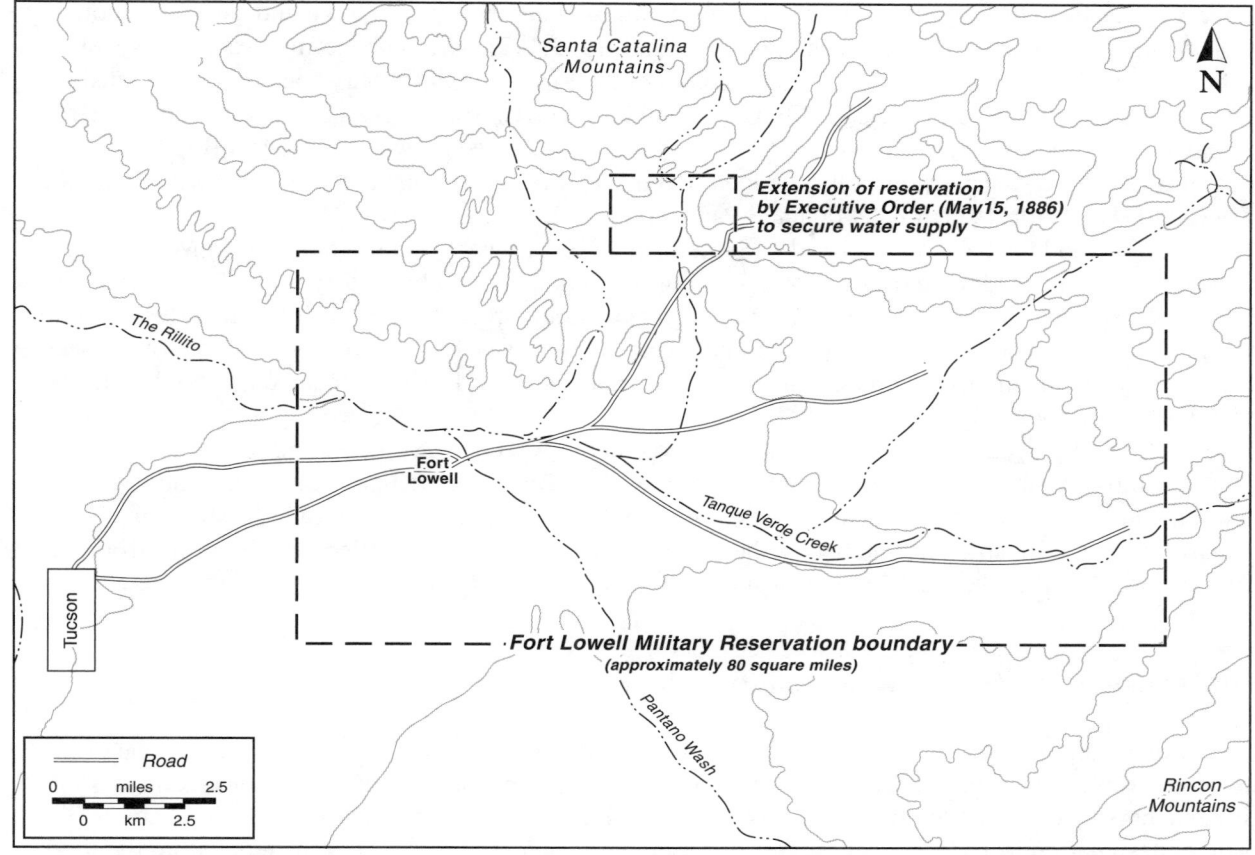

Figure 32. Map of the Fort Lowell Military Reservation (based on Turner 1982a:Map 2).

premises on the same; traveling to and fro in same; stock running over parade [ground] and into corrals and gardens; etc., etc., and I have deemed it my duty to take some action [quoted in Turner 1982a:10].

Carr never found an effective solution to these problems, but the fort managed to function in spite of them. From 1873 through the 1880s, troops at Fort Lowell escorted wagon trains along the overland routes, provided protection to settlers, patrolled the international border, and conducted scouting and offensive operations against the Apache. In addition, the post was an important supply depot, supporting field operations around the region. Supplies arrived from Yuma and Sonora and were stored at the fort before being shipped to other posts in Arizona. The post also supplied reinforcements to units actively engaged in fighting the Apache (Peterson 1963:5). Troop strength at the fort averaged two to four companies. In April 1882, the escape of several hundred Apaches from the San Carlos Indian Reservation to the north resulted in a massive troop build-up in Arizona. Fort Lowell's troop strength nearly tripled. In 1885, a large band of Chiricahua Apache led by Geronimo fled the reservation, prompting a large-scale manhunt that captured national headlines. One year later, at the height of the struggle to capture the renegade band, Fort Lowell was operating at full capacity with 18 officers and 239 enlisted men (Peterson 1963:14–15).

In addition to its military role, the fort was important to Tucson in a number of ways. The Army proved to be the local merchants' best customer. John B. "Pie" Allen built the sutler's store at the post in 1873 and provided goods to the fort. The post had its own garden, but it also bought fresh vegetables and other produce from the farmers along the Rillito. Soldiers spent their pay in town and Tucson's economy "was fattened on Federal military subsidies" (Cosulich 1953:192). Tucson benefitted socially as well. Officers held dinners, concerts, dances, and picnics at the fort. The 6th Cavalry Band provided music for the concerts and dances, and occasionally performed in town. Tucson baseball teams traveled to the fort to play the post team (Figure 33) and traffic flowed regularly between town and the fort (Figure 34). However, until the Apache were fully subdued in the late 1880s, civilians rarely traveled without a military escort (Hughston 1911; Lockwood and Page n.d.:81–82; Peterson 1963:11).

Geronimo and his band surrendered in September 1886 and were sent by train to Fort Marion, Florida. This episode ended the most extensive U.S. military campaign in the history of the Southwest (Thrapp 1967:366). Over the next few years, several breakouts from the San Carlos Indian Reservation required troops from Fort Lowell to pursue and arrest the fugitives, but the Apache were no longer seen as a military threat, and troop strength at the fort was reduced. Fort Lowell remained an active military post until February 14, 1891.

Fort Lowell played an indirect but important role in the Apache wars, operating primarily as a supply depot for those posts that were closer to the hostilities. For Tucson residents, the post provided a strong, continual military presence and acted as a deterrent to Apache attacks. By employing a strategy of aggressive pursuit of hostile Apache bands, the Army pushed the Apache frontier east and south from the Tucson Basin, paving the way for significant settlement of the study area.

Settlement in the Fort Lowell Vicinity before 1891

The extract from the proceedings of an 1883 Board of Officers meeting, mentioned above, is one of the few sources we have found on early settlement in the Río Antiguo study area. It includes the names of five ranchers who had settled within the bounds of the Fort Lowell Military Reservation prior to its official designation in 1875; it also implies that there were at least a few more ranchers within the reservation from the time of its designation. Four of the five named ranchers were located upstream of the fort and were using water from the Rillito (i.e., Tanque Verde Creek) that the Army had decided it needed for its own use. The discussion in the proceedings centered on what the holdings of the ranchers were worth and whether the Army should buy them out (the original document apparently included a map of the reservation indicating the locations of individual ranches; the map does not accompany the typed transcription consulted at Arizona Historical Society in Tucson). The following paragraphs summarize the information on the five named ranchers provided in the proceedings extract, with notes on their other connections to the study area.

David Dunham

The 1883 proceedings extract indicates David Dunham (spelled "Durham" in the transcription at Arizona Historical Society) as the current owner of the property first settled by Robert Rolette. Dunham had an important early connection to the area as the man contracted by the government to build Fort Lowell. Newspaper stories from the 1920s and 1930s, near and at the end of Dunham's life, state that Dunham first came to Tucson from Cincinnati, Ohio, shortly after the end of the Civil War. He settled first in Tucson proper, but soon bought a farm in the vicinity of Fort Lowell. The accounts are somewhat conflicting, but Dunham was evidently the primary contractor for the construction of both Fort Lowell and Fort Huachuca, and possibly other posts in southern Arizona. His purchase of property near Fort Lowell was undoubtedly prompted by his role in construction of the fort (*Arizona Daily Star [ADS]*, 9 December 1932; *Tucson Citzen [TC]*, 25 March 1928, 30 May 1932, 8 September 1932).

According to the proceedings extract, Rolette sold the "squatter's rights" to his property to the Robertson brothers in 1862. We have no other information on the Robertson brothers. In 1864, the Robertsons sold the property to Granville Oury, who sold it in an unspecified year to Goldman (or

Figure 33. Tucson baseball team at Fort Lowell, ca. 1890 (photograph courtesy of the Arizona Historical Society, Tucson, Accession No. 2635).

Goldberg—both names are used in the transcription at Arizona Historical Society) and the Drachman brothers. Granville Oury was the brother of William Sanders Oury, a prominent figure in Tucson history who arrived in Arizona in 1856. William Oury eventually established a ranch about 7 miles east of Fort Lowell on Tanque Verde Creek, and operated it until his death in 1887. Gilbert Cole Smith, the son-in-law of William Oury, served as quartermaster at Fort Lowell during the 1880s.

Granville Oury arrived in Tucson the same year as William and eventually served in the territorial legislature. In 1871, he moved to Phoenix to further pursue his political career (C. Smith 1967); perhaps the move prompted his sale of the Rillito property. We know nothing about the Goldman (or Goldberg) to whom Granville Oury reportedly sold his property. The Drachmans, on the other hand, were from a prominent family headed by Philip Drachman, who arrived in Tucson in the 1850s. The various Drachman descendants have been involved in a variety of successful businesses in Tucson from the 1860s until today (Drachman 1999; Sonnichsen 1982:96).

According to the proceedings extract, Goldman and the Drachmans never lived on their Rillito property, but one of their tenants, Juan Montijo, filed a claim for it in 1873. It is unclear what the basis of such a claim would have been, given the prior claims of Goldman and the Drachmans, but it was not granted because it fell within the bounds of the (not yet officially designated, but apparently demarcated) military reservation. Juan Montijo was presumably related to the Jesús Montijo and Jesús Montijo, Jr., who patented homesteads with the GLO in 1900 and 1903, respectively, immediately east and northeast

Figure 34. Civilian visitors on the parade ground at Fort Lowell, 1885. Jennie Crepin (later Mrs. Willis P. Haynes) is fourth from the left. Willis Pearson Haynes, Tucson businessman and real estate developer, is fifth from the left. Note Cottonwood Lane and Officers' Quarters in background (photograph courtesy of the Arizona Historical Society, Tucson, Accession No. 93062).

of the fort after it was abandoned (see below). On the 1893 Roskruge map (see Figure 15), Dunham is indicated as the owner of a parcel in the NE ¼ of Section 31 (Township 13 South, Range 15 East). This location is consistent with the general location given by Smith (1910:98) for his Arkansas pioneer's bottomland parcel, and probably the best indication of where the Dunham ranch was located in 1883.

Dunham bought Goldman's share of the property in 1873, and the Drachman brothers' share in 1876. The proceedings extract states that the Drachman brothers "had agreed never to interfere with the water supply of the Post," a condition that Dunham tacitly accepted when he bought the parcel. However, in 1881, Dunham interrupted the flow of water several times and was ordered off the reservation by the commanding officer. Dunham claimed to have dug the ditch that supplied the fort with water, a claim disputed by the Board of Officers. Apparently, he also requested compensation for improvements he had made to his property, including a three-room adobe house, a well, fencing around his claim, other irrigation ditches, and some fruit trees. It is not clear from the proceedings extract how or when the dispute was resolved, or if Dunham vacated the land.

George Doe

The property belonging to George Doe in 1883 belonged first to John B. "Pie" Allen, better known for building and running the sutler's store adjacent to the newly erected fort (see above). According to the proceedings extract, Doe's property was first occupied by Allen in 1874. Allen filed a claim on the property, but presumably this claim would have been denied when the military reservation was established. Allen sold the property in 1876 to Doe, who was apparently unfazed by the designation of the reservation a year earlier. By 1883, Doe had made various improvements, including a five-room adobe house, 30 acres of cleared and fenced land, 400 fruit trees, a large corral (apparently used by the fort), and irrigation ditches. Doe also ran horses and cattle on the reservation. In a letter to the post commander in November, 1885, Doe expressed his willingness to sell the rights to all of the land he had occupied in the military reservation for $2,500.00 (Doe 1885). We do not know if his offer was accepted.

The location of the Doe property referred to in the proceedings extract is uncertain. On the 1893 Roskruge map of Pima County (see Figure 15), Doe is indicated as the owner of property in the NE $\frac{1}{4}$ of Section 36 (Township 13 South, Range 14 East), immediately east of the fort, but the 1893 map may not reflect land ownership during the period the fort was occupied. In 1900, the same quarter-section was patented by Jesús Montijo, which means Doe must have abandoned it by 1895. In 1897, as noted earlier, Doe purchased his own 160-acre parcel from the GLO along the south bank of Tanque Verde Creek, adjacent on the east to the quarter-section later patented by Montijo. A ditch built by Doe and originating in the bed of Tanque Verde Creek was in use at least as early as 1908, and probably earlier (see below). Perhaps when Doe purchased the Tanque Verde Creek parcel in 1897, he was reoccupying land that he had sold to the government some 12 years earlier, when the fort was attempting to secure its water supply.

Like Dunham, Doe was involved in the construction of Fort Lowell, although exactly how is uncertain. His obituary claims, "He built Fort Lowell" (*TC*, 10 March 1929), but this probably overstates his actual role. Perhaps he was a subcontractor to Dunham, or a hired craftsman. As we discussed earlier in the chapter, Doe was the carpenter for a failed irrigation project along the Rillito in 1887, a project supervised by Alexander Davidson, the primary contractor. Doe apparently did build an adobe wall near the Officer's Quarters preserved today west of Craycroft Road (see Chapter 5). According to brief biographical notes prepared by one of his descendants, Doe used the farm he had bought from John B. Allen to raise "hay and grain for Fort Lowell, fruit and milk for Tucson" (Arizona Historical Society n.d.). He was later a partner in a contracting firm, Doe and Parsons, that built a number of prominent buildings in downtown Tucson, including the Carnegie Library (*TC*, 10 March 1929).

Branlía Elías

The Elías property may have been one of the first locations settled along the Rillito. According to the proceedings extract, the current owner Branlía Elías claimed to have been willed the property by its original occupant, Miguel Pacheco, in 1882. Pacheco had reportedly settled there 25 years earlier (i.e., 1858), but Elías had no papers to document his claim. Improvements on the property in 1883 consisted of 75 acres of cleared and fenced land, a well, and a pole house. Elías had 4 horses and 40 head of cattle, "which interfere seriously with the grazing of the post herd."

We have not found any other information about Branlía Elías, but he may have been related to the Elías family, originally from Sonora, that formed a prominent part of the Mexican elite in Tucson both prior to and after the Gadsden Purchase (Sheridan 1986:42). Elías's predecessor on the property, Miguel Pacheco, was presumably the same man who had served as a judge in Tucson in 1846, a member of an equally prominent Sonoran family with long roots in Tucson. According to Sonnichsen (1982:53–54), Miguel Pacheco owned land and operated both a dairy and a large mezcal distillery, although these two businesses were presumably based in or near Tucson proper.

Emilio Carrillo

According to the proceedings extract, this ranch was established in 1875 by Emilio Carrillo himself, who was not living on the property in 1883. The ranch was occupied by three hired men, "Bruno, Lava and M. J. Elías," probably members of the same clan as Branlía Elías. The ranch had 75 cattle, "which interfere with the grazing of the post herd." Improvements on the ranch consisted of a two-room pole house, a pole corral, and a well. The location of the ranch is uncertain, but it was presumably in close proximity to the fort. Around 1877, Carrillo established La Cebadilla Ranch, about 11 miles east of the fort, near the head of Tanque Verde Creek and in the foothills of the Rincon Mountains. The ranch was the predecessor of the well-known Tanque Verde Ranch, a guest ranch that opened for business in the 1930s and is still in operation (Smith n.d.; Gregonis and Huckell 1980:75–76; Martin 1983:14).

In addition to ranching along Tanque Verde Creek, Emilio Carrillo farmed land along the Santa Cruz River near Tucson. He was one of several farmers with relatively small-scale operations along the Santa Cruz who brought a suit against Sam Hughes and two other Tucson businessmen in 1885 for diverting irrigation water from the river for fields upstream (Sheridan 1986:64–65).

Leopoldo Carrillo

The proceedings extract mentions two ranches owned by Leopoldo Carrillo in the vicinity of the fort, but it does not provide a specific discussion of either property. In his 1885 endorsement of the proceedings, Hughes notes that one of the two Carrillo ranches was downstream from the fort and thus not a threat to the water supply. This is probably the same property depicted as belonging to Carrillo on both the 1873 GLO survey plat of the township (see Figure 30) and on the 1893 Roskruge map (see Figure 15), less than a mile west of the fort and just south of the Rillito. The location of Carrillo's other ranch is not specified in the proceedings extract or by Hughes in his endorsement. It may be depicted on the 1893 map, which indicates Carrillo as the owner of a parcel in Sabino Canyon, about 3 miles north of Tanque Verde Creek.

Leopoldo Carrillo was one of nineteenth-century Tucson's most successful entrepreneurs. He immigrated to Tucson in 1859 from Sonora and soon became a major property owner, with a wide range of business interests. He was best known for his development of Carrillo's Gardens, a lushly landscaped resort on the east bank of the Santa Cruz River near downtown. Carrillo's Gardens served as the social center of the city during the late 1880s and 1890s (Sheridan 1986:50–52; Sonnichsen 1982:84–85). Leopoldo Carrillo was apparently not related to Emilio Carrillo, his fellow landholder near Fort Lowell. In fact, Leopoldo Carrillo was one of the two businessmen allied with Sam Hughes against Emilio Carrillo and others in the Santa Cruz River water dispute mentioned above.

Settlement in the Fort Lowell Vicinity, 1891–1939

Whatever the number of settlers in the vicinity of Fort Lowell when it was first established, our search of GLO records for the study area has indicated that no settler had managed by 1873 to establish a formal claim to their land under the Homestead Act. This probably reflects a combination of factors, including the difficulty of "proving up" a claim in the 5 years specified by the act, and the lack of a sense of urgency in the early days of settlement to establish a formal claim. The same situation prevailed across Arizona, where the first homestead patent was not granted until 1878 (Stein 1990:7). When Fort Lowell was abandoned by the Army in 1891, the lands of the military reservation once again became available for claim or purchase from the GLO, and it is at this time that GLO transactions became common in the study area.

GLO Transactions in the Study Area

Our GLO research was conducted primarily at the State Office of the BLM in Phoenix, with some additional research at the BLM's Tucson Field Office. We also made limited use of the BLM's on-line database of GLO records (http://www.glorecords.blm.gov/), but the database was unavailable for public use during most of our period of research. The results of our research are summarized in Table 1, a list of completed GLO transactions in the study area. The distribution of the parcels covered by these transactions is depicted in the Appendix A map; a concordance of claimant names and the numbers for claims used in the map is provided in Table 2. Only successful claims by private individuals are included in Table 1 and on the Appendix A map; unsuccessful claims, the occasional corporate claim (e.g., a canal ROW), and claims by public entities (e.g., the state of Arizona) are not included. The map depicts

Table 1. GLO Transactions in the Río Antiguo Study Area

Map No.	Claimant	Year	Entry Type	Acres	T __ S	R __ E	Section	Aliquot
104	Aguirre, Manuel F.	1911	C	40	13	15	31	SE $\frac{1}{4}$ NE $\frac{1}{4}$
15	Andrews, Joseph D.	1891	C	160	13	13	25	SW $\frac{1}{4}$
87	Atkinson, Kathryn D.	1938	P	320	13	14	24	S $\frac{1}{2}$
103	Baker, Edward	1914	H	119.76	13	15	31	SW $\frac{1}{4}$ NE $\frac{1}{4}$ S $\frac{1}{2}$ NW $\frac{1}{4}$
106	Baker, John, Jr.	1924	H	160	13	15	31	SE $\frac{1}{4}$
69	Bearinger, Margaret J.	1936	H	640	13	14	23	NW $\frac{1}{4}$ NW $\frac{1}{4}$
					15	16	26 [a]	N $\frac{1}{2}$ SE $\frac{1}{4}$ N $\frac{1}{2}$ SW $\frac{1}{4}$ SE $\frac{1}{4}$ SW $\frac{1}{4}$
8	Benedict, Farrand O.	1903	H	80	13	13	24	NW $\frac{1}{4}$ NE $\frac{1}{4}$ NE $\frac{1}{4}$ NW $\frac{1}{4}$
19	Campbell, Al E.	1912	C	160	13	14	19	N $\frac{1}{2}$ NE $\frac{1}{4}$ SE $\frac{1}{4}$ NE $\frac{1}{4}$
							20	SW $\frac{1}{4}$ NW $\frac{1}{4}$
57	Caple, John T.	1931	H	80	13	14	27	N $\frac{1}{2}$ NE $\frac{1}{4}$
52	Carson, Francis K.	1933	H	480	13	14	14	SW $\frac{1}{4}$ S $\frac{1}{2}$ SE $\frac{1}{4}$
							15	SE $\frac{1}{4}$ SE $\frac{1}{4}$
							22	S $\frac{1}{2}$ NE $\frac{1}{4}$ NE $\frac{1}{4}$ SE $\frac{1}{4}$ NW $\frac{1}{4}$ SE $\frac{1}{4}$ [b] NE $\frac{1}{4}$ NE $\frac{1}{4}$
25	Ciarrapico, Florindo	1892	C	160	13	14	30	SE $\frac{1}{4}$
58	Colbert, Oscar Jrnio [*sic?*]	1935	H	40	13	14	27	SE $\frac{1}{4}$ NE $\frac{1}{4}$
34	Cole, Vance M.	1911	H	160	13	14	29	SE $\frac{1}{4}$
76	Cole, William H.	1904	H	40	13	14	26	SE $\frac{1}{4}$ SW $\frac{1}{4}$
91	Collins, Joseph M.	1914	C	40	13	14	25	SW $\frac{1}{4}$ SW $\frac{1}{4}$
105	Conley, Henry	1908	H	159.82	13	15	31	SW $\frac{1}{4}$
26	Conover, Florence L.	1932	H	40	13	14	20	NW $\frac{1}{4}$ NW $\frac{1}{4}$
65	Curry, Charles W.	1908	C	160	13	14	34	SW $\frac{1}{4}$
66	Dale, Robert J.	1913	C	160	13	14	34	SE $\frac{1}{4}$
46	Daly, John C.	1910	C	160	13	14	33	N $\frac{1}{2}$ N $\frac{1}{2}$

continued on next page

Map No.	Claimant	Year	Entry Type	Acres	T __ S	R __ E	Section	Aliquot
102	Doe, George H.	1897	C	159.67	13	15	31	N ¹/₂ NE ¹/₄ N ¹/₂ NW ¹/₄
14	Edmunds, Thomas M.	1891	C	161	13	13	25	S ¹/₂ NE ¹/₄
					13	14	30	W ¹/₂ NW ¹/₄
74	Elliot, Stella Pritchard	1937	H	320	13	14	26	NE ¹/₄ NE ¹/₄ NW ¹/₄
					14	15	28 [a]	W ¹/₂ NW ¹/₄ SE ¹/₄ NW ¹/₄
70	Failor, Gillmor	1937	H	160	12	13	20 [a]	S ¹/₂ NW ¹/₄ SW ¹/₄ NE ¹/₄
					13	14	23	SW ¹/₄ NW ¹/₄
54	Failor, Olive G.	1933	H	40	13	14	22	SE ¹/₄ SE ¹/₄
88	Finney, Elwood C.	1930	H	639.11	13	14	25	N ¹/₂ NE ¹/₄ SE ¹/₄
					13	15	30	NW ¹/₄ NW ¹/₄ NE ¹/₄ SW ¹/₄ [b]
30	Franco, Agapito	1896	H	160	13	14	20	SE ¹/₄
29	Franco, Rosa S.	1895	H	160	13	14	20	SW ¹/₄
13	Freaner, John E.	1891	C	160	13	13	25	N ¹/₂ NE ¹/₄ N ¹/₂ NW ¹/₄
3	Gannon, John Henry	1922	H	160	13	13	13	NW ¹/₄ SW ¹/₄
							14	NE ¹/₄ SW ¹/₄ N ¹/₂ SE ¹/₄
21	Garcia, Jesus	1891	C	160.9	13	14	19	S ¹/₂ SE ¹/₄ S ¹/₂ SW ¹/₄
33	Garstang, Lela	1905	H	160	13	14	29	SW ¹/₄
39	Geyer, Robert W. [c]	1938	H	655.68	13	14	14	S ¹/₂ NW ¹/₄ [b] S ¹/₂ NE ¹/₄ [b]
							15	SW ¹/₄ S ¹/₂ NW ¹/₄
							21	E ¹/₂ NE ¹/₄
							22	N ¹/₂ NW ¹/₄
					13	15	19	N ¹/₂ SW ¹/₄ SW ¹/₄ NW ¹/₄ SW ¹/₄ SW ¹/₄

Map No.	Claimant	Year	Entry Type	Acres	T __ S	R __ E	Section	Aliquot
51	Gillis, Robert I.	1934	H	480	13	14	15	N $\frac{1}{2}$ SE $\frac{1}{4}$ SW $\frac{1}{4}$ SE $\frac{1}{4}$ S $\frac{1}{2}$ NE $\frac{1}{4}$
							22	SW $\frac{1}{4}$ NW $\frac{1}{4}$ NE $\frac{1}{4}$ S $\frac{1}{2}$ NW $\frac{1}{4}$
48	Glanville, William J.	1907	C	160	13	14	33	SW $\frac{1}{4}$
89	Glover, James B.	1902	C	80	13	14	25	N $\frac{1}{2}$ SW $\frac{1}{4}$
100	Gonzales, Nazario A.	1921	C	160	13	15	20	SW $\frac{1}{4}$ SW $\frac{1}{4}$ [b]
							29	NW $\frac{1}{4}$ NW $\frac{1}{4}$ [b]
							30	E $\frac{1}{2}$ NE $\frac{1}{4}$
50	Gonzalez, Miguel V.	1908	H	197.01	13	14	33	E $\frac{1}{2}$ SE $\frac{1}{4}$
					14	14	3 [a]	NW $\frac{1}{4}$ NE $\frac{1}{4}$ NW $\frac{1}{4}$ NW $\frac{1}{4}$
							4 [a]	NE $\frac{1}{4}$ NE $\frac{1}{4}$
73	Goulding, Emma E.	1902	C	80	13	14	26	SE $\frac{1}{4}$ NW $\frac{1}{4}$ SW $\frac{1}{4}$ NE $\frac{1}{4}$ [b]
49	Grant, John Breck	1909	H	80	13	14	33	W $\frac{1}{2}$ SE $\frac{1}{4}$
24	Grihalva, Jesus	1891	C	79.75	13	14	30	S $\frac{1}{2}$ SW $\frac{1}{4}$
60	Hall, John H.	1903	C	157.24	13	14	27	E $\frac{1}{2}$ SW $\frac{1}{4}$ SW $\frac{1}{4}$ SE $\frac{1}{4}$ SW $\frac{1}{4}$ SW $\frac{1}{4}$
32	Hancock, James F.	1892	H	160	13	14	29	NE $\frac{1}{4}$
38	Hatrick, Alonzo B.	1911	H	160	13	14	32	SE $\frac{1}{4}$
36	Hausner, John	1910	C	160	13	14	32	NE $\frac{1}{4}$
77	Haynes, William	1901	C	80	13	14	26	E $\frac{1}{2}$ SE $\frac{1}{4}$
10	Haynes, Willis Pearson	1890	C	161.1	13	13	24	N $\frac{1}{2}$ SE $\frac{1}{4}$ SW $\frac{1}{4}$ NE $\frac{1}{4}$
					13	14	19	NW $\frac{1}{4}$ SW $\frac{1}{4}$
42	Hernandez, Nieves	1894	H	120	13	14	28	W $\frac{1}{2}$ NW $\frac{1}{4}$ NW $\frac{1}{4}$ SW $\frac{1}{4}$
68	Huffman, Ira E.	1931	H	640	12	13	29 [a]	S $\frac{1}{2}$ S $\frac{1}{2}$ N $\frac{1}{2}$
					13	14	14	N $\frac{1}{2}$ SE $\frac{1}{4}$
							26	NW $\frac{1}{4}$ NW $\frac{1}{4}$ [b]
					13	15	28 [a]	SE $\frac{1}{4}$ NW $\frac{1}{4}$

continued on next page

Map No.	Claimant	Year	Entry Type	Acres	Legal Description			
					T __ S	R __ E	Section	Aliquot
53	Huffman, Martha E.	1931	H	640	12	13	20[a]	S $\frac{1}{2}$ SE $\frac{1}{4}$ NE $\frac{1}{4}$
							29[a]	N $\frac{1}{2}$ N $\frac{1}{2}$
					13	14	22	NW $\frac{1}{4}$ SE $\frac{1}{4}$ [d]
							23	W $\frac{1}{2}$ SW $\frac{1}{4}$
2	Huntley, Dewitt C.	1932	H	400	13	13	12	SE $\frac{1}{4}$ SW $\frac{1}{4}$ S $\frac{1}{2}$ SE $\frac{1}{4}$
							13	NE $\frac{1}{4}$ NE $\frac{1}{4}$ NW $\frac{1}{4}$ S $\frac{1}{2}$ NW $\frac{1}{4}$
55	Ingersoll, Carrie P.	1900	C	160	13	14	27	SW $\frac{1}{4}$ NE $\frac{1}{4}$ SE $\frac{1}{4}$ NW $\frac{1}{4}$ W $\frac{1}{2}$ NW $\frac{1}{4}$
4	Jackson, George Archibald	1916	C	40	13	13	13	NE $\frac{1}{4}$ SW $\frac{1}{4}$
31	Jones, Charles G.	1890	C	160	13	14	29	NW $\frac{1}{4}$
86	Keith, Leo B.	1937	H	640	13	14	13[a]	S $\frac{1}{2}$
							24	N $\frac{1}{2}$
84	Kendall, Frank B.	1910	C	160	13	14	35	SW $\frac{1}{4}$
6	Kennedy, Benjamin	1896	H	160	13	13	13	SW $\frac{1}{4}$ SW $\frac{1}{4}$
							14	SE $\frac{1}{4}$ SW $\frac{1}{4}$ S $\frac{1}{2}$ SE $\frac{1}{4}$
67	Knox, Florence W. [c]	1933	H	478.84	13	12	24[a]	SE $\frac{1}{4}$ SW $\frac{1}{4}$
							25[a]	NE $\frac{1}{4}$ NW $\frac{1}{4}$
					13	14	14	S $\frac{1}{2}$ NE $\frac{1}{4}$ S $\frac{1}{2}$ NW $\frac{1}{4}$
40	Latter Day Saints	1937	C	40	13	14	21	SE $\frac{1}{4}$ SE $\frac{1}{4}$
99	Lester, Anna M.	1937	H	480	13	15	30	SW $\frac{1}{4}$ NE $\frac{1}{4}$
					14	15	10[a]	S $\frac{1}{2}$ SE $\frac{1}{4}$ SE $\frac{1}{4}$ SW $\frac{1}{4}$
							14[a]	W $\frac{1}{2}$
7	Levin, Alexander	1881	C	160	13	13	13	SE $\frac{1}{4}$ SW $\frac{1}{4}$ S $\frac{1}{2}$ SE $\frac{1}{4}$
							24	NE $\frac{1}{4}$ NE $\frac{1}{4}$
45	Lohrum, John	1910	H	160	13	14	28	S $\frac{1}{2}$ S $\frac{1}{2}$
90	Los Reyes, Francisco de	1913	H	40	13	14	25	NW $\frac{1}{4}$ SE $\frac{1}{4}$
62	Martin, Philip J.	1910	C	160	13	14	34	NW $\frac{1}{4}$

Map No.	Claimant	Year	Entry Type	Acres	T __ S	R __ E	Section	Aliquot
81	McCormick, Gregory	1913	H	40	13	14	35	SE $^1/_4$ NW $^1/_4$
20	Meineke, William H.	1898	H	160	13	14	19	N $^1/_2$ SE $^1/_4$ SW $^1/_4$ NE $^1/_4$ NE $^1/_4$ SW $^1/_4$
37	Merino, Juan C.	1915	H	160	13	14	32	SW $^1/_4$
18	Molina, Alejandro	1880	C	162.8	13	14	19	NW $^1/_4$
94	Montijo, Jesus	1900	H	160	13	14	36	NE $^1/_4$
93	Montijo, Jesus, Jr.	1903	H	159.65	13	14	25	S $^1/_2$ SE $^1/_4$
					13	15	30	S $^1/_2$ SW $^1/_4$
64	Moreno, Juan	1923	H	80	13	14	34	SE $^1/_4$ NE $^1/_4$
							35	SW $^1/_4$ NW $^1/_4$
82	Mule, Gios and Egnazio	1912	C	40	13	14	35	SW $^1/_4$ NE $^1/_4$
27	Murphey, John W.	1939	H	640	13	14	20	NE $^1/_4$ NE $^1/_4$ NW $^1/_4$
							21	NW $^1/_4$ N $^1/_2$ SW $^1/_4$ N $^1/_2$ SE $^1/_4$ W $^1/_2$ NE $^1/_4$
					13	15	18 [a]	SE $^1/_4$ SW $^1/_4$
41	Plummer, Paul	1890	H	160	13	14	21	S $^1/_2$ SW $^1/_4$ SW $^1/_4$ SE $^1/_4$
							28	NE $^1/_4$ NW $^1/_4$
72	Powell, Hubert F.	1932	H	480	13	14	23	E $^1/_2$ E $^1/_2$ W $^1/_2$
16	Prince, Levi M.	1895	H	160	13	13	25	SE $^1/_4$
92	Provencio, Petronilo	1912	H	40	13	14	25	SE $^1/_4$ SW $^1/_4$
80	Ramband, Severin	1897	C	40	13	14	35	NE $^1/_4$ NE $^1/_4$
71	Romero, Carmen	1899	H	120	13	14	26	W $^1/_2$ NW $^1/_4$
							35	NW $^1/_4$ NW $^1/_4$
61	Romero, Jesus	1902	H	160	13	14	27	N $^1/_2$ SE $^1/_4$ SE $^1/_4$ SE $^1/_4$
							34	NE $^1/_4$ NE $^1/_4$
47	Roth, William F.	1896	H	160	13	14	33	S $^1/_2$ N $^1/_2$
43	Rowland, William Edwin	1890	H	160	13	14	28	SW $^1/_4$ NE $^1/_4$ SE $^1/_4$ NW $^1/_4$ NE $^1/_4$ SW $^1/_4$ NW $^1/_4$ SE $^1/_4$

continued on next page

Map No.	Claimant	Year	Entry Type	Acres	T __ S	R __ E	Section	Aliquot
17	Ryan, Simpson S.	1925	H	41.38	13	14	18	SW $\frac{1}{4}$ SW $\frac{1}{4}$
23	Samuels, Mark V.	1911	H	160	13	14	30	NE $\frac{1}{4}$
85	Schoenen, John N.	1913	C	160	13	14	35	SE $\frac{1}{4}$
1	Schulze, Herman	1926	H	160	13	13	12	W $\frac{1}{2}$ SW $\frac{1}{4}$
							13	NW $\frac{1}{4}$ NW $\frac{1}{4}$
							14	NE $\frac{1}{4}$ NE $\frac{1}{4}$
44	Schwenker, Refugio J.	1891	H	160	13	14	28	N $\frac{1}{2}$ NE $\frac{1}{4}$ SE $\frac{1}{4}$ NE $\frac{1}{4}$ NE $\frac{1}{4}$ SE $\frac{1}{4}$
22	Scrivner, Claud E.	1908	C	160.05	13	14	30	NE $\frac{1}{4}$ SW $\frac{1}{4}$ E $\frac{1}{2}$ NW $\frac{1}{4}$ NW $\frac{1}{4}$ SW $\frac{1}{4}$
78	Sirrine, Ernest E.	1904	C	80	13	14	26	SW $\frac{1}{4}$ SE $\frac{1}{4}$
							35	NW $\frac{1}{4}$ NE $\frac{1}{4}$
35	Stattelman, Georg Martin	1910	H	160	13	14	32	NW $\frac{1}{4}$
5	Sykes, Glenton G.	1930	H	80	13	13	13	N $\frac{1}{2}$ SE $\frac{1}{4}$
75	Tapia, Mercedes	1897	C	80	13	14	26	NE $\frac{1}{4}$ SW $\frac{1}{4}$ NW $\frac{1}{4}$ SE $\frac{1}{4}$
56	Tompkinson, Albert	1930	H	40	13	14	27	NE $\frac{1}{4}$ NW $\frac{1}{4}$
96	Vinson, Harold F.	1936	H	200	13	15	17 [a]	S $\frac{1}{2}$ SW $\frac{1}{4}$ SW $\frac{1}{4}$ SE $\frac{1}{4}$
							19	NW $\frac{1}{4}$ NE $\frac{1}{4}$ NE $\frac{1}{4}$ NW $\frac{1}{4}$
97	Vinson, Harold F.	1939	H	440	13	15	19	SE $\frac{1}{4}$ S $\frac{1}{2}$ NE $\frac{1}{4}$ NE $\frac{1}{4}$ NE $\frac{1}{4}$ SE $\frac{1}{4}$ NW $\frac{1}{4}$
							20	W $\frac{1}{2}$ NW $\frac{1}{4}$ NW $\frac{1}{4}$ SW $\frac{1}{4}$
95	Vinson, Thomas B.	1939	H	519.58	13	15	19	NW $\frac{1}{4}$ NW $\frac{1}{4}$
				13	16	29 [a]	SE $\frac{1}{4}$ S $\frac{1}{2}$ SW $\frac{1}{4}$ NE $\frac{1}{4}$ SW $\frac{1}{4}$
							33 [a]	E $\frac{1}{2}$ NE $\frac{1}{4}$ NE $\frac{1}{4}$ SE $\frac{1}{4}$
					14	16	18 [a]	S $\frac{1}{2}$ SE $\frac{1}{4}$
59	Wakefield, Harvey B.	1911	C	42.76	13	14	27	NW $\frac{1}{4}$ SW $\frac{1}{4}$
83	Wakefield, Lyman W.	1897	C	40	13	14	35	SE $\frac{1}{4}$ NE $\frac{1}{4}$

Map No.	Claimant	Year	Entry Type	Acres	Legal Description T __ S	R __ E	Section	Aliquot
79	Walker, Edward C.	1913	H	40	13	14	35	NE $\frac{1}{4}$ NW $\frac{1}{4}$
11	Way, Frank Arthur	1908	C	40	13	13	24	SE $\frac{1}{4}$ NE $\frac{1}{4}$
12	Welsh, Maurice E.	1907	H	160	13	13	24	S $\frac{1}{2}$ SW $\frac{1}{4}$ S $\frac{1}{2}$ SE $\frac{1}{4}$
9	Wetmore, Edward L.	1892	H	160	13	13	24	S $\frac{1}{2}$ NW $\frac{1}{4}$ N $\frac{1}{2}$ SW $\frac{1}{4}$
63	Wheatcroft, Joseph E.	1916	H	80	13	14	34	W $\frac{1}{2}$ NE $\frac{1}{4}$
98	Wolfley, Silas D.	1936	H	639.59	12	12	31 [a]	E $\frac{1}{2}$ SE $\frac{1}{4}$ SE $\frac{1}{4}$ NE $\frac{1}{4}$
					12	14	6 [a]	S $\frac{1}{2}$ NE $\frac{1}{4}$ W $\frac{1}{2}$ NE $\frac{1}{4}$ NE $\frac{1}{4}$
					13	15	19	SE $\frac{1}{4}$ SW $\frac{1}{4}$
101	Worley, Jesse S.	1911	C	160	13	15	30	SE $\frac{1}{4}$
28	Yepis, Alfonso F.	1924	C	40	13	14	20	SE $\frac{1}{4}$ NW $\frac{1}{4}$

Note: With the exception of a few obvious errors, the spellings of claimant names provided by the corresponding GLO record are not corrected here.

Key: C = cash sale; H = Homestead Act patent; P = private land claim

[a] The portion of the claim falling within this section is outside the project area.

[b] This portion of the claim was part of an earlier claim.

[c] The acreage of this claim does not match the apparent total of the aliquot fractions. We were unable to resolve the discrepancy.

[d] The description of this portion of the claim on the claim record differs slightly from its depiction on the master title plat. We were unable to resolve the discrepancy and have partially inferred the intended boundaries of the claim.

only the earliest claimant for a parcel; the few claims that include previously claimed land are depicted without the previously claimed portion. Also, if part of a claim falls outside the study area, it is depicted on the map only if it is contiguous with a part of the claim within the study area. Depictions of claims are approximate when a claim is not a regular section aliquot (e.g., a claim for 42.76 acres is depicted as a 40-acre quarter-quarter-section).

A portion of the abandoned Fort Lowell Military Reservation, including most of the ruins of the fort and an area around them (Township 13 South, Range 14 East, Section 36, NW $\frac{1}{4}$ and S $\frac{1}{2}$), became state property in 1910 (see the Appendix A map). Most of the rest of the reservation within and near the study area was eventually claimed by private parties. A total of 106 successful private claims was made in the study area in the period 1880–1939, including 40 cash sales, 65 homestead patents (granted under either the original Homestead Act of 1862 or a later version of the same act), and 1 private land claim (granted under an act preceding the Homestead Act).

The overall depiction on the Appendix A map is a composite of land ownership in the Río Antiguo study area over a period of 59 years. Thus, it is not a meaningful picture of settlement for any particular moment. Nonetheless, a sense of the sequence of settlement in the study area can be had by looking at the distribution of claims in different periods. The map uses colors to distinguish claims made in different periods, including all claims prior to the abandonment of Fort Lowell (1880–1890), and

**Table 2. Concordance of GLO Claimant Names and
Map Index Numbers Used in Appendix A**

Number	Name	Number	Name
1	Schulze, Herman	54	Failor, Olive G.
2	Huntley, Dewitt C.	55	Ingersoll, Carrie P.
3	Gannon, John Henry	56	Tompkinson, Albert
4	Jackson, George Archibald	57	Caple, John T.
5	Sykes, Glenton G.	58	Colbert, Oscar Jrnio
6	Kennedy, Benjamin	59	Wakefield, Harvey B.
7	Levin, Alexander	60	Hall, John H.
8	Benedict, Farrand O.	61	Romero, Jesus
9	Wetmore, Edward L.	62	Martin, Philip J.
10	Haynes, Willis Pearson	63	Wheatcroft, Joseph E.
11	Way, Frank Arthur	64	Moreno, Juan
12	Welsh, Maurice E.	65	Curry, Charles W.
13	Freaner, John E.	66	Dale, Robert J.
14	Edmunds, Thomas M.	67	Knox, Florence W.
15	Andrews, Joseph D.	68	Huffman, Ira E.
16	Prince, Levi M.	69	Bearinger, Margaret J.
17	Ryan, Simpson S.	70	Failor, Gillmor
18	Molina, Alejandro	71	Romero, Carmen
19	Campbell, Al E.	72	Powell, Hubert F.
20	Meineke, William H.	73	Goulding, Emma E.
21	Garcia, Jesus	74	Elliot, Stella Pritchard
22	Scrivner, Claud E.	75	Tapia, Mercedes
23	Samuels, Mark V.	76	Cole, William H.
24	Grihalva, Jesus	77	Haynes, William
25	Ciarrapico, Florindo	78	Sirrine, Ernest E.
26	Conover, Florence L.	79	Walker, Edward C.
27	Murphey, John W.	80	Ramband, Severin
28	Yepis, Alfonso F.	81	McCormick, Gregory
29	Franco, Rosa S.	82	Mule, Gios and Egnazio
30	Franco, Agapito	83	Wakefield, Lyman W.
31	Jones, Charles G.	84	Kendall, Frank B.
32	Hancock, James F.	85	Schoenen, John N.
33	Garstang, Lela	86	Keith, Leo B.

126

Number	Name	Number	Name
34	Cole, Vance M.	87	Atkinson, Kathryn D.
35	Stattelman, Georg Martin	88	Finney, Elwood C.
36	Hausner, John	89	Glover, James B.
37	Merino, Juan C.	90	de los Reyes, Francisco
38	Hatrick, Alonzo B.	91	Collins, Joseph M.
39	Geyer, Robert W.	92	Provencio, Petronilo
40	Latter Day Saints	93	Montijo, Jesus, Jr.
41	Plummer, Paul	94	Montijo, Jesus
42	Hernandez, Nieves	95	Vinson, Thomas B.
43	Rowland, William Edwin	96	Vinson, Harold F.
44	Schwenker, Refugio J.	97	Vinson, Harold F.
45	Lohrum, John	98	Wolfley, Silas D.
46	Daly, John C.	99	Lester, Anna M.
47	Roth, William F.	100	Gonzales, Nazario A.
48	Glanville, William J.	101	Worley, Jesse S.
49	Grant, John Breck	102	Doe, George H.
50	Gonzalez, Miguel V.	103	Baker, Edward
51	Gillis, Robert I.	104	Aguirre, Manuel F.
52	Carson, Francis K.	105	Conley, Henry
53	Huffman, Martha E.	106	Baker, John, Jr.

subsequent claims in spans of 10 years (1891–1900, 1901–1910, and so on) up to the latest private claims in 1939.

Almost all of the successful claims in the study area date to 1891 or later, or the period after abandonment of the fort. This is true even for the portions of the study area well to the west of the fort and outside the bounds of the former military reservation. The only exceptions are six claims made west of the reservation and adjacent to the Rillito in the period 1880–1890 (see the claims of Haynes, Jones, Levin, Molina, Plummer, and Rowland in Table 1). Not surprisingly, these earliest claims, and most of the claims made in the first 10 years after the fort was abandoned, fall at least partially on the floodplain of the Rillito, where the best soil for farming was found and irrigation was easiest. In the period 1901–1910, claims were still being made on the floodplain, but relatively level parcels on the terraces south of the river were also being claimed. By this period, pumping water from deep wells was becoming feasible, and these parcels were probably destined for a combination of stock raising and farming with well water. In the period 1911–1920, basically the same pattern is evident, with a few incursions into the foothills north of the river. Beginning in 1921 and continuing to 1939, most of the foothills property in the study area was finally claimed. The earliest of these claims may have been made with stock raising in mind, but the long-term plans of many claimants undoubtedly included residential development. An important example of this is the 640-acre claim patented by John W. Murphey in 1939, in Sections 20 and 21 of Township 13 South, Range 14 East. This claim was joined to other acreage acquired by Murphey in the 1920s and 1930s to form the Catalina Foothills Estates, an important early suburban development discussed later in the chapter.

As noted, Table 1 and the Appendix A map do not include the many failed land claims recorded by the GLO in the study area. We did not make a comprehensive search for failed claims, but in the portion of Township 13 South, Range 14 East encompassed by the study area (21 sections, or about 78 percent of the study area), there were 69 relinquished or canceled Homestead Act and Desert Lands Act claims during the period 1885–1931. The relinquished and canceled claims, ranging in size from 40 to 320 acres and distributed more or less evenly across the township, represent failed attempts at making the fairly minimal improvements required by either act. We have not pursued this aspect of the GLO records any further, but doing so would conceivably yield a few insights into what constituted a successful approach to settlement in the study area.

Of the 106 claimants in Table 1, 22 (or about 21 percent) had Spanish names and were probably of Mexican descent. (For a few claimants, Mexican ancestry can be assigned only loosely: Refugio Schwenker was presumably of German-Mexican descent; and Gios and Ignazio Mule, whose claim eventually served as the site of San Pedro Chapel, were of Italian descent, though with close ties to the Mexican community [Turner 1990:52]). The other 84 claimants were of Anglo-American or other Euroamerican extraction. While these proportions reflect a substantial Mexican presence in the study area, the percentage of Mexican claimants is actually lower than other farming and ranching areas in the Tucson Basin during the same period, most notably the Santa Cruz River valley between downtown Tucson and San Xavier del Bac. The difference is due in part to the relatively late date that the Rillito Valley began to be settled: when Fort Lowell was abandoned and GLO transactions began carving up the area, only a limited number of settlers of any ethnicity had settled in the vicinity. By then, Anglo-Americans were a major presence in the Tucson Basin, and their dominance of GLO transactions in the agriculturally promising Rillito Valley is not surprising. In contrast, settlement along the Santa Cruz River near Tucson at the start of the GLO period was already well advanced and heavily Mexican, which meant that a higher percentage of private land claims (28 of 60 claims, or about 47 percent) were made by people with Mexican ancestry (O'Mack and Klucas 2001).

Since GLO claims could be (and often were) sold soon after being finalized, comparing such percentages may not mean much. Landownership in the study area as represented on the 1893 Roskruge map (see Figure 15) suggests that, shortly after Fort Lowell was abandoned, the percentage of landowners of Mexican descent was actually around 50 percent (Table 3), and this figure does not include what was undoubtedly a significant number of Mexican-Americans squatting on unclaimed portions of the former military reservation. The largest concentration of such squatters was in and among the ruins of the fort itself. The Mexican-American community that formed around the ruins after abandonment of the fort was known by its inhabitants as El Fuerte ("The Fort"), which even today retains some of its distinctiveness as an ethnic enclave.

El Fuerte

As already noted, two of the earliest documented settlers in the vicinity of Fort Lowell were Pedro Romero and Leopoldo Carrillo, both of Mexican descent. The 1873 GLO survey plat of Township 13 South, Range 14 East (see Figure 30) depicts a house owned by Romero in the NE ¼, NE ¼ of Section 34, and one owned by Carrillo in the NW ¼, NW ¼ of Section 35. Carrillo probably remained the owner of the same property until at least 1893, the year he was indicated as a landowner in the same vicinity on the Roskruge map (see above). Romero was also indicated as a landowner in the same vicinity on the 1893 map, as was C. Romero. The latter was probably Carmen Romero, who patented a 120-acre claim immediately east of Pedro's property in 1899 (see Table 1), a claim that must have included Carrillo's original property. Carmen was presumably the wife of Pedro. In 1902, Jesús Romero, perhaps a son of Pedro and Carmen, patented a 160-acre claim in the same area that must have included Pedro's original

Table 3. Individual Landholders in the Río Antiguo Study Area, 1893
(based on Roskruge 1893)

Name	Township	Range	Section	Aliquot	GLO
Andrews	13 S	13 E	25	SW $\frac{1}{4}$	yes
Barcelo	13 S	14 E	27	SW $\frac{1}{4}$	
Carrillo	13 S	14 E	26	SW $\frac{1}{4}$	
Conlee	13 S	14 E	26	SE $\frac{1}{4}$	
Davidson	13 S	14 E	28	SE $\frac{1}{4}$	
Doe	13 S	14 E	36	NE $\frac{1}{4}$	
Dunham	13 S	15 E	31	NE $\frac{1}{4}$	
Edmunds	13 S	13 E	25	NE $\frac{1}{4}$	yes
Franco	13 S	14 E	20	SW $\frac{1}{4}$	yes
Franco, J.	13 S	14 E	20	SE $\frac{1}{4}$	yes
Henault	13 S	14 E	30	SE $\frac{1}{4}$	
Hernandez	13 S	14 E	28	SW $\frac{1}{4}$	yes
Jacobs	13 S	13 E	13	SE $\frac{1}{4}$	
Kennedy, B.	13 S	13 E	13	SW $\frac{1}{4}$	yes
Lopez	13 S	14 E	28	SE $\frac{1}{4}$	
Martin	13 S	14 E	29	NW $\frac{1}{4}$	
Molino	13 S	14 E	19	NW $\frac{1}{4}$	yes
Montijo	13 S	14 E	36	NE $\frac{1}{4}$	yes
Plummer	13 S	14 E	21	SW $\frac{1}{4}$	yes
Prince	13 S	13 E	25	NW $\frac{1}{4}$	yes
Romero, C.	13 S	14 E	27	SE $\frac{1}{4}$	yes
Romero, P.	13 S	14 E	27	SE $\frac{1}{4}$	yes
Salazar	13 S	14 E	27	SW $\frac{1}{4}$	
Schwenker	13 S	14 E	28	SE $\frac{1}{4}$	yes
Verduga	13 S	14 E	33	NE $\frac{1}{4}$	
Wetmore	13 S	13 E	24	SW $\frac{1}{4}$	yes

Note: The 1893 map is sometimes hard to interpret because of the crowding of details. The locational information provided here constitutes our best reading of the map. All spellings on the map are preserved here, except for obvious errors (e.g., "Corrillo" for Carrillo). A "yes" in the GLO column indicates a probable correspondence with a GLO transaction involving the same individual or family (see the text).

property (see Table 1). Thus, for at least a few years before Fort Lowell was built and continuing for at least a decade after it was abandoned, a substantial area immediately east of the fort was occupied (legally, for at least part of that period) by Mexican-Americans.

An established Mexican-American presence was undoubtedly what encouraged other Mexican-Americans to settle in the area after Fort Lowell was abandoned, but most of the Mexican-Americans who settled there after 1891 made no formal claims on the land. As a result, their presence in the area and the development of the Mexican-American enclave known as El Fuerte are known largely from oral-historical research. The most important effort in this regard was initiated by two anthropologists, Edward and Rosamond Spicer; Edward Spicer was a professor of anthropology at the University of Arizona for his entire career. The Spicers moved into the El Fuerte neighborhood in 1946 at a time when the Fort Lowell area was beginning to be absorbed by greater Tucson and the Mexican-American residents of El Fuerte were either dying off or moving away. The Spicers bought and repaired an old adobe house in the neighborhood and soon took an active interest in the history of the area. That interest led, after several decades, to the Fort Lowell Community History Project, a grant-funded project carried out in 1981 to research the history of the Fort Lowell area in all its aspects, with special attention to the previously neglected history of El Fuerte (Cheek 1992; Spicer n.d.).

With county, city, and neighborhood participation, the community history project became an important part of an ongoing preservation effort in the neighborhood (Spicer 1980). Perhaps more importantly, it prompted the collection of a substantial body of oral-historical data from current and former members of the El Fuerte community. Teresa Turner, a resident in the community, was responsible for most of the oral-historical work, which she carried out as part of a more general overview of the history of the Fort Lowell area. The overview, originally published as a guide for a walking tour of the Old Fort Lowell Neighborhood, has been revised twice and is the only substantial published source on the history of El Fuerte (Turner 1982a, 1982b, 1990). Other important oral-historical testimony relating to El Fuerte has been collected and published independently by Martin (1983).

The first Mexican-Americans to settle at Fort Lowell following its abandonment occupied the abandoned buildings of the fort itself and built small adobe houses nearby. According to Turner (1990:21), the settlers came from towns in Sonora and Baja California, drawn to the Tucson area by family members already living there. Like so many Mexicans who came to southern Arizona after the Gadsden Purchase, these immigrants did not perceive the change from Sonora to Arizona as a radical one. Instead, it was a move from one part of a familiar desert environment to another part, where basically the same way of life could be carried on, often in the company of previously settled friends and family members (Turner 1990:21; see also Sheridan 1986:71). El Fuerte quickly grew to "a scattering of twenty-five to thirty adobe homes" (Turner 1990:26). The people supported themselves by farming on the nearby floodplain of the Rillito, grazing livestock in the vicinity, gathering wild plant foods and hunting, and working for wages on the larger farms and ranches in the area (Turner 1990:29–32).

Apart from specific fort buildings known to have been reoccupied by Mexican-Americans, the distribution of El Fuerte residences during the first decades of the community is not well documented. By the 1930s, the community centered on the area immediately west of Craycroft Road, on either side of Fort Lowell Road, including the fort buildings preserved in this area (see Chapter 5 for a discussion of these buildings). A map prepared by Rosamond Spicer in 1981 (Turner 1990:51) is the most detailed record of Mexican-American and other residences in the area, and it probably does not represent all of the houses used at different times in the life of the community. One part of this area that still retains much of its original character is El Callejón, "The Alley," a cul de sac on the north side of Fort Lowell Road where several houses dating to the early days of El Fuerte still stand, some still owned and occupied by the original Mexican-American families (Turner 1990:40).

Another surviving part of the El Fuerte community is San Pedro Chapel, located on a low rise just south of Fort Lowell Road and west of El Callejón. The chapel was built relatively late in the life of El Fuerte—it was completed in 1932—but the same location had previously held two other chapels. The first of these, built around 1915, was too small to hold more than a priest celebrating mass (the people attending stood outside); the second, larger chapel, dedicated to San Angel de la Guarda, was finished around 1920, but it was destroyed in a rare tornado in 1929. San Pedro Chapel served the El Fuerte community until 1948, when St. Cyril's Catholic Church opened at Swan Road and Pima Street, just to the south. At that time, the Diocese of Tucson, which had been owner of the chapel property since its donation by the family that had homesteaded it, sold the property and deconsecrated the chapel. Over the next 30 years, the chapel was reused intermittently for residential and minor commercial purposes, until it became one of the focal points of preservation efforts in the neighborhood. It was purchased by the Old Fort Lowell Neighborhood Association in 1993 and has since been largely restored to its original condition. It currently serves as a kind of community center and as a place for private weddings, baptisms, and other functions (J. Turner n.d.; T. Turner 1990:52–53, 56).

The Mormon Presence along the Rillito

Among the Anglo-Americans to settle along the Rillito shortly after the abandonment of Fort Lowell was Nephi Bingham, a Mormon from Utah who first came to southern Arizona as a freighter. Bingham bought land along the north bank of the Rillito near the center of the study area, at the large right-angle bend in the river. He brought his extended family from Utah to live there, and soon other Mormons joined them, creating a community of Mormons that eventually expanded to both sides of the river. Known as Binghampton, the community thrived for about 40 years before being absorbed by Tucson. The history of Binghampton ties the Río Antiguo study area to the wider history of Mormons in the West, which we sketch in the following paragraphs before looking more closely at the history of Binghampton.

Mormons in the West

Mormons were among the first Anglo-Americans to settle in Arizona. They first entered the region that would become the modern state in the 1840s, explored scattered parts of it in the 1850s and 1860s, and made their first systematic attempt to establish permanent settlements in the 1870s. Despite physical hardships, persecution by non-Mormon Anglo-Americans, and the failure of their earliest settlements, Mormons had a significant and rapidly growing presence in Arizona by the 1880s. Today, Mormons continue to be concentrated in the areas first settled in the nineteenth century by their predecessors, but they have long since become a part of mainstream society and now form a significant part of the population in just about every part of the state (Brown et al. 1994:128–129).

"Mormon" is the name commonly applied to members of the Church of Jesus Christ of Latter-day Saints, a Protestant faith originating in the northeastern United States in the early 1800s. The common name alludes to the Book of Mormon, the sacred text delivered to the Latter-day Saints by their founder and prophet, Joseph Smith. A fundamental belief of the Saints, and the source of their optimistic name for themselves, is that they have been chosen to prepare the world for the Second Coming of Christ. Two events that will precede the Second Coming, and accepted by the Saints as their special responsibility, are the restoration of the gospel of Christ and the "building up of Zion," the establishment of the ideal society and nation over which Christ will rule on his return (Church Educational System 1993:1). Since Joseph Smith's time, restoring the gospel has meant spreading the message of the prophet through missions, and building up Zion has meant living exemplary lives in towns and communities founded and organized according to the principles laid down by Mormon leaders.

Joseph Smith and his followers first attempted to establish communities dedicated to their faith in the Midwest, but the Mormon penchants for political autonomy and economic separatism, as well as their faith-based practice of polygamy, were met with mistrust and hostility by non-Mormons. The Mormons suffered repeatedly from persecution and eventually left the Midwest following the murder of Smith by a mob in Nauvoo, Illinois, in 1844 (Hansen 1998). In 1847, Brigham Young, successor to Smith as leader of the Mormons and the group's first president, settled the main body of the faithful at Great Salt Lake in what is now Utah. There the Mormons flourished, spreading out from Great Salt Lake in orderly settlements, building irrigation systems and roads, and successfully farming land that most non-Mormon settlers would have passed over as useless. Building on Smith's ambitions, Brigham Young hoped to establish a Mormon kingdom in Utah that would serve as the center of the new Zion. Shortly after arrival to Great Salt Lake, Young and the Mormon leadership proposed creation of the state of Deseret (after the word for "honeybee" in the Book of Mormon), a vast area that included Utah and portions of eight other western States, including all of Arizona north of the Gila River. Deseret never became a state, but a pared-down version of it became Utah Territory in 1850, with Brigham Young as governor (Brown et al. 1994:90–91).

Early Mormon Settlement in Arizona

The Latter-day Saints in Utah would soon extend their colonization efforts into what is now Arizona, but the first Mormons to enter Arizona actually came a year before Brigham Young made it to Great Salt Lake. These Mormons came not as settlers but as a U.S. military expedition, charged with blazing a wagon trail from the Great Plains to the Pacific coast. The Mormon Battalion was a volunteer company of Latter-day Saints assembled in the Midwest by church leaders in an effort to demonstrate the patriotism of the church and thus defuse growing anti-Mormon sentiments in the region. The U.S. Army, responding to its recently declared war with Mexico, welcomed what would prove to be a dedicated and well-disciplined company. The route of the Mormon Battalion across the Southwest, including a stop in Tucson in December 1846, is discussed later in the chapter.

Mormons made another brief appearance in southern Arizona during the period just prior to the Gadsden Purchase. In the fall of 1851, five years after the Mormon Battalion passed through Tucson, a party of Mormon settlers headed to California stopped in the Santa Cruz Valley. The settlers were offered land concessions at Tubac by the local commander of the Mexican army, which had recently reoccupied the presidio site. Establishing themselves on irrigated lands near the presidio, the settlers plowed their fields and planted crops, assuming the river would supply water through the winter. That winter it did not, and the following spring the frustrated settlers moved on to California. The identity of the people in this small party and their exact place of origin in the east are unknown, but their time at Tubac represented the first Mormon settlement in what is now Arizona (McClintock 1985:56–57; Officer 1987:255).

For the next three decades, Mormon entries into what is now Arizona came exclusively from the north as planned expansions of the colony in Utah. A steady increase in the population of Utah soon led Mormon leaders to seek out new lands to settle, and as with most things Mormon, the effort was deliberate and organized. In 1873, a scouting expedition was sent by Brigham Young to the Little Colorado River in northeastern Arizona with the hope of discovering suitable new lands. The expedition returned with news of a bleak and rugged area with little hope for settlement. A second expedition in 1875 reached a point farther up the same valley and returned with a more favorable report, prompting Young to send four parties of 50 men each and their families to found four settlements. The settlers were to live according to the principles of the United Order, a recently conceived Mormon plan for communal living that required the community to pool its resources and labor for the common good. The social experiment was largely a failure, as was this initial effort to settle along the lower Little Colorado. The temperamental river alternated between providing too little water and washing away carefully erected irrigation works, and after a few years of struggle three of the four towns were abandoned. Only St. Joseph survived, and only as a small group of families (McClintock 1985:138–148; Peterson 1973:15–23; Sheridan 1995: 191–195).

But Mormons soon founded towns farther up the Little Colorado, along its tributaries, and eventually farther south, along the Salt and Gila Rivers. Eventually, about 20 successful towns were established in the basin of the Little Colorado River, most of which survive today as predominantly Mormon communities. Along the Salt River, the town of Mesa was first settled in 1878 near a large, refurbished Hohokam irrigation canal. Thanks in large part to the agriculture made possible by the canal, Mesa was a relatively affluent community, a model of Mormon town planning, and soon the largest of several Mormon communities in what is now the Phoenix area (McClintock 1985:211–224). In 1927, a massive temple was dedicated at Mesa, still the only Mormon temple in Arizona, although a second Arizona temple has recently been proposed for Snowflake, one of the early Mormon settlements along Silver Creek, a tributary of the Little Colorado River (Julien 2000).

Mormon settlement of southernmost Arizona occurred at about the same time as the settlement of the Salt and Gila Valleys, but the numbers of Mormons south of the Gila never compared with their numbers farther north. In 1877, a Mormon party headed south from the Salt River Valley hoping to settle in either the upper Gila Valley or the San Pedro Valley. The party spent several months in the Santa Rita Mountains south of Tucson while the men worked in a sawmill. After earning enough money to buy more supplies and livestock, the group moved on to a spot along the San Pedro River about 9 miles south of modern Benson. In 1880, after two years of hardship in a temporary camp, the settlers laid out the town of St. David, named for David Patten, an early Mormon martyred with Joseph Smith in Nauvoo. A second Mormon settlement, MacDonald, was established just up the river from St. David in 1882, and a third settlement, Miramonte, was founded 9 miles west of St. David in 1913 (McClintock 1985:232–236).

The San Pedro settlements benefited briefly from the short-lived economic prosperity of nearby Tombstone, which enjoyed a mining boom in the early 1880s, but the settlements never became much more than small farming communities. They did, however, play an important role as stepping stones for Mormon colonization of northern Mexico. With the consent of Mexican president Porfirio Díaz, Mormon settlement parties began entering the Mexican states of Chihuahua and Sonora in 1886, establishing themselves in a series of colonies on large tracts of land purchased from or granted by the Mexican government. These colonies (named as such, e.g., Colonia Juárez, Colonia Oaxaca, Colonia Morelos) followed the typical Mormon pattern of settlement, with careful town plans, cooperative agricultural works, and schools, and the Mormons were generally well received by the local Mexican population. The Mormon tenure in the region came to an end with the Mexican Revolution, when the favors granted them by Díaz became a source of resentment for rebel forces, and their crops and livestock became constant targets of rebel confiscations. By 1915, halfway through the revolution, most of the Mormon settlers in Mexico had fled back to the United States (Burns and Naylor 1973; McClintock 1985:266–275).

The Mormon Community at Binghampton

One destination for the Mormons returning from Mexico was Nephi Bingham's recently established settlement along the Rillito. Binghampton was unusual among Mormon settlements in Arizona in not having been settled as part of a planned effort directed by Mormon leaders in Utah. Accounts of the actual origins of the settlement are somewhat confused (see the discussion by Ciolek-Torrello and Homburg 1990:73), but it is clear that Nephi Bingham first bought the property on the north bank of the Rillito around 1898. Bingham brought his second wife and their children to his new property (his first wife remained in Utah), and he was soon joined by his father, Erastus Bingham, who arrived from Colorado with his entire family. Nephi Bingham bought his land from Alexander Davidson, a non-Mormon who continued to have ties to Bingham and the rest of the Mormon community for many years later. The

Bingham family, which included 35 children, cleared land for farming, built houses and a small adobe school, planted vegetable gardens, and, by 1905, had started a dairy operation. In 1899, a cemetery plot was designated on the north edge of the little settlement; the cemetery still exists and includes the grave of Nephi Bingham, who died in 1916 (Ciolek-Torrello and Homburg 1990:73–74; Day 1988; Parkhurst 2001).

The first extrafamilial additions to the community came in 1908, when a Mormon resident of Colonia Dublán in Chihuahua visited the Binghams and decided that he would transfer his family there. The move ultimately involved four or more families from Chihuahua and led to more house-building, land-clearing, and irrigation works. From our research into the history of irrigation in the study area (see above), it appears that the principal irrigation ditches in the vicinity of Nephi Bingham's original property probably predated Bingham's arrival, although he undoubtedly made improvements and modifications to the system, including the construction of a large reservoir just behind his house. The community soon expanded to the south side of the Rillito, where a school was built as early as 1905 on land donated by Alexander Davidson. The school remained in Mormon hands until 1928, when it was taken over by Pima County. The original building still stands, although it has been modified beyond recognition and is incorporated into the auditorium of modern Davidson Elementary School (Ciolek-Torrello and Homburg 1990:73–74; Day 1988; Gursky 1994; Parkhurst 2001; Rogers 1993; Sterner 1996:16–17).

Most important among the changes that followed the initial influx of settlers from Mexico was the organization of the first branch of the Mormon church in Tucson, in 1910. The organization proceedings and the ordination of Heber Farr as the first branch president were officiated by the president of the Mormon California Mission and took place in Nephi Bingham's home, right after Nephi and his family were baptized in the settlement's irrigation reservoir. The name chosen for the branch was Binghampton. Six years later, Farr purchased a 60-acre parcel on the south side of the Rillito and platted the Lohrum subdivision, where members of the community bought lots and built houses. The subdivision was bounded on the south by what is now Fort Lowell Road, on the east by Alvernon Way, on the west by Dodge Boulevard, and on the north by Kleindale Road. This area subsequently became the core of the growing Mormon settlement, (Ciolek-Torrello and Homburg 1990:74; Parkhurst 2001).

Achieving the status of branch in 1910 may have been part of the reason that Binghampton became a destination for Mormons leaving Mexico in the wake of the revolution, although, as noted above, a connection between Binghampton and at least one of the Chihuahua colonies was already established. In any case, the exodus from Mexico began to deposit Mormon families in Binghampton as early as 1911. By 1913, the branch membership had tripled. Many new families lived temporarily in tents along the south side of the Rillito and at Jaynes Station, a stop along the Southern Pacific Railroad near the confluence of the Rillito and the Santa Cruz Rivers. The Jaynes Station settlement arose in response to a company located there that employed the newly arrived Mormons in clearing land. After the work was completed, the Mormon families either settled at Binghampton or moved on to Mormon communities elsewhere in Arizona. The new arrivals at Binghampton eventually settled up and down the Rillito River, as far east as the confluence of Tanque Verde Creek and Pantano Wash, and as far west as Country Club Road (Ciolek-Torrello and Homburg 1990:76; Parkhurst 2001; Rogers 1993).

Binghampton remained a small, largely self-contained Mormon community until the 1940s, when it finally began to be absorbed into the city of Tucson. By 1926, the Binghampton branch of the Mormon church had grown large enough to become a ward, the next level in the church hierarchy. A new church was completed at Binghampton in 1928, along the south side of Fort Lowell Road. Additions to the church in the period 1959–1962 and in the 1970s expanded it to its current size, and it now serves three Tucson wards. Examples of early pioneer houses survive in the neighborhood, and the original cemetery remains in Mormon control, but Binghampton is no longer a primarily Mormon settlement. Nonetheless, recognition of Binghampton as the original center of Mormon life in Tucson has prompted an ongoing effort by residents, former residents, and descendants of former residents, as well as Pima County, to preserve the historic character of the area (Mann 1991; Parkhurst 2001). A discussion of Binghampton as an archaeological site, AZ BB:9:238, and the proposed NRHP Binghampton Rural Historic Landscape is provided in Chapter 5.

Residential and Other Development after 1920

Between 1880 and 1920, Tucson's population grew from around 7,000 to over 20,000. By 1940, the population was almost double the latter figure. As early as the late 1880s, Tucson had become a mecca for the ill, and people suffering from a variety of ailments, including arthritis, asthma, and tuberculosis, were flocking to southern Arizona for its arid climate and year-round sunshine. Healthy tourists also contributed to the city's growing population and economy, as Easterners traveled west to experience the natural wonders of Arizona. The Tucson Sunshine Climate Club, organized in 1922, worked hard to promote Tucson as a haven of pleasure and health, as well as the city's role as the preeminent tourism, trade, and distribution center in southern Arizona (Luckingham 1982:29, 86). Other factors contributed to Tucson's rapid growth, but the climate remained the city's prime attraction, and each winter saw an increase in visitors over the previous year. Some visitors became permanent residents, whereas others purchased second homes for the winter months. The influx of people forced newcomers to locate ever farther from the city center. To keep pace with Tucson's growth, residential subdivisions and related development sprang up around the city, including along and near the Rillito.

In this section, we look at one important example of residential development in the vicinity of the Río Antiguo study area and several examples of related local developments, including churches, schools, and entertainment and recreation opportunities.

Catalina Foothills Estates

In the late 1920s and early 1930s, John and Helen Murphey acquired nearly 8,000 acres of federal and state land in the Catalina foothills for an average of $15 per acre (Figure 35). This was prime real estate that they would soon transform into Tucson's most prestigious residential area—the Catalina Foothills Estates. Murphey, a Tucson native, was the city's first big land speculator and home builder. With his wife, Helen, who was both a business and artistic partner, and Swiss architect Josias T. Joesler, they formed an architectural and construction team that made significant contributions to the modern Tucson landscape. Leo B. Keith became a partner and financial manager of the Murphey Building Company in 1929, and five years later the company changed its name to the John W. Murphey–Leo B. Keith Building Company to reflect Keith's increasing involvement (City of Tucson 1994:6).

The first phase in Murphey's development strategy focused on the area north of the intersection of Campbell Avenue and River Road, 3 miles from what were then the Tucson city limits. With county approval, Murphey carved roads into the foothills and dug a large well to supply the development with water. Power and telephone lines were extended from the city and construction of the first homes began in 1930. In the early 1930s, Pima County built a bridge across the Rillito at Campbell Avenue, providing direct access to the new residential development. To fully develop the subdivision, Murphey had to market the area's desirability as a place for home sites. He did this by promoting the qualities of open space, spectacular views, mild winter climate, and natural vegetation—country living with city conveniences. An advertisement in a local newspaper described the "distinctive livable homes on four- to ten-acre lots covered with beautiful desert growth. Quiet, restful, practically no dust . . . and only 10 minutes from town" (ADS, 9 October 1938). To attract prominent buyers, Murphey controlled the development with comprehensive deed restrictions which gave his company final say in all decisions regarding real estate, design, and construction. Covenants governing the Catalina Foothills Estates limited development to residential purposes only, prohibited the removal or destruction of native vegetation, and

SALE RECEIPT   **Original**

Grant *SL.*

STATE LAND DEPARTMENT

Tucson Arizona, *Sept. 15-30*

Place of Sale

Sold to *John H Murphy Blg. G*

Address *N.E.º G ~* *Tucson*

Tract *NE¼ S ~*

Sec. *16* T *13 S* R *14 E* Acres *480*

Appr. of Land Under Lease to .... $ *7200* ⁰⁰

Appr. of Impr. Claimed by *John H Murphy* $ *6700* ⁰⁰

Highest bid for Land .... $ *1*

Highest bid for Improvements .... $

Rent due from .... $

Interest due from .... $

Total Rent and Interest .... $

Total Appr. and Sale Cost .... $

Receipt To Purchaser:

.... per cent of Sale Price of Land .... $ *360.00*

Amount to cover Cost of Sale .... $

.... per cent of Purchase Price of Impr. .... $

Class and Appr. fee (2%) on Land .... $ *144.00*

Class and Appr. fee (2%) on Impr. .... $

Certificate of Purchase Fee .... $ *3.00*

Patent Fee .... $

Total Rent and Interest .... $

Miscellaneous .... $

.... $

Total Paid by Purchaser .... $ *507* ⁰⁰

Sales Report No. *4929*
C. P. or Pat. No.

Geo. A. Macdonall

Sales Agent.

PAID
12318
SEP 18 1930

Figure 35. Sales receipt for land in the Santa Catalina foothills
purchased by John Murphey (Murphey 1930).

136

required that the architecture of all homes conform to the natural landscape of southern Arizona, thereby preserving both the landscape and the views (City of Tucson 1994:12–14). By the fall of 1939, Murphey had sold 38 separate residences with another six under construction (Murphey 1939).

Josias T. Joesler designed many of the homes in the initial and later phases of the Catalina Foothills Estates and supervised the other architects working for Murphey. Born in Zurich, Switzerland in 1895, Joesler studied architecture, engineering, drawing, and history. He traveled extensively through Europe, North Africa, and Latin America. In 1926, Joesler and his Spanish wife, Natividad, moved to Los Angeles where he established himself as an architect. Upon the recommendation of a fellow architect, Joesler moved to Tucson in 1927 to work with Murphey. Joesler was well known for his ability to blend regional, historic, and contemporary styles to create his own Southwestern look. He drew heavily upon the Southwestern Revival tradition—Mission Revival, Spanish Colonial Revival, Pueblo Revival, and Sonoran Revival, all of which were popular in the United States. Many of the Joesler-designed showcase houses in the Catalina Foothills Estates followed a Southwestern theme—Casa Mexicana, Pueblo House, and Santa Fe House.

In 1940, Joesler and Murphey moved their offices from Fourth Avenue near downtown to St. Philip's Plaza, a Mexican-style plaza designed and constructed by the architect and builder team and consisting of five buildings around a central park (Figure 36). The buildings, constructed between 1936 and 1940, include St. Philip's in the Hills church (1936), El Merendero Tea Room and Gift Shop (1937), Catalina Foothills Estates Sales Office/Joesler Studio (1937), Hutton Webster Art Studio and residence (1939), and Murphey-Keith Building Company Office (1940). Located at the intersection of Campbell Avenue and River Road, St. Philip's Plaza served as the community center to the foothills development (Tucson Magazine 1936; City of Tucson 1994:13, 14–16).

The Murpheys' created an upscale community of southwestern style homes, nestled in the foothills on large lots with spectacular mountain views (Figure 37). By combining rural character with municipal conveniences such as public utilities, transportation facilities, and a public school, Catalina Foothills Estates provided a complete lifestyle and was one of the first master-planned communities in southern Arizona.

St. Philip's in the Hills Episcopal Church

The history of St. Philip's in the Hills Episcopal Church has been covered extensively in previous studies (Abbott 1986; Strittmatter 2000) and only an outline is presented here. Central to this discussion is the property's significance as an example of a major local architectural style.

St. Philip's in the Hills church, located at the northeast corner of the intersection of Campbell Avenue and River Road, is a religious and architectural landmark (Figure 38). The inspiration for the church came from George W. Ferguson, a seminary-trained reverend without a parish, and builder John W. Murphey. Ferguson and his wife, May, moved to Tucson in 1935. Murphey built the Ferguson's home, to which the reverend considered adding a chapel. Murphey countered with an offer to build a small church in the Catalina foothills on land that he would donate. Moreover, he agreed to construct the church at cost. Swiss-born architect Josias T. Joesler designed the Spanish Colonial–style church, which is considered one of his most important works. The church was completed on December 23, 1936, and the Reverend Ferguson conducted the first service, a midnight Eucharist, on Christmas Eve. The final bill was a nominal $17,700 (Abbott 1986:2–5, 8).

Southwest of St. Philip's is a Joesler-designed central courtyard, modeled after a typical Mexican plaza. The plaza predates the church and served as the gateway to the Catalina Foothills Estates. Bounded by River Road to the south and Campbell Avenue to the west, the original walled park included benches, an exterior wall fountain, central courtyard fountain, landscaping, and dirt paths to the three entries.

Figure 36. St. Philip's Plaza, view to the north-northwest, ca. 1950. The intersection of Campbell Avenue and River Road is at the lower left. The old River Road alignment, visible at left, jogged to the north of the three Joesler-designed buildings to the west of Campbell (photograph courtesy of the Arizona Historical Society, Tucson, Magee Photograph Collection, Accession No. 753).

Figure 37. Catalina Foothills Estates residential subdivision, view to the northwest, May 1941 River Road runs from left to right. Note the paved residential road extending north of River (photograph courtesy of the Arizona Historical Society, Tucson, Magee Photograph Collection, Accession No. 5943).

In 1937, Murphey built the Catalina Foothills Estates sales office on the west side of Campbell. Later that same year, he added a tea room east of the park and just north of River Road. In 1939, he constructed a studio just north of the sales office and the following year he erected the new offices of the Murphey-Keith Building Company directly south of the tract office (Figure 39). All of the buildings surrounding the plaza were designed by Joesler and reflected his distinctive southwestern style. Collectively, the five buildings surrounding the plaza constituted the community center for the Catalina Foothills Estates. John and Helen Murphey deeded the courtyard to the church in 1949, with the proviso that it remain a park in perpetuity (Strittmatter 2000:8–9).

St. Philip's was the fourth Episcopal church in Tucson and, in its early years, experienced rapid growth. On February 2, 1939, St. Philip's received parish status. The following year, an addition was built for a church school and counseling facility for the Rector. Joesler drew up the plans at no charge and Murphey once again agreed to do the work at cost. Church member Scott B. Appleby pledged $2,500 and the congregation raised the remainder to finance the $7,500 addition. Several years later, Appleby

**Figure 38. St. Philip's in the Hills Episcopal Church today,
view to the north.**

worked with Joesler to design a transept to enlarge the church. The addition, completed in 1947, provided seating for 125 more parishioners (Abbott 1986:21). In 1950, the parish purchased El Merendero Tea Room from Murphey and renamed it La Parroquia, Spanish for "parish hall" (Abbott 1986:22). The following year the church added classrooms, a gallery, a cloistered patio, and storage room. Joesler worked with the church to design other additions and modifications until his death in 1956. Gordon Leupke, Joesler's former student and a St. Philip's parishioner, took over as church architect. He relied upon Joesler's notes and drawings to ensure that future additions retained the original style (Abbott 1986:25).

Over the years, improvements and realignments to Campbell and River have adversely affected the plaza. A 1965 widening project along Campbell Avenue resulted in the loss of property on the west side, and the reconstruction of a new west wall caused the fountain to lose its central location. Road construction in 1984 damaged the southwest corner of the plaza wall, requiring its reconstruction. A realignment

Figure 39. Murphey-Keith Building Company office today, view to the northwest. The Murphey Investment Trust currently occupies this historic building designed by noted architect Josias T. Joesler.

of River Road east of Campbell the following year necessitated the removal of the south wall and its reconstruction to the north (Strittmatter 2000). The current project to widen the intersection of Campbell Avenue and River Road has compromised the integrity of the plaza once again (Figure 40), this time taking a strip approximately 15 feet wide across the south side of the plaza, requiring the reconstruction of both the south and west walls.

St. Philip's in the Hills has a strong presence in Tucson. Apart from its religious significance, St. Philip's is an important example of the collaborative efforts of Murphey and Joesler and represents a major local architectural style. The additions, modifications, and renovations of the church have significantly altered the original structure. Nevertheless, the integrity of style has been retained because of the efforts of Joesler, Leupke, and later architects. In terms of function, over the years the church has benefitted the larger community by serving as a meeting place for secular groups and hosting cultural events.

Schools

Several private and public schools, catering to a variety of needs and ages, have existed within the study area. Hacienda del Sol, founded in 1929, had the distinction of being the first private school for girls in the Southwest. Joesler designed the southwestern-style adobe main building, and John and Helen Murphey built and helped operate the school. Situated in the foothills of the Santa Catalina Mountains on Hacienda del Sol Road, east of Campbell Avenue and north of River Road, the school offered students a traditional college preparatory curriculum and a varied recreational program, including horseback riding,

141

**Figure 40. St. Philip's Plaza courtyard today, view to the northwest.
Note the newly constructed bare block wall in the background, the impact of the
current project to widen Campbell Avenue and River Road.**

tennis, archery, and basketball. In 1937, the school established an accredited two-year junior college program that included specialized courses in Spanish and the art, architecture, and archaeology of the Southwest (Tucson Magazine 1938a). The school closed in 1944 and reopened shortly thereafter as the Hacienda del Sol Ranch Hotel, which offered guests the rugged beauty of the southwestern desert with comfortable amenities and recreational activities. Over the years, the hotel went through a succession of owners. In 1993, a limited partnership acquired the property in a foreclosure for $1.6 million in cash. The new owners restored the property to its 1940s splendor and the Hacienda del Sol currently operates as a guest ranch resort (*ADS*, 27 June 1993). It is interesting to note that the 1940 Tucson City Directory lists George W. Ferguson, Rector of St. Philip's in the Hills Episcopal Church, as president of Hacienda del Sol School for Girls.

John and Helen Murphey started the River Road School in 1931 to serve the growing number of children living in their housing development, the Catalina Foothills Estates. The Murpheys, along with other taxpayers in the foothills, did not want their district annexed to the Amphitheater School District, and in June 1931, they successfully petitioned the Pima County School Superintendent and Board of Supervisors to create School District Number 16, later known as Catalina Foothills School District (School District No. 16 1931). Nine children attended the first session with Helen Murphey providing many of the school supplies. The school met in the garage of a house in the subdivision that had not sold. In January 1939, Murphey sold 2.2 acres on River Road to the Catalina Foothills School District for the sole purpose of erecting a public school building. The district purchased the land for $10.00. That

142

summer, architect Joesler designed a two-room Mission Revival–style schoolhouse with a bell tower. The Works Progress Administration constructed the school under the supervision of the Murphey–Keith Building Company (Figure 41). Heavy beams supported the flat roof, which Joesler designed to provide an unobstructed view of the Santa Catalina Mountains to the north. Adobe bricks used in the construction were manufactured on the school grounds.

The River Road School met the needs of the growing foothills community, providing a public education to students in grades 1–6 (grades 7–8 were added in the late 1960s). In 1966, the district added five classrooms and a multipurpose room to accommodate the burgeoning student enrollment. In 1972, the school was renamed the Murphey School in honor of the man who had envisioned it. The original building at 2101 E. River Road now houses the Catalina Foothills District's administrative offices (Figure 42) (Catalina Foothills School District 1988; Jewett 1986:10–11, 46).

The Valley School for Girls, a private school located off Swan Road just north of the river, opened in Tucson in 1952 after four years at Tumacacori. Resident students and local day students at the non-sectarian girls school followed a traditional college preparatory curriculum with an emphasis on foreign languages, art, and music (*ADS*, 17 May 1956). The school apparently closed in 1972 after a brief and unsuccessful merger with Southern Arizona School for Boys. Originally situated on a 60-acre parcel that had been a dude ranch in the 1930s and early 1940s, much of the land has given way to residential development. Several of the original, single-story buildings remain and currently serve as private residences.

The Verde Desert Ranch School (later known as the Desert Ranch School of Arizona), a private school for Jewish boys grades 4–12, was located east of the intersection of present day Fort Lowell and Swan Roads, south of the Rillito. Students received instruction in Judaism in addition to their regular course work. Classes were held outdoors under shaded ramadas, and recreational activities included horseback riding, baseball, tennis, badminton, and shuffleboard. Students at Desert Ranch School of Arizona, according to the promotional literature, lived, studied, and recreated in an environment where "[i]mproved sinews of brain, character and body are inevitably accomplished under the sun and stars of the historical romantic Southwest" (Tucson Magazine 1938b, 1939). We have not found any solid information on the dates of operation of the school, only references as early as 1938 and as late as 1940 (Tucson City Directory 1940).

Entertainment and Recreation

During the same period that the Río Antiguo study area was experiencing the beginnings of residential development and the construction of churches and schools, it was also hosting a variety of businesses devoted to entertainment and recreation. Some of these businesses were unique to the study area; others linked the area to categories of businesses springing up around the Tucson Basin and elsewhere in the Southwest.

Dude Ranches

During the Depression years, raising cattle was an unpredictable business and many cattle operations folded. Dude ranching, on the other hand, enjoyed a boom. Ranches like the Flying V near present-day Ventana Canyon Resort (Figure 43) went from primarily cattle operations with a few guest cottages to full-fledged resorts with polo fields, tennis courts, and other amenities (Sheridan 1995:242; Sonnichsen 1982:221). Dude ranches first developed in Arizona in the 1920s, and proliferated during the 1930s, 1940s, and 1950s. The first dude ranch in southern Arizona was probably Rancho Linda Vista, which opened near Oracle in 1925. The Flying V started taking guests in the fall of 1927 and at its peak boasted a 14-month waiting list (Henry 1992:212; *ADS*, 17 October 1971).

Figure 41. Catalina Foothills School under construction, view to the northeast, 1939. River Road is in the foreground (photograph courtesy of the Arizona Historical Society, Tucson, Accession No. 7417).

Figure 42. River Road School today, view to the northeast.

The early dude ranches catered to the affluent from the East and California who stayed for several months while participating in regular ranch activities like roundups and fence-mending. By contrast, the typical dude ranch guest of the 1940s and 1950s preferred to look, sound, and feel like a cowboy rather than work like one. While the early dude ranches were working cattle ranches, by the mid-1930s the facilities began offering guests fewer genuine ranch activities. Instead, ranch owners created an atmosphere that paid homage to the rustic life on the range with horseback riding, hayrides, chuck wagon cookouts, and sing-alongs under the stars. This touch of western realism was balanced with resort-style comforts—all in a healthy, scenic, and socially intimate environment (Norris 1976:220).

Dude ranches began to appear in the study area around 1930 (Figure 44). Some lasted for only a year or two, while others survived well into the 1950s by adopting a stronger resort orientation. The Harding Guest Ranch, Desert Manor Ranch, and Catalina Guest Ranch were all located at 3838 North Campbell Avenue (current site of the University of Arizona Campus Agricultural Center), operating at different times during the period 1930–1952. Hacienda del Sol Ranch Hotel, originally a private girls school, was located in the Catalina foothills. El Rancho Rillito operated from 1946 to 1954 just off of River Road near the river's big bend. The Vista al Norte Ranch, on Fort Lowell Road east of Columbus Boulevard, provided guests with a western-style experience from 1935 to 1958. Las Moras Ranch, located at 3801 N. Swan Road, opened in 1931 and changed its name to Rancho Las Moras three years later. Rancho Las Moras ceased operations in 1937, and in 1940, the Valley Ranch opened for business but folded the same year. The Valley Ranch property would later become the site of the Valley School for Girls, a private, nonsectarian girls school. From 1942–1943, Rancho de la Sombra operated on the present site of Tucson Country Club.

Figure 43. Flying V Dude Ranch, ca. 1941 (photograph courtesy of the Arizona Historical Society, Tucson, Magee Photograph Collection, Accession No. 1288).

There were basically two types of ranches: the working cattle ranch with guest facilities and the nonworking guest ranch, which was not on the grounds of a working ranch but featured riding and other Western-style activities. With the exception of the Flying V, all of the ranches in the study area were of the latter type (Norris 1976:233, 250–255). The ranches varied in size, able to accommodate anywhere from a half dozen to four dozen guests. Most of the dude ranches discriminated against Jews and convalescents. An advertisement for one ranch stated unequivocally, "No person having a communicable disease will be accepted as a guest" (Henry 1992:212).

The western-oriented dude ranch reached its greatest popularity in the late 1940s with approximately 100 ranches in and around Tucson, prompting the tourism-promoting Sunshine Climate Club to proclaim Tucson "The Capitol of the Dude Ranch Country" (Norris 1976:222; Luckingham 1982:66). Today, only a handful of ranches remain, all on the outskirts of town. Guests now stay for a few days or weeks rather than months. The term "dude ranch" has given way to "guest ranch," or the more contemporary "ranch resort." Regardless of the name, the ranches remain a western institution.

146

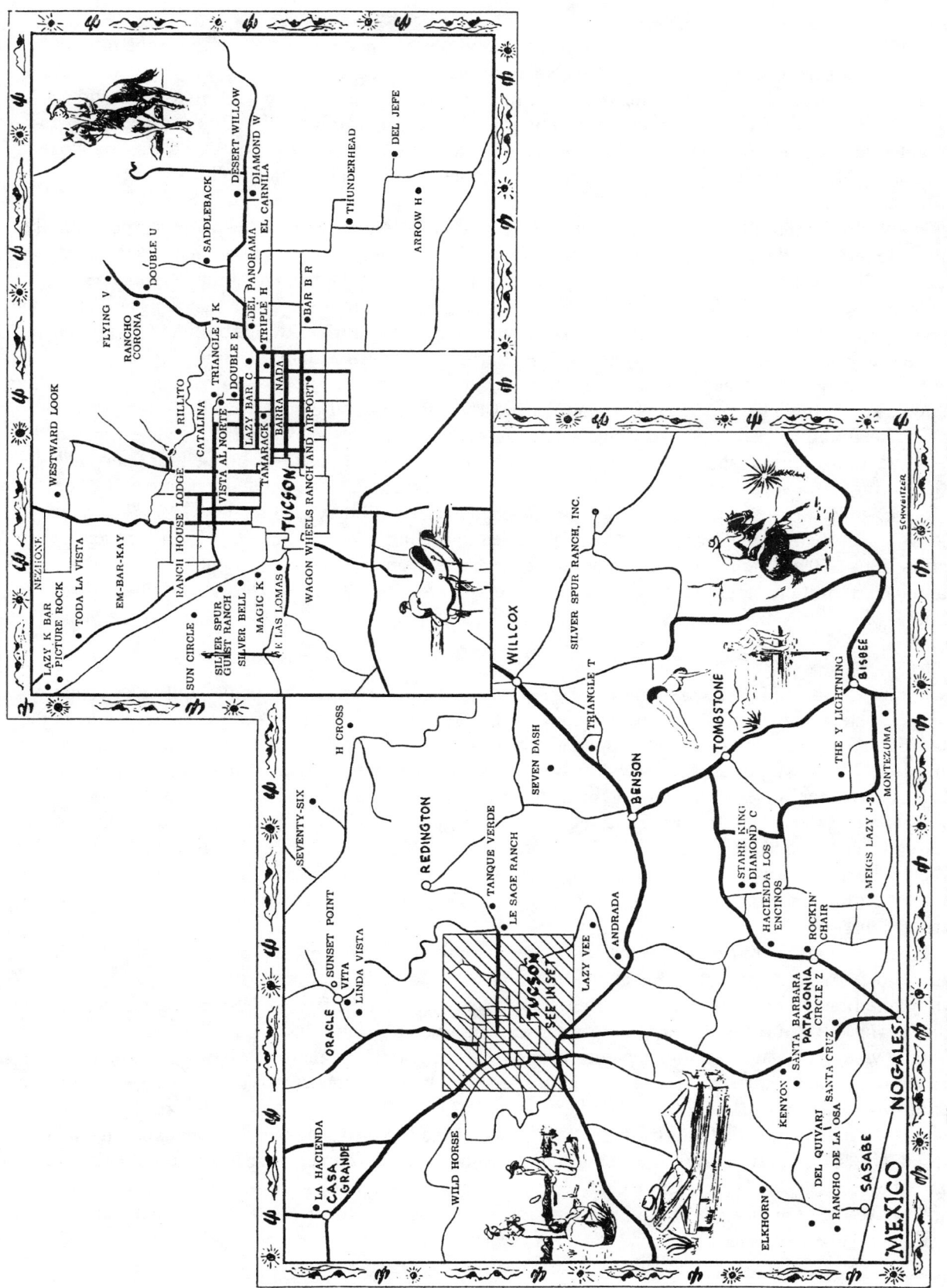

Figure 44. Portion of a 1948 map of guest ranches in the Tucson area (Chamber of Commerce 1948).

147

Wetmore Amusement Park

Edward L. Wetmore, Sr., moved to Tucson in 1878, and settled on 160 acres of land near the present-day intersection of Limberlost and Oracle Roads, south of the Rillito River. The Tucson Mall, which opened in March 1982, now stands on the site of the Wetmore family home. Wetmore was an assayer and cattle rancher, and operated Tucson's first nursery. His sons, Edward and Ralph, raised their respective families on the family homestead. Ralph Wetmore drilled water wells and mining holes all over Arizona, and is credited with creating many of the roads that snaked into the Santa Catalina foothills by hauling his drilling equipment (Wetmore n.d.).

The Wetmore family holds the distinction of building the first Olympic-size swimming pool and the first outdoor movie theater in the state. In 1918, Edward Wetmore, Jr., built a pool measuring 20 by 40 feet for his brother and sister-in-law, Ralph and Helen Wetmore. Helen taught the neighborhood kids how to swim, and soon the locals who came out to buy produce from the Wetmore gardens and orchards were taking a dip to cool off. The Wetmore pool became so popular that Edward built an Olympic-size pool with a 30-foot-high diving board and a slide. Early on, the pool had no filtration system, so the Wetmores changed the water twice a week and let it run out to irrigate the rows of fruit trees surrounding the pool. The family charged 25 cents for adults and 15 cents for children to swim.

The Wetmore property became a favorite recreation spot for Tucsonans. In 1922, the family added other attractions, thus creating the Wetmore Amusement Park, which featured an open-air dance hall with a spring-suspended double maple floor, outdoor movie theater, roller rink, and picnic park. The Wetmore family ran the dance floor, pool, and other facilities until they sold them in 1945. The dance hall subsequently burned down but the pool remained in use until the mid-seventies. Among their many contributions to the area, the Wetmores built Wetmore Road, an east-west thoroughfare, and paved and maintained it until the early 1920s when they turned it over to Pima County (Henry 1992:3–4; Jewett 1986:64–65).

Rillito Racetrack

The Rillito Racetrack is located on the north bank of the Rillito between Campbell and First Avenues, near the western limit of the Río Antiguo study area. The Rillito Racetrack Chute, an integral part of the Rillito Racetrack, is listed on both the State and National Register of Historic Places. The track was first built in 1943 by J. Rukin Jelks, who was raising quarter horses on the 88-acre parcel. Beginning in the late 1930s, quarter horse racing enjoyed considerable local and regional popularity, with crowds of up to 3,000 attending the Sunday afternoon races at the Moltacqua Turf Club on Sabino Canyon Road. Bob Locke, owner of the Moltacqua track, sold the property in 1942 (Henry 1992:195). In 1943, Jelks carved a track in his backyard and with the help of fellow horse breeders Jake Meyer and Melville Haskell, made the Rillito Racetrack the site of the first organized and regulated quarter horse racing in the United States (Figure 45).

There are a number of other "firsts" associated with the Rillito Racetrack. The Rillito was the first quarter horse track to have a $^3/_8$-mile chute independent of the oval track, the first to have pari-mutuel betting, the first to experiment with weight to handicap races, and the first to use a photoelectric timer. Melville Haskell teamed with Tucson veterinarian Van Smelker, Jr., to develop and perfect an electronic timing device to measure race times precisely and to determine the winners of close races. The device was simple. Haskell and Smelker placed a high-speed clock next to the track on the finish line and filmed the finish with a movie camera from the judges' stand. Race officials would examine the film frame by frame as each horse touched the finish line. The clock in the background showed how much time had elapsed. Haskell's contributions to the sport did not end there. He adapted the rules and regulations for quarter horse racing from the Jockey Club rules for racing thoroughbreds, earning him the title "The Father of Modern Quarter Horse Racing" (Committee to Preserve Historic Rillito Racetrack n.d.; Rillito Race Track 1988; Vinik and Wegner 1984).

Figure 45. Rillito Racetrack, built by J. Rukin Jelks, view to the northeast, ca. 1946.
The three-eighths of a mile chute is adjacent to the south side of the oval track. River Road is visible at top
(photograph courtesy of the Arizona Historical Society, Tucson, Magee Photograph Collection, Accession No. 272).

The chute at Rillito Racetrack is a straight leg of prepared dirt measuring three-eighths of a mile long by 45 feet wide and is adjacent to the south side of the oval track. By 1945, every track holding quarter horse races was using the "chute system" and the Rillito regulations. In 1953, the adjoining oval track was enlarged to accommodate trotters and thoroughbreds.

The racetrack closed in May 1982 and Pima County acquired the property. Shortly thereafter a community effort began to preserve the property and to have it recognized as a historic property. A group known as the Committee to Preserve Historic Rillito Racetrack successfully petitioned the county to designate the track as the official Pima County racetrack for a period of at least 25 years. The Rillito Racetrack Historical Review Committee was formed to take on the task of preserving and reopening the track. On May 21, 1986, the Pima County Board of Supervisors voted to make the Rillito Racetrack a county park in perpetuity, and on January 23, 1988, the track reopened. The Rillito Racetrack is significant for its pivotal role in the development of a national sport and its overall impact on the horse racing industry.

Valley of the Moon

The Valley of the Moon (AZ BB:9:111), located just east of Tucson Boulevard and not far south of the Rillito, is a simulated fairyland for children created by George Phar Legler. Legler came to Tucson in 1916 as an electrician for the railroad and later worked until retirement as a postal clerk. In 1923, he purchased 2.5 acres of land on Allen Road. He hauled in tons of rock and cement and over the next several years constructed a fantasy land of tunnels, towers, caves, and waterfalls. The Valley of the Moon opened to the public in 1932 (Figure 46).

Legler guided children and adults on nighttime tours through the eerie landscape of fairy temples, enchanted castles, and mystic grottoes. Adults could make reservations for nocturnal metaphysical health tours of the grounds. Admission was free but a donation box at the gate collected enough money to help with the utility bills. In a 1945 handbill, Legler described his creation:

> Mineralized rock cliffs, caves, pools, and garden miniatures have been blended with tropical and desert flora to create the fantasy "touch of three": Edgar Allen Poe, Robert Louis Stevenson, and Alice in Wonderland. A tour through this scenic center has been a memorable experience for thousands of people [Valley of the Moon Memorial Association 1945].

Beginning in the 1940s, Saturday afternoon visitors were treated to Bunnyland Theater, an 11-act program that featured a troupe of trained rabbits. Legler and his rabbits performed at the Los Angeles County Fair in 1948 and the Valley of the Moon gained popularity, receiving favorable press in 1953 issues of *McCall's* and *Life* magazines. Known as the "Gnome of Tucson" or the "Mountain Gnome," Legler made his home in one of the caves he created.

Throughout the 1950s and 1960s, Legler continued to give tours, but in 1971, declining health forced him to close the Valley of the Moon. The site had fallen into a state of disrepair when a group of teenagers who had visited the amusement park as children set out to restore the fantasy world they remembered. With Legler's approval, the teenagers and their families formed the Valley of the Moon Restoration Association. Before his death in 1982 at the age of 97, Legler deeded the property to the Association, which later became the George Phar Legler Memorial Society. During the 1980s and 1990s the Valley of the Moon was open intermittently for productions and tours. Today, the amusement park is closed temporarily, but it maintains a telephone listing with a voice message soliciting volunteers to repair the facility for future programs. The Valley of the Moon has been listed in the State Register of Historic Places since 1975.

Figure 46. Entrance to George Phar Legler's Valley of the Moon fantasy land, n.d. (photograph courtesy of the Arizona Historical Society, Tucson, Accession No. 78096).

Tucson Country Club

Today, public and private golf courses abound in Tucson, but that was not always the case. Prior to World War II, Tucson's golf enthusiasts had few options. Long-time Tucsonan Roy Drachman remembered a nine-hole course at the northwest corner of Campbell Avenue and Speedway Boulevard that operated for a few years in the early 1900s. The Tucson Golf and Country Club opened in August 1914 and closed in the early 1940s to make way for a residential subdivision. The city's only public course, located at Randolph Park, was built in the early 1920s and patronized by those who could not afford a country club membership. El Rio Country Club opened in 1929 and served as the principal course for Tucson golfers until 1948, when the Tucson Country Club was built on the east side, far from the city center (Drachman 1999:95–97).

The history of the Tucson Country Club has been reviewed by Healy (1990), whose discussion is followed here. In 1946, a group of influential Tucsonans, eager to establish a new country club, formulated a plan to create a for-profit corporation, with initial funding of $500,000, to be raised by 100 subscriptions of $5,000 each. Under the plan, the subscribers would receive shares of corporate stock and charter membership in the eventual country club. With the capital, the group planned to purchase a large tract of land suitable for a country club and adjoining residential subdivision. The original corporation was named Country Club Estates, Inc. Approximately 50 Tucsonans paid $5,000 each for subscriptions, with the remaining units sold to nonresidents, many of whom recognized Tucson's growth potential.

In September 1946, Country Club Estates paid $220,000 for approximately 580 acres of land along the south bank of Tanque Verde Creek, east of its confluence with Pantano Wash. Prior to its purchase by the corporation, the land had been bought and sold many times over the preceding years. With its close proximity to the still-active underflow ditches originating in Tanque Verde Creek, the area was prized for its fertile soil and access to water. The corporation set aside 205 acres for the country club with the remainder earmarked for the subdivision. Country Club Estates then formed a nonprofit organization, naming it Tucson Country Club. To this new entity, the corporation deeded, at no cost, the land set aside for a country club. Moreover, they lent $250,000 to Tucson Country Club for the construction of an 18-hole golf course and the remodeling of an existing residence for use as a clubhouse.

Upon completion of the golf course and clubhouse, the Tucson Country Club began selling regular memberships for $1,500. February 8, 1948, marked the formal opening of the facility. Members and guests celebrated the occasion with breakfast, a round of golf, and a buffet supper. Country Club Estates proceeded to sell lots in the subdivision known as Indian Ridge Estates because of its proximity to University Indian Ruin (AZ BB:9:33), a major Hohokam site.

Transportation

The Río Antiguo study area, like the Rillito Valley more generally, has always been slightly removed from the transportation system that developed in southern Arizona during the historical period. The Apache threat that long delayed Euroamerican settlement of the Rillito Valley also kept the valley from becoming a major transportation route, and even after settlement began in earnest in the late nineteenth century, the major transportation routes through the Tucson Basin had already been established, largely bypassing the valley. Nonetheless, the history of the routes that eventually did pass through the Rillito Valley was determined by the history of the major routes of the Tucson Basin, especially those in the Santa Cruz Valley to the east of the study area. In this section, we consider the impacts of transportation throughout the Tucson Basin on the history of the Río Antiguo study area, and how events in the study area have in turn affected the development of regional transportation.

Early Spanish Routes

The precise routes of the Spanish explorers who traversed southern Arizona in the sixteenth and seventeenth centuries are largely unknown, but they likely followed existing Native American trails. Chroniclers of the early expeditions rarely bothered to mention the Native Americans who accompanied the Spanish, but it is unlikely that any *entrada* ever set out without at least one Native American guide, and major expeditions like that of Coronado included many. The Native Americans who accompanied an expedition might not have been directly familiar with the territory they were entering, but it is safe to assume that they sought advice from their local counterparts as to where trails were and where they led. As daring as Spanish explorers might have been, they would not have chosen to blaze a new trail over using an existing one. And Native American trails were followed by travelers long after the early *entradas* had come and gone. As Stein (1994:3) put it, "In Arizona, historic routes almost always have prehistoric roots."

As we noted earlier in this chapter, Kino's interest in exploring the Pimería Alta was not limited to finding new places where he might extend his missionary enterprise. He also hoped to find a land route to Baja California, which, among other things, would make it easier to move supplies and livestock to the Jesuit missions there. During the period 1687–1711, Kino made numerous trips into almost every part of the Pimería Alta, with repeated trips down the Santa Cruz River to its confluence with the Gila, then down the Gila to its confluence with the Colorado. In addition to these natural corridors, Kino also crossed the formidable western desert of the Pimería Alta many times and by several different routes, using ancient trails that would later serve miners, trappers, and the occasional military expedition (Bolton 1948:end map).

Following the establishment of missions and *visitas* along the Santa Cruz, the river quickly became the principal Spanish route—often the only Spanish route—of commerce, communication, and settlement in southern Arizona, maintaining the region's ties with Spanish settlements in Sonora and Sinaloa. Transportation into and through the region during most of the Spanish Colonial period varied little from this north-south orientation, and the missions of the middle Santa Cruz served both as the northern terminus of the Spanish colony and as the starting point for further exploration. Expeditions heading west to California followed the route established by Kino (down the Santa Cruz to the Gila, then down the Gila to the Colorado). The most famous and consequential of these after Kino's day were the California expeditions of the Tubac presidio commander, Juan Bautista de Anza, in the last quarter of the eighteenth century.

The Anza Trail

By the 1770s, the Spanish had established missions and presidios on the California coast, but their hold on the region was tenuous at best. The small outposts (consisting of roughly 70 people each) relied on supplies brought in from more-established settlements in Mexico. The two principal supply routes—one for ships and one on land—followed the California coast, and both routes were treacherous and unreliable. To complicate matters, Russia was encroaching on the northern Pacific frontier, and French and English vessels were cruising the coast, threatening to take advantage of Spanish vulnerability. In 1773, Antonio María de Bucareli y Ursúa, viceroy of New Spain, commissioned Juan Bautista de Anza, commander of the presidio at Tubac, to establish an overland route from northern Sonora to the California missions. On January 8, 1774, the Anza expedition set out from Tubac, well equipped with pack animals, horses, and cattle for butchering en route. Marauding Apaches forced Anza to abandon his original plan of following Kino's trail down the Santa Cruz to the Gila. Instead, Anza headed south toward the Sonoran missions, then northwestward across the desert to the Colorado River. From there, the expedition continued west, eventually reaching the presidio at Monterey. This was the first continuous overland journey from northern New Spain to the coast of California Alta (Wagoner 1975:118–120).

The King of Spain promoted Anza to lieutenant colonel and chose him to lead a second expedition to colonize the San Francisco Bay area. Anza recruited settlers and soldiers in Sinaloa and Sonora, and on October 23, 1775, the expedition departed from Tubac. Francisco Garcés, the Franciscan assigned to San Xavier del Bac, accompanied the expedition, as he had the earlier expedition. On this trip, Anza followed Kino's old route to the Colorado River: down the Santa Cruz to the Gila, then west to the Colorado. From the Colorado, the expedition headed west across the California desert. The expedition reached Monterey in March 1776, and San Francisco Bay three months later, where Anza established a presidio and mission. The colonial government hoped to secure Anza's route by establishing a mission and military colony on the lower Colorado River. The Quechan living in the valley rose against the Spanish in July 1781, killing many of the missionaries and colonists, including Garcés. The massacre effectively closed the route between northern Sonora and the California settlements (Officer 1987:21; Wagoner 1975:139).

Routes of the Nineteenth and Early Twentieth Centuries

The overland route to California remained closed for over 40 years. In 1823, two years after Mexican independence, the new emperor of Mexico, Agustín de Iturbide, ordered that the road be reopened. The task fell to José Romero, commander of the Tucson presidio, who left Tucson in June 1823, accompanied by Felix Caballero, the Franciscan in charge of the California mission at Santa Catalina. Caballero had recently traveled from California to Arispe, Sonora, and his knowledge of the route proved useful on the expedition. Romero reached Santa Catalina in mid-July and reestablished the connection between southern Arizona and the settlements on the Pacific coast. Although the Quechan were at peace with Mexico throughout most of the Mexican period, few Sonorans migrated to California via the overland route. Not until the end of the Mexican-American War and the discovery of gold in California did large-scale migration take place (Officer 1987:21–22, 101–102).

Despite its relative proximity to the long-established Spanish colony in northern New Mexico, no permanent route between Arizona and New Mexico was established until Anglo-Americans pioneered one late in the period of Mexican occupation, shortly after the U.S. government declared war on Mexico. In 1846, Col. Stephen Watts Kearny, after assembling his new Army of the West at Fort Leavenworth, Kansas, embarked on a mission to conquer Mexico's northwest frontier. On August 18, Kearny and a company of 1,700 men captured Santa Fe without firing a shot. The following month Kearny and a contingent of dragoons headed south, intent on blazing a wagon trail to the Pacific coast. The expedition turned west at the head of the Gila River, then followed close along the river through rugged and desolate country all the way to its confluence with the Colorado. From there, they continued west, finally reaching San Diego in December (Wagoner 1975:260–268).

The Mormon Battalion

Kearny purposely bypassed the Mexican garrison at Tucson to avoid a confrontation, but the route he chose along the Gila proved too rugged for wagon travel. The first practical wagon route across southern Arizona was not blazed until several months later, when the Mormon Battalion, assembled in Missouri and led by Capt. Philip St. George Cooke, traveled from Santa Fe to San Diego, crossing Arizona well south of the Gila. The Mormon Battalion originally consisted of about 500 Latter-day Saints who volunteered to demonstrate their patriotism and to escape religious persecution in the Midwest (Sheridan 1995:51). Cooke dismissed a large number of Mormons as unfit for combat, and on October 19, 1846, with a force of about 340 men, the Mormon Battalion departed Santa Fe with orders to establish a wagon road to California.

The trek of the Mormon Battalion, combined with the Gadsden Purchase, would forever change the focus of travel through southern Arizona. Instead of following Kearney's route along the Gila River, Cooke and the Mormon Battalion departed from the former route in southwestern New Mexico and headed southwest (Figure 47). They entered what is now Arizona through Guadalupe Pass in the Peloncillo Mountains and, from there, headed west until they reached the San Pedro River. From the San Pedro, Cooke decided to press overland to Tucson. The Mormon Battalion passed through Tucson in December 1846, unopposed by the presidio troops. The garrison commander, Capt. Antonio Comadurán, had quietly withdrawn his men to San Xavier to avoid an armed confrontation. After an uneventful stay in Tucson, Cooke and the Mormon Battalion traveled down the Santa Cruz River to the Gila where they rejoined Kearny's route and continued west to California (Wagoner 1975:270–272).

Cooke and the Mormon Battalion created the first viable wagon road across the deserts of southern Arizona and showed that wagons could be brought into and through the region from the east, an important discovery for the years ahead. Beginning in 1848, the year the Mexican-American War ended and most of Arizona became part of the United States, the principal route of entry into the region

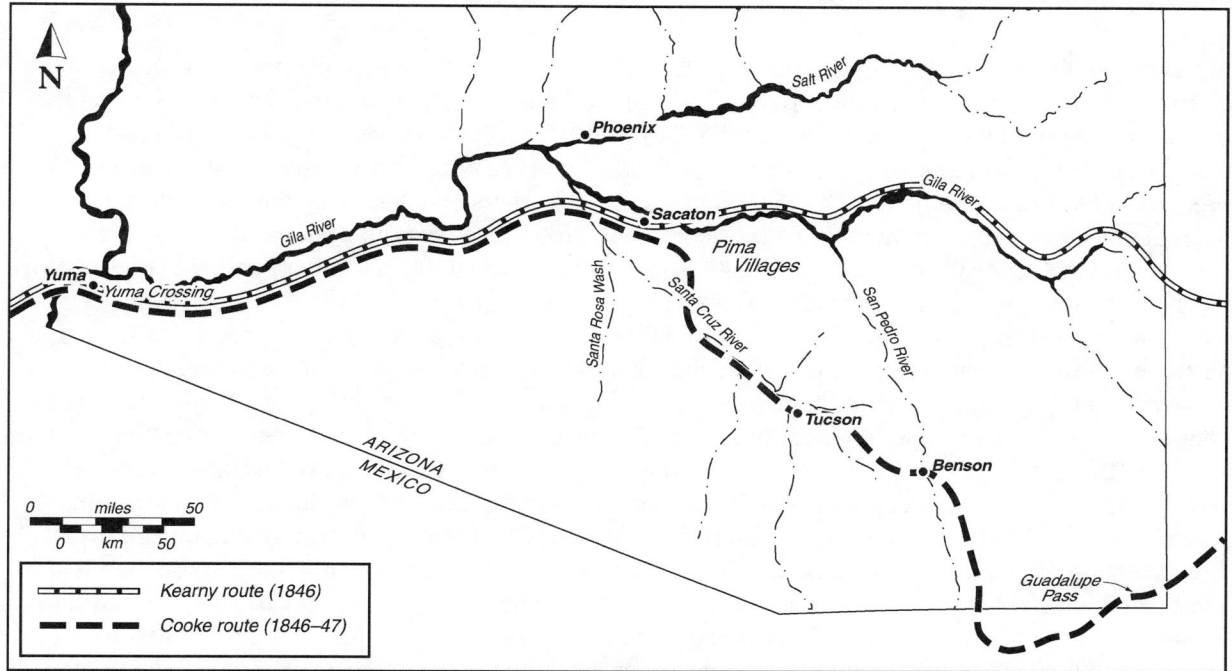

Figure 47. Routes of the Mexican-American War (after Walker and Bufkin 1979:Figure 18).

changed from the south to the east. From then on, transportation into Tucson would no longer focus on the Santa Cruz River but would follow the general route taken by the Mormon Battalion, which became known as Cooke's Wagon Road. Several alternate routes emerged along this general route, but the new focus of travel was firmly established (O'Mack and Klucas 2001). In the ensuing years, wagon trains, stage lines, and the Southern Pacific Railroad would follow the general route pioneered by the Mormon Battalion.

The Southern Emigrant Trail

The Southern Emigrant Trail was an important variant of Cooke's Wagon Road, taking a more southerly route before linking with the established Gila Trail. Following the end of the Mexican-American War in 1848, a battalion of Second Dragoons under the command of Maj. Lawrence Pike Graham journeyed west from Chihuahua, Mexico, to California. The group entered what is now southeastern Arizona at San Bernardino Springs, then headed west to the San Pedro River. Rather than follow the river northward as Cooke had done, Graham's force proceeded west then southwest to the Santa Cruz River. They followed the river downstream to Tucson, where they reconnected with Cooke's Wagon Road and continued on to California (Officer 1987:210–214). Graham's route, eventually known as the Southern Emigrant Trail, was used by many people headed to California during the gold rush of the late 1840s.

The discovery of gold in California in 1848 resulted in the migration of thousands of fortune seekers from the eastern states, many of whom came through southern Arizona along the routes established by Kearny, Cooke, and Graham. The Southern Emigrant Trail alone was used by more than 15,000 travelers between 1849 and 1850 (Etter 1995).

155

Government Surveys

The Treaty of Guadalupe Hidalgo, signed in February 1848, officially ended the war with Mexico and gave the United States what is now Arizona north of the Gila River. The U.S. government soon sent surveyors to explore the region. In 1851, John Bartlett began surveying the new boundary between Mexico and the United States. Critics of the 1848 treaty pointed out that the United States conceded to Mexico the land south of the Gila, even though Cooke and others had demonstrated the importance of this region as a valuable segment in the transcontinental route to California. This oversight was corrected in 1854 with the acquisition of another 30,000 square miles through the Gadsden Purchase (Figure 48), which established the present international boundary (Wagoner 1975:277).

To strengthen its hold on the newly acquired territory, the U.S. government appropriated funds for the survey, development, and marking of wagon roads across Arizona. At the same time, interest in a transcontinental railroad began to increase. In 1854, Lt. John G. Parke, on assignment with the Department of War's Corps of Topographical Engineers, surveyed a possible railroad route connecting the Gila River and El Paso. From the Gila, Parke traveled upstream along the Santa Cruz to Tucson, then surveyed a route to the east, eventually crossing Apache Pass in the Chiricahua Mountains and meeting Cooke's Wagon Road in New Mexico. The following year, Parke surveyed the route again and discovered an alternate pass between the Chiricahuas and Mount Graham, which led him to the San Pedro River and downstream to the Gila, bypassing Tucson altogether. In 1855, the Texas Western Railroad Company hired Andrew B. Gray, who had been a member of Bartlett's boundary commission, to survey for a potential rail line across southern Arizona. Gray recommended two possible routes, both by way of Tucson. The most expeditious route went through Apache Pass and headed directly west to Tucson. The second, longer route went through the Chiricahua Mountains south of Apache Pass, crossed the San Pedro River, continued west to Tubac, and then down the Santa Cruz Valley to Tucson. Gray's survey then followed the familiar trail to the Gila and Colorado Rivers, and on to Los Angeles (Wagoner 1975: 323–327). Portions of the routes surveyed by Parke and Gray were eventually followed by stage lines, the Southern Pacific Railroad, the first automobile highway, and Interstate 10.

Stage Lines

With the acquisition of land through the Gadsden Purchase and the growing population in California, there was an increasing demand for improved and regular communication with the east. In 1857, Tucson became a stop along the 1,476-mile San Antonio and San Diego Mail Line, commonly known as the "Jackass Mail" because travel between Yuma and San Diego was by mule. Organized by James E. Birch to provide semi-monthly service, the "Jackass Mail" suffered from financial problems, Birch's untimely death, and the overwhelming competition of the Butterfield Overland Mail (Conkling and Conkling 1947:92–93; Sonnichsen 1982:43). In October 1858, the U.S. government canceled its contract with the San Antonio and San Diego because it duplicated the service of the Butterfield, organized by John Butterfield of Utica, New York (Stein 1994:15). Operating a stage line required way stations for supplies and fresh horses or mules, and the Butterfield had more stations than its predecessor. Twenty-six stations dotted the landscape across the 437-mile Arizona portion of the overland route between Stein's Pass in New Mexico and Fort Yuma on the Colorado River (Ahnert 1973:13). These way stations, spaced at regular intervals, provided food, water, grain, equipment, fresh horses, and austere overnight accommodations.

The Butterfield Overland Mail followed the Southern Overland Trail, a variation of the Southern Emigrant Trail that entered Arizona through Apache Pass along the route surveyed by Parke. Westbound stagecoaches passed through several stations, including those at San Simon, Dragoon Springs, and Cienega Springs, before reaching Tucson. The Tucson station consisted of three adobe buildings near

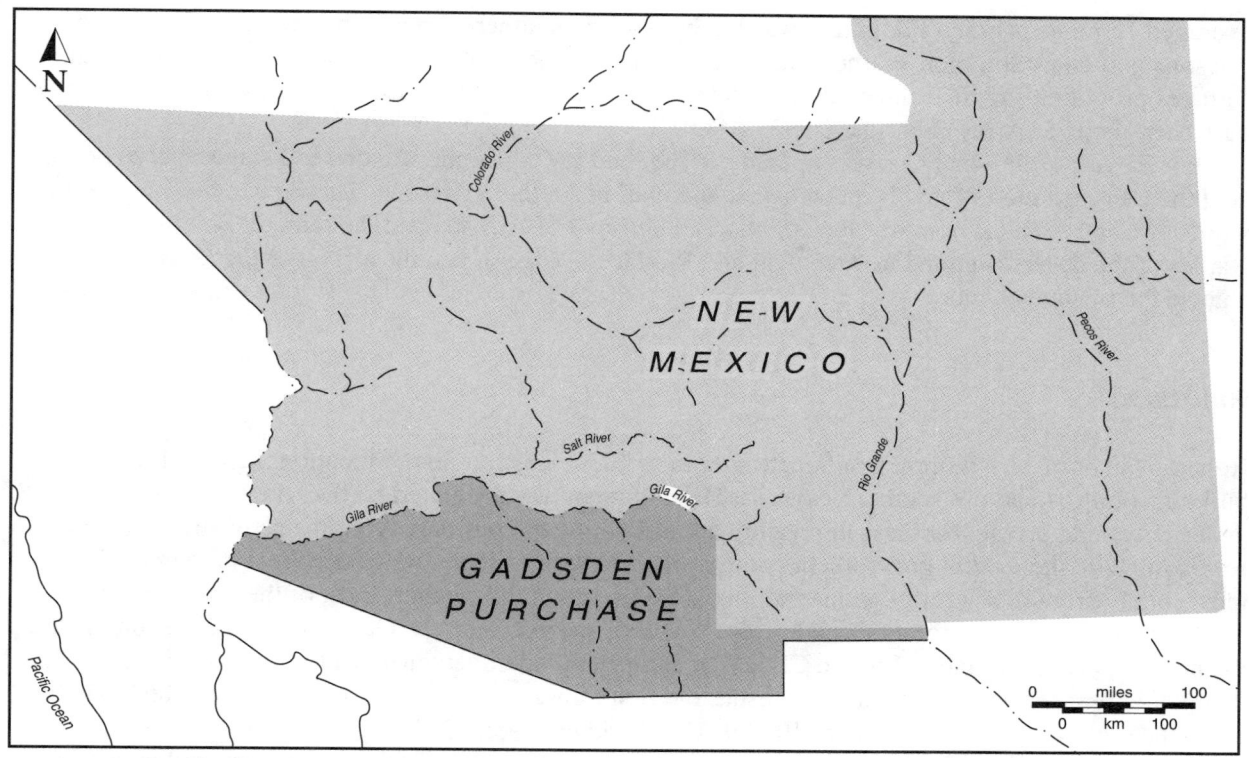

Figure 48. The Gadsden Purchase (after Walker and Bufkin 1979:Figure 22).

what is now the intersection of Main Avenue and Alameda Street. Butterfield Superintendent William Buckley appointed William S. Oury his local manager, and Tucson merchant Samuel Hughes served as the station keeper until the route was suspended in 1861. Operating as a time-table station, Tucson received the westbound mail on Tuesdays and Fridays at 1:30 p.m., and the eastbound mail on Wednesdays and Saturdays at the disagreeable hour of 3:00 a.m. (Conkling and Conkling 1947:157–158; Sonnichsen 1982:43). From Tucson, the route continued north along the east side of the Santa Cruz River to its confluence with the Rillito, where it crossed the Santa Cruz and followed the river generally northwest to Point of Mountain (at the north end of the Tucson Mountains), a distance of about 18 miles (Ahnert 1973:49; Conkling and Conkling 1947:157–161).

The Butterfield Overland Company operated successfully until the outbreak of the Civil War, when the U.S. government canceled the contract and rerouted the mail through states farther north. Other mail and transportation services continued to use the trail and way stations, including the Texas and California Stage Line, the Arizona Stage Company, the Tucson, Arizona City and San Diego Stage Company, the Tucson and Tombstone Stage Lines, and the National Mail and Transportation Company (Whittlesey et al. 1994:308, 311). The stage lines moved passengers, mail, and light cargo, serving as the primary and sometimes only means of transportation before the railroad came to Tucson. The overland stage route through southern Arizona served as the corridor for the Southern Pacific Railroad and Interstate 8.

By the late 1850s, heavy wagons became the primary means of transporting goods between southern Arizona and the East. Most of the equipment, supplies, and food required by the growing settlements had to be brought in by wagon. Freighters typically consisted of two or three wagons (some huge, with rear wheels measuring 8 feet high), hitched in tandem to a team of 12–20 mules, and capable of carrying cargo loads of up to 18,000 pounds (Sherman and Ronstadt 1975; Walker 1973). Wagon freighters averaged 15 miles per day. Freighting was big business in southern Arizona before the railroad, and Tucsonans such as Solomon Warner and partners Pinckney Randolph Tully and Estevan Ochoa made fortunes providing supplies and equipment to miners, ranchers, and townspeople, as well as their biggest customer, the U.S. Army (Sheridan 1995:104–105).

For 35 years following Cooke's opening of the road to California, wagons and stagecoaches dominated the transportation of goods, passengers, and mail in southern Arizona. Tucson had become, in the words of Capt. John G. Bourke, "the commercial *entrepôt* of Arizona and the remoter Southwest . . . the Naples of the desert" (quoted in Greenleaf and Wallace 1962:24). But the arrival of the railroad would change the town even more.

Railroads

Robert Walker of Mississippi, in a Senate speech in 1836, was the first to mention the possibility of building a railroad across southern Arizona. His comment was prompted by the wider interest of the U.S. government and private business in creating a transcontinental railroad. After the acquisition of California in 1848, the federal government commissioned a series of surveys of the West in search of the most suitable route for a transcontinental line. Surveys along the southernmost of the proposed lines established the feasibility of a railroad across southern Arizona, and the Gadsden Purchase soon made the necessary land available. But the Civil War dampened federal enthusiasm for a transcontinental line that would best service the South. As a result, the first transcontinental line, completed in 1869, passed far to the north of Arizona (Cowdery 1948:9–10; Sheridan 1995:112–114).

In 1869, the Central Pacific and Union Pacific lines met in Utah. Seeking to control rail traffic in and out of California, the owners of the Central Pacific acquired ownership of the Southern Pacific Railroad in 1868. Construction of the Southern Pacific line began soon thereafter, and by 1876, the new line had connected San Francisco with Los Angeles and a line was being built east toward Yuma. The original intent of the line to Yuma was to meet the transcontinental Texas and Pacific Railroad at the California-Arizona border, because the Southern Pacific did not have authority to build east of the California state line. However, its political and financial clout enabled the Southern Pacific to convince the territories of Arizona and New Mexico to permit them to continue eastward from Yuma. The Southern Pacific Railroad, moving east from San Diego on track laid primarily by Chinese laborers, crossed the Colorado River into Arizona in 1877 and the following year started up the Gila River valley. Reaching the lower Santa Cruz River in early 1879, the railroad turned south toward Tucson, stopping at Casa Grande in May 1879. After a delay of several months, track was laid once again up the Santa Cruz River valley, and on March 20, 1880, a cheering crowd of Tucsonans welcomed the arrival of Southern Pacific engine No. 41 (Janus Associates 1989; Myrick 1975:15, 19–55). Tucson soon became the largest rail center in the state.

In the spring of 1880, workers extended the Southern Pacific Railroad line east from Tucson, and by May, had reached Pantano, 28 miles away. The original Southern Pacific line proceeded southeast from Tucson, avoiding the Santa Cruz River and generally following the Southern Overland Trail used by wagon trains and stage lines. By September of the same year, the line was completed into New Mexico. In December 1881, the line met the Texas and Pacific line east of El Paso, thus completing the transcontinental connection. During the next 40 years, the Southern Pacific became the backbone of a series of branch railroads extending throughout southern Arizona, servicing towns, mining districts, and the Mexican border. Meanwhile, the Santa Fe Railroad had built a line south from Albuquerque, which connected with the Southern Pacific Railroad line at Deming, New Mexico, providing another transcontinental link.

The arrival of the railroad in southern Arizona launched a new era of economic development in the region by providing relatively easy and inexpensive access to national markets. Mines and ranches had outlets for their products and could receive necessary supplies. With development came decline, however, as wagon freighters could not compete with the cheaper and faster rail freight. Wagon freighters charged 5½ to 14 cents per pound and took twenty days to make the trek between Yuma and Tucson. The Southern Pacific Railroad transported goods for 1½ cents per pound and could make the trip in one day. While this turn of events forced many long-distance freighters out of business, some local wagon lines actually prospered by connecting mining camps and outlying ranches to the rail lines (Sheridan 1995: 104; Walker 1973:202). The railroad impacted stage lines as well. Travel by stagecoach was cramped, dusty, uncomfortable, and expensive. A passenger traveling in 1879 from Gila Bend to Tucson could expect to pay thirty dollars for the 129-mile, 29-hour trip (Myrick 1975:14). Despite the obvious competition from the railroads, the stagecoach short lines survived into the twentieth century, conveying passengers between outlying settlements and the rail stations (Stein 1994:22).

During the early 1900s, the railroad transformed Tucson into a trade and tourist center. Mining towns in the vicinity were connected to Tucson by spur lines, namely, the Silver Bell in 1904 and the Twin Buttes in 1906. In 1910, the Tucson and Nogales Railroad, a subsidiary of the Southern Pacific, was built from the border city of Nogales to Tucson, a run of 65 miles. The Tucson and Nogales offered affiliate connections to the interior and west coast of Mexico.

Automobiles

By the end of the 1920s, railroad trackage in southern Arizona began to decline, largely because of the ascendancy of the automobile. Cheaper transportation became available by truck, and many rail lines became unprofitable. Mining in the region also declined, especially after World War I, leading to a decreased need for mining-focused rail transportation.

Throughout the first decades of the twentieth century, the population of southern Arizona increased steadily, as did the popularity of the automobile, and the demand for better roads grew apace. In 1912, the first year of statehood, the Arizona legislature passed the State Road Law, which called for a network of approximately 1,500 miles of road connecting all county seats and most principal towns (ADOT 1977:1). In 1920, Arizona ranked ninth in the nation in per capita ownership of automobiles, and there was great concern about poor road conditions in the southern portion of the state (Sonnichsen 1982:212). A 1921 amendment to the Federal Aid Act of 1916 allocated money to states for the construction of a comprehensive and connected system of primary and secondary highways equal to seven percent of each state's total road mileage. Between 1880 and 1927, Arizona's population grew from roughly 40,000 to over 400,000. During the same period, roadways in the state expanded from 2,000 to 22,000 miles, mainly because of the advent of the automobile (ADOT 1977:13).

In 1930, Arizona had an estimated 24,000 miles of road, 2,771 of which were part of the state highway system (ADOT 1977:17). New road construction during the 1920s and 1930s consisted of graded dirt roads, usually covered in gravel. The State of Arizona supplemented federal funding by gasoline taxes, vehicle registration fees, common carrier taxes, certificate of title fees, and chauffeurs' license fees (Dowell 1933:4).

By the late 1920s, the major north-south road in the state ran from Ash Fork to Nogales through Prescott, Phoenix, Florence, and Tucson. The only east-west road across southern Arizona entered the state near Safford and passed through Globe, Phoenix, Gila Bend, and Yuma (Sheridan 1995:239). People traveling north from Tucson along U.S. 80, the Tucson-Florence highway, enjoyed a paved road for several miles before it turned to gravel near Pusch Ridge on the western edge of the Santa Catalina Mountains. State Route (SR) 84, also known as the Casa Grande Highway, headed roughly northwest of Tucson to Casa Grande, where it continued west through Gila Bend and on to Yuma. The Casa Grande highway became the corridor for Interstate 8.

Transportation in the Río Antiguo Study Area

Within the Río Antiguo study area, transportation became a significant public concern only after the establishment of Fort Lowell in 1873. Roads to and along the Rillito proliferated in the late nineteenth century, in large part because of the military presence at the fort. Soon after the fort was built, the U.S. Army built a road extending southeast along Pantano Wash, across the southern edge of the Rincon Mountains, and then to Tres Alamos. This road was used by the Southern Pacific Mail line from 1874 to 1878, and by other stage lines thereafter (Jones and Ciolek-Torrello 1991:48).

By the 1880s, the Apache threat had been eliminated from the Tucson Basin, and the number of farms, ranches, and rural settlements quickly grew. There was a similar growth in the number of roads connecting these places to Tucson. The 1893 Roskruge map of Pima County (Figure 49) shows a road heading east from Tucson to Fort Lowell, then continuing eastward along the south bank of Tanque Verde Creek. At the confluence of Tanque Verde and Sabino Canyon Creeks, it bifurcated, with one branch heading northeast to Agua Caliente Spring and the other continuing east along the Tanque Verde, passing by the Oury, Martínez, and Carrillo ranches before continuing on to Cebadilla (now Redington) Pass.

In the same period, there were two main routes heading north from Tucson and passing immediately west of the study area. One route was the Fort Yuma Road, which followed the old Southern Overland Trail north to Casa Grande, and the other was the Tucson–Camp Grant Wagon Road, which headed north-northeast around the western and northern edges of the Santa Catalina Mountains to the San Pedro River valley. Both roads were in use by the time Fort Lowell was established, and both appear on the 1873 GLO survey plat of Township 14 South, Range 13 East (see Figure 30). Both became major transportation corridors (SR 84 and U.S. 80/89, respectively) in the twentieth century.

The earliest depiction we have found of roads running north from the study area is the 1905 Tucson 15-minute USGS quadrangle map (Figure 50), which depicts numerous north-south roads crossing the Rillito and heading north into the Santa Catalina Mountains. These roads probably began as footpaths, following the natural contours. They developed over time with use by horses, wagons, and, eventually, automobiles, connecting farms, ranches, and mines north of the river to businesses and services in Tucson. With the exception of Oracle and Sabino Canyon Roads, and First and Campbell Avenues, these roads were informal and unimproved.

Before bridges spanned the Rillito, travelers crossed the river via unimproved fords at numerous locations. Fourteen fords are depicted on the 1905 USGS map between Oracle Road (the western limit of the study area) and abandoned Fort Lowell. The same map depicts two fords crossing Pantano Wash between the fort and the eastern limit of the study area, and one ford crossing Tanque Verde Creek at Sabino Canyon Road (originally known as Doe Lane), at the eastern limit of the study area. Crossing the Rillito and its two tributaries could be a leisurely undertaking (Figure 51) or an exercise in survival, depending on the season. Summer and winter floods were common, making crossings dangerous or impossible, and whatever the water level, the subsurface flow in the valley created its own special hazard, what George E. P. Smith called "the menace of quicksand" (1964:7). In 1905, a record-setting rainfall caused the streams and rivers in and around Tucson to run at flood levels for months. During the period of high water, Smith and an acquaintance by the name of Cochran made a trip to Sabino Canyon, which required them to cross Tanque Verde Creek at the head of the Narrows, where Doe Lane ended (Figure 52). According to Smith's later reminiscence, they rode in a light wagon drawn by a pair of mules, with Cochran carrying a brand new shotgun for hunting rabbit along the way. Thanks to the quicksand, the gun served another purpose that day:

> We drove down Doe Lane and came to the Rillito River (i.e., Tanque Verde Creek). It was in flood. Without hesitating [Cochran] drove in and, as soon as the small mules got into the water, they began to flounder for the quicksand was deep. We could not turn

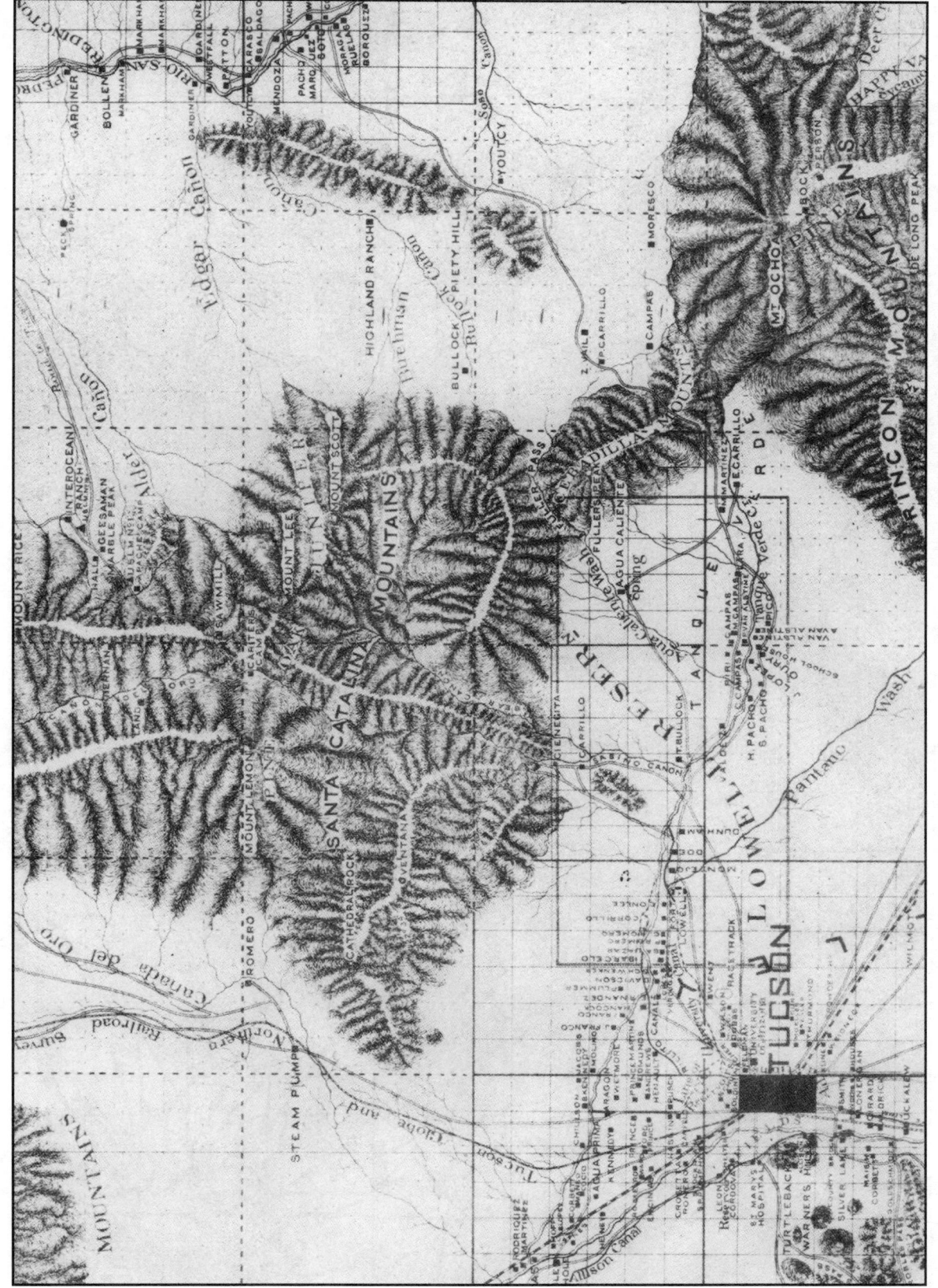

Figure 49. Portion of 1893 map of Pima County (Roskruge 1893).

161

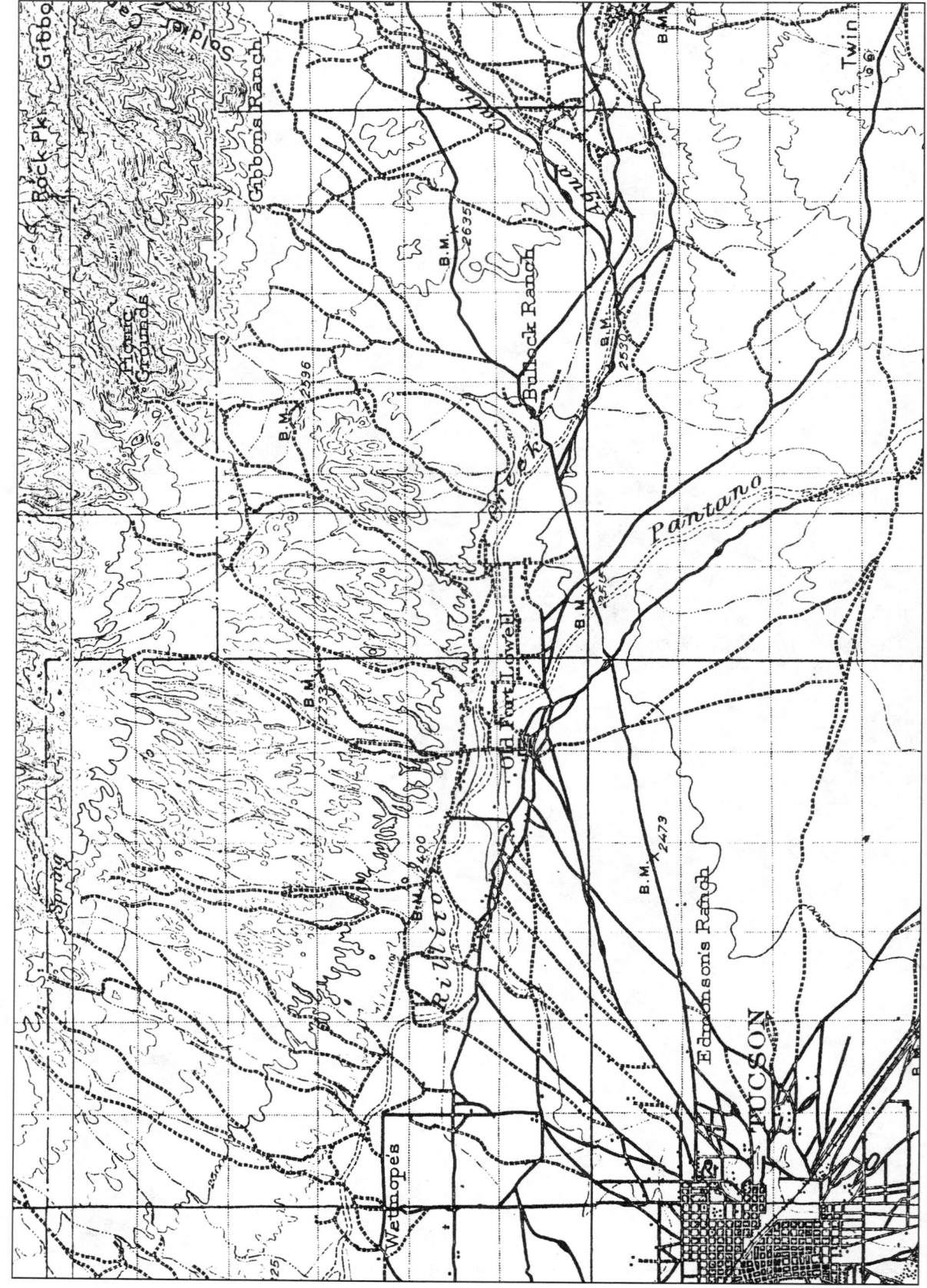

Figure 50. Portion of 1905 Tucson 30-minute USGS quadrangle map.

162

Figure 51. Rillito River crossing at Rincon Road, ca. 1906. The location of Rincon Road is unknown (photograph courtesy of the Arizona Historical Society, Tucson, MacDougal Collection, Accession No. A1-3).

163

Figure 52. The bed of Tanque Verde Creek at Doe's Lane (now Sabino Canyon Road) in 1906 (photograph courtesy of Special Collections, University of Arizona Library, Tucson, Ms. 280, box 13, folder 16).

back. Mr. Cochran lashed his mules and yelled at them and they did their best. But if they pulled one leg out of the deep sand, they would sink their other legs into the quicksand. He used his whip until it was broken, and he threw it away. Then he took his hundred dollar gun and struck the mules over the back with the gun, bending it so badly that he had to send it back to the factory where it had been made for straightening. He was standing up and shouting. I leaned away to give him room, expecting that the next minute I would be floundering in the water also. But the little mules never gave up and eventually they got us out [G. Smith 1967:18–19].

Similar references to difficult crossings attempted elsewhere along the Rillito can be found in a variety of sources on the history of the river. An especially entertaining story is provided by Bartley Cardon, who was born in the Mormon community at Binghampton in 1913 and as a child was occasionally fool enough to cross the Rillito during high water (Cardon 1993).

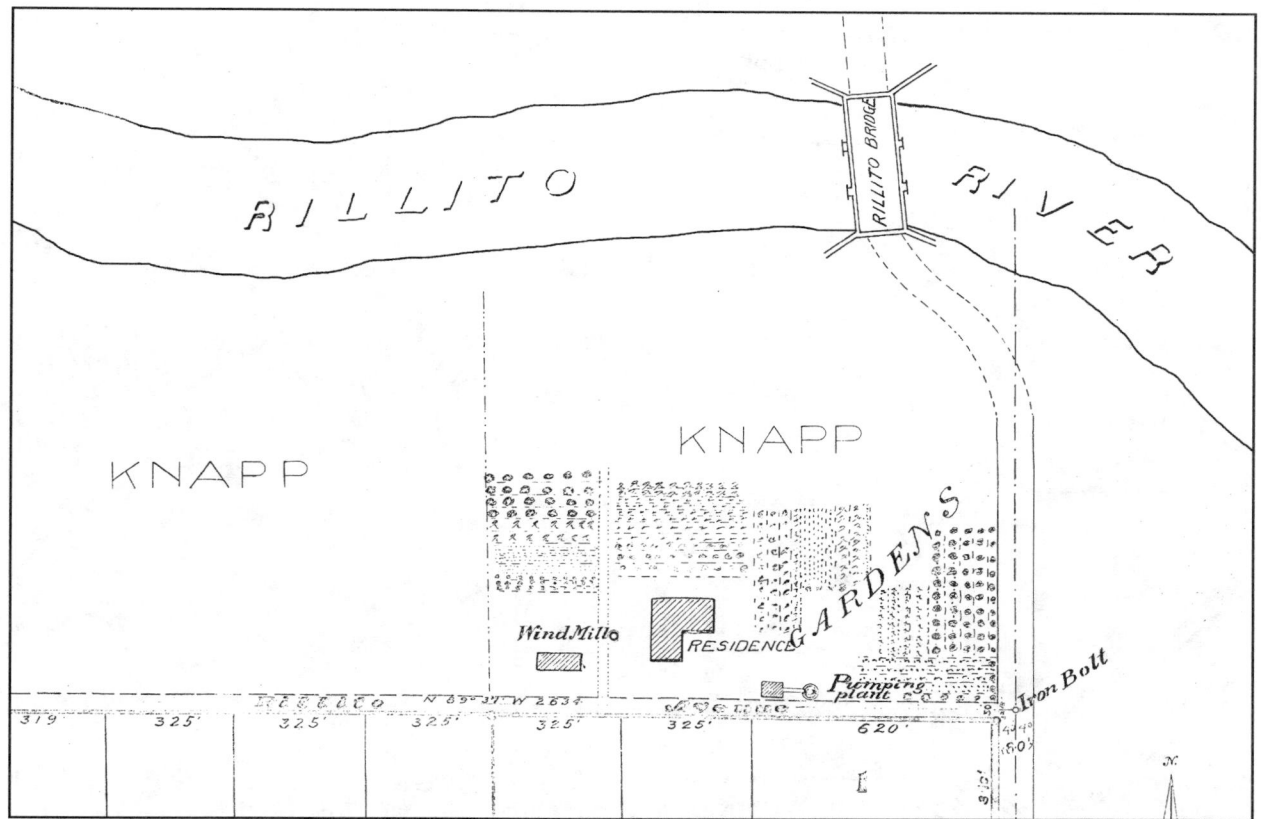

Figure 53. Portion of the 1909 plat map of Haynes Rillito Park subdivision (Wright 1909).

Bridges

Fords across the Rillito, whether bladed or simply tracks across the sandy river bottom, were prone to closure or washout during heavy rains. As traffic across the Rillito increased, so did the need for bridges. The Oracle Road crossing at the western limit of the study area was an important one for many years, serving a major north-south route, and it was a logical location for a bridge. When the 1905 Tucson 30-minute USGS quadrangle map (see Figure 50) was prepared, the crossing still lacked a bridge, but it soon had one. In fact, Smith (1967:19), in his account of the episode at Doe Lane in 1905, remembered that there was a bridge at Oracle Road by that year, but it was apparently not finished until October 1908 (see Smith 1910:111). The earliest map depiction that we have found of a bridge at Oracle Road is on the 1909 plat map of the Rillito Park residential subdivision (Figure 53).

In 1915, Oracle Road was improved to create an 18-foot-wide, two-lane concrete road running north from the intersection of Drachman and Main Streets to the Rillito. North of the Rillito, the road remained dirt. Torrential rains in the summer of 1921 caused major flooding along the river, washing away the south bank section of the bridge. In 1951, Pima County engineers realigned Oracle Road to the east and constructed a new, 30-foot-wide bridge to replace the old one. The present bridge spanning the Rillito was built in 1970 and measures 68 feet across (Jewett 1986:4–6).

The First Avenue crossing was not provided with a bridge until around 1960, judging from the first appearance of a bridge there on a 1961 map (Chamber of Commerce 1961). On a 1936 map of the area (Figure 54), First Avenue was a bladed road extending north across the bed of the Rillito to River Road, which was itself bladed from Oracle Road east to Campbell Avenue and the entrance to the Catalina

165

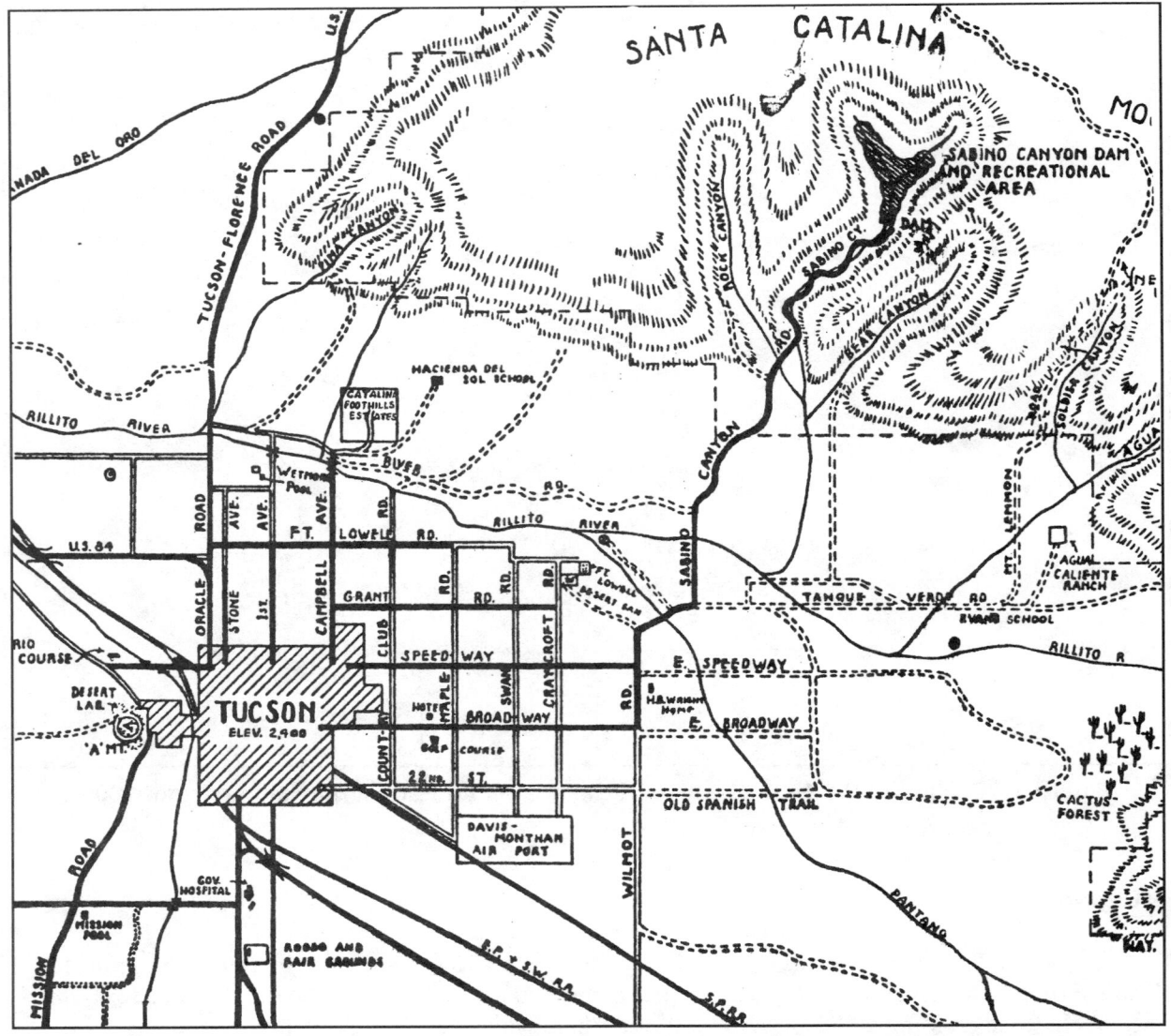

Figure 54. Portion of a 1936 map of points of interest around Tucson (Chamber of Commerce 1936).

Foothills Estates. Beginning in 1943, Tucsonans regularly traveled along First Avenue to attend horse races at the Rillito Racetrack, located on the north bank of the river just east of First Avenue. The segment of First Avenue across the Rillito River remained bladed until 1953, when it was paved (Chamber of Commerce 1950, 1953, 1959).

In the early 1930s, a 254-foot wooden bridge was constructed across the Rillito at the Campbell Avenue crossing to provide access to the Catalina Foothills Estates, a large residential development. The county later paved the bridge with asphalt. In 1963, the county tore down the original bridge—the last major wooden bridge in the county—to make way for a four-lane prestressed concrete structure (*ADS*, 3 May 1963). This bridge, built by the Murray J. Schiff Construction Company, measured 360 feet from bank to bank and cost Pima County taxpayers $219,417. With great fanfare, including a parade of

166

antique cars, Scottish bagpipers, riders on horseback, and can-can dancers from a local high school, county and city officials dedicated the bridge on November 2, 1963 (*ADS*, 3 November 1963).

Residents of the Mormon community at Binghampton, on the north bank of the Rillito, had long lobbied the Pima County Board of Supervisors for a bridge at Dodge Boulevard, the neighborhood's main transit point across the river. Pima County subsequently dismantled the wooden bridge that originally spanned the Santa Cruz River at St. Mary's Road and installed it across the Rillito at Dodge. A bridge does not appear on a 1950 map of the area (Chamber of Commerce 1950), but a 1953 edition of the same map (Chamber of Commerce 1953) shows one in place. Deanna Gursky (1994:32), in her history of the Davidson School located near the south bank of the river, gives 1950 as the date of construction. On May 3, 1962, a fire caused by a leaking gas line destroyed the bridge. County engineers designed a two-lane, precast concrete structure to replace it, with construction beginning in November 1962. While awaiting its completion, motorists drove across the river bed (*ADS*, 9 May 1962). The new, 300-foot bridge opened on February 2, 1963 (*ADS*, 2 February 1963).

By the fall of 1961, the Board of Supervisors was moving forward with its plan to extend Swan Road north from Fort Lowell Road, across the Rillito to meet River Road. People living north of River Road ardently supported the extension and presented County officials with a petition containing 134 signatures. The Swan Road extension would give them easy access to businesses on Tucson's east side. Local developers were equally supportive because an extended Swan Road would provide access to their subdivisions in the eastern Catalina foothills (*ADS*, 3 October 1961). After securing the necessary ROWs, Pima County had its contractors build a two-lane paved road across the bed of the river, in anticipation of eventually building a bridge. The crossing opened to traffic in the fall of 1962 (*ADS*, 9 October 1962). In March 1969, construction began on a 485-foot-long, 44-foot-wide concrete girder bridge across the Rillito. Built by the Ashton Company with county and federal funds, motorists began using the structure on September 30, 1969 (*ADS*, 16 November 1969).

River Road

River Road, the first major east-west route north of the Rillito River, developed through use over time. Access to the area north of the Rillito by farmers, ranchers, and land speculators gradually increased, creating the demand for a continuous east-west route along the river. Around 1912, a road was extended a short distance east from Oracle Road, north of the Rillito; this was the beginning of River Road as a formal route. In 1913, it was extended east to First Avenue. River Road became an official Pima County road in 1929 and was bladed from Oracle Road to just beyond Campbell Avenue. From there, it headed east as an unimproved road, roughly parallel to the Rillito for much of the way, and finally meeting Sabino Canyon Road (Ayres 2001:90).

In 1936, River Road was still an improved dirt road (Chamber of Commerce 1936), but Pima County soon started paving it one section at a time. The first section, from Campbell Avenue to Camino Real, was paved in the late 1930s to handle the increase in traffic from Catalina Foothills Estates, a recent major product of Tucson developer John W. Murphey. In the late 1920s and early 1930s, Murphey acquired several thousand acres of land north of River Road and east of Campbell Avenue. Shortly thereafter he began selling lots and building houses. In 1936, Murphey built St. Philip's in the Hills Episcopal Church at the northeast corner of the intersection of Campbell Avenue and River Road. More people in the area meant more automobiles and more dust. As traffic increased, road conditions worsened. Murphey and the residents of Catalina Foothills Estates lobbied Pima County to improve the roads to the subdivision. A proposal to pave River Road from Campbell Avenue east to Camino Real, and Campbell Avenue north of River Road, went before the Board of Supervisors. In a letter to the board, George W. Ferguson, Rector of St. Philip's in the Hills, wrote:

The new church of St. Philip's in the Hills represents a substantial investment and there is no question in our minds as to the adviseability [sic] of the proposed paving. The accumulation of dust and dirt which is constantly sifting into the church as a result of the traffic is a constant problem and source of consideration. To this might also be added the protests of numerous members of the congregation as to the deplorable state of the road in its present condition [Ferguson 1937].

The county complied with the residents' demands and paved the segment of River Road along the southern boundary of the Catalina Foothills Estates. Apart from this improvement, little else was done to the road until the early 1950s. Maps and aerial photographs of the area indicate that by 1954, River Road had been paved between Campbell Avenue and Alvernon Way. Four years later, it was paved from Alvernon east to Swan Road, and from Oracle Road to First Avenue. By 1961, the segment from La Cañada to Oracle was paved (Pima County 1954, 1958, 1960, 1961). The segments between First and Campbell Avenues and Swan and Sabino Canyon Roads were paved by 1962 (Ayres 2001:91).

Today, River Road extends from La Cholla Boulevard on the west to Sabino Canyon Road on the east. Once used primarily as a route for local residents, it now serves as a major east-west transportation corridor.

Rillito Parkway

As Tucson's population grew, so did traffic problems. In 1961, regional planners envisioned an east-west transportation corridor north of the Rillito to link the growing eastern Catalina foothills with the Tucson-Phoenix highway. River Road was the only continuous east-west transportation route along the Rillito; however, Pima County Transportation Engineer Walter Burg described the roads's serpentine alignment as "totally inadequate" for handling a large volume of traffic (ADS, 15 December 1961).

A transportation study completed in 1965, part of a comprehensive regional plan developed five years prior, proposed to upgrade the main arteries and build freeways and parkways to handle the increasing congestion. Tucsonans wanted a solution, but nobody liked the idea of a freeway or interchange in their backyard. Plans for intra-city limited-access roads met with intense opposition and were tabled for several years. In 1981, the Pima Association of Governments approved a long-range plan to build two parkways: one to connect the southeast side with the city center and the other to funnel traffic in an east-west orientation parallel to the Rillito and Pantano channels (ADS, 22 July 1961; Sonnichsen 1982:294).

The proposed Rillito Parkway was intended to preserve the foothills and the big bend (or Binghampton) area of the Rillito while enhancing neighborhoods by concentrating vehicular traffic on the parkway. Comprising four to eight traffic lanes, with a landscaped median and landscaped buffers on either side of the road, the parkway would parallel the Rillito River for approximately 13.5 miles, with a western terminus at the intersection of Orange Grove and Thornydale Roads and an eastern terminus at the juncture of Grant and Tanque Verde Roads. In an effort to assuage public concern over the displacement of residential sites, planners selected an alignment that would roughly follow along the north bank of the Rillito River from La Cañada Drive to Oracle Road. Continuing along the north bank in a southeasterly direction, the parkway would cross to the south bank of the river at Mountain Avenue and parallel the river to Craycroft Road. From there the parkway would parallel the west bank of Pantano Wash between Craycroft and Wilmot Roads. From Wilmot Road, the parkway would merge with Grant Road and continue to its eastern terminus at the intersection of Grant and Tanque Verde Roads. Transportation planners envisioned six grade-separated intersections, four of which would have access ramps, and signalized intersections at major cross streets along the parkway. Concomitant to the Rillito Corridor proposal were 29 miles of major arterial improvements and additional river crossings at Stone Avenue,

Mountain Avenue, and Alvernon Way, the last crossing intended to replace the substandard Dodge Boulevard bridge (Ruiz Engineering Corporation 1985:44–49).

Regional planners estimated $300 million for the project, but opponents of the plan feared the actual amount would far exceed that figure. In a 1984 referendum, voters rejected the Rillito Parkway. This resounding "no" was due in large part to the 1984 "Keep It Kinky" campaign, a grass-roots effort to maintain the scenic River Road rather than have it swallowed by a parkway. Despite feasibility studies and repeated attempts to resurrect the plan, the Tucson City Council and Pima County Board of Supervisors, smarting from fierce public opposition to the parkway, backed away from the proposed project. Instead, transportation planners moved forward with more popular, if shortsighted programs to upgrade the main arteries as a means of easing congestion and facilitating traffic flow. As an alternative to the Rillito Parkway, city transportation officials favored extending Prince Road east to connect with River Road, crossing the river somewhere near Swan Road. Pima County administrators envisioned a bridge across the Rillito at Alvernon Way. Neither plan came to fruition (*ADS,* 8 May 1986). Although the parkway did not materialize, the Pima County Flood Control District, with the help of the COE, constructed the Rillito River Park trail along the Rillito from Craycroft Road to its confluence with the Santa Cruz River. This 10.5-mile scenic route is now used by walkers, cyclists, and skaters.

Sabino Canyon and Mount Lemmon Roads

When the residents of Tucson first ventured into the surrounding countryside for recreational purposes in the late nineteenth century, one of the places that attracted their interest was Sabino Canyon, just northeast of the Río Antiguo study area. Sabino Canyon cuts into the southern slope of the Santa Catalina Mountains and has a flowing creek, tall cottonwoods, and relatively cool mountain air. It was an important source of water for Fort Lowell during its day (see below), and it later became a favorite getaway for picnickers, swimmers, and hikers. The 1893 Roskruge map (see Figure 49) shows a road leading up the canyon and few houses in the canyon's lower reaches. Around 1920, a graded two-lane road suitable for automobiles replaced the rutted trail (Figure 55). Doe Lane, the scene of George E. P. Smith's adventure on Tanque Verde Creek (see above), was eventually subsumed by Sabino Canyon Road, which now forms the eastern limit of the Río Antiguo study area.

Just as popular as Sabino Canyon but much harder to reach was Mount Lemmon, the highest point in the Santa Catalina Mountains. For years, picnickers, campers, and vacationers made the trek up to Mount Lemmon to escape the oppressive summer heat. Burros and mules packed supplies along the trail leading up Sabino Canyon to the village of Summerhaven, atop Mount Lemmon. The first road to Summerhaven for automobiles was built in 1920 on the north side of the range, beginning in the town of Oracle—a total distance of 75 miles from downtown Tucson. In March 1933, Secretary of Agriculture Henry A. Wallace approved $1.153 million to build a two-lane surfaced road up the south side of the mountains. Prisoners provided much of the labor for the 18-year project. The road was christened the Catalina Highway and still serves as the principal route to Summerhaven (Henry 1992:59).

Redington Road

Redington Road was an early route through the pass between the Santa Catalina and Rincon Mountains, used in succession by Native Americans, settlers, ranchers, military expeditions, stagecoaches, and wagon freighters (Figure 56). Today, Redington Road begins where Tanque Verde Road ends, at the foothills of the Tanque Verde Mountains, winding its way northeast to the tiny community of Redington in the San Pedro Valley.

169

Figure 55. The graded dirt road to Sabino Canyon, a popular recreation spot, view to north, ca. 1920s (photograph courtesy of the Arizona Historical Society, Tucson, Wallace Photograph Collection, Accession No. 0745).

Figure 56. Redington Road today, view to the west toward Tucson.

In the nineteenth century, the pass between the Santa Catalinas and the Rincons was known as Cebadilla Pass, from the Spanish name for a wildflower (it is not clear whether the name of the pass came from La Cebadilla Ranch, which was established along Tanque Verde Creek by Emilio Carrillo around 1877 (see above), or if the ranch took its name from the pass). Prior to the establishment of Fort Lowell, Cebadilla Pass was seldom used by anyone but Apaches. People traveling to the San Pedro Valley preferred the wagon road that headed north out of Tucson around the west side of the Santa Catalina Mountains before bearing northeast toward Camp Grant (Schellie 1968:137). The trail through the pass is evident on an 1870 map of southern Arizona (Figure 57) and is depicted as following the course of Tanque Verde Creek (National Archives 1870).

In December 1865, Tucsonan Mark Aldrich and five partners trekked east over Cebadilla Pass to the San Pedro Valley with plans to create a farming and cattle empire. The men and their families built an irrigation canal, ploughed and planted fields, and had a successful first harvest. In late 1866, the community was raided by Apaches and its members fled back to Tucson. The area remained unsettled until the arrival of brothers Henry and Lem Redfield in 1875 (McKelvey 1958). The Redfields built a successful cattle ranching operation in the San Pedro Valley, and other ranchers soon followed. In October 1879, the Redfields and their neighbors established a post office. For reasons unknown, the federal government would not permit them to use the name Redfield, so they coined "Redington" (Barnes 1988:358).

Four years prior to the arrival of the Redfield brothers, the men who carried out the infamous Camp Grant Massacre rendezvoused on the banks of Pantano Wash before marching over Cebadilla Pass to attack an unsuspecting band of Aravaipa Apaches near Camp Grant (see above). Other Euroamericans also occasionally used the trail, and soldiers traveling between Fort Lowell and Camp Grant, or in pursuit of Apaches, frequented it. In 1885, George J. Roskruge surveyed the area for the construction of a county road that would run from the Martinez Ranch on the north bank of Tanque Verde Creek through the Cebadilla Pass to the San Pedro River. In his notes, Roskruge described the specifications for the road:

> The road bed is to be left constructed not less than twelve feet wide and all curves are to be built wide enough to allow full swing for a team of six animals drawing a wagon. The road bed [is] to be left in a smoothe [*sic*] condition. The ravines or gulches are to be substantially filled so as to form a good road for the passage of wagons of all kinds [Roskruge 1885].

According to Gregonis and Huckell (1980:77), stagecoaches once made their way over Cebadilla Pass, following the route between the San Pedro and Santa Cruz Valleys. After the closing of Fort Lowell in 1891, the military abandoned the wagon road. In the early twentieth century, access to Redington by automobile required taking either the roundabout route through Benson, southeast of Tucson, and down the San Pedro Valley, or by way of Oracle to the north (McKelvey 1958). Automobiles had a difficult time traversing the old wagon trail over the pass until the mid-1930s when the Civilian Conservation Corps, as part of several federal works projects in the Tucson area, carved a two-lane dirt road out of the trail. Today, motorists wishing to travel the winding, unpaved road are in for a dusty, bumpy ride.

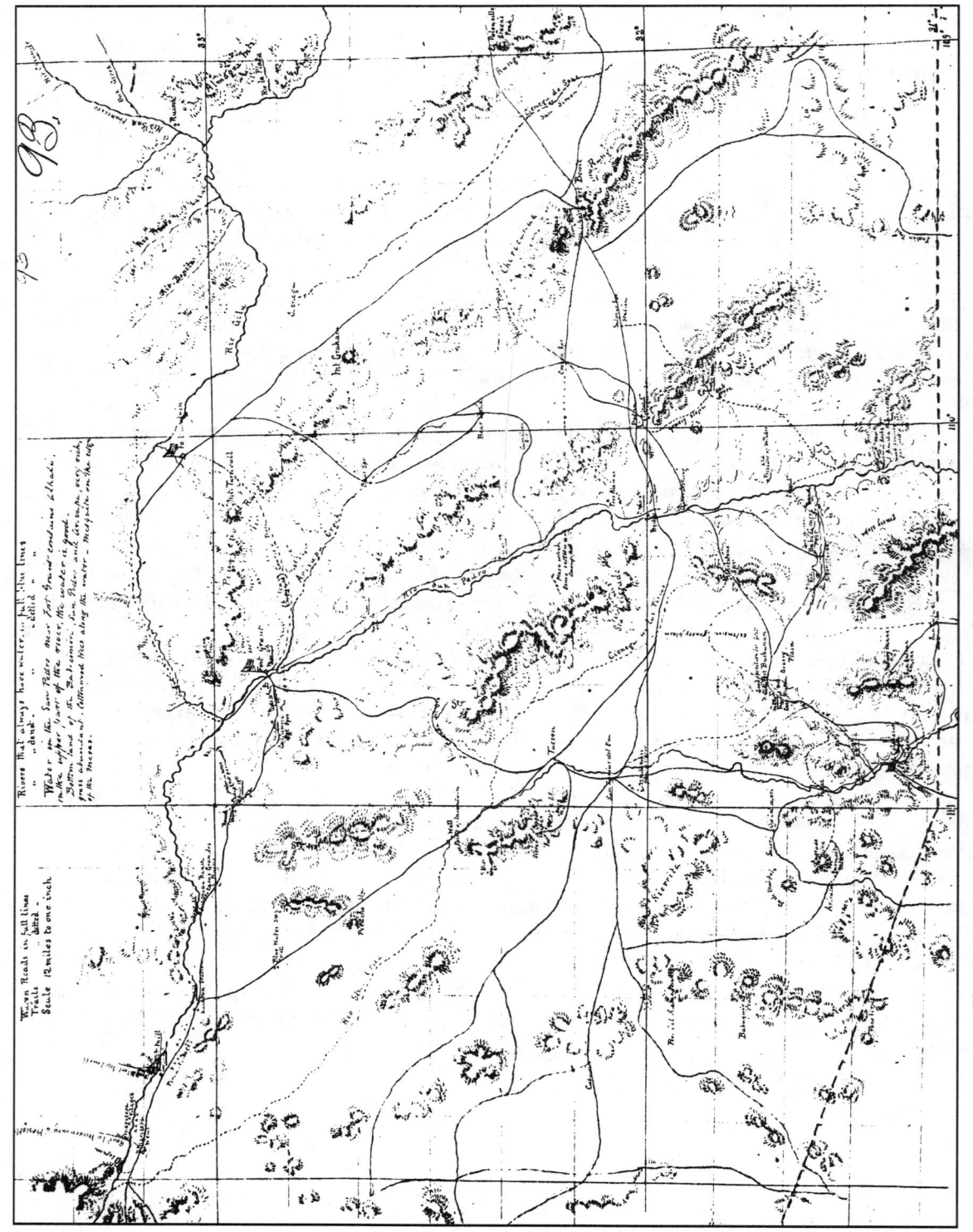

Figure 57. Portion of 1870 map of wagon roads and trails in southern Arizona. Note trails heading east of Tucson to the San Pedro River valley (National Archives 1870).

172

CHAPTER 5

Historic Properties and Survey Coverage in the Study Area

In this chapter, we summarize existing data on the nature and distribution of historic properties in the Río Antiguo study area and discuss the extent of previous archaeological survey coverage. We also discuss the subsurface archaeological potential of the study area based on a consideration of its geomorphology. We identify locations of particular subsurface concern, including the presumed locations of historical-period sites known only from documentary references. The chapter begins with notes on the range of sites found in the study area, then provides detailed descriptions of four major sites (two prehistoric, two historical-period). Basic information on the other sites in the study area is provided in Table 4, and descriptions of these sites appear in Appendix B.

Previously Recorded Archaeological Sites

We reviewed the archaeological site files of ASM in Tucson for the locations of archaeological sites previously recorded in the study area. This review included both the paper files kept at ASM—site cards, USGS quadrangle maps with hand-plotted site locations, and project reports—and AZSITE, the recently established online database for ASM archaeological site information. We transferred by hand the site plots on the ASM quadrangle maps to our own copies of the same maps. We also obtained from ASM copies of the electronic AZSITE files of digitized site locations and survey coverage, which we overlaid on digital raster graphic (DRG) images of the corresponding USGS maps. A comparison of the hand-plotted and digitized site locations showed few discrepancies, but we noted numerous discrepancies between the site plots on either set of maps and the site plots on individual site cards and in project reports. We prepared our own map (not included here) of the locations of previously recorded archaeological sites within or adjacent to the study area based on a combination of information from the ASM quadrangle maps, the ASM site cards, the digitized AZSITE maps, and project reports. Whenever possible, we relied on the latest available report on a site for information on site location and size. It is worth emphasizing that the location and size of some sites on our map varied significantly from their depictions on the ASM maps and site cards.

Table 4 lists the sites previously recorded in the study area and provides basic information about site temporality, function, and size. A total of 51 sites has been recorded in the study area. Of these, 20 sites date exclusively to the prehistoric period, 15 date exclusively to the historical period, and 16 have both prehistoric and historical-period components.

The period names used for the prehistoric sites in Table 4 and Appendix B generally reflect the names used by the recorders or excavators of a given site, with occasional minor changes to show a site's connection to our discussion of prehistoric culture history in Chapter 3. The period names used for historical-period sites are also those commonly used by archaeologists, but in the many cases the site recorders did not assign period names, we did. The historical periods we distinguish are Territorial (1854–

Table 4. Summary of Archaeological Sites in the Río Antiguo Study Area, by ASM Number

ASM Site No. [a]	Site Name	Site Area [b]	Prehistoric Period	Prehistoric Function	Historical Period	Historical Function	References
BB:9:5		3.28 acres (1.33 ha)	undifferentiated Hohokam	limited activity	Early Statehood	adobe brick manufacture	Ciolek-Torrello and Homburg 1990; Sliva 1998
BB:9:6		< 0.36 acres (< 0.14 ha)	undifferentiated Hohokam	limited activity			Midvale 1937
BB:9:7		9.79 acres (3.96 ha)	undifferentiated Hohokam	habitation	Early Statehood	guest ranch	Sliva 1998
BB:9:8		< 0.36 acres (< 0.14 ha)	undifferentiated Hohokam	habitation or limited activity			Sliva 1998
BB:9:9		3.67 acres (1.49 ha)	undifferentiated Hohokam	habitation	Early Statehood	residential	Dart 1983
BB:9:11		< 0.36 acres (< 0.14 ha)	undifferentiated Hohokam	habitation	Territorial (?) and Early Statehood	irrigation; topsoil borrow area	Midvale 1937
BB:9:12		< 0.36 acres (< 0.14 ha)	undifferentiated Hohokam	limited activity	Territorial and Early Statehood	residential; irrigation	Ciolek-Torrello and Homburg 1990; Midvale 1937
BB:9:13		< 0.36 acres (< 0.14 ha)	undifferentiated Hohokam	limited activity	Territorial and Early Statehood	campsite and lookout	Sliva 1998
BB:9:14	Hardy site	209.82 acres (84.95 ha)	Colonial (Snaketown phase) through Classic (Tanque Verde phase)	habitation			Dart 1988; Gregonis 1997; Jones 1998b
BB:9:16		< 0.36 acres (< 0.14 ha)	undifferentiated Hohokam	limited activity			Midvale 1938
BB:9:17		< 0.36 acres (< 0.14 ha)	undifferentiated Hohokam	limited activity			Ciolek-Torrello and Homburg 1990; Midvale 1938
BB:9:18		< 0.36 acres (< 0.14 ha)	Colonial (Rillito phase)	habitation			Ciolek-Torrello and Homburg 1990; Harry and Ciolek-Torrello 1992
BB:9:19		< 0.36 acres (< 0.14 ha)	undifferentiated Hohokam	limited activity	Territorial or Early Statehood	irrigation	Ciolek-Torrello and Homburg 1990; Sliva 1998

ASM Site No.[a]	Site Name	Site Area[b]	Prehistoric Period	Prehistoric Function	Historical Period	Historical Function	References
BB:9:20		<0.36 acres (<0.14 ha)	undifferentiated Hohokam	fortified hilltop (*trincheras?*)			Sliva 1998
BB:9:21		<0.36 acres (<0.14 ha)	Sedentary (Rincon phase)	habitation or limited activity			Mayro 1987a, 1987b
BB:9:22	Pottery Hill	<0.36 acres (<0.14 ha)	undifferentiated Hohokam	limited activity			Midvale 1938
BB:9:23		<0.36 acres (<0.14 ha)	undifferentiated Hohokam	limited activity	Territorial or Early Statehood	irrigation	
BB:9:24		1.36 acres (0.55 ha)	Sedentary (Rincon phase); Classic (Tucson phase)	habitation or limited activity			Old Pueblo Archaeology Center 2000
BB:9:25		<0.36 acres (<0.14 ha)	undifferentiated Hohokam	habitation or limited activity			Midvale 1938
BB:9:26		<0.36 acres (<0.14 ha)	undifferentiated Hohokam	habitation			Midvale 1938
BB:9:33	University Ruin	<0.36 acres (<0.14 ha)	Sedentary (Rincon phase) through Classic (Tanque Verde and Tucson phases)	habitation	Territorial (?) to post–World War II	ranching; archaeological laboratory	Fontana and Cormack 1956; Hayden 1957
BB:9:35		<0.36 acres (<0.14 ha)	undifferentiated Archaic (?)	habitation			
BB:9:40	Fort Lowell	33.62 acres (13.61 ha)			Territorial and Early Statehood	military; residential	Dart 1988; Jones 1998b; Peterson 1963; Turner 1990; Weaver 1947
BB:9:54		1.28 acres (0.52 ha)	Colonial (Rillito phase) through Classic (Tanque Verde phase)	habitation			Huntington 1982
BB:9:72	Band Quarters Kitchen	1.03 acres (0.42 ha)			Territorial	military	Dart 1988; Huntington 1982; Jones 1998b; Kinkade and Fritz 1975; Turner 1990
BB:9:95		0.48 acres (0.19 ha)	undifferentiated Hohokam	undetermined			

continued on next page

ASM Site No. [a]	Site Name	Site Area [b]	Prehistoric Period	Prehistoric Function	Historical Period	Historical Function	References
BB:9:100	Lazy Creek site	< 0.36 acres (< 0.14 ha)	undifferentiated Hohokam	limited activity	Territorial or Early Statehood	irrigation; horse track	Sliva 1998
BB:9:111	Valley of the Moon	< 0.36 acres (< 0.14 ha)			Early Statehood and post–World War II	entertainment	
BB:9:118	Hill Farm site	1.75 acres (0.71 ha)	undifferentiated Hohokam	habitation	Territorial and Early Statehood	irrigation	Urban 1982
BB:9:141	Mesquite Creek site	2.43 acres (0.98 ha)	Colonial (Rillito phase); Sedentary (Rincon phase)	limited activity			
BB:9:219		2.11 acres (0.85 ha).	undifferentiated prehistoric	limited activity			Mayro 1987c
BB:9:220		< 0.36 acres (< 0.14 ha)			Territorial or Early Statehood	residential	Chavarria 1996
BB:9:238	Binghampton	370.64 acres (150.06 ha)	undifferentiated Hohokam	habitation or limited activity	Territorial to post–World War II	residential; farming; irrigation; cemetery	Ciolek-Torrello and Homburg 1990; Gursky 1994; Harry and Ciolek-Torrello 2001; Parkhurst et al. 2001; Turner 1990
BB:9:246		< 0.36 acres (< 0.14 ha)			undetermined	undetermined	
BB:9:247		< 0.36 acres (< 0.14 ha)			Territorial and Early Statehood	irrigation	Hohmann 1989
BB:9:253		< 0.36 acres (< 0.14 ha)	undifferentiated Hohokam	limited activity			Harry 1990
BB:9:254		< 0.36 acres (< 0.14 ha)			Early Statehood and post–World War II	residential	Harry 1990
BB:9:255		< 0.36 acres (< 0.14 ha)	undifferentiated Hohokam	limited activity	undetermined	irrigation	Harry 1990
BB:9:256		< 0.36 acres (< 0.14 ha)			Early Statehood and post–World War II	residential	Harry 1990
BB:9:259		< 0.36 acres (< 0.14 ha)	undifferentiated prehistoric	limited activity			Dart 1991

ASM Site No. [a]	Site Name	Site Area [b]	Prehistoric Period	Prehistoric Function	Historical Period	Historical Function	References
BB:9:302	Davidson Flume and Schroeder's Well	3.11 acres (1.26 ha)			Territorial to post–World War II	irrigation	Sterner 1996
BB:9:306		< 0.36 acres (< 0.14 ha)			post–World War II	residential	Lenhart 1996
BB:9:309		3.12 acres (1.26 ha)	undifferentiated Hohokam	limited activity	Territorial and Early Statehood	residential	
BB:9:310		< 0.36 acres (< 0.14 ha)	undifferentiated Hohokam		Territorial and Early Statehood	residential	
BB:9:314		1.97 acres (0.8 ha)	undifferentiated Hohokam	limited activity	undetermined	irrigation	Jones and Dart 1997; Stephen 1997
BB:9:315		2.08 acres (0.84 ha)	Sedentary (Rincon phase)	habitation			Stephen 1997
BB:9:321		0.49 acres (0.2 ha)			Territorial and Early Statehood	irrigation	Thiel 1997; Thurtle 2001
BB:9:322		< 0.36 acres (< 0.14 ha)			Early Statehood	residential (?)	Sliva 1998
BB:9:324		< 0.36 acres (< 0.14 ha)			Early Statehood and post–World War II	undetermined	Jones 1998b; Stephen 1998; Turner 1990
BB:9:325	Corbett Ditch	< 0.36 acres (< 0.14 ha)			Territorial and Early Statehood	irrigation	Stephen 1998; Turner 1990
BB:9:356		1.65 acres (0.67 ha)	Sedentary (Rincon phase)	limited activity	Territorial and Early Statehood	residential; irrigation	Homburg and Kurota 2000; O'Mack and Riggs 2001

[a] All site numbers preceded by "*AZ*." Sites in boldface indicate sites located in the APE.
[b] Site areas are calculated from our digital plots and may differ significantly from those given on ASM site cards.

1912), Early Statehood (1912–1945), and post–World War II (1945–present). Consistent with documentary evidence for a lack of settlement in the Rillito Valley during the Spanish Colonial (1539–1821) and Mexican (1821–1854) periods (see Chapter 3), the historical-period sites that can be assigned a temporal association all date to the Territorial period or later.

As the function columns in Table 4 suggest, and as is more specifically evident in the individual site descriptions in Appendix B, the variety of prehistoric and historical-period sites in the study area is considerable. Among the prehistoric sites, two large habitation sites stand out, both in terms of size and complexity and in terms of the amount of research carried out at them. These sites are described in detail below. Two historical-period sites also stand out in size and importance, although neither has been subject to the amount of archaeological work seen at either of the major prehistoric sites. Both sites are described below, with an emphasis on historical context.

Major Prehistoric Sites

Hardy Site (AZ BB:9:14)

The Hardy site is a large, dispersed, multicomponent Hohokam habitation site located just south of the confluence of Pantano Wash and Tanque Verde Creek. The site covers approximately 85 hectares (210 acres), with its eastern boundary falling at the west bank of Pantano Wash and its northern boundary on the floodplain of the Rillito. The site is situated primarily on the first terrace above the modern entrenched channels of Pantano Wash and the Rillito. It is known locally as the prehistoric site on which Fort Lowell was built in the 1870s.

The earliest known description of the prehistoric remains constituting the Hardy site is that of Adolph Bandelier, who visited Fort Lowell in December 1884. Bandelier noted "traces of low mounds, of undistinguishable disposition, and also much ancient pottery after the pattern of the lower Gila and Verde" (Bandelier 1970:206). Bandelier also described what were likely the remains of a Classic period adobe structure located northeast of the fort. No such architectural vestiges of the Classic period are currently visible at the Hardy site, and Gregonis (1997:5) has suggested that Bandelier was referring to nearby University Indian Ruin (AZ BB:9:33), located on the other side of Pantano Wash, approximately 1.5 km (0.93 mile) east of the Hardy site.

The land encompassing abandoned Fort Lowell was leased by the University of Arizona between 1929 and 1943 (Cummings 1935). During this period, Frank Midvale formally recorded the prehistoric remains at the site as AZ BB:9:14. These remains consisted of several trash mounds and scattered artifacts in the vicinity of the fort. Midvale also noted several Hohokam sherds visible in the adobe walls of the extant fort buildings (Gregonis 1997:6). With the exception of this initial documentation, little attention was given to the prehistoric component of the site during this period, with the major effort given to the investigation and preservation of the remains of the historical-period fort. This trend continued into the 1970's, with archaeological investigations at the Hardy site limited to small-scale monitoring associated with improvements to the park.

In late 1975, Pima County purchased a 25-acre parcel of land adjacent to the northeastern margin of the park. The following spring, volunteers from ASM began what became the most intensive archaeological investigations of the prehistoric component of the site (Gregonis 1997). It was during this period that the prehistoric component was christened the Hardy site. Work at the site continued through the 1977–1978 field season, when the Department of Anthropology at the University of Arizona ran the project as a field school (Gregonis 1997:8). The work comprised both surface survey of the site and its immediate surroundings, and subsurface investigations within a 20-by-20-m area in the northwestern portion of the newly acquired parcel. Several discrete artifact scatters and trash mounds were identified within the parcel, suggesting a moderately intense prehistoric occupation.

The ASM-sponsored investigations of the Hardy site resulted in the excavation of a total of 36 sub-surface features including pit houses, borrow pits, caliche-mixing basins, extramural pits, and a cemetery/offertory area (Gregonis 1997:11). Ceramic data indicated an occupation extending from the Snaketown phase of the Pioneer period through the Sedentary period. A small number of Tanque Verde Red-on-brown sherds recovered from the site suggest some Classic period activity as well, although the absence of features clearly attributable to the Classic period suggests that this activity was minimal.

Data collected during the ASM excavations allowed for the investigation of a number of research questions that, at the time, were little understood in the Tucson Basin. The relatively large areal exposures provided important data on village structure and the use of space, including changes through time. Gregonis (1997:63–65) has argued that although the excavated area contained evidence of nearly continuous occupation for a period of 500 years, the occupation could not be considered intensive, perhaps reflecting the shifting activities of one or two households. The pattern appeared to reflect the simultaneous presence of two or three houses plus related extramural features associated with a trash mound. The location of this set of features changed through time, perhaps tied to the periodic abandonment and rebuilding of the pit houses, features whose use-life has been estimated to range from as long as 100 years (Wilcox et al. 1981:192) to as brief as seven years (Ahlstrom 1985:638).

The ASM excavations at the Hardy site also contributed important data on the transition from the Rincon phase of the Sedentary period to the Tanque Verde phase of the Classic period, when rapid changes in settlement structure, mortuary behavior, and material culture occurred in the Tucson Basin. In the approximate period A.D. 1100–1200, the typical Sedentary period "house-in-a-pit" was replaced by a rectangular to subrectangular structure, occasionally with low adobe walls set only a few centimeters into the ground. Entryways frequently had adobe "step-risers" forming one or two steps leading down into the main part of the structure (Gregonis 1997:67). Changes in religious ceremonies and beliefs in this period are reflected in the appearance of inhumation burials alongside the cremation burials typical of the Sedentary period. Innovations occurred in pottery as well. The curvilinear designs characteristic of late Rincon phase ceramics are replaced by more-geometric, linear patterns, though not as elaborate as those found on vessels dating to the Tanque Verde phase proper. These designs also occur primarily on the interior surfaces of bowls, which is characteristic of the Rincon phase. The combination of Classic period design motifs with Sedentary period design placement, along with the transitional architectural forms, prompted Gregonis to reintroduce the Cortaro phase, originally proposed by Harold Gladwin to "bridge the gap" between the Rincon and Tanque Verde phases (Kelly 1978:47). Others (e.g. Wallace 1995) have assigned the transitional ceramics to the late Rincon phase and have suggested that the Cortaro designation be limited to associations of Classic period architecture with late Rincon phase ceramics.

University Indian Ruin (AZ BB:9:33)

University Indian Ruin is a large prehistoric habitation site located on the first river terrace east of Pantano Wash, on the broad point of land lying between Pantano Wash and Tanque Verde Creek. The site lies about 1.5 km (0.93 mile) due east of the Hardy site. The most densely occupied portion of the site falls within an 11-acre parcel owned by the University of Arizona (Hayden 1957:1). Precise site boundaries have never been defined, and the depiction of the site on the ASM maps does not represent the probable areal extent of the site. Two discrete occupation areas have been identified within the University of Arizona parcel. The two areas are separated by a shallow wash running perpendicular to the terrace. South of the wash there is a low artificial mound upon which an adobe compound was constructed. Immediately north of the wash lies the probable main portion of the settlement, referred to as the village area. Although no direct stratigraphic link was demonstrated between these two areas, associated artifacts indicate considerable temporal overlap in their respective occupations (Hayden 1957:5).

The most intensive archaeological work at University Indian Ruin took place in January–March 1940, under the direction of Julian Hayden (Hayden 1957). With a crew of Civilian Conservation Corps laborers from Pennsylvania, Hayden conducted excavations within both the village and mound areas of the site. In spite of the limited areal exposures, the excavations provided important data on settlement structure and growth. During the Tanque Verde phase, the primary occupation locus of the site appears to have been the village area, where a diverse assortment of pit houses and walled compounds of above-ground adobe houses were identified. Two of the excavated pit houses were found below later above-ground adobe structures, suggesting significant temporal depth to the occupation. During the later Tucson phase, the focus of the community shifted to the platform mound, the most conspicuous feature at the site.

The analysis of temporally diagnostic artifacts recovered from excavations at University Indian Ruin has indicated occupation in the Tanque Verde and Tucson phases of the Classic period. Pottery types at the site include Tanque Verde Red-on-brown, Pantano Red-on-brown (a term sometimes used to refer to Tanque Verde Red-on-brown with abundant schist in the paste), Gila and Tucson Polychrome, and small quantities of Gila Red, San Carlos Red, and San Carlos Red-on-brown (Hayden 1957:121). Hayden also reported that an earlier and unpublished excavation by Ben Wetherill had found several sherds from a Spanish majolica bowl below the collapsed roof of one of the later architectural features in the village portion of the site (Hayden 1957:178). The context of this find suggests that a portion of the site was occupied into the middle of the seventeenth century, perhaps by Sobaipuri who had obtained the vessel through trade with the Spanish. Given the limited record of the recovery of these artifacts, it is difficult to evaluate this claim.

The excavations at University Indian Ruin have provided one of the few substantial data sets on the Tucson phase of the Classic period. The presence of materials from the earlier Tanque Verde phase also provides an opportunity to explore questions about the transition between the two phases. The architectural features identified at the site exhibited the variability characteristic of the Classic period. The Tanque Verde phase component included both semirectangular pit structures similar in form to their Sedentary period predecessors, and rectilinear surface rooms with walls of post-reinforced adobe. In terms of settlement structure, the Sedentary period courtyard groups, with their extramural spaces defined by the orientation of their constituent houses, gave way to a more formalized division of space reflected in the construction of compound walls. But perhaps the most telling evidence of the increasing formalization of the use of space can be seen in the construction of the platform mound and its associated architectural features.

Given the apparent intensity of the Classic period occupation at the site, a surprisingly small number of burials were encountered during the 1940 excavations. Both inhumation and cremation burials were noted, reflecting the diversity of burial practices that characterized the Classic period. The three excavated cremations were all of the urn variety and were generally placed along the courtyard walls (Hayden 1957:97). The four inhumations were placed in pits excavated through the floors of abandoned rooms. Although the small sample limits the confidence with which comparisons can be made, the mixed burial treatment observed at the site appears to remain constant between the Tanque Verde and Tucson phases, leading Hayden to speculate that two distinct ethnic communities resided at the site: a local population continuing the practices of the preceding Sedentary period, and an immigrant Salado population that brought with it new styles of architecture and ceramics, along with a suite of mortuary practices including inhumation. Further evidence for this view may be the architectural diversity and innovations in village structure discussed above.

Major Historical-Period Sites

Binghampton (AZ BB:9:238)

As we discussed in some detail in Chapter 4, the Mormon community of Binghampton was established on the banks of the Rillito, near the center of the Río Antiguo project area, at the very end of the nineteenth century. Here we briefly summarize the history of Binghampton and then describe both the archaeological site, AZ BB:9:238, and the proposed NRHP Binghampton Rural Historic Landscape.

Around 1898, Nephi Bingham, a Mormon freighter from Utah, purchased 60 acres from Alexander Davidson in the SW $\frac{1}{4}$ of the NE $\frac{1}{4}$ of Section 28 (Township 13 South, Range 14 East) (Parkhurst 2001). The parcel was located on the north side of the river, at the center of what came to be known as the river bend area, after the two right-angle turns the river takes as it passes through the area. Bingham was attracted by the rich alluvial soils and the potential for irrigation, and he and his extended family were soon clearing trees, digging ditches, and practicing a variety of desert agriculture first developed 50 years earlier by Mormons in Utah. Within a few years, the Binghams were joined by other Mormon settlers, most notably from northern Mexico, where Mormon colonies first established in the 1880s were forced to disperse because of the civil unrest brought about by the Mexican Revolution. The influx of settlers from Mexico, especially after 1911, led to intensive use of the floodplain on the north side of the river, and to the eventual expansion of the original Bingham colony to the river's south side. In 1910, a branch of the Mormon Church was established in the community, the first branch in the Tucson area. The branch was named Binghampton in honor of the original settlers (Ciolek-Torrello and Homburg 1990:73–78; Parkhurst 2001; see also Chapter 4).

Binghampton was a thriving, distinctively Mormon community for about 40 years. By the start of World War II, the community had become much less rural in character and was beginning to be absorbed by greater Tucson. Nonetheless, the Binghampton neighborhood today retains a significant Mormon presence, and a number of the buildings and landscape features associated with the early Mormon settlement survive. A 584-acre tract on the north bank of the Rillito, centered on Nephi Bingham's original 60-acre parcel, has recently been nominated to the NRHP as the Binghampton Rural Historic Landscape. The NRHP nomination form (Parkhurst 2001) is now an important source on the history of Binghampton, adding significantly to the information compiled in a cultural resources survey of the Rillito Valley by SRI in 1989 (Ciolek-Torrello and Homburg 1990).

The archaeological site of Binghampton, AZ BB:9:238, was first recorded in the 1989 SRI survey. As defined by SRI, the site occupies approximately 371 acres on the north bank of the Rillito, bounded on the south and west by the incised river channel, on the north by the front edge of the Santa Catalina foothills, and on the east by Alvernon Way. This boundary is roughly the same as the boundary of the proposed Binghampton Rural Historic Landscape (see below), although the latter encompasses significantly more acreage, reflecting a more deliberate assessment of the historical associations of architecture and landholdings in the area. The site boundary established by SRI, considered a provisional boundary from the start, was based more on the known historical association of the river bend area with the Binghampton community than on the actual distribution of extant structures, archaeological features, or artifacts. SRI did briefly describe a variety of features within AZ BB:9:238—houses, a cemetery, irrigation features, and earthen berms—all of which are also described in the NRHP nomination form. Surprisingly, SRI found only occasional scatters of historical-period artifacts on the site, which may reflect either the consistent use of pits for trash disposal or natural and cultural processes that have obscured surface artifacts. Scarce as surface artifacts may be, the intensive use of the area by Mormons and others during the first half of the twentieth century undoubtedly left much more in the way of both artifacts and features than was identified in the SRI survey (this is also suggested by the results of a recent survey of a portion of the site by Parkhurst et al. 2001).

Irrigation was central to the success of farming at Binghampton, as it was for farming all along the Rillito during the historical period (see Chapter 4). Numerous abandoned irrigation features survive in the area, many undoubtedly of Mormon origin. A map of irrigation features owned by the Rillito Irrigation District in the Binghampton area was prepared by a civil engineer, J. Moss Ruthrauff, sometime in the period 1910–1918 (Ruthrauff n.d.; see Chapter 4 for a discussion of the district). The features on the map are apparently the major parts of the system long used by the Bingham community (Ciolek-Torrello and Homburg 1990:63–64), but as we discuss in Chapter 4, the Binghams might have built their system around existing features. The map depicts a large ditch originating in the bed of Tanque Verde Creek, just upstream of its confluence with Pantano Wash, then running along the north bank of the Rillito for more than 2 miles to a large, earthen reservoir just north of the original Bingham property. Two smaller ditches exited the reservoir, one running north to the foothills, then west along the north edge of the floodplain, and the other south and west to meet the Rillito, where it passed under the river via a siphon. Remnants of both the northern distribution ditch and the reservoir were noted in the field by Ciolek-Torrello and Homburg (1990:63), and probable remnants of the southern distribution ditch have been noted by Parkhurst (2001). Other probable fragments of the same system, including smaller distribution ditches and segments of pipe were noted recently in a survey for River Road improvements (Parkhurst et al. 2001). A segment of canal recorded by Hohmann (1989) as AZ BB:9:247 just east of the AZ BB:9:238 boundary is probably also part of the Binghampton system. We discuss the relationship of Binghampton-associated irrigation features with other irrigation systems in the study area in Chapter 4.

With the fall of the water table in the Rillito Valley after 1930, Binghampton farmers, like other farmers along the Rillito, turned to wells as their primary source of irrigation water. The Binghampton area has numerous wells of a wide range of dates, some still actively used, others abandoned. A variety of water-storage features have also been recorded in the area (cisterns, aboveground tanks) some originally fed by ditches, others built to hold well water (Parkhurst 2000; Parkhurst et al. 2001).

One of the most important and culturally sensitive archaeological features of AZ BB:9:238 and the Binghampton Rural Historic Landscape is the Latter-day Saints Cemetery, located in the northeastern corner of the site and district, and first used by the Mormon community around 1899. The cemetery was used without formal title to the land until 1927, when John Murphey, a real estate developer, included the area in a claim he filed with the GLO for a large tract of foothills land. Murphey demanded removal of the graves from the property, a demand the Mormon community fought by sending a representative to the GLO in Phoenix. Eventually, the community was allowed to purchase a 40-acre parcel (Township 13 South, Range 14 West, Section 21, SE ¼, SE ¼; see Table 1), which continues to serve as a Mormon cemetery today. The cemetery is a noncontributing element of the proposed Binghampton Rural Historic Landscape (Parkhurst 2001).

A small prehistoric site, AZ BB:9:23, recorded in the 1930s, falls within the bounds of AZ BB:9:238, near its northern limit. This site is a small sherd and lithic scatter of undifferentiated Hohokam association. The site was apparently not re-located by SRI during its 1989 survey (Ciolek-Torrello and Homburg 1990). The ASM site card for AZ BB:9:23 includes a note that a historical-period ditch passed near it. The ditch was probably another segment of the Mormon distribution canal noted in this area during the SRI survey.

Fort Lowell (AZ BB:9:40)

Camp Lowell, later designated Fort Lowell, was moved from its original location in downtown Tucson to a location along the Rillito in March 1873. The move was prompted by substandard living conditions, a polluted water supply, and social problems arising from the close proximity of the post's enlisted men to the temptations of Tucson. General Order 33 established the Fort Lowell Military Reservation, an area extending 5 miles north, 5 miles south, 11 miles east, and 4 miles west of the post's center just south of the confluence of Pantano Wash and Tanque Verde Creek (Arizona State Parks Board 1978). Lt. Col. Eugene Asa Carr, accompanied by the governor of Arizona Territory, Anson P. K. Safford, selected the site for its grazing potential, firewood, and steady supply of potable water. The troops dug wells and erected windmills to pump water, and irrigation ditches carried water from the Rillito to the post (Peterson 1963:8, 10).

Over the next 17 years, the post served primarily as a supply depot for outposts in southern and eastern Arizona actively engaged in the Apache wars. In addition, troops from the fort provided protection for wagon trains, scouted against the Apache, and policed the international border. Fort Lowell's continual military presence during the 1870s and 1880s served as a deterrent to Apache raiding in the Tucson Basin. Moreover, the post contributed to the social and economic well-being of Tucson. Soldiers at the fort and citizens of Tucson regularly entertained each other with dinners, dances, concerts, and sporting events. Fort Lowell contributed $150,000 annually to the local economy through the purchase of food and building and outfitting supplies, and soldiers frequented the hotels, saloons, and gaming houses in town (Peterson 1963:11). Local craftsmen and laborers were hired for the building and subsequent maintenance of the post, and laundresses kept the troops in clean uniforms. In addition, the fort employed civilians with specialized skills such as blacksmiths, wheelwrights, teamsters, and schoolteachers (Arizona State Parks Board 1978). This social and economic interdependency terminated when the fort was abandoned in February, 1891. The end of the Apache wars a few years earlier and the subsequent troop reductions rendered the fort obsolete in the overall military strategy of the area.

The layout of Fort Lowell followed the general plan of other military posts in the Southwest. Skilled craftsmen and laborers from Tucson, assisted by the troops, constructed permanent adobe buildings around a rectangular parade ground (Figure 58). David Dunham was the government contractor in charge of building Fort Lowell. Dunham supervised approximately 100 men, serving as foreman, timekeeper, and paymaster. Lumber for the building project was cut from the pine forests in the Rincon Mountains, trimmed, and hauled in by ox-drawn wagons (TC 1928). Lord and Williams, a Tucson business, supplied 600,000 adobe bricks for the construction project, all made on the premises with the raw material at hand (Peterson 1963:9). An archaeological investigation conducted a century later (Kinkade and Fritz 1975) found prehistoric sherds and lithics, as well as historical-period sherds, embedded in the adobe used in construction of the fort.

Concerning the layout of Fort Lowell, the Records of the War Department, Office of the Quartermaster General, lists the following buildings:

> The buildings consist of seven sets of officers' quarters built of adobe, with dirt roofs; three adobe buildings for the enlisted men, 122 by 18 feet; band quarters, 92 by 18 feet; a hospital of eight rooms; guard house; commissary and quartermaster's store house; quartermaster's corral 300 feet square containing the wheelwright and blacksmith shop; forage house and sheds for about 100 animals; cavalry corral 158 by 160 feet; [and] five sets of laundresses' quarters . . . [quoted in Cosulich 1953:210].

To the north of the parade ground were two Company Barracks, the Band Quarters, and the Quartermaster and Commissary Storehouse. A corridor of cottonwood trees lined the south side of the parade ground (Figure 59), separating it from a row of Officers' Quarters. On the east side were the Post Hospital and another Company Barrack. The Adjutant's Office, Guard House, Schoolhouse, and Bakery stood in a row on the west edge. North of the Company Barracks were the corrals, and even farther north were irrigation ditches and the post gardens. To the west of the post, John B. Allen built the Sutler's Store, which provided goods to the fort. The buildings at Fort Lowell had walls of adobe bricks, with pine logs and saguaro ribs supporting dirt roofs. Porches, shutters, and tin roofs were added in the mid-1880s.

After the fort was abandoned in 1891, the reservation lands were turned over to the Department of the Interior. Squatters who for years had encroached on the military reservation finally took steps to

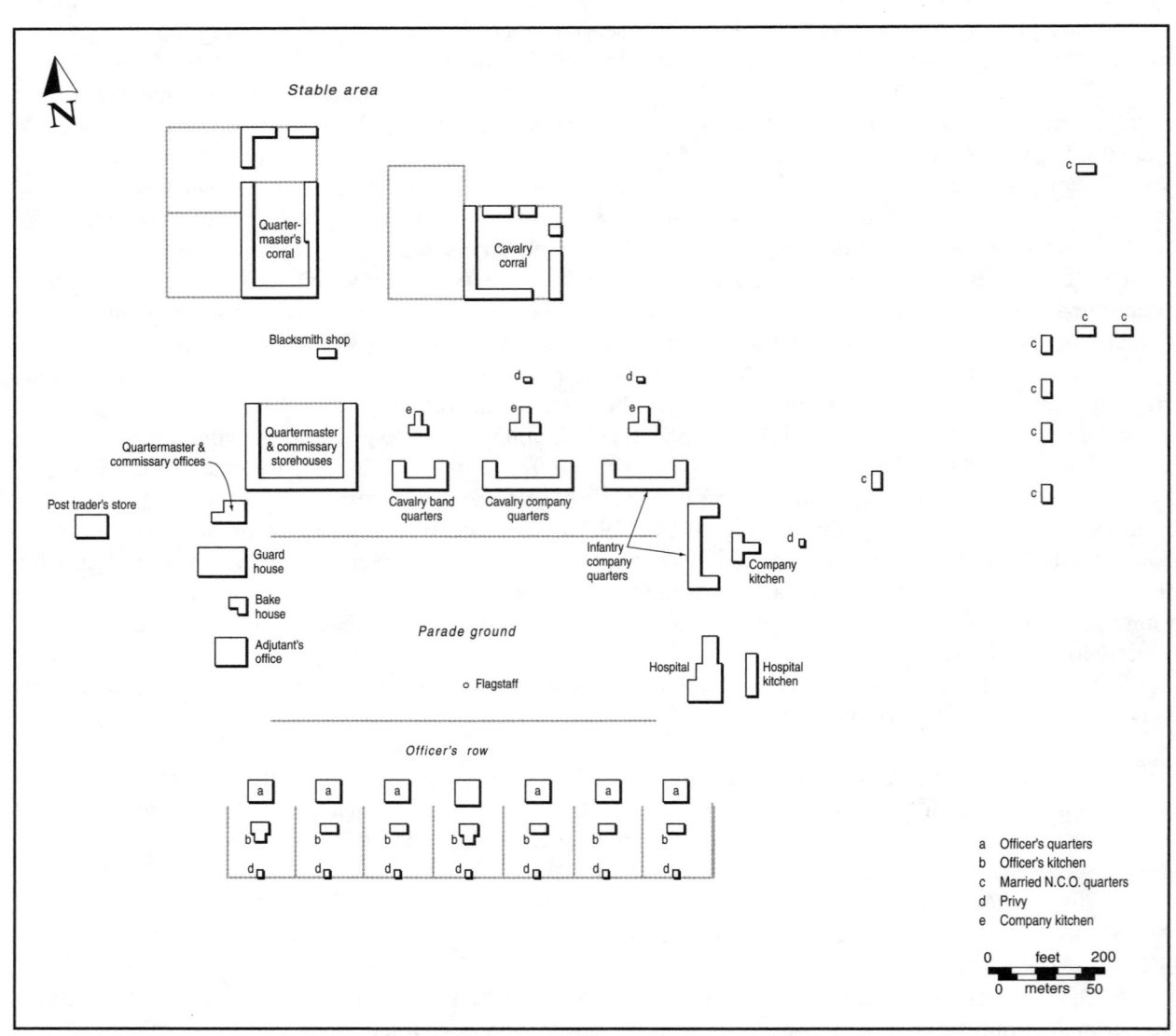

Figure 58. Map of Fort Lowell, ca. 1880 (after Bufkin, in Peterson 1963:13).

Figure 59. Cottonwood Lane, view to west, 1888. The Officers' Quarters are on the left, and the parade ground is on the right behind the picket fence (photograph courtesy of the Arizona Historical Society, Tucson, Accession No. 29123).

legally acquire the lands. The doors, window sashes, tin roofing, beams, glass, and picket fences were sold at the public auction of the post. The townspeople even cut down the cottonwood trees to use as fire wood. With nothing to protect the adobe walls, the buildings soon decayed (Figures 60 and 61). Despite the dilapidated state of the former military post, the Tucson Chamber of Commerce billed it as a point of historic interest and a popular spot for picnics, and many visitors to Tucson made the trek east of town to see the crumbling ruins of old Fort Lowell (Chamber of Commerce 1904:4; Hughston 1911) (Figure 62). Sometime in the early twentieth century, the federal government transferred the property to the Arizona State Land Office, which leased or sold parcels to private individuals. It was during this period prior to 1929 that settlers built homes both in and among the ruins. Known as La Barriada de Rillito, or El Fuerte, this small, predominantly Mexican-American community farmed the fertile lands along the Rillito (Arizona State Parks Board 1978; see also Chapter 4).

In 1929, the University of Arizona obtained 40 acres for the purpose of preserving the ruins of Fort Lowell. Several years later, University of Arizona dean Byron Cummings led an effort to preserve the ruins as a historic monument. With the help of University of Arizona students and the Arizona Archaeological and Historical Society, Cummings had the land surveyed, filled in the holes dug by treasure hunters, and cleaned up the property (Cummings 1935). Plans were underway to restore the Commanding Officer's Quarters and the Post Hospital when the project was dropped for lack of funds. The university sold the property to George R. Babbitt, Jr., of Flagstaff. Babbitt donated the land to the Boy Scouts, who placed a protective shelter over the Post Hospital ruins (Figure 63) in 1952, but did little else to preserve the property. In 1957, Pima County purchased the fort. Five years later, the Pima County Parks Department completely reconstructed the Commanding Officer's Quarters and kitchen, on a site just northeast of their original location (Figure 64). The adobe bricks used in the reconstruction were made from raw material excavated on site and, like the ones used in the original structures, contain

Figure 60. Fort Lowell Hospital ruins, view to the southeast, ca. 1910
(photograph courtesy of the Arizona Historical Society, Tucson, Accession No. 5943).

Figure 61. Fort Lowell ruins, view to the north, ca. 1915. The Cavalry Band Quarters are at the center, and the east edge of the Quartermaster and Commissary Storehouse is visible at far left (photograph courtesy of the Arizona Historical Society, Tucson, Accession No. B113637).

Figure 62. J. Knox Corbett's stagecoach being "held up" at the ruins of old Fort Lowell, date unknown (photograph courtesy of the Arizona Historical Society, Tucson, Accession No. 13797).

Figure 63. Fort Lowell, ruins of the Post Hospital today, view to the north.

Figure 64. Fort Lowell, Commanding Officer's Quarters (reconstructed) today, view to the northwest.

Figure 65. Fort Lowell, Cottonwood Lane today, view to the west. The reconstructed Commanding Officer's Quarters and kitchen are visible at the upper left.

prehistoric sherds. In 1962, the county replanted Cottonwood Lane in its approximate original location (Figure 65). Since 1963, the Arizona Historical Society has operated a branch museum at the Commanding Officer's Quarters. In the 1970s, the Pima County Board of Supervisors designated the 58 acres of the Fort Lowell Park and 126 additional acres to the west as the Fort Lowell Historic District. The City of Tucson, under a similar ordinance, followed suit in 1981, designating a 13-acre area within its jurisdiction as a historic district (Peterson 1963:17–18; Mabry 1990a:2–3).

Today, the remains of the old fort fall within a single political jurisdiction (Figure 66). The City of Tucson acquired Fort Lowell Park from Pima County in a 1984 land swap and purchase deal. The ruins of the Post Hospital and Hospital Kitchen are protected by a sheet-metal *ramada* and fence. Along the northern boundary of the park, the remains of the Infantry Company Quarters and its kitchen, and the Cavalry Band Quarters have been fenced off. Portions of the adobe walls still stand, but most have eroded to ground level. North of the park are the ruins of the Cavalry Corral and Shops and the Quartermaster Corral and Shops. The Post Garden is on the grounds of St. Gregory's College Preparatory School, located at 3231 N. Craycroft Road south of the Rillito. The original garden comprised 5 acres and received water via an irrigation ditch (Ciolek-Torrello and Homburg 1990:83).

Outside the park boundaries, only a few structures associated with the fort remain. In 1900, Dolly Cates purchased a large tract of land comprising the remains of the Guard House, Bakery, Adjutant's Office, three of the Officer's Quarters, and their attendant kitchens and privies. Five years later, Cates established a tuberculosis sanatorium in the Officer's Quarters nearest Craycroft Road (Mabry 1990a:2). Cates resided in one of the former Officer's Quarters from 1908 to 1928. Harvey Adkins purchased the property in 1928 and established the Adkins Steel and Tank Manufacturing Company in 1934. Adkins stuccoed the building used as a sanatorium and added a porch to convert it into a dwelling (Figures 67 and 68). Today, the remains of three Officer's Quarters, two of their attendant kitchens, ruins of an

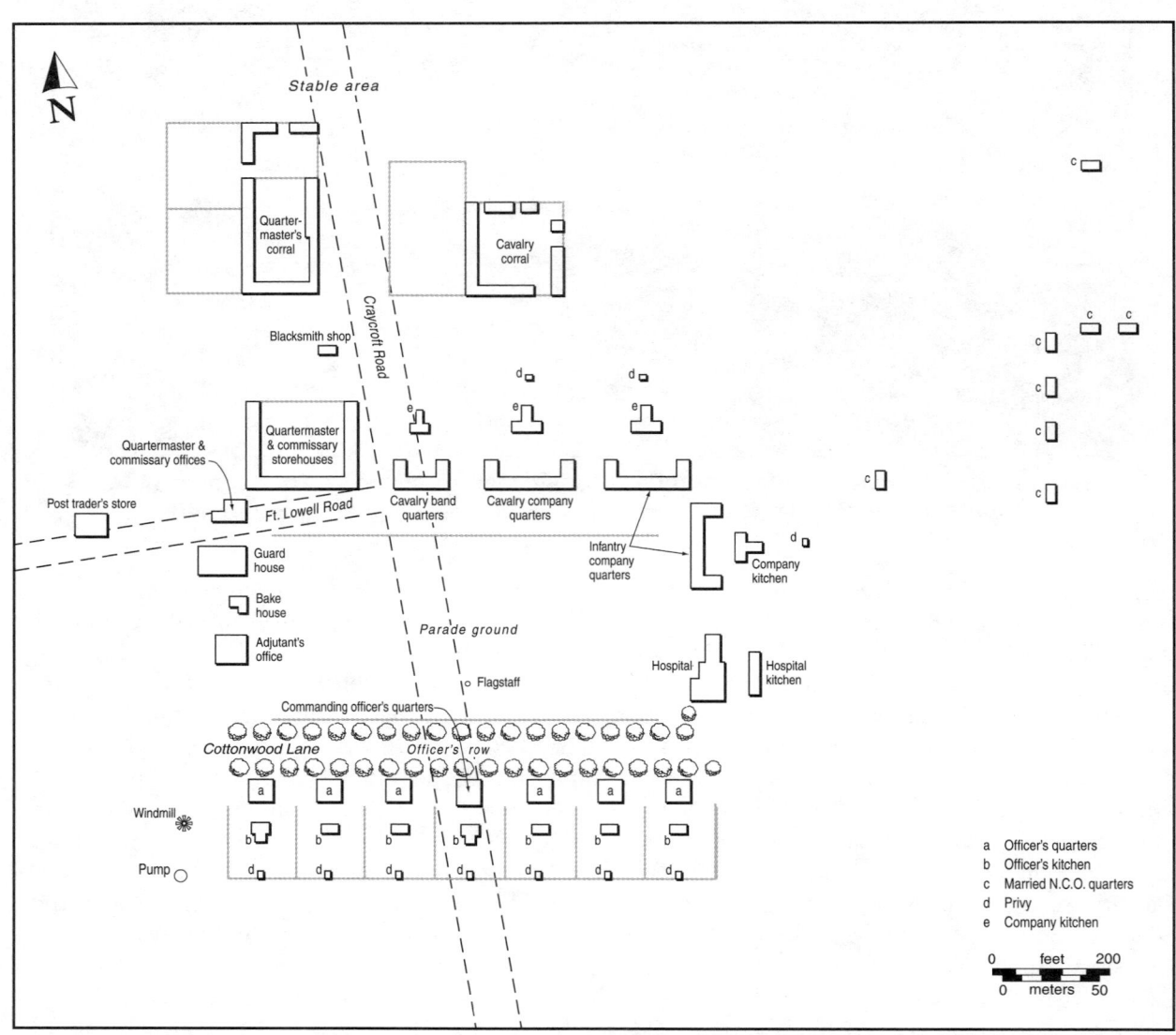

Figure 66. Map of Fort Lowell, with road additions (after Bufkin, in Peterson 1963:13).

190

Figure 67. Fort Lowell Officer's Quarters, view to the west, January 1938 (HABS 1941).

adobe wall, and ruins of the stone Guard House stand to the west of Craycroft Road. Of the three Officer's Quarters, one is in ruins, the one used by Cates was gutted by fire in 1970, and the third functions as a dwelling. One of the kitchens, probably stuccoed at or near the time Adkins renovated the Officer's Quarters (Figure 69), was also destroyed in the 1970 fire. The other kitchen is in ruins. The original adobe wall running behind and between the Officer's Quarters was built by George H. Doe in 1877. Doe owned a ranch east of the post and may have been called upon for other building and maintenance projects during his association with the fort (see Chapter 4). The Guard House, built in 1873, contained several rooms for the guards and four cells made of stone, the only stone used on the post. All that remains of the structure is a stone wall ruin south of Fort Lowell Road (Arizona State Parks Board 1978).

The Quartermaster and Commissary Storehouse is located at the northwest corner of the intersection of Craycroft and Fort Lowell Roads. In 1938, residents of El Fuerte converted this structure into five apartments. Today, it still serves as a row of apartments and retains its original architectural integrity. Adjacent to this structure are the stone ruins of the Commissary cellar and a small adobe mound where the Quartermaster and Commissary Offices once stood. Immediately west of these structures is the Post Sutler's store, built by John B. "Pie" Allen in 1873. Allen sold the store the following year to Frederick L. Austin, who operated the store until 1891 when the post closed. After the fort was abandoned, the property changed hands several times. In the 1930s it was converted into a private residence, and although the owners added a south facade in the mid-1970s, the interior still retains its original architectural integrity (Arizona State Parks Board 1978).

Several archaeological and historical investigations have shown that significant prehistoric and historical-period remains occur within the boundaries of the Fort Lowell Historic District. A 1941 Historic American Building Survey (HABS) report on Fort Lowell identifies the locations of the Post Hospital and the Officer's Quarters and adjacent kitchen. The same report briefly reviews the history of occupation and use of the Officer's Quarters as a private residence (HABS 1941). Alfred E. Johnson (1960),

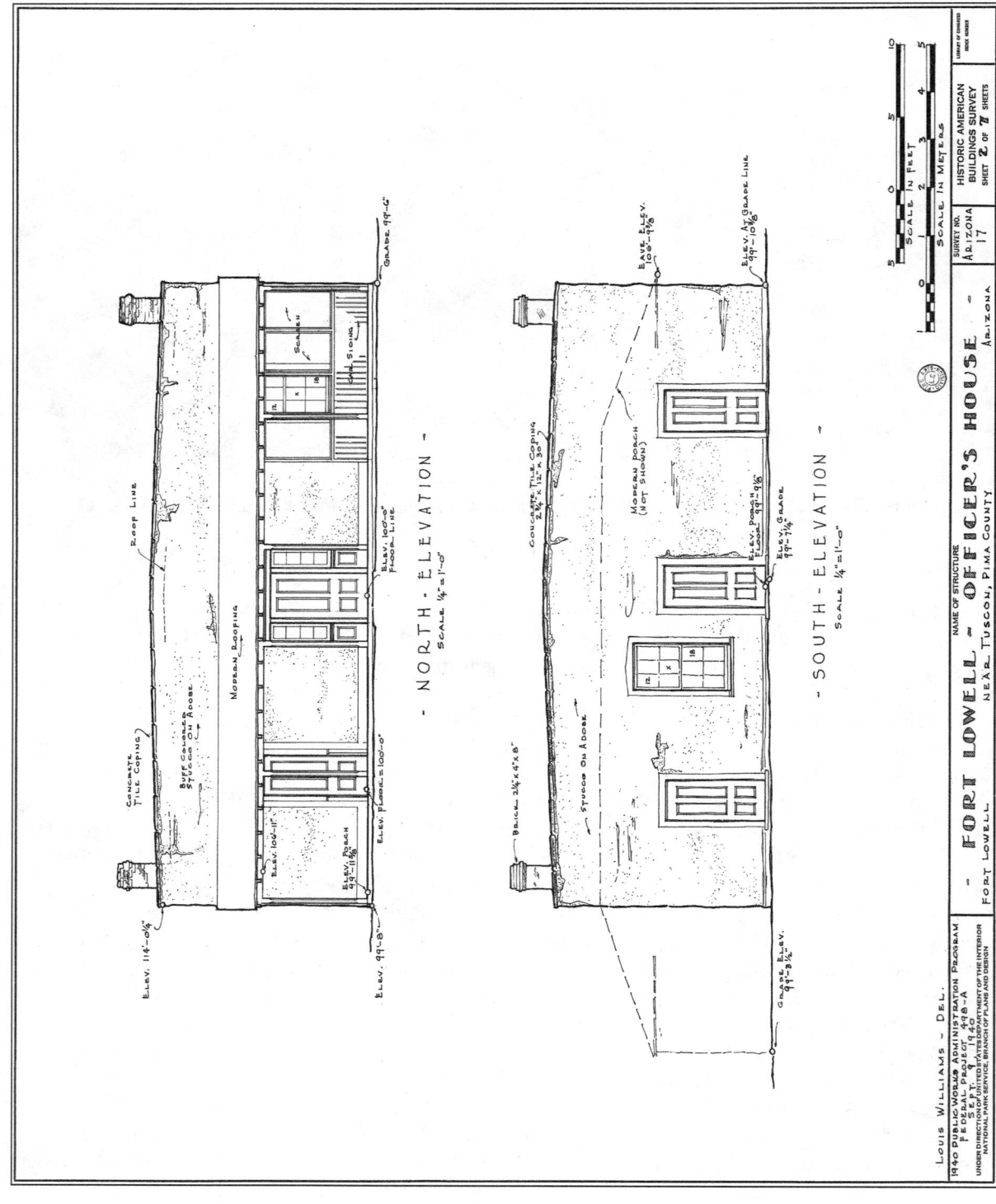

Figure 68. 1940 line drawing of Fort Lowell Officer's Quarters, converted into a private dwelling (HABS 1940).

Figure 69. Fort Lowell kitchen behind Officer's Quarters, view to the southwest, Historic American Buildings Survey, July 6, 1940 (HABS 1941).

under the auspices of the Arizona State Museum, excavated several of the Officer's Quarters and attendant outbuildings in the southeast corner of the fort, producing information on military architecture and material culture. In 1975, ASM archaeologists excavated in and around the building foundations of the Band Quarters kitchen complex as part of the Tucson Sewage Project (Kinkade and Fritz 1975). The authors of the report identified a three-room adobe building that served as a mess hall, kitchen, and storage room for members of the regimental band at the fort. Based on the abundance of prehistoric artifacts in the adobe bricks, the authors concluded that local soil from the underlying Hohokam site was used for construction of the kitchen. Kinkade and Fritz also apparently identified distinct interior and exterior cooking areas, based on the occurrence of burned surfaces and fired brick. Finally, they noted a number of discrepancies in construction from the typical patterns described in War Department plans and historical-period accounts (Huntington 1982:7–8). The Band Quarters kitchen was assigned its own ASM number, AZ BB:9:72, which has never been formally subsumed under the original Fort Lowell designation.

ASM revisited the Band Quarters kitchen complex and a nearby corral in 1982 as part of a project to mitigate the impact of widening Craycroft Road. In his report of these investigations, Huntington (1982: 9–10) reexamined several of the research issues originally addressed by Kinkade and Fritz, notably the construction, use, and post-military occupation of the Band Quarters kitchen complex. His particular concerns involved documentation of construction techniques and the use of local building materials, comparison of the information collected from the Band Quarters kitchen complex with the results of the architectural study of the Officer's Quarters and kitchen (Johnson 1960), and the post-military occupation of the fort by the Mexican immigrants who established the community of El Fuerte. Based on his investigations, Huntington (1982:29–30) concluded that differences in construction between the enlisted men's and officer's kitchens did not reflect status, but were the product of the different periods during which the buildings were built. The kitchen complex was built at a time when the fort employed skilled civilian craftsmen, and better building techniques were used in its construction. In contrast, the Officer's Quarters investigated by Johnson were actually occupied by noncommissioned officers and were built at a later date when skilled civilian labor was no longer used for lack of funds. The construction techniques reflected in the remains suggest it was built by unskilled troop labor. Huntington analyzed pollen extracted from the bricks and mortar to confirm Kinkade and Fritz's hypothesis regarding the use of local materials to fabricate the adobe bricks. Huntington (1982:31) failed, however, to find anything other than circumstantial evidence for reoccupation of the kitchen complex by the Diaz family, who, according to Turner (1982), occupied the nearby band barracks after the fort was abandoned in 1891.

Desert Archaeology (Mabry 1990b) monitored soil testing at the Adkins property at the southwest corner of Fort Lowell and Craycroft Roads, which the City of Tucson sought to acquire for the purpose of expanding Fort Lowell Park. Although no artifacts were brought to the surface, the possibility of significant prehistoric and historic remains below the surface warranted a recommendation for archaeological monitoring of all future ground disturbance.

Designated Historic Sites and Districts in the Study Area

Five historic properties in the Río Antiguo study area have received official designation as historic sites or districts. The locations of the five properties are depicted in Figure 70. Table 5 lists the properties and provides a brief description of each one.

In addition to the five officially designated historic properties, four archaeological sites have been determined eligible for listing in the NRHP. The four sites are: AZ BB:9:18, a dense Rillito phase artifact scatter; AZ BB:9:238, the original site of the Mormon community of Binghampton; AZ BB:9:302, the Davidson Flume and Schroeder's Well; and AZ BB:9:356, an early twentieth-century irrigation drop box. Discussions of all four sites are provided in Appendix B.

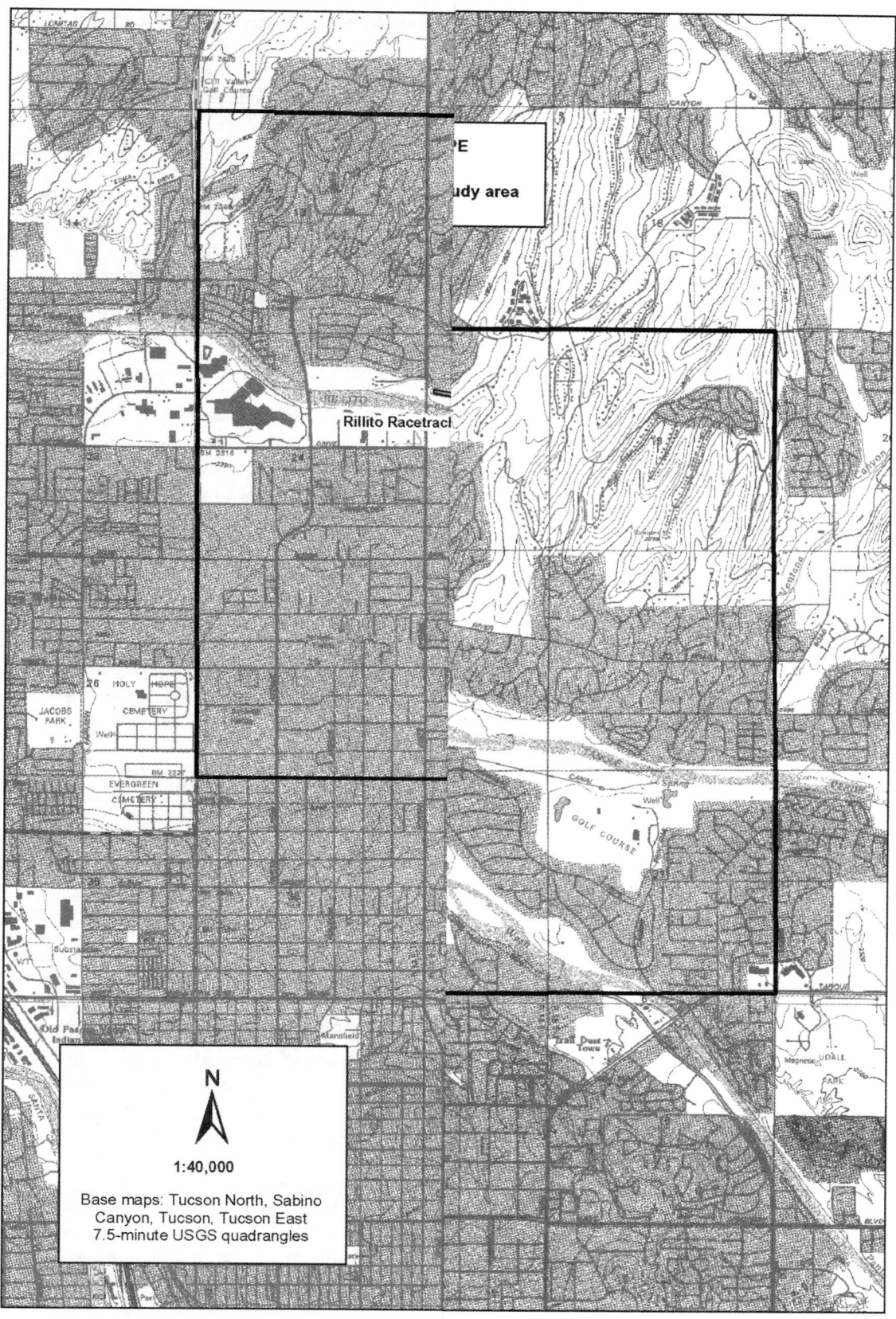

PE

udy area

Rillito Racetrack

N

1:40,000

Base maps: Tucson North, Sabino
Canyon, Tucson, Tucson East
7.5-minute USGS quadrangles

Table 5. Designated Historic Sites and Districts in the Río Antiguo Study Area

Name	Type and Year of Designation	Comments
Binghampton Rural Historic Landscape	NRHP District (proposed)	The proposed district consists of 67 contributing landscape units, for a total of 584 acres. The landscape units, 20 of which include a contributing house, correspond to ownership parcels. The proposed district has been nominated under NRHP Criteria a, c, and d, based primarily on its association with the Mormon farming community of Binghampton, from its founding in 1898 to the 1920s. Contributing houses include post-Mormon examples from as recent as 1953, and much of the current rural character of the district reflects post-Mormon uses of the area.
Fort Lowell Multiple Resource Area	NRHP District 1978 THD 1981	Pima County first established the Fort Lowell Historic District in 1976, encompassing an area north of Fort Lowell Road. Two years later, the Fort Lowell Multiple Resource Area (MRA) was listed in the NRHP. The MRA did not include a significant portion of the county district west and east of the fort ruins. In 1981, the City of Tucson created its own Fort Lowell Historic District, encompassing an area south of Fort Lowell Road. In 1992, the city annexed the area north of Fort Lowell Road and combined the city and county districts into the current city Fort Lowell Historic District. There are slight differences in the current NRHP and THD boundaries; the boundary shown in Figure 70 combines the two districts.
Rillito Racetrack Chute	NRHP 1986 SRHP 1986	Both nominations refer specifically to the $^3/_8$-mile "chute" or straightaway at the Rillito Racetrack. The chute, like other aspects of racing at Rillito Racetrack during its early history, was an important innovation in quarter horse racing.
San Pedro Chapel	THL 1982 SRHP 1993 NRHP 1993	San Pedro Chapel, an integral part of the Mexican-American community that grew up around the ruins of Fort Lowell in the early twentieth century, was the first City of Tucson Historic Landmark. The chapel was not completed until 1932, but it was preceded by two other chapels at or near the same site.
Valley of the Moon	SRHP 1975	This unique amusement park, the creation of George Phar Legler, opened in 1932 and closed in 1971. It was open intermittently in the 1980s and 1990s, but its nonprofit owners (currently, the George Phar Legler Memorial Society) have found it difficult to find funding to restore and maintain the property.

Key: NRHP = National Register of Historic Places individual property; SRHP = Arizona State Register of Historic Places individual property; THD = City of Tucson Historic District; THL = City of Tucson Historic Landmark

Archaeological Survey Coverage in the Study Area

Archaeological survey coverage in the Río Antiguo study area is concentrated largely on the floodplain of the Rillito. Almost all of the Río Antiguo APE falls within the floodplain, and about 75 percent of the APE has been surveyed. Outside the APE, only a small percentage of the overall study area has been surveyed. In most of the area to either side of the floodplain, development took place well before archaeological surveys became a usual element of planning, but the prehistoric archaeological potential of these areas is nonetheless limited (see below). Along the Rillito floodplain as a whole, where both prehistoric and historical-period archaeological potential is high, the largest surveys have been prompted by COE-sponsored flood-control projects, as noted in Chapter 3. The survey covering the largest area within the Río Antiguo study area and APE was a 1989 SRI survey for a COE channelization project of the Rillito and Tanque Verde Creek (Ciolek-Torrello and Homburg 1990). This survey provided essentially uninterrupted coverage of a wide swath of the Rillito floodplain from Craycroft Road to Campbell Avenue. Several other substantial surveys have included portions of the same area, reflecting a general recognition of the floodplain as an area of high archaeological sensitivity. Table 6 lists the other surveys in the study area with the corresponding report references and acreage.

Geoarchaeological Assessment of the Río Antiguo Study Area

This section serves two purposes. First, it provides an overview of geological and geoarchaeological information pertinent to the Río Antiguo study area. Second, it uses this information to assess buried and surficial archaeological potential in the study area. The assessment considers the potential for both prehistoric and historical-period sites.

Previous Geological Studies

The first study of the Quaternary geology of the Tucson Basin was the work of Smith (1938), who identified three Pleistocene terraces. From oldest to youngest, these terraces were named the University, Cemetery, and Jaynes terraces. The Tertiary deposits of the Santa Catalina foothills, the northern part of the Río Antiguo study area, have been described more recently by Pashley (1966) and Dickinson (1999).

The surficial geology of the Río Antiguo study area has been mapped by the Arizona Geological Survey, first by McKittrick (1988), who mapped surficial Tertiary deposits, Quaternary terraces, and Holocene terrace and channel deposits on 12 7.5-minute USGS quadrangle maps (1:24,000 scale). Klawon et al. (1999) later refined two of McKittrick's 7.5-minute maps, the Tucson North and Sabino Canyon quadrangles; these two maps provide complete coverage for the geology of the Río Antiguo study area. McKittrick's geologic maps provided relative age estimates, also subsequently revised by Klawon et al. (1999). The age estimates were based chiefly on aerial photography, surficial field examination, and limited subsurface inspections. Criteria for the age estimates included elevational differences between alluvial surfaces, depth of channel incision, amount of rock varnish on surface clasts, degree of rounding on interfluves, and the stage of soil formation.

It is important to note that the maps of McKittrick and Klawon et al. were prepared without the benefit of deep stratigraphic exposures and absolute dating. Thus, their age estimates must be regarded as

Table 6. Archaeological Surveys in the Río Antiguo Study Area

ASM Project No.	References	Acres	Focus of Survey
1979-031	Brew 1980 Schaefer and Brew 1979	260	2 areas plus 400 feet of right-of-way
1981-43		14	Lazy Creek I development
1981-45		3	Windwood development
1981-48		0.33	low-income housing development
1981-75		10	Desert Fountain Patio Homes
1981-102		6.33	Stonybrook Apartments
1981-99		0.17	low-income housing development
1980-4		375.5	Quail Canyon development
1980-55		40	Primavera development
1980-110		0.13	low-income housing development
1980-158		72.11	Rio Verde Vista II development
1982-7		n/a	Winterhaven Townhomes development
1982-142		5.84	Hill Farms II development
1982-148		1.22	Sahuaro Village development
1982-147		10	Hacienda del Río development
1982-179		70	University of Arizona Campbell Avenue Farm
1983-7		4.36	Racquet Club Village development
1983-68		1.32	Roger Lane Townhomes
1983-80		2.68	Elysian Garden Apartments
1983-81		41	River Road property
1983-83		5	Cactus Boulevard development
1984-70	Dart 1984	40	Tanque Verde Wash subdivision
1984-108	Hartmann 1984	88	Rillito Racetrack property
1985-76	Weed 1985	0.7	Kaphing's Kasitas
1985-79	Brew 1985	4.5	La Sonrisa Townhomes
1987-201		55	road expansion/bridge construction
1987-203	Mayro 1987a	n/a	Hacienda del Sol Road improvement
1987-213	Mayro 1987b	n/a	Alamo Wash
1988-186	Dart 1988	29	Rillito riverbank
1988-201	Maldonado 1988	72+	Stone Avenue extension
1989-2	Ciolek-Torrello and Homburg 1990	1,730+	Rillito/Tanque Verde Creek
1989-121	Hohmann 1989	259	water recharge complex
1989-164	Eppley 1989	n/a	Sabino Canyon/River Roads improvements

ASM Project No.	References	Acres	Focus of Survey
1990-137	Harry 1990	27	Foothills Park development
1991-174	Dart 1991	57	Catalina Foothills High School
1996-127	Lenhart 1996	5	North Mountain Park development
1996-160	Eppley 1996	4	Tucson Racquet Club expansion
1996-466	Madsen 1996a	66.85	Christopher City land planning
1996-467	Madsen 1996b	6.77	University of Arizona Parcel C
1996-468	Madsen 1996c	3.83	University of Arizona Parcel B
1997-9	Tompkins 1997	5.6	River Park Apartments development
1998-61		n/a	traffic signal, Grant/Rosemont intersection
1998-148	Sliva 1998	n/a	4 areas for water-main alignments
1998-303	Stephen 1998	9	Presidio/Craycroft NWC project
2000-157	Diehl 2000	n/a	Prince/Stone intersection
2000-224	Jones 2000	0.9	St. Philip's Plaza expansion
2000-264	Homburg and Kurota 2000 O'Mack and Riggs 2001	n/a	Pantano Wash bank protection project
2000-453	Tucker 2000	47.52	Craycroft Road expansion
—	Rowe and Slawson 1999	n/a	Tanque Verde Interceptor
—	Perry 2000	n/a	Pantano Wash–Tanque Verde Creek bank protection project
—	Villalobos 2002	68	Rillito ecosystem restoration project

Note: No references are indicated for surveys documented only by an ASM project registration form. An "n/a" in the Acres column means the survey acreage was not available or the survey was linear. The last two entries have not been registered at ASM.

approximations. In reality, none of the Quaternary terraces are well dated, and the stratigraphic relationships among most terraces in the Tucson Basin are poorly known (Haynes and Huckell 1986). This situation is particularly true for the older terraces, because their scarps (terrace edges) have been modified or obliterated by erosional processes.

Table 7 shows how the surficial geologic units of previous studies are correlated. As is apparent from the table, many of the units used by McKittrick and Klawon et al. (1999) are correlated, but the maps of the latter study were more useful for the present geoarchaeological assessment, as discussed later in this section. Detailed descriptions for the geologic units identified by Klawon et al. (1999:4–9) are provided below.

River Deposits

Sediments deposited by the Rillito River (including Tanque Verde Creek) and Pantano Wash cover most of the southern portion of the study area. Surfaces consist of active channels, young stream terraces composing the geologic floodplain, and several broad, older relict terraces dating to the Pleistocene. Deposits are a mix of gravel and sand with finer material, and exhibit mixed clast lithologies, reflecting the large

Table 7. Correlation of Geologic Map Units in the Northern Tucson Basin and Their Archaeological Sensitivity

Geologic Units Modified from Klawon et al. (1999:Table 1)	Age Estimate	Description	McKittrick (1988)	Dickinson (1999)	Pashley (1966)	Anderson (1987)	Smith (1938)	Archaeological Sensitivity	
								Buried Sites	Surface Sites
River alluvium									
Qycr	<100 y	modern river channel deposits	cha					low	low
Qyr	<10 ka	Holocene floodplain and terrace deposits	T1, T2					high	high
Qlr	10–130 ka	Late Pleistocene river terrace deposits	T3		Jaynes		Jaynes	low	high
Qmr	~130–500 ka	Middle Pleistocene river terrace deposits	T4		Cemetery		Cemetery	low	moderate
Qor	~500 ka–2 ma	Middle to early Pleistocene river deposits	T5		University		University	low	moderate
Fan alluvium									
Qy2	<2 ka	Late Holocene alluvium	ch	Qa1				high	high
Qy1	0–10 ka	Holocene alluvium	Y	Qa1				high	moderate
Ql	10–130 ka	Late Pleistocene alluvium	M2	Qpc/Qfr/Qss				low	moderate
Qm	~130–500 ka	Middle Pleistocene alluvium	M1	Qpc/Qfr/Qss				low	low
Qml	10–500 ka	Middle to late Pleistocene alluvium	M1, M2	Qpc/Qfr/Qss				low	low
Qmo	~500 ka–2 ma	Middle to early Pleistocene alluvium	O, QTbf	Qpc/Qfr?				low	low
QT	1–5 ma	Early Pleistocene to Pliocene alluvium	O, QTbf	QTca, Qpc	basin fill	Ft. Lowell		low	low
Qtvb		Ventana Benchlands fan complex	QTbf	Qtvb	basin fill	Ft. Lowell?		low	low
Older Foothills deposits									
Tsc	5–20 ma	Miocene alluvium	QTbf	Tsc	Rillito III	Tinaja		low	low
Tpa	20–30 ma	Late Oligocene to early Miocene deposits	Ts	Tpa	Rillito I and II	Pantano		low	low

Key: y = years ago; ka = thousand years before present; ma = million years before present drainage areas of the Rillito and Pantano Wash watersheds. Most of the area covered by river deposits has been altered by intense urban of unit contacts is less certain than in piedmont areas.

Qycr: Modern River Channel Deposits (< 100 Years)

This unit consists of river channel deposits composed primarily of sand and gravel. Modern channels are typically entrenched several meters below adjacent young terraces. The current entrenched channel configuration began to form with the development of arroyos in the late 1800s, and continued to evolve through the twentieth century (Pearthree and Baker 1987). Historically, channels had variable widths and were braided, but modern channels in much of the map area are relatively uniform within artificially stabilized banks. Channels are extremely flood prone and are subject to deep, high velocity in moderate to large flow events. Channel banks along the Rillito have been stabilized by soil cement, and the channel will convey the calculated 100-year flood without overtopping. The banks of the small length of the Pantano Wash channel in the map area and most of the banks of Tanque Verde Creek are unprotected and are subject to lateral erosion during floods.

Qyr: Holocene Floodplain and Terrace Deposits (< 10 ka [Thousand Years before Present])

The Qyr unit consists of floodplains and low terraces flanking the main channel system. Most Qyr areas were part of the active floodplain prior to arroyo development in the past century or so. Terrace surfaces are flat and uneroded, except immediately adjacent to channels. Qyr deposits consist of weakly consolidated to unconsolidated sand, silt, and clay, with gravel lenses in former channels. Stratigraphic investigations of Qyr deposits indicate that several sequences of arroyo development and filling have occurred in the past 5,000 years (Haynes and Huckell 1986). Soils are weakly developed, with some carbonate filaments and fine masses and weak soil structure in near-surface horizons. Locally, Qyr surfaces may experience sheetflooding during large floods, and as a result of flooding on local tributaries that debouch onto Qyr surfaces. Unprotected channel banks formed in Qyr deposits are very susceptible to lateral erosion.

Qlr: Late Pleistocene River Terrace Deposits (10–130 ka)

The Qlr unit consists of Pleistocene river terraces that are 1–3 m higher than the historical floodplain. Deposits consist of gravel, sand, silt, and clay. Soils are somewhat reddened, have weak argillic horizons, and have moderate calcic horizon development. These terraces are generally narrow and have fairly irregular surfaces, implying that they have undergone substantial erosional modification. Qlr terraces were labeled the Jaynes terrace by Smith (1938) and Pashley (1966), and Qt3 by McKittrick (1988). Qlr deposits are probably inset into and banked against older Qmr deposits. Haynes and Huckell (1986) reported a radiocarbon date of 18 ka from carbonate in a Qlr soil, which is likely a minimum age for the Jaynes terraces.

Qmr: Middle Pleistocene River Terrace Deposits (~130–500 ka)

Unit Qmr consists of middle Pleistocene river terraces that cover much of the floor of the northern Tucson Basin. Qmr terraces are typically ~2 m higher than adjacent Qlr terraces and are inset below Qor terraces. Deposits consist of sand, silt, clay and gravel. Soils are reddened and have variable development, but moderate to strong, clay-rich argillic horizons are typical. Calcic horizon development is also quite variable, but typically stage III or IV (cemented). Terraces are quite broad and terrace surfaces are quite flat away from drainage and terrace margins. Qmr terraces were labeled the Cemetery terrace by Smith (1938) and Pashley (1966), and Qt4 by McKittrick (1988). Based on the strong soil development associated with Qmr terraces, they are likely of middle Pleistocene age.

Qor: Middle to Early Pleistocene River Deposits (~500 ka–2 ma [Million Years before Present])

The Qor unit consists of relict, very old basin-floor deposits in the central portion of the Tucson Basin. Qor surfaces form elongate ridges. They are found at the topographically highest locations in the central basin, and thus record the highest level of basin filling. Deposits consist primarily of sand and gravel, and are generally coarser than younger terrace deposits. These surfaces are distinguished by strongly cemented calcic horizons with laminar caps suggestive of great antiquity. Qor surfaces were labeled the University terrace by Smith (1938) and Qt5 by McKittrick (1988).

Piedmont Alluvium

Quaternary and late Tertiary deposits cover most of the Santa Catalina foothills piedmont between the Santa Catalina Mountains and the Rillito. This sediment was deposited primarily by larger streams that head in the mountains; smaller streams that head on the piedmont have eroded and reworked some of these deposits. The deposits range in age from modern to early Pleistocene or Pliocene. The lower margin of the foothills piedmont is defined by its intersection with the planar, very gently northwest-sloping Holocene floodplain of the Rillito. Approximate age estimates for the various units are given in parentheses after the unit name.

Qy2: Late Holocene Alluvium (< 2 ka)

Unit Qy2 consists of channels, low terraces, and small alluvial fans composed of cobbles, sand, silt, and boulders that have been recently deposited by modern drainages. In areas proximal to the mountain front, sediment load is generally sand and cobbles with some boulders; terraces may be mantled with finer sediment. On lower piedmont areas, young deposits consist predominantly of sand, silt, and cobbles. Channels generally are incised less than 1 m below adjacent Qy2 terraces and fans, but locally, incision may be as much as 2 m. Channel morphologies generally consist of single-thread high-flow channels with gravel bars adjacent to low-flow channels. Downstream-branching distributary channel patterns are associated with the few young alluvial fans in the area. Local relief varies from fairly smooth channel bottoms to the undulating bar-and-swale topography characteristic of coarser deposits. Soil development associated with Qy2 deposits is minimal, and terrace and fan surfaces are brown. Channels appear light-colored on aerial photographs, whereas Qy2 terraces generally appear darker than surrounding areas. Vegetation density is variable. Channels typically have sparse, small vegetation, but the densest vegetation in the map area is found along channel margins and on Qy2 terraces along channels. Along the larger washes, tree species include mesquite, cottonwood, willow, and sycamore; smaller bushes and grass may also be quite dense. Smaller washes typically have palo verde and mesquite trees, large creosote bush, and other bushes along them.

Qy1: Holocene Alluvium (0–10 ka)

Unit Qy1 consists of low terraces and alluvial fans found near the mountain front and at scattered locations along drainages throughout the foothills. Qy1 surfaces are slightly higher than adjacent Qy2 surfaces and are generally subject to inundation only in extreme floods. Surfaces are planar to broadly rounded and typically are 1–2 m above adjacent active channels. Surfaces typically are sandy and brown in color, but where a gravel lag is present, vegetation is sparse and surfaces are light colored. Channel patterns consist of tributary or distributary networks. Qy1 surfaces support mesquite and palo verde trees, and typically smaller bushes are quite dense. Qy1 soils typically are weakly developed, with some soil structure but no obvious clay accumulation and stage 1 calcium carbonate development.

Ql: Late Pleistocene Alluvium (10–130 ka)

Unit Ql consists of moderately dissected terraces and relict alluvial fans found on the upper, middle, and lower piedmont. Active channels are typically incised up to about 3 m below these surfaces, with incision generally increasing toward the mountain front. Ql fans and terraces commonly are inset below adjacent Qm and older surfaces, but the lower margins of Ql deposits lap out onto more dissected Qm surfaces in many places on the middle and upper piedmont. Weakly to moderately incised tributary drainage networks are typical on Ql surfaces. Ql deposits consist of pebbles, cobbles, and finer-grained sediment. Ql surfaces commonly have loose, open lags of pebbles and cobbles; surface clasts exhibit weak rock varnish. Ql surfaces appear light orange on aerial photographs, reflecting slight reddening of surface clasts and the surface soil horizon. Ql soils are moderately developed, with orange to reddish brown clay loam argillic horizons and stage II calcium carbonate accumulation. Dominant vegetation types include creosote, bur sage, and ocotillo.

Qm: Middle Pleistocene Alluvium (130–500 ka)

Unit Qm consists of moderately dissected relict alluvial fans and terraces with strong soil development found throughout the foothills. Qm surfaces are typically several meters above adjacent active channels. Qm surfaces are drained by well-integrated, moderately incised tributary channel networks. Planar Qm surfaces are smooth with pebble and cobble lags; rock varnish on surface clasts is typically orange. More eroded Qm surfaces are characterized by loose cobble lags with moderate to strong varnish, ridge-like topography and carbonate litter on the surface. Qm surfaces have a distinctive dark orange color on aerial photographs, reflecting reddening of the surface soils and surface clasts. Soils typically contain reddened, clay argillic horizons, with obvious clay skins and subangular blocky structure. Soil carbonate development is typically III to IV, but strongly cemented petrocalcic horizons are uncommon. Qm surfaces generally support ocotillo, creosote bush, cholla, and saguaro.

Qml: Middle and Late Pleistocene Alluvium (10–500 ka)

Unit Qml consists of middle or late Pleistocene alluvium that could not be differentiated.

Qmo: Middle to Early Pleistocene Alluvium (500 ka–2 ma)

Unit Qmo consists of moderately to deeply dissected relict alluvial fans and terraces with variable soil development found mainly in the western foothills. Qmo surfaces are typically 5–10 m above adjacent active channels. Well-preserved planar Qmo surfaces are uncommon. Where they exist, they are smooth with pebble and cobble lags; rock varnish on surface clasts is typically orange to red. Well-preserved soils typically contain reddened, clay argillic horizons, with obvious clay skins and subangular blocky structure. Soil carbonate development is typically stage IV (cemented petrocalcic horizons, little or no laminar cap). More-eroded Qmo surfaces are characterized by loose cobble lags with moderate to strong varnish, ridge-like topography and carbonate litter on the surface. On aerial photographs, ridge crests on Qmo surfaces are dark reddish brown, reflecting reddening of the surface soils and surface clasts, and eroded slopes are gray to white. Qmo surfaces generally support bur sage, ocotillo, creosote bush, cholla, and saguaro.

QT: Early Pleistocene to Pliocene Alluvium (1–5 ma)

Two subunits are used to designate very old, deeply dissected and highly eroded alluvial fan deposits across the map area, modifying the usage of Dickinson (1999). The QT unit is used for the high-level, undeformed deposits in the central part of the map area (the Campbell Avenue fan complex of Dickinson [1999]) and similar, less extensive deposits in the western part of the map area. QT ridge crests are typically at least 10 m above adjacent active channels. QT surfaces are alternating eroded ridges and deep valleys. They are drained by well-integrated, deeply incised tributary channel networks. Even the highest surfaces atop QT ridges are rounded, and original highest capping fan surfaces are not preserved. QT deposits are dominated by gravel ranging from boulders to pebbles, with minor lenses of brown or reddish sand and silt. Clast lithology is predominantly gneiss. Deposits are weakly to moderately indurated, but are quite resistant to erosion because of the large clast size. Soils typically are dominated by pedogenic carbonate development, which is typically stage V (cemented petrocalcic horizons with laminar cap) on ridge crests. Carbonate litter is common or ridge crests and side slopes. On aerial photographs, QT surfaces are gray to white. QT surfaces generally support mesquite, palo verde, ocotillo, creosote bush, cholla, and saguaro. QT deposits record the highest levels of sediment accumulation in the foothills, an they predate the down-cutting and erosion that have dominated the Quaternary evolution of the foothills. Beds dip from 2° to 3° basinward and are not tilted. Locally, QT deposits overlie older, tectonically tilted Tsc and Tpa deposits in an angular unconformity. At the mountain front west of Finger Rock Canyon, QT deposits clearly onlap the Catalina detachment fault and are not displaced. QT deposits cover much of the foothills piedmont in the area of Campbell Avenue (Tucson North quadrangle). Isolated remnants of QT deposits in the middle and upper piedmont indicate that these deposits mantled the entire piedmont in the area of Campbell Avenue, and have subsequently been eroded from much of the upper piedmont.

QTvb: Ventana Benchlands Fan Complex

This second Quaternary–late Tertiary map unit consists of bouldery gravel deposits that form the high Ventana benchlands on the piedmont downslope from Sabino and Ventana Canyons (east-central part of the map area, Sabino Canyon quadrangle). Beds dip from 0° to 3° basinward, and there is no evidence of tilting of these deposits. These coarse sediments were probably deposited by ancestral Sabino Creek and Ventana Wash; they apparently filled a broad paleovalley on the downthrown (southwest) side of the Finisterra fault. QTvb deposits may have thinned to the northwest onto an erosion surface cut on the upthrown side of the fault. There are no exposures of the stratigraphic relationship between QTvb deposits and the fault, but QTvb deposits are undeformed and were probably deposited after the fault was active (Dickinson 1999). QTvb deposits on the upthrown northeast side of the Finisterra fault may have been restricted to the bottoms of valleys cut into the underlying Pantano Formation. If so, they have been completely removed by erosion.

Older Foothills Deposits

The following discussion of older foothills deposits is based on Dickinson (1999).

Tsc: Miocene Alluvium (5–20 ma)

This map unit consists of dissected, tectonically deformed alluvial fan deposits of probable Miocene age. Deposits consist of moderately indurated, cobbly to bouldery gravel with finer sand deposits; clasts are predominantly gneiss and schist. Beds commonly dip 10° to 15° to the southwest, and are cut by minor faults. Tsc deposits are widely exposed in the middle part of the map area, where Quaternary deposits are relatively sparse. Because they are dominated by clasts of rock currently exposed in the Santa Catalina Mountains and are deformed, Tsc deposits probably record the late phase of displacement on the Catalina detachment fault and the Finisterra fault splay. Accordant ridges formed in Tsc deposits suggest that two distinct erosional surfaces were cut across Tsc deposits during the late Pliocene to early Quaternary in the area of Swan and Craycroft Roads (Dickinson 1999). These erosion surfaces were likely mantled by thin early Pleistocene to late Pliocene deposits (unit QT or QTvb) at one time, but no clear evidence of these deposits exists at present. Qm and younger surfaces are inset below the level of the erosion surfaces cut on Tsc deposits.

Tpa: Late Oligocene to Early Miocene Deposits (10–30 ma)

This map unit consists of tectonically deformed, moderately indurated beds of the Pantano Formation. Deposits are pebble and cobble clast-supported conglomerate, bouldery matrix supported on conglomerate, and clay-rich beds that may represent ancient playas. The fine-grained matrix of these deposits is a distinct maroon color. Volcanic and granitic clasts are dominant in the conglomerates, and gneissic clasts are rare. These deposits thus record early displacement on the Catalina detachment fault and predate exposure of the gneissic rocks that are the predominant rock type in the southern Santa Catalina Mountains today. Strata are tilted by various amounts, but are typically in the range of 12° to 30°; minor faults are common (Dickinson 1999).

Bedrock and Bedrock Pediment

R: Bedrock

Bedrock was not mapped in detail for this project. Exposed bedrock in the southern Santa Catalina Mountains is primarily granitic gneiss, in the footwall of the Catalina-Rincon metamorphic core complex.

Rp: Bedrock Pediment

Bedrock pediment consists of fairly planar erosional surfaces cut onto bedrock on the upper margin of foothills piedmont. Pedimented surfaces are narrow and dissected. They are perched several meters or more above active channels. Based on their topographic position, the pediments probably formed in the Pliocene to early Pleistocene, concurrent with deposition of the highest levels of QT deposits (Morrison 1985).

Previous Geoarchaeological Studies

Virtually no geomorphic or geoarchaeological studies have been conducted to study the alluvial stratigraphy of the Rillito. Consequently, it is uncertain how its geomorphic history compares to that of other drainage systems. A detailed geomorphic reconstruction of the Rillito alluvium is needed to determine how it relates to better-studied areas, especially along the Santa Cruz River. Geomorphic studies of the alluvial history of the latter river have identified cycles of aggradation and channel entrenchment during the Holocene (Haynes and Huckell 1986; Huckell 1998; Waters 1987). It is possible that changes in the Rillito parallel these cycles, but because of high spatial and temporal variability in alluvial geomorphic systems in the Southwest (Kottlowski et al. 1965; Waters 1985, 1987), the relationship between the Rillito and the Santa Cruz is unknown. Because the Rillito is a tributary of, and grades to, the Santa Cruz, the geomorphic history of the lower reach of the Rillito should be similar to that of the Santa Cruz.

To better assess the effect of the Rillito on prehistoric and historical-period human settlement and land use, it is important that its geomorphic history be reconstructed independently from previous geoarchaeological work in other parts of the Tucson Basin. It is especially important that its cycles of aggradation and erosion be determined, because these will have a strong effect on preservation and burial of the alluvial archaeological record. Such cycles also strongly affect the carrying capacity of subsistence systems dependent on floodplain agriculture, as has been noted along the Santa Cruz (Doelle 1985; Doelle et al. 1985; Huckell 1998) and elsewhere in the Southwest (Dean 1988; Dean et al. 1985; Euler et al. 1979).

Although no detailed geoarchaeological investigations have been conducted on the Rillito, it is useful to review previous studies along different reaches of the Santa Cruz, because these studies have demonstrated that a rich archaeological record is preserved in the Holocene alluvium. Haynes and Huckell (1986), Waters (1987), and Freeman (1997) have shown that the Santa Cruz, the major through-flowing drainage in the Tucson Basin, experienced cycles of alluvial aggradation and channel entrenchment during the Holocene, and it likely that the Rillito River experienced many of the same changes, though not necessarily contemporaneously. Haynes and Huckell (1986) documented the alluvial history of the Santa Cruz by recording the stratigraphy of arroyo cuts, gravel pits, and backhoe trenches, focusing on Brickyard Arroyo on the San Xavier Indian Reservation, Airport Wash in the southern Tucson Basin, and the Ina Road–Interstate 10 area near the Santa Cruz. Diagnostic artifacts and radiocarbon dating of natural and cultural deposits were used to date five erosional-aggradational cycles over the last 6,000 years. At least three erosional-aggradational epicycles were identified in the last 2,500 years, suggesting that the frequency of cutting and filling increased during the late Holocene. Haynes and Huckell's stratigraphic model is an important contribution, and particularly significant is their finding that alluvium dating from 8000 to 6000 B.P. has been removed by erosion. The 8000–6000 B.P. period corresponds to the warm and dry conditions of the Altithermal. Haynes and Huckell also found that late Archaic period cultural deposits are preserved in the Santa Cruz alluvium, a finding that was confirmed by both their fieldwork and the extensive excavations conducted by Desert Archaeology along Interstate 10. Haynes and Huckell documented a number of prehistoric charcoal concentrations at AZ AA:12:111, between 0.3 and 1.5 m deep, in a trench dug at Interstate 10 and Ina Road. Three distinct cultural layers were found, each separated by culturally sterile strata. Radiocarbon dating indicates that the lower cultural layer dates to 4260 B.P. (A-2234); four dates from the middle layer clustered between 2700 B.P. and 2900 B.P.; and the upper layer yielded a date of 1400 B.P. (A-3141). At the Ina Road Landfill site (AZ AA:12:130), located between the mouths of Cañada del Oro Wash and the Rillito on the east side of the Santa Cruz, as many as 80 small to large, rock-filled hearths were found buried under 4 m of alluvium. Dates from charcoal in three hearths and a carbonized log ranged between 3100 and 3700 B.P. Haynes and Huckell (1986) reported a single radiocarbon date of A.D. 1240 ± 210 (A-2236) obtained from charcoal collected at a depth of 1.5 m in a trench excavated just north of the Rillito River and east of First Avenue. This date is apparently the only one obtained thus far from Rillito alluvium. At this same location, a weak to moderately developed paleosol was identified at a depth of 1 m. In assessing the potential for buried archaeological sites in Holocene alluvium of the Tucson Basin, Haynes and Huckell (1986) concluded that "it is clear that any land modification activities entailing earthmoving operations on any of the major wash floodplains may well impact buried sites that have no surface indications." Unfortunately, it is impossible to predict precisely where sites are buried, but the subsequent work of Desert Archaeology along Interstate 10 has clearly demonstrated the high sensitivity of the Holocene alluvium for buried sites along the Santa Cruz (Freeman 1999). The Rillito River probably has a similarly high sensitivity for prehistoric sites.

Waters's (1987, 1988b) investigation of the San Xavier reach of the Santa Cruz River concentrated on geomorphic changes during the span of Hohokam settlement, thus complementing and refining Haynes and Huckell's stratigraphic model for the late Holocene. Waters's geoarchaeological study integrated data from excavations at the San Xavier Bridge site (AZ BB:13:14), off-site bank exposures, and corroborative data compiled by Haynes and Huckell from other reaches of the Santa Cruz. Waters reported that significant environmental changes have occurred on the river, thus echoing Haynes and Huckell's previous assessment. Waters concluded that aggrading conditions before 6000 B.C. were followed by channel erosion and widening until about 5500 B.C., and then a return to an aggradational phase interrupted by brief periods of channel cutting. These major geomorphic changes were considered to be climate induced, but he attributed four cut-and-fill epicycles during the last 2,500 years to other causes, including localized oversteepening of the floodplain, differences in the water table level relative to the channel, and human impacts.

Accompanying the geomorphic changes of the last 2,500 years were dramatic settlement shifts, with periods of alluvial aggradation coinciding with times of increased riverine settlement (Doelle 1985;

Doelle et al. 1985; Effland and Rankin 1988, Waters 1987, 1988b). Aggrading conditions are known to increase the carrying capacity of subsistence systems dependent on floodplain agriculture (Dean 1988). Thus, it is not surprising that settlement shifts paralleling those of the Tucson Basin have been identified in other regions of the Southwest (e.g., Dean et al. 1985; Euler et al. 1979). Based on the timing of cut-and-fill epicycles, Waters's (1987, 1988b) geomorphic model of the San Xavier reach of the Santa Cruz River bolstered Doelle's assertion (Doelle 1985; Doelle et al. 1985) that Hohokam settlement change between A.D. 300 and 1450 was strongly related to environmental shifts on the floodplain. Waters argued that farming would have been impractical as the entrenched Santa Cruz River was slowly filling between 50 B.C. and A.D. 800. He noted that Snaketown and Cañada del Oro phase settlements, dated A.D. 300–800, are poorly represented by surface expressions because they are deeply buried. Waters noted that floodwater farming was possible only after the river channel became filled during the later Rillito phase (A.D. 800–950) and early Rincon subphase (A.D. 950–1,000), a time corresponding to intensive settlement along the Santa Cruz River. An entrenched channel began migrating upstream during the middle Rincon subphase (A.D. 1000–1100), and it continued to migrate through the late Rincon phase (A.D. 1100–1150), thus lowering agricultural productivity as floodwater farming was confined to a delta fan at the arroyo terminus. Channel stabilization and filling resulted in a *cienega* environment near Martínez Hill during the Tanque Verde phase (A.D. 1150–1300), a setting that would have been suitable to agriculture along the margin of the *cienega*; settlements abandoned on the west side of the river were apparently relocated to the east side during this time. There was little change in settlement location during the Tucson phase (A.D. 1300–1450) and the *cienega* appears to have contracted in size as the channel refilled, thus making floodwater farming possible once again. After A.D. 1450, the Santa Cruz became severely entrenched, which may explain the widespread abandonment of Classic period settlements at that time.

Historical records indicate that farming was practiced along the Santa Cruz River during the aggrading conditions that existed from at least A.D. 1696 through the 1880s. Heavy floods in 1887 and 1890, however, eroded a continuous channel more than 6 m deep through Tucson (Betancourt and Turner 1988; Cooke and Reeves 1976), thus undermining the agricultural systems. This most recent period of erosion is still in effect today, but the main changes now involve channel widening rather than down-cutting. In addition to flooding, this entrenchment has been attributed to the combined effects of a lowered water table and natural climatic change (Betancourt and Turner 1988; Cooke and Reeves 1976). A soil-cement revetment program, sponsored by Pima County Flood and Water Control and the U. S. Army Corps of Engineers, has been in progress more more than a decade. This work is aimed at stabilizing the banks and keeping the channel from migrating from its present course.

The studies of Haynes and Huckell (1986), Waters (1987), and Freeman (1999) are major contributions, and their work has established a strong foundation for future geoarchaeological work along the Santa Cruz River and its tributaries. It is unknown how their stratigraphic units correlate to cultural deposits in tributaries of the Santa Cruz River. Dynamic geomorphic changes, similar to those described by Waters for the San Xavier reach of the Santa Cruz River, likely occurred along the Rillito, and such changes must have also profoundly affected the amount of arable land, as well as the preservation and burial of the archaeological record. Because of the time-transgressive nature of these changes over different reaches of the river, and between different drainages, lag times likely existed. The archaeological implications of such lags and variability in the magnitude of different geomorphic processes are uncertain. The numerous discoveries of Archaic and early Formative period farming settlements (e.g., Gregory 1999; Roth 1992, 1995), which relied on irrigation agriculture on the basin's major floodplains, demonstrate that large portions of drainages in the Tucson Basin were not entrenched between 500 B.C. and A.D. 500. In all likelihood, the first prehistoric settlers along the Rillito were drawn to reaches marked by stable or aggrading conditions that could be cultivated by irrigation, as was the case for historical-period settlement along the Rillito (see Chapter 4).

One of the most exciting recent developments in Tucson Basin archaeology is the discovery of numerous small irrigation canals throughout much of the basin. Late Archaic wells and Hohokam canals have been documented at Los Morteros (Bernard-Shaw 1988, 1989; Bernard-Shaw and Doelle 1991; Katzer 1989), a village located on the Santa Cruz River floodplain at the northern end of the Tucson Mountains. Small irrigation canals have also been identified at AZ AA:12:90 (Kinkade and Fritz 1975), a Hohokam field house site located southwest of Hodges Ruin at the Tucson sewage treatment plant, and at several late Archaic and Formative period settlements along Interstate 10 (e.g., Ciolek-Torrello et al. 1999; Fish et al. 1992; Gregory 1996).

Archaeological Sensitivity in the Río Antiguo Study Area

The review of geoarchaeological studies of the Tucson Basin presented above clearly indicates a high probability that Holocene alluvium along the Rillito contains buried prehistoric archaeological deposits. Surficial prehistoric sites may be found on older, elevated landforms predating the Holocene, but they are likely to be concentrated near the Rillito and its tributaries, or near other water sources such as seep springs that may exist away from the river.

To assess the association of prehistoric and historical-period sites with the geologic units discussed above, the site-locational information summarized earlier in the chapter was laid over a map of the study area depicting the geologic units defined by Klawon et al. Table 8 summarizes the information provided by the overlay, showing which sites, distinguished by period of occupation, are associated with each geologic unit. The table and Figure 71 indicate that archaeological components are concentrated in five units: Qyr, Qlr, Qmr, Qy2, and Ql.

Table 9, which correlates the same site locations with the geologic units defined by McKittrick (1988), provides a slightly different perspective. This table indicates that 14 components were associated with recently active channel deposits (unit "ch"), 11 with the T1 terrace, and 12 with the T2 terrace. Several of these components are actually older than McKittrick's age estimates for these terraces, which can be attributed to errors in McKittrick's mapping of the geologic units. Most of these errors were corrected in the subsequent mapping by Klawon et al. (Philip Pearthree, personal communication 2002), and we have relied on the mapping of Klawon et al. because it was generally more accurate than that of McKittrick. Nonetheless, McKittrick did distinguish between T1 and T2 units where Klawon et al. defined the single unit Qyr, based on their inability to consistently distinguish two units in the field. The distinction between T1 and T2 may prove valid after further field study and, thus, it may have some relevance to the distribution of archaeological sites. In fact, further data on the distribution of sites in the study area may eventually help gauge the validity of McKittrick's distinction.

To better assess the association between archaeological sites and geologic units, data was compiled on the areal extent of the units (as a percentage of the entire 17,304 acres in the study area). Similarly, the amount of land that has been surveyed for archaeological sites was determined (1,806 acres), including the acreage falling on each geologic unit. This information is presented in Table 10 and Figure 72, along with information on the percentage distributions of all prehistoric (n = 39) and historical-period components (n = 27). Figure 72 shows that the study area is largely composed of the Qyr, Qlr, Qmr, Qy2, QT, and Tsc units. Archaeological survey, however, has concentrated on units Qycr, Qyr, Qy2, and Tsc. If archaeological sites were randomly distributed across the study area, then they would be expected to approximately parallel the distribution of the survey coverage. The percentage of both prehistoric and historical-period components is less than that of the surveyed area for Holocene unit Qyr, but this difference may be at least partly explained by the high potential for buried sites, and thus the failure to identify much of the archaeological record. The percentage of archaeological components is much higher than that for the surveyed area in units Qlr, Qmr, Qy2, Ql, and Qm. All of these units but Qy2 consist of stable Pleistocene landforms, where sites and artifacts are expected to be highly visible. Consequently, surficial archaeological surveys conducted on the Pleistocene landforms are probably sufficient to find most sites present, depending on their site size, artifact density, and the transect spacing of the survey.

Table 8. Corre Site Number

Cultural Period & Phase	Age Estimate	Qycr (< 100 y)	(QTvb)	Older Foothills Deposits Tsc (5–20 ma)	Tpa (20–30 ma)	Bedrock R	Total No. of Site Components
Historical	A.D. 1540–1950	302	12, 246, 306,				27
Classic							
Tucson	A.D. 1300–1450						2
Tanque Verde	A.D. 1150–1300						2
Sedentary							
Rincon	A.D. 950–1150		141,				8
Colonial							
Rillito	A.D. 850–950						3
Cañada del Oro	A.D. 800–850						1
Pioneer							
Snaketown	A.D. 750–800						1
Tortolita	A.D. 450–650						0
Agua Caliente	A.D. 1–450						0
Archaic	6500–1 B.C.						2
Paleoindian	11,000-6500 B.C.						
Formative	A.D. 1–1450		12, 2⁄				27
Prehistoric	11,000 B.C.–A.D. 1450						1
Total		1	0	0	0	0	74

Note: All site numbers are ASM designations with the prefix AZ BB
Key: y = years ago; ka = thousand years before present; ma = millior

209

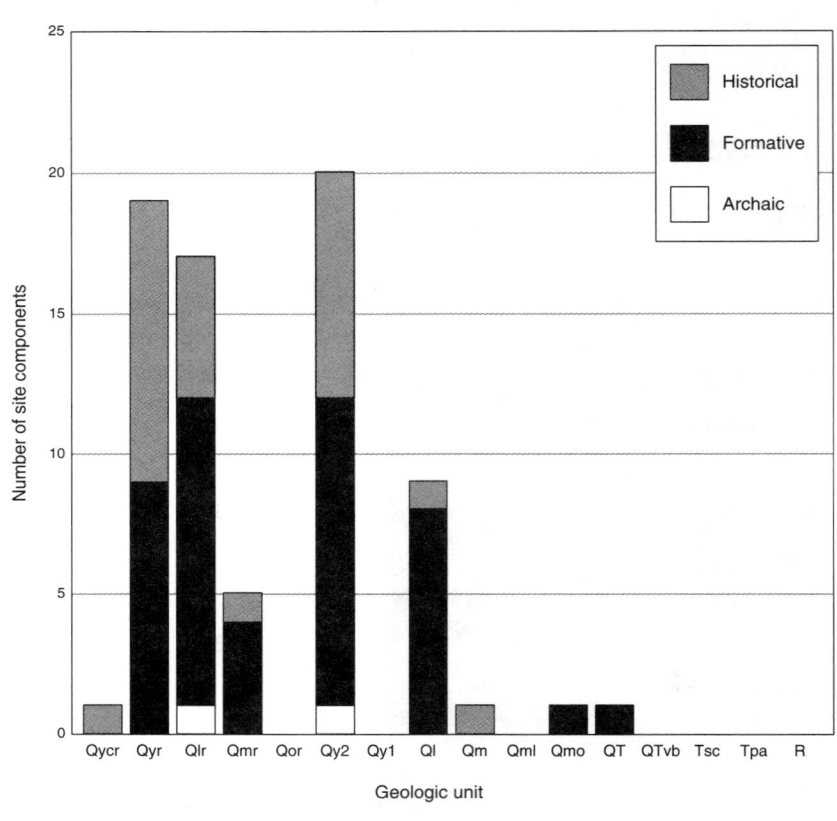

Figure 71. Frequency of sites by geologic unit.

Table 9. Correspondence of Archaeological and Historical-Period Components with Geologic Units of McKittrick (1988), by Abbreviated Site Number

Cultural Period & Phase	Age Estimate	Geologic Unit											Total No. of Site Components
		cha	ch	T1	T2	T3	T4	T5	M2	M1	O	QTbf	
Historical	A.D. 1540–1950	302	23, 118, 220, 246, 324	5, 19, 321, 325	111, 238, 247, 254, 356, 306	7, 9, 11, 12, 40, 72, 309, 310	33			322		13	27
Classic													
Tucson	A.D. 1300–1450		24				33						2
Tanque Verde	A.D. 1150–1300					14	33						2
Sedentary													
Rincon	A.D. 950–1150		24	315	141, 356	14, 21	33			54			8
Colonial													
Rillito	A.D. 850–950			18	141	14							3
Cañada del Oro	A.D. 800–850					14							1
Pioneer													
Snaketown	A.D. 750–800					14							1
Tortolita	A.D. 450–650												0
Agua Caliente	A.D. 1–450												0
Archaic	6500–1 B.C.					35			259				2
Paleoindian	11,000–6500 B.C.												0
Formative	A.D. 1–1450		16, 23, 118, 246, 255	5, 17, 19, 310, 314	238, 253, 256	7, 8, 9, 11, 12, 100, 309				6, 25, 26		13, 20, 22, 95	27
Prehistoric	11,000 B.C.–A.D. 1450		219										1
Total		1	13	11	12	22	4	0	1	5	0	5	74

Note: All site numbers are ASM designations with the prefix AZ BB:9:.

Table 10. Areal Distribution of Geologic Units of Klawon et al. (1999) in Río Antiguo Study Area Relative to Archaeological Survey Coverage and Associated Archaeological and Historical-Period Sites

Geologic Units	Area of Geologic Units		Survey Coverage		Associated Archaeological Sites and Components							
	Acres[a]	%	Acres	%	All Sites		Prehistoric Components			Historical-Period Components		
					No.	%	Site Nos.	No.	%	Site Nos.	No.	%
River alluvium												
Qycr	552	3.2	240	13.3	1	2.0				302	1	3.7
Qyr	3,091	17.9	1,050	58.1	15	29.4	12, 14, 17, 141, 238, 246, 256, 315, 356	9	23.1	12, 111, 238, 246, 247, 254, 306, 324, 325, 356	10	37.0
Qlr	1,448	8.4	46	2.5	9	17.6	7, 8, 9, 11, 21, 35, 100	7	17.9	7, 9, 11, 40, 72	5	18.5
Qmr	3,488	20.2	10	0.6	2	3.9	33, 219	2	5.1	33	1	3.7
Qor	104	0.6										
Subtotal	8,683	50.3	1,346	74.5	27	52.9		18	46.2		17	63.0
Fan alluvium												
Qy2	1,666	9.6	110	6.1	14	27.5	5, 16, 18, 19, 23, 118, 253, 255, 259, 309, 310, 314	12	30.8	5, 19, 23, 118, 220, 309, 310, 321	8	29.6
Qy1	114	0.7										
Ql	326	1.9	0.002	0.0	7	13.7	13, 20, 24, 25, 26, 54, 95	7	17.9	13	1	3.7
Qm	751	4.3	1	0.0	1	2.0				322	1	3.7
Qml	47	0.3										

Geologic Units	Area of Geologic Units		Survey Coverage		Associated Archaeological Sites and Components							
					All Sites		Prehistoric Components			Historical-Period Components		
	Acres[a]	%	Acres	%	No.	%	Site Nos.	No.	%	Site Nos.	No.	%
Qmo	790	4.6	1	0.1	1	2.0	6	1	2.6		1	2.6
QT	1,484	8.6	0.1	0.0	1	2.0	22	1	2.6		1	2.6
Qtvb	374	2.2	85	4.7								
Subtotal	5,552	32.01	197.1	10.9	24	47.1		21	53.8		10	37.0
Older Foothills deposits												
Tsc	2,903	16.8	262	14.5								
Tpa	142	0.8	1	0.1								
Subtotal	3,045	17.6	263	14.6	0	0.0		0	0.0		0	0.0
Bedrock												
R	22	0.1	0	0.0	0	0.0		0	0.0		0	0.0
Total	17,304	100.0	1,806	100.0	51	100.0		39	100.0		27	100.0

Note: All site numbers are ASM designations with the prefix AZ BB:9:; numbers have been rounded in most instances.

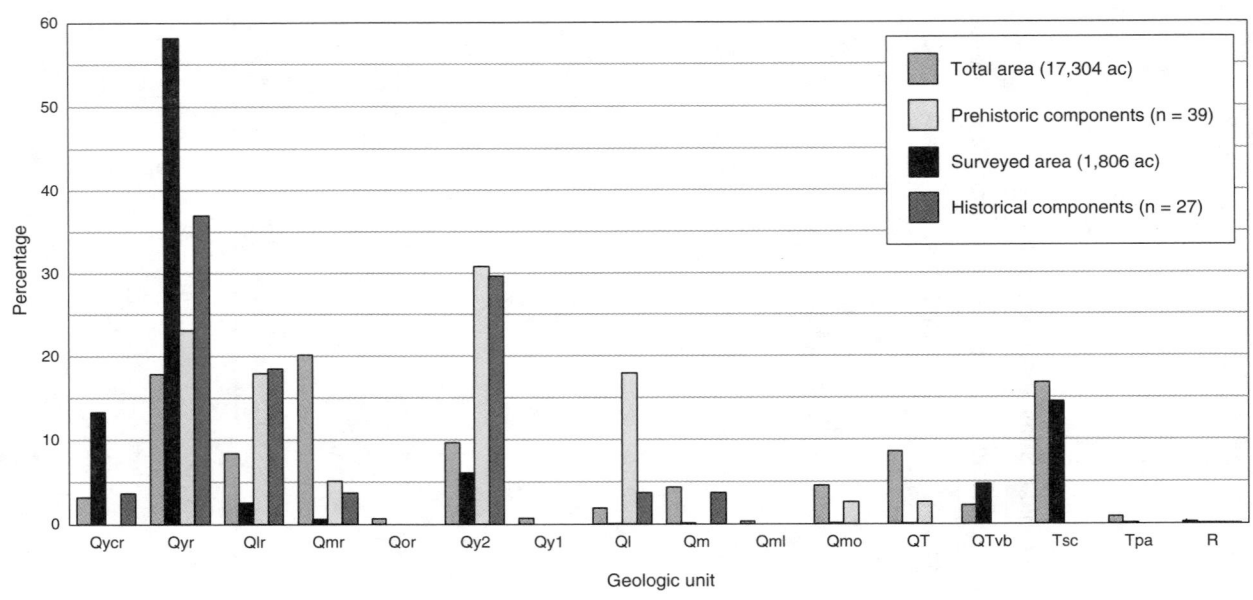

Figure 72. Distribution of geologic units, surveyed areas, and archaeological sites.

Summary of Geoarchaeological Assessment

The results of our geoarchaeological assessment of the Río Antiguo study area indicate that archaeological testing or monitoring of construction projects is warranted where Holocene deposits will be disturbed. The Holocene units discussed above should be used to pinpoint Holocene landforms in the field. Archaeological sites, including those with prehistoric or historical-period components, may be found on more-elevated landforms, but surface surveys are probably sufficient for these Quaternary and Tertiary deposits. In this regard, we emphasize that our designation of a given landform as having low archaeological sensitivity (see Table 7) does not mean the landform should be exempt from archaeological survey prior to disturbance.

Unrecorded Historical-Period Features

The two major historical-period archaeological sites in the Río Antiguo study area, Binghampton and Fort Lowell, undoubtedly preserve numerous unrecorded buried features. Detailed surface mapping of both sites probably would also yield a variety of previously unrecorded surface features, as well as information on site structure through time. Significant features associated with both sites undoubtedly exist outside the currently defined limits of the two archaeological sites. This is especially true in the case of Binghampton, where an accurate site boundary would correspond with the eventual extent of Mormon settlement, which by 1910 included a large area on the south bank of the river, opposite Nephi Bingham's original property on the north bank. Aside from these obvious examples, three other kinds of unrecorded historical-period features in the study area are worth mentioning here: features associated with the Mexican-American community of El Fuerte, irrigation features, and other water-control features.

214

The community of El Fuerte, which sprang up around the ruins of Fort Lowell after 1891, is likely represented by a significant archaeological record. At least one site already recorded in the study area, AZ BB:9:220, just south of Fort Lowell Road and adjacent to the east bank of Alamo Wash, includes a set of three privy pits probably associated with specific Mexican-American families. The discovery of similar, well-preserved domestic features in the neighborhood would present an excellent opportunity to study the social and economic context of life in a rural Mexican-American community at the turn of the century. The fact that significant portions of the original El Fuerte neighborhood like El Callejón (see Chapter 4) have escaped major development suggests a high probability that more buried domestic features still exist. As a part of the Fort Lowell Historic District, the archaeological remains of El Fuerte are probably best considered a part of the Fort Lowell site (AZ BB:9:40), but the archaeology of El Fuerte would benefit from research designed specifically to address questions of Mexican-American life and identity.

Irrigation features are probably the most abundant historical-period features already recorded in the study area. In addition to irrigation features recorded as a part of Binghampton (AZ BB:9:238), portions of at least two of the major underflow ditches originating in Tanque Verde Creek survive in the study area (see the descriptions of AZ BB:9:325 and 326 in Appendix B; also see Chapter 4). Numerous segments of lesser ditches have also been recorded in the study area on the Rillito floodplain (see the descriptions of AZ BB:9:11, 12, 19, 23, 100, 118, 247, 255, 314, and 321 in Appendix B), and there are probably many more unrecorded ditch segments preserved there, even within areas already surveyed: an indifference to minor historical-period features has meant that irrigation ditches are often mentioned in site descriptions as sources of disturbance but not as features in themselves.

The most substantial unrecorded irrigation features that may exist in the study area are sections of the buried flumes that formed parts of the major underflow ditches. Sterner (1996) documented substantial portions of the Davidson Flume just east of Craycroft Road, buried in the bed of the Rillito. Amazingly, portions of the flume were covered with only a thin layer of river sand but had somehow survived largely intact. SRI's recent recording of a concrete drop box, apparently the connection between the aboveground University ditch and the buried flume of the Bingham ditch (Homburg and Kurota 2000; O'Mack and Riggs 2001; also see Chapter 4) suggests that other buried flumes are still preserved in the study area, even in the highly active channels of the Rillito, Tanque Verde Creek, and Pantano Wash.

Other historical-period water-control features that may be present in the study area are ones designed to contain flooding on and near the Rillito floodplain. To date, no such features have been recorded formally in the study area, but the possibility that they exist is suggested by a sketch map prepared by Frank Midvale in 1937 when he recorded the prehistoric site AZ BB:9:5 (Figure 73). The map depicts the vicinity of the intersection of River Road and Campbell Avenue and shows a series of earthen dikes paralleling the north bank of the Rillito and both sides of Mountain Estates Wash where it empties into the river. All of these features have undoubtedly been destroyed by realignments and improvements to River Road, but other parts of the study area that have not experienced the same degree of disturbance may preserve similar features.

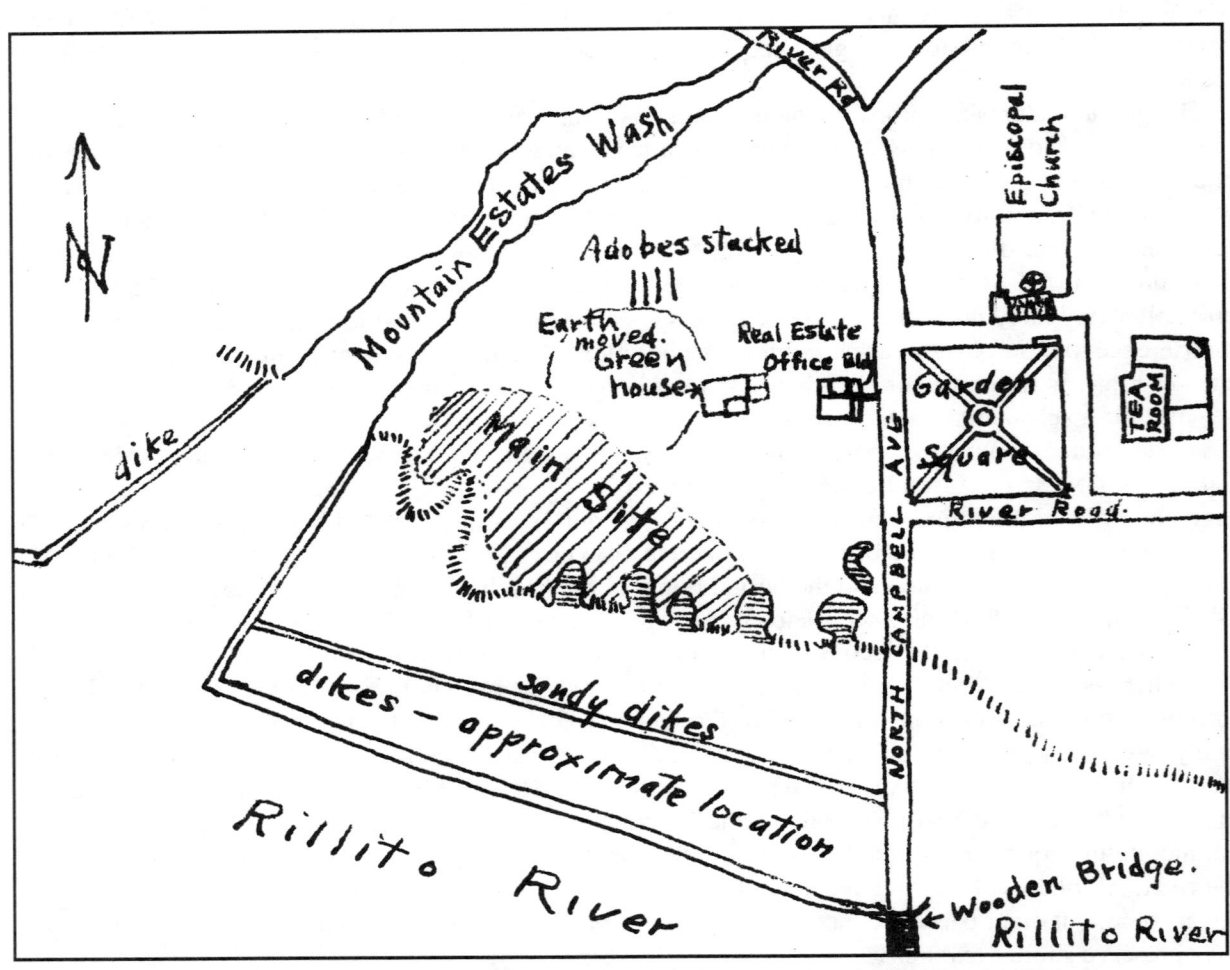

Figure 73. Sketch map of area near intersection of River Road and Campbell, prepared in 1937 by Frank Midvale for the AZ BB:9:5 (ASM) site card.

Map of GLO Transactions in the Río Antiguo Study Area

• See back pocket

Archaeological Site Descriptions

The 51 archaeological sites recorded to date in the study area are described in turn below, with the exception of the four major sites discussed in Chapter 5. The descriptions are based on the corresponding ASM site cards, supplemented by associated survey and excavation reports. To the extent possible, we have provided the most current available information for every site, which occasionally contradicts the information on the site cards. For many sites, the ASM site card is the only source of information, and many site cards, especially for sites recorded decades ago, provide only limited information.

AZ BB:9:5 (ASM)

Prehistoric period: undifferentiated Hohokam
Prehistoric function: limited activity
Historical period: Early Statehood
Historical function: adobe brick manufacture

The principal source of information for this site is the ASM site card, prepared by Frank Midvale in 1937. The material culture he found included ground stone, cores, hammer stones, flakes, and chips. Pottery was present, but was not described. During the 1930s, the site was affected and possibly destroyed by trash dumping and large-scale adobe brick manufacture, with associated soil mining. An attempt was made to relocate the site during a survey of water-main alignments, but it had been completely destroyed (Sliva 1998).

AZ BB:9:6 (ASM)

Prehistoric period: undifferentiated Hohokam
Prehistoric function: limited activity

ASM site card from 1937 is the only source of information on this site, which is located on a finger escarpment on the north side of River Road. Frank Midvale recorded a scatter of sherds here, with few or no other material remains. He suggested that the material on the site derived from people traversing the area to access the river, or possibly from an unidentified larger site nearby.

AZ BB:9:7 (ASM)

Prehistoric period: undifferentiated Hohokam
Prehistoric function: habitation
Historical period: Early Statehood
Historical function: guest ranch

Most of the information on this site comes from Frank Midvale's 1937 ASM site card. The site was a small Hohokam village with six or more trash mounds. In 1937, material culture was abundant on the surface and included pottery, mano fragments, a hammer stone, cores, and a fragment of a stone hoe. In the 1930s, the area was part of the Desert Manor Guest Ranch, which was not recorded as a part of the site. The site was revisited by Sliva (1998) and found to have been destroyed by modern development.

AZ BB:9:8 (ASM)
Prehistoric period: undifferentiated Hohokam
Prehistoric function: habitation or limited activity

Little is known about this site apart from what appears on the 1937 ASM site card prepared by Frank Midvale. The site was a small campsite or village located on a low terrace south of the Rillito, with no surface indication of features. Artifacts consisted of a thin scatter of sherds, plus unspecified numbers of hammer stones and cores. According to a recent report, modern development has destroyed the site (Sliva 1998).

AZ BB:9:9 (ASM)
Prehistoric period: undifferentiated Hohokam
Prehistoric function: habitation
Historical period: Early Statehood
Historical function: residential

This site was characterized as a small prehistoric village by Frank Midvale, who first recorded it in 1937. The site occupies the front edge of the first river terrace on the south side of the Rillito. According to Midvale's ASM site card, material culture at the site included pottery, hammer stones, cores, and choppers. In the 1930s, the site lay partially beneath the home of a Mrs. Weimer, who collected a number of artifacts from the site, including a large olla, a stone cup, a metate, a stone axe, and polishing stones. Doty's Goat Dairy also owned a portion of the site. The site was revisited by ASM archaeologists in 1981 and again in 1983 (Dart 1983), at which time no prehistoric remains were observed. However, they did observe historical-period artifacts in two trash pits cut by construction trenches. The artifacts dated to the 1910s–1930s and were probably associated with the Weimer house.

AZ BB:9:11 (ASM)
Prehistoric period: undifferentiated Hohokam
Prehistoric function: habitation
Historical period: Territorial (?) and Early Statehood
Historical function: irrigation; topsoil borrow area

Information about this site comes exclusively from the ASM site card prepared in 1937 by Frank Midvale, who recorded a number of pit houses disturbed by a topsoil borrow area. Few artifacts were found in the area, and sherds were especially scarce. He did find hammer stones, choppers, cores, and one little-used metate. Midvale's map shows the remains of a historical-period canal (labeled "historic pioneer canal") running through the site. He does not comment on this feature, but it apparently struck him as fairly old. At the time of his visit, the area was being used by the University of Arizona as a topsoil borrow area. The soil was being hauled to campus and used to establish lawns. Much of the prehistoric site had been destroyed by this activity before Midvale was able to record it.

AZ BB:9:12 (ASM)

Prehistoric period: undifferentiated Hohokam
Prehistoric function: limited activity
Historical period: Territorial and Early Statehood
Historical function: residential; irrigation

The 1937 ASM site card prepared by Frank Midvale is the only source of information on this site. The prehistoric artifacts were not abundant, and Midvale speculated that changes in the course of the Rillito had washed away the main part of the site. An unspecified number of sherds were found, and a few pieces of flaked stone. Historical-period occupation of the site was also recorded on the site card. The area was the home of a Mr. Diaz, who had apparently lived in the area since around 1900. The site was also the location of a canal intake built in the 1890s and destroyed by changes in the course of the river.

AZ BB:9:13 (ASM)

Prehistoric period: undifferentiated Hohokam
Prehistoric function: limited activity
Historical period: Territorial, Early Statehood
Historical function: campsite and lookout

The principal source of information on this site is the ASM site card prepared by Frank Midvale in 1937. Midvale describes the site as "a natural lookout station" because of its location on a prominent hill, affording a good view of the Rillito Valley. Midvale cited oral-historical sources ("old timers") that referred to the hill as an Apache camp and gathering spot during the period when Fort Lowell was in use. The area was being used for picnicking in 1937. Some prehistoric use of the hill was indicated by a light scatter of sherds, choppers, hammer stones, and flaked stone. The site fell within the bounds of a recent survey (Sliva 1998), but there is no evidence that it was either relocated or reexamined at that time.

AZ BB:9:14 (ASM): Hardy site

Prehistoric periods: Colonial (Snaketown phase) to Classic (Tanque Verde phase)
Prehistoric function: habitation

See Chapter 5 for a description of this site. This site underlies nineteenth-century Fort Lowell, which has its own designation, AZ BB:9:40. Another historical-period site, AZ BB:9:72, which forms a part of Fort Lowell, also overlies portions of this prehistoric site. The Band Quarters Kitchen is included in the discussion of Fort Lowell in Chapter 5.

AZ BB:9:16 (ASM)

Prehistoric period: undifferentiated Hohokam
Prehistoric function: limited activity

This site is known only from the 1938 ASM site card prepared by Frank Midvale. The site was described as a light scatter of artifacts on a gravelly terrace north of the Rillito. Artifacts in the scatter included sherds, hammer stones, choppers, chips, flakes, cores, and mano fragments. One lightly ground metate was also present.

AZ BB:9:17 (ASM)
Prehistoric period: undifferentiated Hohokam
Prehistoric function: limited activity

This site is known only from the 1938 ASM site card prepared by Frank Midvale. The site was described as a scatter of artifacts on the north bank of the Rillito, including sherds, hammer stones, cores, scrapers, manos, and flaked stone.

AZ BB:9:18 (ASM)
Prehistoric period: Colonial (Rillito phase)
Prehistoric function: habitation

This site is known only from the 1938 ASM site card prepared by Frank Midvale. The site was found adjacent to a large wash leading into the north bank of the Rillito and is described as a "sherd area or small settlement." Sherds were abundant, as were hammer stones, chipped stone, and cores. All ceramics were from the Santa Cruz (i.e., Rillito) phase. By the time of Midvale's visit, a portion of the site had been destroyed by erosion.

AZ BB:9:19 (ASM)
Prehistoric period: undifferentiated Hohokam
Prehistoric function: limited activity
Historical period: Territorial or Early Statehood
Historical function: irrigation

This site is known primarily from the 1938 ASM site card prepared by Frank Midvale. The site is described as "a sherd area or small campsite," with a small amount of pottery and a few pieces of chipped stone visible on the surface. According to a note on the site card, a ditch with running water passed 40 yards south of the site; this was presumably an irrigation ditch. The entire site has since been destroyed (Sliva 1998).

AZ BB:9:20 (ASM)
Prehistoric period: undifferentiated Hohokam
Prehistoric function: fortified hilltop (*trincheras*?)

Little is known of this site beyond the data contained on its site card, completed by Frank Midvale in 1938. The site was located on a hill just north of the Rillito. A wall or terrace 685 feet long surrounded the hilltop, with traces of one or two possible rooms connected to it. The enclosed area was about 225 feet long by 150 feet wide. Fairly abundant material culture was found within the terraced area, and outside it up to 60 feet away. Artifacts included pottery, fragments of a mortar, small manos, a stone hoe, hammer stones, and choppers. Although no phase designation was given, Midvale notes that the site may be related to the Hardy site, AZ BB:9:14 (Snaketown through Tanque Verde phases), and that pottery samples suggest it is earlier in date than University Ruin, AZ BB:9:33. AZ BB:9:20 fell within the bounds of a recent survey (Sliva 1998), but there is no evidence that it was relocated or reexamined at that time.

AZ BB:9:21 (ASM)
Prehistoric period: Sedentary (Rincon phase)
Prehistoric function: habitation or limited activity

This site was first described by Frank Midvale on the ASM site card he prepared in 1938. The site was a camp or small village, with fairly abundant pottery and other material culture, including hammer stones, cores, and many pieces of chipped stone, as well as mano and trough metate fragments. The site was revisited in 1987 (Mayro 1987a, 1987b) during an expansion of Alvernon Road. At that time, very little evidence of the site was found. The area had been extensively modified by modern development, and the only sign of prehistoric occupation was a small area of lithic debitage, several cores, a hammer stone and one middle Rincon–phase sherd. The area of the site was smaller and the density of artifacts lighter than Midvale had described. The site was tested with a backhoe for subsurface features, but none were found. Mayro concluded that AZ BB:9:21, for all intents and purposes, no longer existed.

AZ BB:9:22 (ASM): Pottery Hill
Prehistoric period: undifferentiated Hohokam
Prehistoric function: limited activity

This site is known only from the 1938 ASM site card prepared by Frank Midvale. The site consisted of abundant pottery remains scattered on the steep slopes of a large hill north of the Rillito. Hammer stones, cores, choppers, and chipped stone were also abundant on the slopes, but there were few artifacts of any kind on the very top of the prominence. Midvale suggested the site was used as a campsite or possibly a lookout, since there was an extended view in all directions from the top of the hill.

AZ BB:9:23 (ASM)
Prehistoric period: undifferentiated Hohokam
Prehistoric function: limited activity
Historical period: Territorial or Early Statehood
Historical function: irrigation

This site is known only from the 1938 ASM site card prepared by Frank Midvale. The site consisted of a light scatter of sherds, along with a low density of hammer stones, cores, choppers, crude scrapers, knives, and other flaked stone. The site sat at the base of a prominent hill (location of the Pottery Hill site, AZ BB:9:22). Midvale noted an "old historic ditch" of unspecified date passing near or through the site.

AZ BB:9:24 (ASM)
Prehistoric period: Sedentary (Rincon phase); Classic (Tucson phase)
Prehistoric function: habitation or limited activity

We were unable to locate the ASM site card for this site, but AZSITE summarizes the contents of the original 1938 card by Frank Midvale. The site was also tested recently by Old Pueblo Archaeology Center (2000). As originally recorded, the site consisted of a light sherd and lithic scatter located on a low ridge and foothill spur just north of the Rillito. Midvale characterized the site as a small hilltop village. A pit dug into the site, apparently by a pothunter, showed cultural materials as deep as 3 feet. Sherds observed at the site include Rincon red wares, one Casas Grandes Polychrome sherd, and one

Jeddito Black-on-yellow sherd. The testing by Old Pueblo failed to find any subsurface features and yielded only a single artifact, a decorated brown ware sherd.

AZ BB:9:25 (ASM)

Prehistoric period: undifferentiated Hohokam
Prehistoric function: habitation or limited activity

This site is known only from the 1938 ASM site card prepared by Frank Midvale. The site was found on the end of a finger ridge overlooking the Rillito. Pottery was fairly abundant, and some cores and flakes were found. A circular depression visible at the surface may have been the remains of a room or pit house.

AZ BB:9:26 (ASM)

Prehistoric period: undifferentiated Hohokam
Prehistoric function: habitation

This site is known only from the 1938 ASM site card prepared by Frank Midvale. Like AZ BB:9:25, this site was found on the end of a finger ridge overlooking the Rillito. Pottery was abundant, and Midvale also found mano and metate fragments, hammer stones, cores, chipped stone, and shell fragments, including a fragment of a bracelet. A possible rock alignment was the only suggestion of architecture at the site.

AZ BB:9:33 (ASM): University Ruin

Prehistoric period: Sedentary (Rincon phase) to Classic (Tucson phase)
Prehistoric function: habitation
Historical period: Territorial (?) to post–World War II
Historical function: ranching; archaeological laboratory

See Chapter 5 for a discussion of the prehistoric component of this site. The historical-period component consists of a ranch house built near the base of the main platform mound at the site. Both the property encompassing the site and the ranch house were donated by the owner, Dorothy Knipe, to the University of Arizona in 1934. The ranch house was originally used by the Department of Anthropology as an archaeological laboratory and dig headquarters (Hayden 1957); the house is still maintained by the University.

AZ BB:9:35 (ASM)

Prehistoric period: undifferentiated Archaic (?)
Prehistoric function: habitation

This site was first recorded in 1941, when workers removing soil from a borrow area on University of Arizona property found in situ artifacts and features. The ASM site card prepared at that time is the only source of information on the site. The card lacks detail and is partially illegible, but it notes the presence of metates, manos, scrapers, choppers, and flaked stone, as well as some hearths. The card's preparers (their names are illegible) suggested that the site was associated with the Archaic period Cochise culture, presumably because it lacked pottery. A note on the card added in 1976 states that this site is the same as

AZ BB:9:11, but the two sites are plotted in different locations on the corresponding ASM quadrangle map. AZ BB:9:11 is also described as having some pottery. Because of the apparent differences in artifacts and location, we have kept the two sites separate.

AZ BB:9:40 (ASM): Fort Lowell
Historical period: Territorial and Early Statehood
Historical function: military; residential

See Chapter 5 for a discussion of this site. AZ BB:9:40 lies over the prehistoric Hardy site, which has its own designation (AZ BB:9:14). Another historical-period site associated with Fort Lowell has been given a separate designation: the Band Quarters Kitchen (AZ BB:9:72). This sites is discussed in Chapter 5 as a part of AZ BB:9:40. Portions of the El Fuerte neighborhood also fall within AZ BB:9:40, as discussed in Chapter 5.

AZ BB:9:54 (ASM)
Prehistoric period: Colonial (Rillito phase) to Classic (Tanque Verde phase)
Prehistoric function: habitation

This site was first recorded in the 1960s, in preparation for a highway salvage project. According to a 1970 note on the ASM site card, the site was destroyed without warning by road construction. An additional note from 1982 indicates that the site was not in fact destroyed in 1970; the surviving portion of the site was excavated by Huntington (1982). Subsurface features included borrow pits and four pit houses. Ceramic types represented at the site included Rincon Red-on-brown, Rincon Polychrome, and Tanque Verde Red-on-brown.

AZ BB:9:72 (ASM): Band Quarters Kitchen
Historical period: Territorial
Historical function: military

See Chapter 5 for a discussion of Fort Lowell (AZ BB:9:40), which includes this site. Prehistoric artifacts found at this site presumably derive from the Hardy site (AZ BB:9:14), which is described separately in Chapter 5.

AZ BB:9:95 (ASM)
Prehistoric period: undifferentiated Hohokam
Prehistoric function: undetermined

The only available information on this site comes from a brief description by Sharon Urban in 1980, on file at ASM (we did not locate a site card). The site is described as a sherd and lithic scatter of undetermined date.

AZ BB:9:100 (ASM): Lazy Creek site
Prehistoric period: undifferentiated Hohokam
Prehistoric function: limited activity

Historical period: Territorial or Early Statehood
Historical function: irrigation; horse track

Information on this site comes from the ASM site card and archaeological survey form. The site was first recorded in 1981 by Sharon Urban, who described it as a sparse sherd and lithic scatter. The site had been heavily disturbed by a horse track built immediately over the site, and by an irrigation ditch that passed through the site, running immediately adjacent to the north side of Fort Lowell Road and feeding into a small reservoir near the site. No decorated wares were found. Sliva (1998) recently reported that the site has been destroyed by a townhome development.

AZ BB:9:111 (ASM): Valley of the Moon
Historical period: Early Statehood and post–World War II
Historical function: entertainment

See Chapter 4 for a discussion of entertainment businesses in the project area, including the Valley of the Moon, first opened in 1932. The Valley of the Moon was at first designated AZ BB:9:35, but when it was discovered that that number had already been assigned to another site, this site was designated AZ BB:9:111.

AZ BB:9:118 (ASM): Hill Farm site
Prehistoric period: undifferentiated Hohokam
Prehistoric function: habitation
Historical period: Territorial and Early Statehood
Historical function: irrigation

This site is located just south of the Rillito in an area that was once mesquite *bosque*. The only available information on the site comes from the ASM site card prepared by Sharon Urban in 1982, and the ASM archaeological survey form prepared the same year. Urban described the site as a sherd and lithic scatter with some fire-cracked rock, possibly a small village site. The area had been plowed and used as a pasture for many years, so it was heavily disturbed. The site may have once extended farther south, but the area has been destroyed by development. Urban also noted the presence of a historical-period irrigation ditch of unspecified date running along the south side of the site. The locational information for this site is a little imprecise, but the ditch probably represents one of the three late-nineteenth- or early-twentieth-century ditches (the Binghampton, Cole, or Corbett) that once passed through the area, or possibly a lateral associated with one of those ditches. The site map attached to the archaeological survey form actually depicts what is apparently a lateral extending from the south side of the ditch noted by Urban. The site map also depicts a small lake just south of this lateral ditch. The lake is undoubtedly the one once (perhaps still) fed by the Corbett ditch, as depicted by Smith (1910:Figure 50).

AZ BB:9:141 (ASM): Mesquite Creek site
Prehistoric period: Colonial (Rillito phase); Sedentary (Rincon phase)
Prehistoric function: limited activity

The Mesquite Creek site consisted of two loci, each about 40 m in diameter, located on the northern edge of the Tanque Verde Wash floodplain. Locus 1 was a sparse lithic scatter with a few plain ware sherds. Locus 2 was a much denser and probably deeper concentration of sherds and lithics. Four painted sherds were found, including a Rincon Red-on-brown sherd from Locus 1, and Rillito and early Rincon Rincon Red-on-brown sherds in Locus 2. Lithic artifacts of mudstone, quartz, and quartzite were found in both loci. The ASM site card was the only source of information we were able to locate for this site.

AZ BB:9:219 (ASM)
Prehistoric period: undifferentiated prehistoric
Prehistoric function: limited activity

AZ BB:9:219 was first described in 1987 (Mayro 1987c). The site was a lithic scatter consisting of cores and flakes of basalt, quartzite, rhyolite, and silicified limestone. All stages of reduction were represented, leading Mayro to suggest that the site was a chipping station associated with the Hardy site (AZ BB:9:14), located some 400–800 m to the east. However, it was not possible to rule out an Archaic period occupation. The site had been damaged by modern development in the area, making site boundaries difficult to determine.

AZ BB:9:220 (ASM)
Historical period: Territorial or Early Statehood
Historical function: residential

This site, first recorded in 1987, consists of three privy pits located just south of Fort Lowell Road and adjacent to the east bank of Alamo Wash, within the El Fuerte neighborhood. Two houses forming part of the neighborhood, the Luján and Jacobo houses, are within 50 m of the pits. On the surface of one pit, SCA glass and other early glass was found. The site is discussed by Chavarria (1996). The development of the El Fuerte neighborhood is discussed in Chapter 4 of the report.

AZ BB:9:238 (ASM): Binghampton
Prehistoric period: undifferentiated Hohokam
Prehistoric function: undetermined
Historical period: Territorial to post–World War II
Historical function: residential, farming, irrigation, cemetery

See the discussion of Mormon settlement along the Rillito in Chapter 4, and a description of the site of the site of Binghampton in Chapter 5. The prehistoric component, consisting of a scatter of ceramics and lithics, is noted on the ASM site card prepared by Jeff Homburg in 1989.

AZ:BB:9:246 (ASM)
Historical period: undetermined
Historical function: undetermined

The only source of information on this site is the ASM site card, prepared in 1989. The site consisted of a clay-lined, basin-shaped hearth, located near the mouth of a small wash entering the Rillito from the north. The hearth, exposed by erosion, was filled with charcoal and ash. The only artifacts present were historical-period glass and metal fragments. The site card associates the hearth with the "prehistoric ceramic period," but no ceramics or other prehistoric artifacts were found.

AZ BB:9:247 (ASM)
Historical period: Territorial and Early Statehood
Historical function: residential; irrigation

The principal source of information on this site is the ASM site card, prepared in 1989. The site consists of a sparse historical-period artifact scatter and a segment of historical-period canal. The artifact scatter, found near the canal, included aqua glass, SCA glass, and metal fragments. The site card notes that prehistoric plain ware sherds were found in the vicinity (citing Ciolek-Torrello and Homburg 1990), but it is unclear that these sherds fell within the bounds of the present site. The site is presumed to have an association with the nearby Mormon settlement of Binghampton (AZ BB:9:238).

AZ BB:9:253 (ASM)
Prehistoric period: undifferentiated Hohokam
Prehistoric function: limited activity

This site was recorded in a 1990 survey by SRI (Harry 1990). The site consists of a light scatter of lithics and one sherd, covering an area about 50 m in diameter on the north bank of the Rillito. One chert biface and a retouched flake tool were noted. The single sherd, found on the periphery of the scatter, was of an unidentified red-on-brown type.

AZ BB:9:254 (ASM)
Historical period: Early Statehood and post–World War II
Historical function: residential

This site, recorded in a 1990 survey by SRI (Harry 1990), consists of a masonry house with stucco exterior, and associated features. The site is located on a low rise just north of the Rillito and east of the Mormon settlement at Binghampton (AZ BB:9:238). A concrete foundation was found about 40 m from the house, next to a pile of melting adobe bricks; the foundation probably also once supported a house. A small number of artifacts were found on the surface of the site, including an old stove. The house appeared to have been abandoned only recently. County records indicate that the house was built in 1926; it may have been associated with the Binghampton settlement.

AZ BB:9:255 (ASM)
Prehistoric period: undifferentiated Hohokam
Prehistoric function: limited activity
Historical period: Territorial and Early Statehood
Historical function: irrigation

This site was recorded in a 1990 survey by SRI (Harry 1990). The site consists of a light scatter of sherds and lithics covering an area 40 m in diameter on the north bank of the Rillito. Approximately 35 artifacts were noted, with more or less equal numbers of chipped stone artifacts and undecorated sherds. The artifacts were observed only in areas of ground disturbance, suggesting that more of the site is still buried. Part of the disturbance was attributed to the presence of three segments of historical-period canal passing through the area. The largest of these unlined canal segments is probably a portion of the Rillito Farms canal first built by Nephi Bingham and depicted on a map of the Rillito Farms irrigation system by Ruthrauff (n.d.). The other two segments may have formed minor parts of the same system, which was apparently abandoned in the early 1940s.

AZ BB:9:256 (ASM)
Historical period: Early Statehood and post-WWII
Historical function: residential

This site, located on the north bank of the Rillito, was recorded in a 1990 survey by SRI (Harry 1990). The site consists of an adobe-and-stucco house, with a later brick addition. According to county records, the house was built in 1940. Other features recorded near the house are a wooden-plank compost bin, a metal storage shed, and another shed made of plywood. A small amount of historical-period debris was observed on the surface of the site.

AZ BB:9:259 (ASM)
Prehistoric period: undifferentiated prehistoric
Prehistoric function: limited activity

This site was recorded in 1991 in a survey of the Catalina Foothills High School building site (Dart 1991). The site centered on a rock feature, consisting of a large angular cobble, 40 by 30 by 15 cm, evidently placed upright on one of its narrow sides. Three other stones, each less than 25 cm long, were found about 1 m north of the large cobble, apparently placed in a line with it and touching each other. The cobble and the three other stones were all of gneiss, the most common material in the area. A small number of artifacts were found in the general vicinity of the feature, including an oval mano of pink sandstone, a uniface scraper of rhyolite, and a mudstone core with an associated flake.

AZ BB:9:302 (ASM): Davidson Flume and Schroeder's Well
Historical period: Territorial to post–World War II
Historical function: irrigation

This site consists of a group of associated historical-period features documented by SRI on the north bank of the Rillito and in the adjacent river channel (Sterner 1996). The principal features are the Davidson Flume and Schroeder's Well; other features include smaller water-control structures, such as a water tank and a canal head gate. The Davidson Flume is of redwood-box design and originates at an undetermined point in Tanque Verde Wash, upstream from the documented portion of the flume. From Tanque Verde Wash, the flume passes below the channel of the Rillito, ending at an undetermined point near Rillito's north bank. The flume was used and maintained into the 1980s. Schroeder's Well is a circular concrete well, 7 feet in diameter and 11 feet deep, connecting to the Davidson Flume. The other water-control features at the site are located adjacent to or near the well. No artifacts were found in association with any of these features.

AZ BB:9:306 (ASM)
Historical period: post–World War II
Historical function: residential

This site consists of a three-room, wood-frame house at 1321 East Prospect Lane, on the south side of the Rillito, just north of the University of Arizona farms. Built in 1946 and renovated in 1957, the house was recorded as an archaeological site in 1996 during a survey for a small residential development (Lenhart 1996). Other foundations were recorded near the house, including barn and trailer footings, both dating to the 1970s. The house was abandoned in 1982 and showed signs of vandalism when it was recorded. Unspecified numbers of glass and metal artifacts were found on the site.

AZ BB:9:309 (ASM)
Prehistoric period: undifferentiated Hohokam
Prehistoric function: limited activity
Historical period: Territorial and Early Statehood (?)
Historical function: residential

According to the 1996 ASM site card, the prehistoric component of this site consists of "a small scatter of Hohokam chipped stone and ground stone," plus some fire-cracked rock. The historical-period component consists of: a surface trash dump containing glass, crockery, tin cans, square nails, and Papago plain and red wares; a trash pit containing similar artifacts; and two small piles of soil representing the backdirt from looter's pits. One looter's pit was refilled with 1960s-era trash. The site card indicates that some of the early historical-period trash may be related to the Leopoldo Carrillo ranch, which was located 500 feet north of the site and occupied in the period 1870s–1890s. Some of the trash may be derived from a Mormon farm that occupied the same land around 1900. Unfortunately, no historical documentation is cited for either occupation.

AZ BB:9:310 (ASM)
Historical period: Territorial and Early Statehood
Historical function: residential

All of the information on this nineteenth-century trash scatter comes from the ASM site card, prepared in 1996. Artifacts in the scatter include fragments of glass, crockery, tin, and iron, square nails, and Papago plain and red wares. The age of the artifacts suggests they are associated with the local El Fuerte neighborhood, occupied in the approximate period 1890–1920. This site was recorded at the same time as AZ BB:9:310, and there seems to have been some confusion in the preparation of the two site cards. The feature descriptions on the card for AZ BB:9:309 seem to have been included by mistake with the card for the present site. Thus, we exclude these features from the discussion here. Nonetheless, the two sites do have similar artifact assemblages. Since they are separated by only 200 feet, it is possible they are parts of the same site.

AZ BB:9:314 (ASM)
Prehistoric period: undifferentiated Hohokam
Prehistoric function: limited activity
Historical period: undetermined
Historical function: irrigation

This site was first recorded as a light scatter of chipped stone and pot sherds in 1997 (Stephen 1997). Backhoe testing the same year discovered a roasting pit with a rock-lined bottom (Jones and Dart 1997).

Seven large rocks formed the base of the pit, all fire-spalled or fire-blackened. The fill held very little charcoal, suggesting that the original sediments had been washed away. No artifacts were found within the feature, but the surface artifacts date the pit to the general Hohokam period. The site map accompanying the ASM site card depicts an irrigation ditch passing immediately adjacent to the artifact scatter, but there is no discussion of this feature on the card. We assume the ditch is historical-period in date.

AZ BB:9:315 (ASM)
Prehistoric period: Sedentary (Rincon phase)
Prehistoric function: habitation

This site was first recorded in 1997 as a light scatter of chipped stone and pot sherds (Stephen 1997). The artifacts were dispersed over a 75-m-diameter area. Backhoe testing the same year discovered a pit house, two extramural pits, and a sheet midden. A second semi-rectangular pit house with a plastered hearth apron and prepared mud floor was found during scraping. The artifacts from the site included chipped stone and Rincon phase pottery. The ASM site card notes that the site was recommended for mitigation, but this has yet to take place.

AZ BB:9:321 (ASM)
Historical period: Territorial and Early Statehood
Historical function: irrigation

This site consists of a historical-period canal, possibly associated with the Mormon settlement at Binghampton (AZ BB:9:238). The canal was recorded by Thiel (1997), who suggested that it was the western end of the Bingham Ditch, a major canal depicted on a map of early irrigation features in the area. The Bingham Ditch was built to irrigate fields associated with the settlement at Binghampton (see Chapter 4). The ditch documented by Thiel is about 3 m wide, paralleled on either side by a low berm, and long abandoned. Few artifacts were found in the area, although pieces of early aqua-colored glass were found, as well as recent trash.

AZ BB:9:322 (ASM)
Historical period: Early Statehood
Historical function: residential (?)

We were unable to locate the ASM site card for this site, but AZSITE summarizes the contents of the 1998 site card by Jane Sliva. The site, located in the foothills about a mile north of the Rillito, consists of three concrete footings with metal straps, and an associated scatter of glass and metal artifacts. Both the footings and the artifacts appeared to date to the 1930s. The function of the site is not indicated, but the footings and artifacts suggest it was residential.

AZ BB:9:324 (ASM)
Historical period: Early Statehood and post–World War II
Historical function: undetermined

This historical-period trash deposit was first recorded in 1998 by David Stephen, who suggested it was associated with the quartermaster's building at Fort Lowell (Stephen 1998). The trash deposit included

Papago red wares, European white wares, glass, and metal, and appeared to have been disturbed by a recent bulldozer push. Subsequent testing by Jones (1998) discovered a mixture of recent and early twentieth-century artifacts in what was obviously a disturbed context. An association of the deposit with the quartermaster's building at Fort Lowell is doubtful, and, in any case, apparently unsubstantiated by documentary sources.

AZ BB:9:325 (ASM): Corbett Ditch
Historical period: Territorial and Early Statehood
Historical function: irrigation

This historical-period unlined irrigation ditch was first recorded in 1998 by David Stephen, who suggested it was a portion of the Corbett ditch, one of the early underflow ditches discussed in Chapter 4. The location of the feature recorded by Stephen does correspond closely with that of the Corbett ditch on early maps.

AZ BB:9:356 (ASM)
Prehistoric period: Sedentary (Rincon phase)
Prehistoric function: limited activity
Historical period: Territorial and Early Statehood
Historical function: residential; irrigation

This site is located on the point of land separating Tanque Verde Creek and Pantano Wash, about a quarter-mile east of their confluence. The site was first recorded in a recent survey by SRI for a bank-protection project on Pantano Wash (Homburg and Kurota 2000). The prehistoric component of the site consists of a scatter of sherds and lithics, including Rincon Red-on-brown sherds. The original recorders suggested the site was a Rincon-phase field house, because of its location near good farm land. Subsequent testing by SRI (O'Mack and Riggs 2001) showed that the prehistoric artifacts derive from a disturbed context also having historical-period and recent materials. Thus, the prehistoric function of the site is uncertain. The historical-period component centers on a masonry house foundation and a concrete irrigation drop box surrounded by a water-catchment berm. Archival research carried out during the archaeological testing and for the present overview (see Chapter 4) strongly suggests that the drop box represents the point where the University ditch, depicted on early maps of the area, fed into the buried flume of the Bingham ditch, which crossed the point of land separating Tanque Verde Creek and Pantano Wash. Historical-period artifacts near the foundation and drop box consisted mainly of glass, including white and SCA glass.

Abbott, Mary Huntington
  1986   *"The Holiness of Beauty," St. Philip's in the Hills Episcopal Church 1936–1986.* Privately published, Tucson.

Ahlstrom, Richard V. N.
  1985   The Interpretation of Archaeological Tree-Ring Dates. Unpublished Ph.D. dissertation, Department of Anthropology, University of Arizona.

Ahlstrom, Richard V. N., and Mark C. Slaughter
  1996   Site Chronology and Dating Methods. In *Excavation of the Gibbon Springs Site: A Classic Period Village in the Northeastern Tucson Basin,* edited by Mark C. Slaughter and Heidi Roberts, pp. 481–489. Archaeological Report No. 94-87. SWCA, Tucson.

Ahnert, Gerald T.
  1973   *Retracing the Butterfield Overland Trail Through Arizona.* Westernlore Press, Los Angeles.

Altschul, Jeffrey H., Trixi Bubemyre, Kellie M. Cairns, William L. Deaver, Anthony Della Croce, Suzanne K. Fish, Lee Fratt, Karen G. Harry, James Holmlund, Gary Huckleberry, Charles H. Miksicek, Arthur W. Vokes, Stephanie M. Whittlesey, Maria Nieves Zedeño, and Lara F. Ziady
  1996   *Archaeological Investigations at the SRI Locus, West Branch Site (AZ AA:16:3 [ASM]): A Rincon Phase Village in the Tucson Basin.* Draft. Statistical Research, Tucson. Submitted to the Pima County Department of Transportation and Flood Control District, Tucson.

Altschul, Jeffrey H., and Edgar K. Huber
  1995   *Archaeological Testing Report and Treatment Plan for the Dairy Site (AZ AA:12:285 [ASM]).* Technical Report 95-8. Statistical Research, Tucson.

Anderson, Adrienne
  1968   The Archaeology of Mass-Produced Footwear. *Historical Archaeology* 2:56–65.

  1970   From Family Home to Slum Apartment: Archaeological Analysis within the Urban Renewal Area, Tucson, Arizona. Unpublished Master's thesis, Department of Anthropology, University of Arizona, Tucson.

Anderson, F. J.
  1968   *Cenozoic stratigraphy and geologic history of the Tucson Basin, Pima County, Arizona.* Water-Resources Investigations Report 876-4190, U.S. Geological Survey, Tucson.

Arizona Daily Citizen (ADC) [Tucson]
  1887   Another Canal. 20 March:4. Tucson.

Arizona Daily Star (ADS) [Tucson]

1887   The Underflow. 9 June.

1926   F. W. Jordan Is Again Head of Pima Farmers. 19 March.

1928   F. W. Jordon [*sic*] Is New Candidate. 5 August.

1932   Fort Builder Is Taken by Death. 9 December.

1938   "Advertisement for the John W. Murphey–Leo B. Keith Building Company." 9 October.

1956   Valley School Graduates First Class. 17 May.

1957   Couple Sees 58 Years of Arizona History Together. 21 April.

1961   Valley Assn. Will Fight Road Plan. 22 July.

1961   Swan Road Extension Postponed. 3 October.

1961   River Road May Be Realigned. 15 December.

1962   New Bridge Set for November. 9 May.

1962   Swan Rd.–Rillito Link Start Slated Monday. 9 October.

1963   Prelude to Bridge Opening. 2 February.

1963   Wooden Bridge on Campbell Will Be Razed. 3 May.

1963   Opening of Rillito Bridge Dedicated in Ceremonies. 3 November.

1969   Davis Helps Dedicate Swan Road Bridge over Rillito River. 16 November.

1971   Where Did the Dude Ranch Go? 17 October.

1976   Dude Ranches. 15 August.

1986   Rillito Corridor Area Is Left Blank in Proposed Transportation Plan. 8 May.

1993   Old Guest Ranch to Be Restored, Hacienda del Sol Has New Owners. 27 June.

Arizona Department of Transportation (ADOT)

1977   *Historical Notes: Existing Road System and Current Regulations of Highway Transport in Arizona.* Transportation Planning Division, Arizona Department of Transportation, Phoenix.

Arizona Historical Society (AHS)

n.d.   Biographical file on George H. Doe, 1845–1927. On file, Arizona Historical Society, Tucson.

Arizona State Parks Board
  1978   Fort Lowell Multiple Resource Area. National Register of Historic Places Inventory-
          Nomination Form. On file, Arizona State Historic Preservation Office, Phoenix.

Atondo Rodríguez, Ana María, and Martha Ortega Soto
  1985   Entrada de colonos españoles en Sonora durante el siglo XVII. In *Historia general de
          Sonora,* vol. 2, edited by Sergio Ortega Noriega and Ignacio del Río, pp. 77–110. Gobierno
          del Estado de Sonora, Hermosillo, Mexico.

Ayres, James E.
  1968   Urban Renewal Salvage Archaeology in Tucson, Arizona. Paper presented at the 33rd
          Annual Meeting of the Society for American Archaeology, Santa Fe. Manuscript on file,
          Arizona State Museum Library, University of Arizona, Tucson.

  1969   Innovations in the Use of Ceramics: A Case from Historical Archaeology. Paper presented at
          the 12th Annual Ceramic Conference, Flagstaff, Arizona. Manuscript on file, Arizona State
          Museum Library, University of Arizona, Tucson.

  1970a   An Early Historic Burial from the Village of Bac. *The Kiva* 36(2):44–48.

  1970b   Problem-Oriented Historical Archaeology in Tucson, Arizona. Paper presented at the 35th
          Annual Meeting of the Society for American Archaeology, Mexico City. Manuscript on file,
          Arizona State Museum Library, University of Arizona, Tucson.

  1971   Buildings and Bottles. *Southern Arizona Genealogical Society Bulletin* 6(3):48–51.

  1978   Archaeological Report: Preliminary Report of Excavations at TUR 1:6 (The Cordova
          House). In *The Restoration of the La Casa Cordova,* compiled and edited by J. B. Hunt,
          pp. 13–17. Junior League of Tucson, Tucson.

  1979   Archaeological Excavations in the Art Center Block: A Brief Summary. In *Master Plan for
          the Tucson Museum of Art,* Appendix 2. James Gresham and Associates, Tucson.

  1980   Analysis of Historic Artifacts from Tucson, Arizona's Urban Renewal Area. Manuscript on
          file, Arizona State Museum Library, University of Arizona, Tucson. Final report submitted
          to the National Endowment for the Humanities, Grant RO-21419-75-217.

  1984a   *Rosemont: The History and Archaeology of Post-1880 Sites in the Rosemont Area, Santa
          Rita Mountains, Arizona.* Archaeological Series No. 147, vol. 3. Cultural Resource
          Management Division, Arizona State Museum, University of Arizona, Tucson.

  1984b   The Anglo Period in Archaeological and Historical Perspective. *The Kiva* 49:225–232.

  1990   *Historic Archaeology at the Tucson Community Center.* Arizona State Museum Archaeo-
          logical Series No. 181. University of Arizona, Tucson.

  1991   Historical Archaeology in Arizona and New Mexico. *Historical Archaeology* 25(3):18–23.

2001   Assessment of River Road as a Historic Route of Travel. In *Cultural Resources Survey and Historical Assessment for the River Road Expansion and Realignment Between Campbell Avenue and Alvernon Way, and the Binghampton Public Park Development in Pima County, Arizona* (draft), by Janet H. Parkhurst, Eric J. Kaldahl, James E. Ayres, and Allen Dart. Technical Report No. 2001.005. Old Pueblo Archaeology Center, Tucson.

Ayres, James E., and Lyle M. Stone
1983   Historic Period Cultural Resources. In *An Archaeological Assessment of the Middle Santa Cruz River Basin, Rillito to Green Valley, Arizona, for the Proposed Tucson Aqueduct, Phase B, Central Arizona Project,* by Jon S. Czaplicki and J. D. Mayberry, pp. 63–77. Archaeological Series No. 164. Cultural Resource Management Division, Arizona State Museum, University of Arizona, Tucson.

Baar, Sam
1996   *Interstate 10 Frontage Road Project: Results of Archaeological Testing, South of Speedway Parcel.* Technical Report No. 96-11. Center for Desert Archaeology, Tucson.

Bahr, Donald
1971   Who Were the Hohokam? The Evidence from Pima-Papago Myths. *Ethnohistory* 18:245–266.

1975   *Pima and Papago Ritual Oratory: A Study of Three Texts.* Indian Historian Press, San Francisco.

Bahr, Donald, Juan Gregorio, David I. Lopez, and Albert Alvarez
1974   *Piman Shamanism and Staying Sickness (Ká:cim Múmkidag).* University of Arizona Press, Tucson.

Bahr, Donald, Lloyd Paul, and Vincent Joseph
1997   *Ants and Orioles: Showing the Art of Pima Poetry.* University of Utah Press, Salt Lake City.

Bahr, Donald, Juan Smith, William Smith Allison, and Julian Hayden
1994   *The Short, Swift Time of Gods on Earth: The Hohokam Chronicles.* University of California Press, Berkeley.

Bahre, Conrad Joseph
1991   *A Legacy of Change: Historic Human Impact on Vegetation in the Arizona Borderlands.* University of Arizona Press, Tucson.

Bancroft, Hubert H.
1889   *History of Arizona and New Mexico, 1530–1888.* The History Company, San Francisco.

Bandelier, Adolph F.
1890   *Final Report of Investigations among the Indians of the Southwestern United States Carried on Mainly in the Years 1880–1885,* pt. 2. Papers of the Archaeological Institute of America, American Series No. 4. John Wilson and Son and Cambridge University Press, Cambridge.

1970   *The Southwestern Journals of Adolph F. Bandelier, 1883–1884,* edited by Charles H. Lange and Carroll L. Riley. University of New Mexico Press, Albuquerque.

Bannon, John Francis

1955   *The Mission Frontier in Sonora, 1620–1687.* United States Catholic Historical Society, New York.

1964   Introduction. In *Bolton and the Spanish Borderlands*, edited by J. F. Bannon, pp. 3–19. University of Oklahoma Press, Norman.

1970   *The Spanish Borderlands Frontier, 1513–1821.* Holt, Rinehart and Winston, New York.

1978   *Herbert Eugene Bolton: The Historian and the Man.* University of Arizona Press, Tucson.

Barnes, Mark R.

1972   Majolica of the Santa Cruz Valley. In *Mexican Majolica in Northern New Spain*, by Mark R. Barnes and R. V. May, pp. 1–23. Occasional Paper No. 2. Pacific Coast Archaeological Society, Ramona, California.

1980   Mexican Lead-Glazed Earthenwares. In *Spanish Colonial Frontier Research,* edited by Henry F. Dobyns, pp. 91–110. Center for Anthropological Studies, Albuquerque.

1983   Tucson: Development of a Community. Unpublished Ph.D. dissertation, School of Arts and Sciences, Catholic University of America, Washington, D.C.

1984   Hispanic Period Archaeology in the Tucson Basin: An Overview. *The Kiva* 49:213–223

Barnes, Thomas C., Thomas N. Naylor, and Charles W. Polzer

1981   *Northern New Spain: A Research Guide.* University of Arizona Press, Tucson.

Barnes, Will C.

1988   *Arizona Place Names.* University of Arizona Press, Tucson.

Basso, Keith H.

1969   *Western Apache Witchcraft.* Anthropological Papers No. 15. University of Arizona, Tucson.

1970   *The Cibicue Apache.* Holt, Rinehart and Winston, New York.

1983   Western Apache. In *Southwest,* edited by Alfonso Ortiz, pp. 462–488. Handbook of North American Indians, vol. 10, William C. Sturtevant, general editor, Smithsonian Institution, Washington, D.C.

1996   *Wisdom Sits in Places: Landscape and Language among the Western Apache.* University of New Mexico Press, Albuquerque.

Bawaya, Michael

2001   A City Searches for Its Roots. *American Archaeology* 5(2):24–30.

Beals, Ralph L.

1943   *The Aboriginal Culture of the Cáhita Indians.* Ibero-Americana No. 19. University of California Press, Berkeley.

1945   *The Contemporary Culture of the Cáhita Indians.* Bulletin No. 142. Bureau of American Ethnology, Smithsonian Institution, Washington, D.C.

1937   *Excavations at Tumacacori, 1934.* Southwestern Monuments Special Report 15. USDI National Park Service, Washington, D.C.

Berge, Dale L.
    1968   Historical Archaeology in the American Southwest. Unpublished Ph.D. dissertation, Department of Anthropology, University of Arizona, Tucson.

Bernard-Shaw, Mary
    1988   Hohokam Canal Systems and Late Archaic Wells: The Evidence from the Los Morteros Site. In *Recent Research on Tucson Basin Prehistory: Proceedings of the Second Tucson Basin Conference*, edited by William H. Doelle and Paul R. Fish, pp. 153–174. Anthropological Papers No. 10. Institute for American Research, Tucson.

    1989   *Archaeological Investigations at Los Morteros, AZ AA:12:57 (ASM), Locus 1, in the Northern Tucson Basin.* Technical Report No. 87-8, Institute for American Research, Tucson.

Bernard-Shaw, Mary, and William H. Doelle
    1991   Tucson Basin Irrigation Systems. In *Prehistoric Irrigation in Arizona: Symposium 1988*, edited by Cory Dale Breternitz, pp. 25-40. Soil Systems Publications in Archaeology No. 17. Soil Systems, Phoenix.

Betancourt, Julio
    1978a   *An Archaeological Synthesis of the Tucson Basin: Focus on the Santa Cruz and Its Riverpark.* Archaeological Series No. 116. Cultural Resource Management Division, Arizona State Museum, University of Arizona, Tucson.

    1978b   *Cultural Resources within the Proposed Santa Cruz Riverpark Archaeological District: With Recommendations and a Management Summary.* Archaeological Series No. 125. Cultural Resource Management Division, Arizona State Museum, University of Arizona, Tucson.

    1990   Tucson's Santa Cruz River and the Arroyo Legacy. Unpublished Ph.D. dissertation, Department of Geosciences, University of Arizona, Tucson.

Betancourt, Julio L., and Raymond M. Turner
    1988   *Historic Arroyo-cutting and Subsequent Channel Changes at the Congress Street Crossing, Santa Cruz River.* Proceedings of Arid Lands Today and Tomorrow, Tucson.

Bieg, Jim, John Jones, and Ann Leviton
    1976   *Fort Lowell.* Pima County, Arizona.

Birkeland, Peter W.
    1984   *Soils and Geomorphology.* Oxford University Press, New York.

Blaine, Peter, Sr. (with Michael S. Adams)
    1981   *Papagos and Politics.* Arizona Historical Society, Tucson.

Bolton, Herbert E.

1948   *Kino's Historical Memoir of Pimería Alta.* University of California Press, Berkeley.

1964   The Mission as a Frontier Institution in the Spanish American Colonies. In *Bolton and the Spanish Borderlands,* edited by John F. Bannon, pp. 187–211. Reprinted. University of Oklahoma Press, Norman. Originally published 1917, University of Oklahoma Press, Norman.

1984   *Rim of Christendom: A Biography of Eusebio Francisco Kino, Pacific Coast Pioneer.* Reprinted. Reprinted. University of Arizona Press, Tucson. Originally published 1936, Macmillan, New York.

Bourke, John Gregory

1891   *On the Border with Crook.* Charles Scribner's Sons, New York.

Brew, Susan A.

1985   *Archaeological Clearance Survey of La Sonrisa Development Area, Pima County, Arizona.* Cultural Resource Management Division, Arizona State Museum, Tucson.

Brew, Susan A., and Bruce B. Huckell

1987   A Protohistoric Piman Burial and a Consideration of Piman Burial Practices. *The Kiva* 52:163–191.

Bronitsky, Gordon R., and James D. Merritt

1986   *The Archaeology of Southeast Arizona: A Class I Cultural Resources Inventory.* Cultural Resource Series No. 2. Arizona State Office, USDI Bureau of Land Management, Phoenix.

Brown, S. Kent, Donald Q. Cannon, and Richard H. Jackson (editors)

1994   *Historical Atlas of Mormonism.* Simon and Schuster, New York.

Buol, S. W., and M. S. Yesilsoy

1964   A Genesis Study of A Mohave Sandy Loam Profile. *Soil Science Society of America Proceedings* 28:254-256.

Burns, Barney T., and Thomas H. Naylor

1973   Colonia Morelos: A Short History of a Mormon Colony in Sonora, Mexico. *The Smoke Signal* 27:142–180.

Burrus, Ernest J.

1971   *Kino and Manje: Explorers of Sonora and Arizona.* Jesuit Historical Institute, Rome, Italy, and St. Louis, Missouri.

Burton, Jeffery F.

1992a   *San Miguel de Guevavi: The Archaeology of an Eighteenth Century Jesuit Mission on the Rim of Christendom.* Publications in Anthropology No. 57. Western Archeological and Conservation Center, USDI National Park Service, Tucson.

1992b *Remnants of Adobe and Stone: The Surface Archaeology of the Guevavi and Calabazas Units, Tumacacori National Historical Park, Arizona.* Publications in Anthropology No. 59. Western Archeological and Conservation Center, USDI National Park Service, Tucson.

Butzer, Karl W.
1980 Context in Archaeology: An Alternative Perspective. *Journal of Field Archaeology* 7:417–422.

1982 *Archaeology as Human Ecology: Method and Theory for a Contextual Approach.* Cambridge University Press, Cambridge.

Canal Company Records
1911 Complaint Filed in the District Court of the First Judicial District of the Territory of Arizona, County of Pima, 8 March 1911. A. R. Swan, Plaintiff, vs. Charles H. Bayless, Rillito Farms Company, Nephi Bingham, and J. Knox Corbett, defendants. Canal Company Records, Ms. 1129, folder 6. On file, Arizona Historical Society, Tucson.

Cardon, Bartley Pratt
1993 Oral history interview with Bartley Pratt Cardon, conducted by Leonard W. Dewhirst. On file, Arizona Historical Society, Tucson.

Castetter, Edward F., and Willis H. Bell
1942 *Pima and Papago Indian Agriculture.* University of New Mexico Press, Albuquerque.

Castetter, Edward F., and Ruth M. Underhill
1935 *The Ethnobiology of the Papago Indians.* Ethnobiological Studies in the American Southwest II. University of New Mexico Bulletin, Biological Series, Vol. 4, No. 3. University of New Mexico, Albuquerque.

Catalina Foothills School District
1988 *Establishing a Tradition of Excellence.* Pamphlet on file, Arizona Historical Society, Tucson.

Center for Desert Archaeology
2001 Tucson Origins: Archaeology and History for the Río Nuevo Project. Electronic document, http://www.rio-nuevo.org/rionuevo/index.html, accessed November 1, 2001.

Chamber of Commerce
1904 *Health, Wealth, Golden Opportunities: Scenes in and about a Prosperous Southwestern City.* Chamber of Commerce, Tucson. Pamphlet on file, University of Arizona Special Collections, Tucson.

1936 *Points of Interest of Tucson and Vicinity.* Chamber of Commerce and Tucson Sunshine Club, Tucson. Map on file, Arizona Historical Society, Tucson.

1948 *Welcome Visitor!* Chamber of Commerce and Tucson Sunshine Climate Club, Tucson. Ms. 1056, box 8, folder 102a. On file, Arizona Historical Society, Tucson.

1950   *Metropolitan Area Tucson, Arizona.* Chamber of Commerce and Tucson Sunshine Climate Club, Tucson. Map on file, University of Arizona Special Collections.

1953   *Map of Tucson, Arizona.* Chamber of Commerce and Tucson Sunshine Climate Club, Tucson. Map on file, University of Arizona Special Collections.

1959   *Map of Tucson, Arizona.* Chamber of Commerce and Tucson Sunshine Climate Club, Tucson. Map on file, University of Arizona Special Collections.

1961   *Map of Tucson, Arizona.* Chamber of Commerce and Tucson Sunshine Climate Club, Tucson. Map on file, University of Arizona Special Collections.

Chambers, George W.
1955   The Old Presidio of Tucson. *The Kiva* 20(2–3):15–16.

Chavarria, Sara P.
1996   *Archaeological Investigations at the Summit at Alvernon Site, AZ BB:9:280 (ASM): Archaic, Hohokam, Protohistoric, and Historic Use of an Upper Bajada Environment in the Tucson Basin.* Archaeology Report No. 4. Old Pueblo Archaeology Center, Tucson.

Cheek, Annetta L.
1974   The Evidence for Acculturation in Artifacts: Indians and Non-Indians at San Xavier del Bac, Arizona. Unpublished Ph.D. dissertation, Department of Anthropology, University of Arizona, Tucson.

Cheek, Lawrence W.
1992   El Fuerte: The Soul of Tucson. *Arizona Highways* December:38–45.

Church Educational System
1993   *Church History in the Fulness of Times.* Church of Jesus Christ of Latter-day Saints, Salt Lake City, Utah.

Ciolek-Torrello, Richard S.
1995   The Houghton Road Site, the Agua Caliente Phase, and the Early Formative Period in the Tucson Basin. *The Kiva* 60:531–574.

Ciolek-Torrello, Richard S. (editor)
1998   *Early Farmers of the Sonoran Desert: Archaeological Investigations at the Houghton Road Site, Tucson, Arizona.* Technical Series 72. Statistical Research, Tucson.

Ciolek-Torrello, Richard S., and Susan A. Brew
1976   *Archaeological Test Excavations at the San Xavier Bicentennial Plaza Site.* Archaeological Series No. 102. Cultural Resource Management Division, Arizona State Museum, University of Arizona, Tucson.

Ciolek-Torrello, Richard S., and Jeffrey A. Homburg
1990   *Cultural Resources Surveys and Overviews of the Rillito River Drainage Area, Pima County, Arizona.* Technical Series 20. Statistical Research, Tucson.

Ciolek-Torrello, Richard S., Edgar K. Huber, and Robert B. Neily
    1999   *Investigations at Sunset Mesa Ruin.* Technical Series 66. Statistical Research, Tucson.

City of Tucson
    1994   *Joesler & Murphey: An Architectural Legacy for Tucson.* City of Tucson Planning
            Department, Pima County, and the University of Arizona, Tucson.

Clonts, John
    1983   Some Long Overdue Thoughts on Faunal Analysis. In *Forgotten Places and Things:
            Archaeological Perspectives on American History,* edited by A. E. Ward, pp. 349–354.
            Contributions to Anthropological Studies No. 3. Center for Anthropological Studies,
            Albuquerque, New Mexico.

Coggin, H. Mason
    1987   A History of Placer Mining in Arizona. In *History of Mining in Arizona,* edited by J. Michael
            Canty and Michael N. Greeley, pp. 177–190. Mining Club of the Southwest Foundation,
            American Institute of Mining Engineers Tucson Section, Tucson, and Southwestern Minerals
            Exploration Association, Tucson.

Collins, William
    2001   Cattle Ranching in Arizona, 1540–1950. Draft National Register of Historic Places Multiple
            Property Documentation Form. On file, USDI National Park Service, Washington, D.C.

Colton, Harold S., and Lyndon L. Hargrave
    1937   *Handbook of Northern Arizona Pottery Wares.* Bulletin No. 11. Museum of Northern
            Arizona, Flagstaff.

Committee to Preserve Historic Rillito Racetrack
    n.d.   Rillito Racetrack. Ms. 1196, box 1, folder 3. On file, Arizona Historical Society, Tucson.

Conkling, Roscoe B., and Margaret B. Conkling
    1947   *The Butterfield Overland Mail, 1857–1869.* 3 vols. Arthur H. Clark, Glendale, California.

Cooke, R. U., and R. W. Reeves
    1976   *Arroyo and Environmental Change in the American Southwest.* Clarendon Press, Oxford.

Cosulich, Bernice
    1953   *Tucson.* Arizona Silhouettes, Tucson.

Cowdery, Richard B.
    1948   The Planning of a Transcontinental Railroad through Southern Arizona, 1832–1870.
            Unpublished Master's thesis, Department of History and Political Science, University
            of Arizona, Tucson.

Craig, Douglas B., and Henry D. Wallace
    1987   *Prehistoric Settlement in the Cañada del Oro Valley, Arizona: The Rancho Vistoso Survey
            Project.* Anthropological Papers No. 8. Institute for American Research, Tucson.

Crosby, Alfred
    1972   *The Columbian Exchange: Biological Consequences of 1492*. Greenwood, Westport, Connecticut.

Cummings, Byron
    1935   Old Fort Lowell Park. *The Kiva* 1:4.

Cunningham, W. S.
    1937   *Dairying in Arizona*. University of Arizona Agricultural Experiment Station Bulletin No. 155. University of Arizona, Tucson.

Curriden, Nancy T.
    1981   *The Lewis-Weber Site: A Tucson Homestead*. Publications in Anthropology No. 14. Western Archeological Center, USDI National Park Service, Tucson.

Danson, Edward B.
    1946   An Archaeological Survey of the Santa Cruz River from Its Headwaters to the Town of Tubac in Arizona. Unpublished Master's thesis, Department of Anthropology, University of Arizona, Tucson.

Dart, Allen
    1983   *Monitoring for Archaeological Remains During Effluent Pipeline Construction at Roger Road and Mountain Avenue, Tucson, Pima County, Arizona: Site AZ BB:9:9 (ASM)*. On file, Arizona State Museum, Tucson.

    1988   *Monitoring for Archaeological Remains During 1988 Construction of Effluent Water Pipeline Through Historic Fort Lowell and the Prehistoric Hardy Site*. Technical Report 88-4. Institute for American Research, Tucson.

    1989   *The Gunsight Mountain Archaeological Survey: Archaeological Sites in the Northern Sierrita Mountains near the Junction of the Altar and Avra Valleys Southwest of Tucson, Arizona*. Technical Report No. 89-1. Center for Desert Archaeology, Tucson.

    1991   *Archaeological Survey of a Proposed High School Location for the Catalina Foothills School District, Tucson, Arizona*. Letter Report 91-146. Desert Archaeology, Tucson.

Davidson, Alexander J.
    1930–1936 Reminiscences of Alexander J. Davidson as Told to Mrs. George F. Kitt, 1930–1936. Manuscript 208, Alexander J. Davidson Papers, 1931 [*sic*]–1936. On file, Arizona Historical Society, Tucson.

Davis, R. N.
    1959   *History of Dairying in Arizona*. University of Arizona Agricultural Experiment Station, Tucson.

Day, Susan
    1988   Binghampton. *City Magazine* June:52–57.

Dean, Jeffrey S.
  1988   Dendrochronology and Paleoenvironmental Reconstruction on the Colorado Plateaus. In *The Anasazi in A Changing Environment*, edited by George J. Gummerman, pp. 119–167. School of American Research Advanced Seminar Series. Cambridge University Press, Cambridge.

Dean, Jeffrey S., Robert C. Euler, George J. Gumerman, Fred Plog, Richard H. Hevly, and Thor N.V. Karlstrom
  1985   Human Behavior, Demography, and Paleoenvironment on the Colorado Plateau. *American Antiquity* 50:537–554.

Deaver, William L.
  1989   Pottery and Other Ceramic Artifacts. In *The 1979–1983 Testing at Los Morteros (AZ AA:12:57 ASM), a Large Hohokam Village Site in the Tucson Basin,* by Richard C. Lange and William L. Deaver, pp. 27–81. Archaeological Series No. 177. Cultural Resource Management Division, Arizona State Museum, Tucson.

Deaver, William L., and Richard S. Ciolek-Torrello
  1995   Early Formative Period Chronology for the Tucson Basin. *The Kiva* 60:481–529.

DeJong, David H.
  1992   "See the New Country": The Removal Controversy and Pima-Maricopa Water Rights, 1869–1879. *Journal of Arizona History* 33:367–396.

Dickinson, W. R.
  1999   *Geologic Framework of the Catalina Foothills, Outskirts of Tucson (Pima County, Arizona).* Contributed Map CM-99-B (Scale 1:24,000). Arizona Geological Survey, Tucson.

Diehl, Alison
  2000   *Cultural Resources Survey of the Intersection of Prince Road and Stone Avenue, Tucson, Pima County, Arizona.* Project Report No. 00-124. Desert Archaeology, Tucson.

Diehl, Allison C., and Michael W. Diehl
  1996   Building Tucson in the Nineteenth and Twentieth Centuries. *Archaeology in Tucson* 10(3):1–5.

Diehl, Allison Cohen, Timothy W. Jones, and J. Homer Thiel
  1996   *Archaeological Investigations at El Dumpé, a Mid-Twentieth-Century Dump, and the Embankment Site, Tucson, Arizona.* Technical Report No. 96-19. Center for Desert Archaeology, Tucson.

Diehl, Michael W.
  1997   *Archaeological Investigations of the Early Agricultural Period Settlement at the Base of A-Mountain, Tucson, Arizona.* Technical Report No. 96-21. Center for Desert Archaeology, Tucson.

Diehl, Michael W., and Allison C. Diehl
  1996   *Archaeological Investigations of the Tucson Pressed Brick Company, Tucson, Arizona.* Technical Report No. 96-13. Center for Desert Archaeology, Tucson.

244

Di Peso, Charles C.

1948   Preliminary Report of a Babocomari Indian Village. *The Kiva* 14:10–14.

1951   *The Babocomari Village Site on the Babocomari River, Southeastern Arizona.* Amerind Foundation Publication No. 5. Amerind Foundation, Dragoon, Arizona.

1953   *The Sobaipuri Indians of the Upper San Pedro River Valley, Southeastern Arizona.* Publication No. 6. Amerind Foundation, Dragoon, Arizona.

1956   *The Upper Pima of San Cayetano del Tumacacori.* Publication No. 7. Amerind Foundation, Dragoon, Arizona.

1967   *The Amerind Foundation.* Amerind Foundation, Dragoon, Arizona.

Doak, David P., Elizabeth Noll, James E. Ayres, and Thomas N. Motsinger

1995   *Archaeological Report for the Tucson, Arizona, Area Nexrad: Data Recovery at AZ EE:2:167 (ASM) and Recording and Evaluation of Two Additional Sites in the Empire Mountains, Pima County, Arizona.* Archaeological Report No. 95-78. SWCA, Tucson.

Dobyns, Henry F.

1976   *Spanish Colonial Tucson: A Demographic History.* University of Arizona Press, Tucson.

1981   *From Fire to Flood: Historic Human Destruction of Sonoran Desert Riverine Oases.* Ballena Press, Socorro, New Mexico.

Doe, George H.

1885   Letter to L. O. Parker, Captain of the 1st Infantry, Fort Lowell, Arizona. November 14, 1885. Typed transcription of microfilm copy. Fort Lowell Records, Ms. 266, 1869–1890, folder 3. On file, Arizona Historical Society, Tucson.

Doelle, William H.

1984   The Tucson Basin during the Protohistoric Period. *The Kiva* 49:195–211.

1985   *Excavations at the Valencia Site: A Preclassic Hohokam Village in the Southern Tucson Basin.* Anthropological Papers No. 3. Institute for American Research, Tucson.

1997   Preface. In *Archaeological Investigations of a Chinese Gardener's Household, Tucson, Arizona,* by J. Homer Thiel, pp. ix–xxiii. Technical Report No. 96-22. Center for Desert Archaeology, Tucson.

Doelle, William H., Allen Dart, and Henry D. Wallace

1985   *The Southern Tucson Basin Survey, Intensive Survey Along the Santa Cruz River.* Technical Report No. 85-3. Institute for American Research, Tucson.

Doelle, William H., and Frederick W. Huntington

1986   Site Description. In *Archaeological Investigations at the West Branch Site: Early and Middle Rincon Occupation in the Southern Tucson Basin,* by Frederick W. Huntington, pp. 17–24. Anthropological Papers No. 5. Institute for American Research, Tucson.

Doelle, William H., Frederick W. Huntington, and Henry D. Wallace
 1987   Rincon Phase Reorganization in the Tucson Basin. In *The Hohokam Village: Site Structure and Organization,* edited by David E. Doyel, pp. 71–96. Southwestern and Rocky Mountain Division, American Association for the Advancement of Science, Glenwood Springs, Colorado.

Doelle, William H., and Henry D. Wallace
 1986   *Hohokam Settlement Patterns in the San Xavier Project Area, Southern Tucson Basin.* Technical Report No. 84-6. Institute for American Research, Tucson.

Dowell, Shelton G.
 1933   The Big Business of Road Building: New Highways Being Constructed to Serve Very Definite Needs of Traffic. *Arizona Highways* 9(9):4–5.

Downs, Winfield Scott (editor)
 1937   *Who's Who in Engineering.* Lewis Historical Publishing Company, New York.

Downum, Christian E.
 1993   *Between Desert and River: Hohokam Settlement and Land Use in the Los Robles Community.* Anthropological Papers No. 57. University of Arizona Press, Tucson.

Doyel, David E.
 1977   *Excavations in the Middle Santa Cruz River Valley, Southeastern Arizona.* Contribution to Highway Salvage Archaeology No. 44. Arizona State Museum, University of Arizona, Tucson.

Drachman, Roy P.
 1999   *From Cowtown to Metropolis: Ninety Years of Arizona Memories.* Whitewing, San Francisco.

Dutt, Andrew, and J. Homer Thiel
 1999   *Results of a Testing Program and a Plan for Archaeological Data Recovery of a Portion of Block 136, Tucson, Arizona.* Technical Report No. 99-8. Desert Archaeology, Tucson.

Effland, Richard W., and Adrianne G. Rankin
 1988   Adaptation within the Santa Cruz River Floodplain near Mission San Xavier: Response to Changing Environments. In *Recent Research on Tucson Basin Prehistory: Proceedings of the Second Tucson Basin Conference,* edited by William H. Doelle and Paul R. Fish, pp. 183–205. Anthropological Papers No. 10. Institute for American Research, Tucson.

Elson, Mark D.
 1986   *Archaeological Investigations at the Tanque Verde Wash Site, a Middle Rincon Settlement in the Eastern Tucson Basin.* Anthropological Papers No. 7. Institute for American Research, Tucson.

Elson, Mark D., and William H. Doelle
 1986   *The Valencia Site Testing Project: Mapping, Intensive Surface Collecting, and Limited Trenching of a Hohokam Ballcourt Village in the Southern Tucson Basin.* Technical Report No. 86-6. Institute for American Research, Tucson.

Eppley, Lisa G.
1989   Letter to Linda Mayro, 18 January 1989. On file at Arizona State Museum site files, University of Arizona, Tucson. Institute for American Research, Tucson.

1996   *An Archaeological Survey for the Tucson Racquet Club Resort.* Letter Report No. 96-152. Desert Archaeology, Tucson.

Erickson, Winston P.
1994   *Sharing the Desert: The Tohono O'odham in History.* University of Arizona Press, Tucson.

Etter, Patricia A.
1995   To California on the Southern Route—1849. *Overland Journal* 13(3).

Euler, Robert C., George G. Gumerman, Thor N.V. Karlstrom, Jeffrey S. Dean, and Richard H. Hevly
1979   The Colorado Plateau: Cultural Dynamics and Paleoenvironment. *Science* 205:1089–1101.

Ewing, Russell Charles
1945   The Pima Uprising of 1751: A Study of Spanish-Indian Relations on the Frontier of New Spain. In *Greater America: Essays in Honor of Herbert Eugene Bolton,* pp. 259–280. University of California Press, Berkeley.

Ezell, Paul H.
1961   *The Hispanic Acculturation of the Gila River Pima.* American Anthropological Association, Menasha, Wisconsin.

Ezzo, Joseph A., and William L. Deaver
1998   *Watering the Desert: Late Archaic Farming at the Costello-King Site.* Technical Series 68. Statistical Research, Tucson.

Fansett, George R.
1952   Small Scale Gold Placering. In *Arizona Gold Placers and Placering,* 5th rev. ed., pp. 87–119. Arizona Bureau of Mines, University of Arizona, Tucson.

Farish, Thomas Edwin
1915–1918 *History of Arizona.* 8 vols. Filmer Brothers Electrotype, San Francisco.

Farrell, Mary
1993   Kentucky Camp: Big Dreams, Small Prospects. *Archaeology in Tucson* 7(2):1–4.

Faught, Michael K.
1995   *Archaeological Testing, Limited Data Recovery, and an In-Place Archaeological Site Preservation Plan for the Madera Reserve Property Development in Green Valley, Pima County, Arizona.* Archaeology Report No. 94-2. Old Pueblo Archaeology Center, Tucson.

Faulk, Odie B.
1969   *The Geronimo Campaign.* Oxford University Press, New York.

Ferguson, George W.
    1937   Correspondence to Warren A. Grossetta. 5 April. Ms. 568, John W. Murphey Papers, box 2, folder 35. On file, Arizona Historical Society, Tucson.

Fish, Paul R., Suzanne K. Fish, Austin Long, and Charles Miksicek
    1986   Early Corn Remains from Tumamoc Hill, Southern Arizona. *American Antiquity* 51:563–572.

Fish, Suzanne K., Paul R. Fish, and John H. Madsen
    1992   Evolution and Structure of the Classic Period Marana Community. In *The Marana Community in the Hohokam World,* edited by Suzanne K. Fish, Paul R. Fish, and John H. Madsen, pp. 20–40. Anthropological Papers No. 56. University of Arizona Press, Tucson.

Fish, Paul R., Suzanne K. Fish, John H. Madsen, Charles H. Miksecek, and Christine R. Szuter
    1992   The Dairy Site: Occupational Continuity on an Alluvial Fan. In *The Marana Community in the Hohokam World,* edited by Suzanne K. Fish, Paul R. Fish, and John H. Madsen, pp. 64–72. Anthropological Papers No. 56. University of Arizona Press, Tucson.

Fontana, Bernard L.
    1960   Assimiliative Change: A Papago Indian Case Study. Unpublished Ph.D. dissertation, Department of Anthropology, University of Arizona, Tucson.

    1965   An Archaeological Survey of the Cabeza Prieta Game Range, Arizona. Manuscript on file, Arizona State Museum Library, University of Arizona, Tucson.

    1971   Calabazas of the Rio Rico. *The Smoke Signal* 24:66–88.

    1983a   Pima and Papago: An Introduction. In *Southwest,* edited by Alfonso Ortiz, pp. 125–136. Handbook of North American Indians, vol. 10, William C. Sturtevant, general editor, Smithsonian Institution, Washington, D.C.

    1983b   History of the Papago. In *Southwest,* edited by Alfonso Ortiz, pp. 137–148. Handbook of North American Indians, vol. 10, William C. Sturtevant, general editor, Smithsonian Institution, Washington, D.C.

    1987   Santa Ana de Cuiquiburitac: Pimería Alta's Northernmost Mission. *Journal of the Southwest* 29:133–159.

    1989   *Of Earth and Little Rain: The Papago Indians.* University of Arizona Press, Tucson.

    1994   *Entrada: The Legacy of Spain and Mexico in the United States.* Southwest Parks and Monuments Association, Tucson.

    1996   Biography of a Desert Church: The Story of Mission San Xavier del Bac. *The Smoke Signal* 3 (rev. ed.).

Fontana, Bernard L., and J. Cameron Greenleaf
    1962   Johnny Ward's Ranch. *The Kiva* 28(1–2).

Fortier, Edward M.
  1980   *Archaeological Excavations at the Stevens House, Tucson, Pima County, Arizona.* Submitted
         to the Tucson Museum of Art, Arizona.

Fratt, Lee
  1981   *Tumacacori Plaza Excavation, 1979: Historical Archeology at Tumacacori National
         Monument, Arizona.* Publications in Anthropology No. 16. Western Archeological and
         Conservation Center, USDI National Park Service, Tucson.

Freeman, Andrea K. L.
  1997   Middle to Late Holocene Stream Dynamics of the Santa Cruz River, Tucson, Arizona:
         Implications for Human Settlement, the Transition to Agriculture, and Archaeological Site
         Preservation. Unpublished Ph.D. dissertation, Department of Anthropology, University of
         Arizona, Tucson.

Freeman, Andrea K. L., William H. Doelle, Mark D. Elson, and Allison Cohen Diehl
  1996   *Archaeological Investigations for the Menlo Park Storm Drain Project: Prehistoric and
         Historic Canal Systems at the Base of A-Mountain.* Technical Report No. 96-14. Desert
         Archaeology, Tucson

Frick, Paul
  1954   An Archaeological Survey in the Santa Cruz Valley, Southern Arizona. Unpublished
         Master's thesis, Department of Anthropology, University of Arizona, Tucson.

Fulton, William S.
  1940   Observations. In *An Archaeological Site Near Gleeson, Arizona,* by William S. Fulton and
         C. Tuthill, pp. 63–64. Papers No. 1. Amerind Foundation, Dragoon, Arizona.

Fulton, William S., and Carl Tuthill
  1940   *An Archaeological Site Near Gleeson, Arizona.* Papers No. 1, Amerind Foundation,
         Dragoon, Arizona.

Gelderman, Frederick W.
  1972   *Soil Survey of the Tucson-Avra Valley Area, Arizona.* U.S. Department of Agriculture, Soil
         Conservation Service, U.S. Government Printing Office, Washington.

Gerhard, Peter
  1993   *The North Frontier of New Spain.* Rev. ed. University of Oklahoma Press, Norman and
         London.

Gile, L. H., F. F. Peterson, and R. B. Grossman
  1966   Morphological and Genetic Sequences of Carbonate Accumulation in Desert Soils. *Soil
         Science* 101:347–360.

Gilman, Catherine
  1997   *Archaeological Monitoring of the NDC/Tucson Lightwave Fiber Optic Network Installation
         Project.* Technical Report No. 97-6. Center for Desert Archaeology, Tucson.

Gilman, Catherine, and Deborah L. Swartz
1998   *Archaeological Testing and Monitoring of the Speedway to Ajo Reclaimed Pipeline Project (Phase I).* Technical Report 98-2. Desert Archaeology, Tucson.

Gladfelter, B. G.
1985   On the Interpretation of Archaeological Sites in Alluvial Settings. In *Archaeological Sediments in Context*, edited by J. K. Stein and W. R. Farrand, pp. 41–52. Center for the Study of Early Man, University of Maine, Orono.

Gladwin, Harold S., Emil W. Haury, E. B. Sayles, and Nora Gladwin
1937   *Excavations at Snaketown: Material Culture.* Medallion Papers No. 25. Gila Pueblo, Globe, Arizona.

Gobierno del Estado de Sonora
1997   *Historia general de Sonora.* 6 vols. 2nd ed. Gobierno del Estado de Sonora, Hermosillo, Sonora, Mexico.

Goodwin, Grenville
1939   *Myths and Tales of the White Mountain Apache.* Memoirs No. 33. American Folklore Society, New York.

1969   *The Social Organization of the Western Apache.* Reprinted. University of Arizona Press, Tucson. Originally published 1942, University of Chicago Press, Chicago.

Graeme, R. W.
1987   Bisbee, Arizona's Dowager Queen of Mining Camps: A Look at Her First 50 Years. In *History of Mining in Arizona*, edited by J. Michael Canty and Michael N. Greeley, pp. 51–76. Mining Club of the Southwest Foundation, American Institute of Mining Engineers Tucson Section, and Southwestern Minerals Exploration Association, Tucson.

Greenleaf, J. Cameron
1975   *Excavations at Punta de Agua in the Santa Cruz River Basin, Southeastern Arizona.* Anthropological Paper No. 26. University of Arizona Press, Tucson.

Greenleaf, J. Cameron, and Andrew Wallace
1962   Tucson: Pueblo, Presidio, and American City. *Arizoniana* 3(2):17.

Gregonis, Linda M.
1997   *The Hardy Site at Fort Lowell Park, Tucson, Arizona.* Archaeological Series 175. Arizona State Museum, Tucson.

Gregonis, Linda M., and Lisa W. Huckell
1980   *The Tucson Urban Study.* Archaeological Series No. 138. Arizona State Museum, Tucson.

Gregory, David A.
1999   *Excavations in the Santa Cruz River Floodplain: The Middle Archaic Component at Los Pozos.* Anthropological Papers No. 20. Center for Desert Archaeology, Tucson.

Griffith, James S.

    1973   The Catholic Religious Architecture of the Papago Reservation, Arizona. Unpublished Ph.D. dissertation, Department of Anthropology, University of Arizona, Tucson.

    1992   *Beliefs and Holy Places: A Spiritual Geography of the Pimería Alta.* University of Arizona Press, Tucson.

Gursky, Deanna

    1994   *Roots and Wings: A History of Davidson School, Its Namesake, and Its Neighborhoods.* Tucson.

Guy, Donna J., and Thomas E. Sheridan (editors)

    1998   *Contested Ground: Comparative Frontiers on the Northern and Southern Edges of the Spanish Empire.* University of Arizona Press, Tucson.

Hackenberg, Robert A.

    1974   Aboriginal Land Use and Occupancy. In *Papago Indians I,* edited by D. A. Horr, pp. 23–308. Garland, New York.

Hadley, Diana, and Thomas E. Sheridan

    1995   *Land Use History of the San Rafael Valley, Arizona (1540–1960).* USDA Rocky Mountain Forest and Range Experiment Station, Fort Collins, Colorado.

Halbirt, Carl D., and T. Kathleen Henderson (editors)

    1993   *Archaic Occupation of the Santa Cruz Flats: The Tator Hills Archaeological Project.* Northland Research, Flagstaff.

Haney, Richard A., Jr. (compiler)

    1985   *College of Agriculture: A Century of Discovery.* College of Agriculture, University of Arizona, Tucson.

Hansen, Klaus J.

    1998   Mormonism. In *World Religions,* pp. 461–464. Macmillan Reference USA, Simon and Schuster Macmillan, New York.

Hard, Robert J., and William H. Doelle

    1978   *The San Augustín Mission Site, Tucson, Arizona.* Archaeological Series No. 118. Cultural Resource Management Division, Arizona State Museum, University of Arizona, Tucson.

Harry, Karen G.

    1990   Letter report on Foothills Park Survey and Rillito Farms Irrigation Canal. Submitted to Pima County Department of Transportation and Flood Control District, Pima County, Arizona. On file, Statistical Research, Tucson.

Harry, Karen G., and Richard S. Ciolek-Torrello

    1992   *Farming the Floodplain: A Look at Prehistoric and Historic Land-Use along the Rillito.* Technical Series 35. Statistical Research, Tucson.

Hartmann, Gayle Harrison
1984   Letter to Donna J. Schober, Arizona State Historic Preservation Office, 10 December 1984. On file, Arizona State Museum, Tucson.

Hartmann, William K.
1989   *Desert Heart: Chronicles of the Sonoran Desert.* Fisher Books, Tucson.

Haury, Emil W.
1932   *Roosevelt 9:6: A Hohokam Site of the Colonial Period.* Medallion Papers No. 11. Gila Pueblo, Globe, Arizona.

1945   *The Excavation of Los Muertos and Neighboring Ruins in the Salt River Valley, Southern Arizona.* Papers of the Peabody Museum of American Archaeology and Ethnology Vol. 24, No. 1. Harvard University, Cambridge.

1953   Discovery of the Naco Mammoth and the Associated Projectile Points. *American Antiquity* 19:1–14.

Haury, Emil W., and Isabel Fathauer
1974   *Tucson from Pithouse to Skyscraper.* Tucson Historical Committee, Tucson.

Haury, Emil W., E. B. Sayles, and William W. Wasley
1959   The Lehner Mammoth Site, Southeastern Arizona. *American Antiquity* 25:2–42.

Hayden, Julian D.
1957   *Excavations, 1940, at University Indian Ruin, Tucson, Arizona.* Technical Series No. 5. Southwest Monuments Association, Tucson, and Gila Pueblo, Globe, Arizona.

Haynes, C. Vance, and Bruce B. Huckell
1986   *Sedimentary Successions of the Prehistoric Santa Cruz River, Tucson, Arizona.* Open-file Report 86-15. Bureau of Geology and Mineral Technology, Tucson.

Healy, William T.
1990   *The History of Tucson Country Club.* Published by the author, Tucson.

Hendricks, David M.
1985   *Arizona Soils.* College of Agriculture, University of Arizona, Tucson.

Henry, Bonnie
1992   *Another Tucson.* Arizona Daily Star, Tucson.

Historic American Buildings Survey (HABS)
1940   Line drawing of Officer's House, Fort Lowell, Tucson, Arizona. HABS No. AZ-17. Electronic document, http://memory.loc.gov/, accessed November 1, 2001. Historic American Buildings Survey/Historic American Engineering Record Web site.

1941   Report, Fort Lowell (Officer's House and Summer Kitchen), near Tucson, Pima County, Arizona. HABS No. AZ-17. Electronic document, http://memory.loc.gov/, accessed

November 1, 2001. Historic American Buildings Survey/Historic American Engineering Record Web site.

Hohmann, John W.
1989   *A Phase I Archaeological Reconnaissance of the Proposed Rillito Creek Recharge Site for Camp Dresser & McKee, Inc., Tucson, Arizona.* Louis Berger and Associates, Phoenix.

Homburg, Jeffrey A., and Alexander Kurota
2000   *Cultural Resources for the Pantano Wash Bank Protection Project: Craycroft Road to Tucson Country Club, Tucson, Pima County, Arizona.* Technical Report 00-47. Statistical Research, Tucson.

Huckell, Bruce B.
1982   *The Distribution of Fluted Points in Arizona: A Review and an Update.* Archaeological Series No. 145. Cultural Resource Management Division, Arizona State Museum, Tucson.

1984a   Sobaipuri Sites in the Rosemont Area. In *Miscellaneous Archaeological Studies in the ANAMAX-Rosemont Land Exchange Area,* by Martyn D. Tagg, R. G. Ervin, and Bruce B. Huckell, pp. 107–146. Archaeological Series No. 147, pt. 4. Cultural Resource Management Division, Arizona State Museum, Tucson.

1984b   The Paleoindian and Archaic Occupation of the Tucson Basin: An Overview. *The Kiva* 49:133–145.

1984c   *The Archaic Occupation of the Rosemont Area, Northern Santa Rita Mountains, South-eastern Arizona.* Archaeological Series No. 147. Arizona State Museum, University of Arizona, Tucson.

1987   Summary and Conclusions. In *The Corona de Tucson Project: Prehistoric Use of a Bajada Environment,* by Bruce B. Huckell, Martyn D. Tagg, and Lisa W. Huckell, pp. 261–296. Archaeological Series No. 147. Cultural Resource Management Division, Arizona State Museum, Tucson.

1993   *Archaeological Testing of the Pima Community College Desert Vista Campus Property: The Valencia North Project.* Technical Report No. 92-13. Center for Desert Archaeology, Tucson.

1995   *Of Marshes and Maize: Prehistoric Agricultural Settlements in the Cienega Valley, South-eastern Arizona.* Anthropological Paper No. 59. University of Arizona Press, Tucson.

1998   Alluvial Stratigraphy of the Santa Cruz River Bend Reach. In *Archaeological Investigations of Early Village Sites in the Middle Santa Cruz Valley: Analyses and Synthesis*, Part 1, edited by Jonathan B. Mabry, pp. 31–56. Anthropological Papers No. 19, Center for Desert Archaeology, Tucson.

Huckell, Bruce B., and Lisa W. Huckell
1982   Archaeological Test Excavations at Tubac State Park. In *Archaeological Test Excavations in Southern Arizona,* compiled by S. A. Brew, pp. 63–102. Archaeological Series No. 152. Arizona State Museum, University of Arizona, Tucson.

Hughes, Lt. Col. R. P.
    1885   Endorsement of an inspection report submitted to the Adjutant General, Division of the Pacific, United States Army, October 14, 1885. Typed transcription of microfilm copy. Fort Lowell Records, Ms. 266, 1869–1890, folder 3. On file, Arizona Historical Society, Tucson.

Hughston, Caroline Mary
    1911   *Old Fort Lowell*. State Consolidated Publishing, Tucson.

Huntington, Frederick
    1982   *Archaeological Data Recovery at AZ BB:9:72 (ASM), the Band Quarters Kitchen and Corral Wall at Fort Lowell, and AZ BB:9:54 (ASM), a Rincon Phase Habitation Site, Craycroft Road, Tucson, Arizona.* Archaeological Series No. 163. Cultural Resource Management Division, Arizona State Museum, Tucson.

Hyde, Charles K.
    1998   *Copper for America: The United States Copper Industry from Colonial Times to the 1990s.* University of Arizona Press, Tucson.

Irvin, G. W.
    1987   A Sequential History of Arizona Railroad and Mining Development, 1864–1920. In *History of Mining in Arizona,* edited by J. Michael Canty and Michael N. Greeley, pp. 253–278. Mining Club of the Southwest Foundation, American Institute of Mining Engineers Tucson Section, Tucson, and Southwestern Minerals Exploration Association, Tucson.

Jackson, Robert H.
    1994   *Indian Population Decline: The Missions of Northwestern New Spain, 1687–1840.* University of New Mexico Press, Albuquerque.

Janus Associates
    1989   *Transcontinental Railroading in Arizona, 1878–1940: A Component of the Arizona Historic Preservation Plan.* Janus Associates, Phoenix. Submitted to the Arizona State Historic Preservation Office, Phoenix.

Jewett, E. D. (editor)
    1986   *Across the Dry Rillito II.* Territorial Publishers, Tucson.

Johnson, Alfred E.
    1960   Archaeological Investigations at Fort Lowell. Manuscript on file, Arizona State Museum Library, University of Arizona, Tucson.

Johnson, William, Alan F. Arbogast, and Jeffrey A. Homburg
    1997   Alluvial Geomorphology and Geoarchaeology of the Lower Verde River. In *Agricultural, Subsistence, and Environmental Studies,* edited by J. A Homburg and R. Ciolek-Torrello, pp. 17–32. Vanishing River: Landscapes and Lives of the Lower Verde Valley: The Lower Verde Archaeological Project, vol. 2. CD-ROM. SRI Press, Tucson.

Jones, Bruce A., and Richard Ciolek-Torrello

1991   *Caverns, Quarries & Campsites: Land Use Among the Prehistoric and Historic Occupants of Colossal Cave Preservation Park, Pima County.* Technical Series 31. Statistical Research, Tucson.

Jones, Oakah L.

1979   *Los Paisanos: Spanish Settlers on the Northern Frontier of New Spain.* University of Oklahoma Press, Norman

Jones, Jeffrey T.

1995a *Archaeological Test Excavations at AZ EE:1:194 (ASM) and Surface Mapping of Nearby Archaeological Sites for the Santa Rita Springs Property Development in Green Valley, Pima County, Arizona.* Archaeology Report No. 94-3. Old Pueblo Archaeology Center, Tucson.

1995b *Archaeological Test Excavations at the Green Valley Electrical Substation Portion of AZ EE:1:32 (ASM) for Tucson Electric Power Company in Green Valley, Pima County, Arizona.* Archaeology Report No. 95-3. Old Pueblo Archaeology Center, Tucson.

1996   *Removal of a Possibly Protohistoric O'odham Human Burial from a Gravel Pit along Indian Agency Road in Tucson, Arizona.* Letter Report No. 95-12. Old Pueblo Archaeology Center, Tucson.

1997   *Archaeological Excavations at the Continental Site in Green Valley, Pima County, Arizona, in 1995: An Investigation of the Portion of Site AZ EE:1:32 (ASM) within Tucson Electric Power Company's Substation Expansion Zone.* Archaeology Report No. 9. Old Pueblo Archaeology Center, Tucson.

1998a Hohokam of the Southern Frontier: Excavations at the Continental Site, a Classic Period Village South of Tucson, Arizona. *The Kiva* 63:197–216.

1998b *Archaeological Test Excavations at the Hardy Site and Site AZ BB:9:324 (ASM) on the Adobes del Bosque Property at Presidio and Craycroft Roads in Tucson, Pima County, Arizona.* Letter Report No. 98-019. Old Pueblo Archaeology Center, Tucson.

1999   *Archaeological Test Excavations for the Genesee Company along Silverbell Road North of Grant Road in Tucson, Arizona.* Technical Report No. 99-2. Old Pueblo Archaeology Center, Tucson.

2000   *Cultural Resources Survey of 0.90 Acres north of River Road and West of Campbell Avenue in Pima County, Arizona (PI200-082).* Letter Report No. 2000.038. Old Pueblo Archaeology Center, Tucson.

Jones, Jeffrey T., and Allen Dart

1997   *Archaeological Testing at Sites AZ BB:9:314 (ASM) and AZ BB:9:315 (ASM) on the Sterling-Pantano Farms Property in Tucson, Arizona, and a Mitigation Plan for Site AZ BB:9:315.* Letter Report No. 97-5. Old Pueblo Archaeology Center, Tucson.

Jordan, Frank W.

    1959   Biographical notes on Frank Wilder Jordan. On file, Arizona Historical Society, Tucson.

Julien, Nephi

    2000   Nephi Julien's Web Pages. Temples of the Church of Jesus Christ of Latter-day Saints. Snowflake Arizona Temple. Electronic document, http://www.nephi.com/temples/ united_states/south_west/snowflake_arizona.htm, accessed April 16, 2002.

Kaldahl, Eric J.

    1999   *Archaeological Test Excavations at AZ BB 13:124 (ASM) near the Los Reales and Wilmot Roads Intersection in Tucson, Arizona.* Technical Report 99-6. Old Pueblo Archaeology Center, Tucson.

Katzer, Keith L.

    1989   The Stratigraphy and Geomorphic History of the Los Morteros Canals (AZ AA:12:57, Locus 1). In *Archaeological Investigations at Los Morteros, AZ AA:12:57 (ASM), Locus 1, in the Northern Tucson Basin,* edited by Mary Bernard-Shaw, pp. 57-72. Technical Report No. 87-8. Institute for American Research.

Kaut, Charles R.

    1957   *The Western Apache Clan System: Its Origin and Development.* Publications in Anthropology No. 9. University of New Mexico, Albuquerque.

Keane, Melissa, and Allen E. Rogge

    1992   *Gold and Silver Mining in Arizona, 1848–1945: A Context for Historic Preservation Planning.* Research Paper No. 6. Dames and Moore, Phoenix.

Keith, Stanton B.

    1974   *Index of Mining Properties in Pima County, Arizona.* Bulletin No. 189. Arizona Bureau of Mines, University of Arizona, Tucson.

Kelly, Isabel T.

    1978   *The Hodges Ruin: A Hohokam Community in the Tucson Basin.* Anthropological Paper No. 30. University of Arizona Press, Tucson.

Kessell, John L.

    1970   *Mission of Sorrows: Jesuit Guevavi and the Pimas, 1691–1767.* University of Arizona Press, Tucson.

    1976   *Friars, Soldiers, and Reformers: Hispanic Arizona and the Sonora Mission Frontier, 1769–1856.* University of Arizona Press, Tucson.

King, Thomas F., Patricia P. Hickman, and Gary Berg

    1977   *Anthropology in Historic Preservation: Caring for Culture's Clutter.* Academic Press, New York.

Kinkade, Gay M., and Gordon L. Fritz

    1975   *The Tucson Sewage Project: Studies at Two Archaeological Sites in the Tucson Basin.* Archaeological Series No. 64. Arizona State Museum, Tucson.

Klawon, Jeanne E., William R. Dickinson, and Philip A. Pearthree
  1999 *Surficial Geology and Geologic Hazards of the Northern Tucson Basin, Pima County, Arizona: Tucson North and Sabino Canyon Quadrangles*. Open-File Report 99-21, Arizona Geological Survey, Tucson.

Kottlowski, R. E., M. E. Cooley, and R. V. Ruhe
  1965 Quaternary Geology of the Southwest. In *The Quaternary of the United States*, edited by H. E. Wright and D. C. Frey, pp. 287–298. Princeton University Press, Princeton, New Jersey.

Kozak, David L., and David I. Lopez
  1999 *Devil Sickness and Devil Songs: Tohono O'odham Poetics*. Smithsonian Institution Press, Washington, D.C.

Kupel, Douglas E.
  1986 Diversity through Adversity: Tucson Basin Water Control Since 1854. Unpublished Master's thesis, Department of History, University of Arizona, Tucson.

Kwiatkowski, Scott
  1996 *Archaeological Investigations in the Vicinity of the Historic Yuma Waterworks, Power Plant, and Gas Plant, Yuma, Yuma County, Arizona*. Project Report No. 96-56. Archaeological Research Services, Tempe.

Lacy, John C.
  1987 Early History of Mining in Arizona: Acquisition of Mineral Rights, 1539–1866. In *History of Mining in Arizona*, edited by J. Michael Canty and Michael N. Greeley, pp. 1–12. Mining Club of the Southwest Foundation, American Institute of Mining Engineers Tucson Section, Tucson, and Southwestern Minerals Exploration Association, Tucson.

Lamar, Howard
  1966 *The Far Southwest, 1846–1912: A Territorial History*. Yale University Press, New Haven, Connecticut.

Leavengood, Betty
  1999 In Search of Pontatoc. *Desert Leaf* (Tucson) 13(10):56.

Lenhart, Austin
  1996 *An Archaeological Survey of the North Mountain Park Property in Tucson, Pima County, Arizona, for ContraVest Properties*. Letter Report No. 96-12. Old Pueblo Archaeology Center, Tucson.

Levi, Laura J.
  1996 *Archaeological Monitoring in the Barrio Libre, Tucson, Arizona*. Technical Report No. 96-9. Center for Desert Archaeology, Tucson.

Limerick, Patricia Nelson
  1987 *The Legacy of Conquest: The Unbroken Past of the American West*. W. W. Norton, New York.

Limerick, Patricia Nelson, Clyde A. Milner, and Charles E. Rankin (editors)
    1991   *Trails: Toward a New Western History.* University Press of Kansas, Lawrence, Kansas.

Lister, Florence C., and Robert H. Lister
    1989   *The Chinese of Early Tucson: Historic Archaeology from the Tucson Urban Renewal Project.* University of Arizona Press, Tucson.

Lockwood, Frank C., and Donald W. Page
    n.d.   *Tucson—the Old Pueblo.* The Manufacturing Stationers, Phoenix.

Logan, Michael F.
    2002   *The Lessening Stream: An Environmental History of the Santa Cruz River.* University of Arizona Press, Tucson.

Luckingham, Bradford
    1982   *The Urban Southwest: A Profile History of Albuquerque-El Paso-Phoenix-Tucson.* Texas Western Press, El Paso.

Lyons, Bettina
    1981   *A History of the J. Knox Corbett House and the J. Knox Corbett Family.* Tucson Museum of Art, Tucson.

Mabry, Jonathan
    1990a   Correspondence, Mabry to City of Tucson, Department of Transportation, Real Estate Division. 31 October. Desert Archaeology Letter Report 90-123. On file, Arizona State Museum, Tucson.

    1990b   Correspondence, Mabry to City of Tucson, Department of Transportation, Real Estate Division. 17 December. Desert Archaeology Letter Report 90-131. On file, Arizona State Museum, Tucson.

    1991   The History of Cattle Ranching in the Cañada del Oro Valley. In *Archaeological Testing at the Romero Ruin,* by Deborah L. Swartz, pp. 57–78. Technical Report No. 91-2. Center for Desert Archaeology, Tucson.

Mabry, Jonathan B. (editor)
    1998   *Archaeological Investigations of Early Village Sites in the Middle Santa Cruz Valley: Analysis and Synthesis.* Anthropological Papers No. 19. Center for Desert Archaeology, Tucson.

Mabry, Jonathan B., and Jeffery J. Clark
    1994   Early Village Life on the Santa Cruz River. *Archaeology in Tucson* 8(1)1–5.

Mabry, Jonathan B., Deborah L. Swartz, Helga Wöcherl, Jeffrey J. Clark, Gavin H. Archer, and Michael W. Lindeman
    1997   *Archaeological Investigations of Early Village Sites in the Middle Santa Cruz Valley: Descriptions of the Santa Cruz Bend, Square Hearth, Stone Pipe, and Canal Sites.* Anthropological Papers No. 18. Center for Desert Archaeology, Tucson.

Mabry, Jonathan B., and J. Homer Thiel
   1995   A Thousand Years of Irrigation in Tucson. *Archaeology in Tucson* 9(4):1–6.

Machette, Michael N.
   1985   Calcic Soils of the Southwestern United States. In *Soils and Quaternary Geology of the Southwestern United States*, edited by D.L. Weide, pp. 1–21. Special Paper 203. Geological Society of America, Boulder, Colorado.

Madsen, John H.
   1996a   *Survey of Christopher City for the University of Arizona, Land Planning*. Letter Report. Cultural Resources Management Division, Arizona State Museum, Tucson.

   1996b   *Survey of University of Arizona Parcel B, Fort Lowell Road at Swan Road*. Letter Report. Cultural Resources Management Division, Arizona State Museum, Tucson.

   1996c   *Survey of University of Arizona Parcel C, Fort Lowell Road at Swan Road*. Letter Report. Cultural Resources Management Division, Arizona State Museum, Tucson.

Majewski, Teresita
   1998   Historical Profiles of the Apache and Yavapai Reservations in Arizona. In *Overview, Synthesis, and Conclusions,* edited by Stephanie M. Whittlesey, Richard Ciolek-Torrello, and Jeffrey H. Altschul, pp. 319–336. Vanishing River: Landscapes and Lives of the Lower Verde Valley: The Lower Verde Archaeological Project. SRI Press, Tucson.

Maldonado, Ronald P.
   1988   *An Archaeological Survey for the Proposed Stone Avenue Extension Alignment*. Cultural and Environmental Systems, Tucson.

Manje, Juan M.
   1954   *Unknown Arizona and Sonora 1693–1721*. Translated by Harry J. Karns and Associates. Arizona Silhouettes, Tucson.

Mann, Christine Toler
   1991   Binghampton Historic District: A Study of an Urban Neighborhood's Attempt to Gain Historic District Status. Unpublished Master's thesis, School of Renewable Natural Resources, University of Arizona, Tucson.

Marmaduke, William S.
   1983   *The Rillito River Project Archaeological Review and Assessment*. Northland Research, Flagstaff, Arizona.

Martin, Douglas D.
   1960   *The Lamp in the Desert: The Story of the University of Arizona*. University of Arizona Press, Tucson.

Martin, Patricia Preciado
   1983   *Images and Conversations: Mexian Americans Recall a Southwestern Past*. University of Arizona Press, Tucson.

Masse, W. Bruce

    1981   A Reappraisal of the Protohistoric Sobaipuri Indians of Southeastern Arizona. In *The Proto-historic Period in the North American Southwest, A.D. 1450–1700,* edited by David R. Wilcox and W. Bruce Masse, pp. 28–56. Anthropological Research Paper No. 24. Arizona State University, Tempe.

    1985   The Peppersauce Wash Project: Excavations at Three Multicomponent Sites in the Lower San Pedro Valley, Arizona. Manuscript on file, Arizona State Museum Library, University of Arizona, Tucson.

Mattison, Ray H.

    1946   Early Spanish and Mexican Settlements in Arizona. *New Mexico Historical Review* 21:273–327.

Mayro, Linda

    1986   *Letter to Becky S. Pearson, 15 October 1986.* On file, Arizona State Museum site files, University of Arizona, Tucson.

    1987a   *Alvernon Way Bridge/Rillito River.* Letter Report. Institute for American Research, Tucson. Submitted to Pima County Transportation and Flood Control District, April 28, W.O. 4BBRGH.

    1987b   *Alvernon Way Bridge/Rillito River.* Letter Report. Institute for American Research, Tucson. Submitted to Pima County Transportation and Flood Control District, September 24, W.O. 4BBRGH.

    1987c   *Alamo Wash: Glenn Street to Rillito River.* Letter Report. Institute for American Research, Tucson. Submitted to Pima County Transportation and Flood Control District, W.O. 4FAWFL.

    1988   Letter to Becky S. Pearson, 9 August 1988. On file, Arizona State Museum site files, University of Arizona, Tucson.

    1999   *Ranching in Pima County, Arizona: A Conservation Objective of the Sonoran Desert Conservation Plan.* Pima County Board of Supervisors, Tucson.

Mazany, Terry

    1981   *Archaeological Test Excavations at the Lee Site, Downtown, Tucson.* Manuscript on file, Arizona State Museum Library, University of Arizona, Tucson.

McCarty, Kieran R., O.F.M.

    1976   *Desert Documentary: The Spanish Years, 1767–1821.* Monograph No. 4. Arizona Historical Society, Tucson.

    1981   *A Spanish Frontier in the Enlightened Age: Franciscan Beginnings in Sonora and Arizona, 1767–1770.* Academy of American Franciscan History, Washington, D.C.

1996   Jesuits and Franciscans. In *The Pimería Alta: Missions and More,* edited by James E. Officer, Mardith Schuetz-Miller, and Bernard L. Fontana, pp. 35–45. Southwestern Mission Research Center, Tucson.

McClintock, James H.
1985   *Mormon Settlement in Arizona.* University of Arizona Press, Tucson.

McDonald, James A., William B. Gillespie, and Mary M. Farrell
1995   Kentucky Camp. In *Tearing Up the Ground with Splendid Results: Historic Mining on the Coronado National Forest,* pp. 49–66. Heritage Resources Management Report No. 15. Southwestern Region, USDA Forest Service, Albuquerque.

McGuire, Randall H.
1979   *Rancho Punta de Agua: Excavations at a Historic Ranch near Tucson, Arizona.* Contribution to Highway Salvage Archaeology in Arizona No. 57. Arizona State Museum, University of Arizona, Tucson.

1983   Ethnic Group Status and Material Culture at the Rancho Punta de Agua. In *Forgotten Places and Things: Archaeological Perspectives on American History,* edited by Albert E. Ward, pp. 193–203. Contributions to Anthropological Studies No. 3. Center for Anthropological Studies, Albuquerque.

McKelvey, Nat
1958   Reckless, Romantic Redington. *Arizona Highways* 31(5):34–39.

McKittrick, Mary Anne
1988   *Surficial Geologic Maps of the Tucson Metropolitan Area.* Open-File Report No. 88-18. Arizona Geological Survey, Arizona.

Meyer, Michael C.
1996   *Water in the Hispanic Southwest: A Social and Legal History, 1550–1850.* University of Arizona Press, Tucson.

Moisés, Rosalio, Jane H. Kelley, and William Curry Holden
1971   *A Yaqui Life: The Personal Chronicle of a Yaqui Indian.* University of Nebraska Press, Lincoln.

Moorhead, Max L.
1975   *The Presidio: Bastion of the Spanish Borderlands.* University of Oklahoma Press, Norman.

Morrison, Roger B.
1985   Pliocene/Quaternary Geology, Geomorphology, and Tectonics of Arizona. In *Soils and Quaternary Geology of the Southwestern United States,* edited by David L. Weide, pp. 123–146. Special Paper 203. Geological Society of America, Boulder, Colorado.

Murphey, John W.
1930   Sales receipt, State Land Department, September 15, 1930. MS 568, John W. Murphey Papers, box 5, folder 84. On file at Arizona Historical Society, Tucson.

1939   Correspondence, John W. Murphey to Mrs. George R. Fansett, November 8, 1939. MS 568, John W. Murphey Papers, box 2, folder 33. On file at Arizona Historical Society, Tucson.

Myrick, David F.
1975   *The Southern Roads. Railroads of Arizona, Vol. 1*. Howell-North, Berkeley.

Nabhan, Gary P.
1982   *The Desert Smells Like Rain: A Naturalist in Papago Indian Country*. North Point, New York.

1983   Papago Fields: Arid Lands Ethnobotany and Agricultural Ecology. Unpublished Ph.D. dissertation, Department of Arid Lands Resource Sciences, University of Arizona, Tucson.

1985   *Gathering the Desert*. University of Arizona Press, Tucson.

National Archives
1870   Map of the southern part of Arizona showing wagon roads, trails, military posts, and the San Pedro River drainage basin. n.p. Map on file, University of Arizona Library, Tucson.

Naylor, Thomas H., and Charles W. Polzer (editors)
1986   *The Presidio and Militia on the Northern Frontier of New Spain: A Documentary History, Vol. 1: 1570–1700*. University of Arizona Press, Tucson.

Noll, Elizabeth, and R. Thomas Euler
1996   *Presidio Cultural Resource Monitoring and Evaluation of Parking Facilities*. Archaeological Report No. 96-107. SWCA, Tucson.

Norris, Frank Blaine
1976   The Southern Arizona Guest Ranch as a Symbol of the West. Unpublished Master's thesis, Department of Geography, Regional Development, and Urban Planning, University of Arizona, Tucson.

Officer, James
1987   *Hispanic Arizona, 1536–1856*. University of Arizona Press, Tucson.

1991   Mining in Hispanic Arizona: Myth and Reality. In *History of Mining in Arizona,* vol. 2, edited by J. Michael Canty and Michael N. Greeley, pp. 1–26. Mining Club of the Southwest Foundation, Tucson, and the American Institute of Mining Engineers Tucson Section, Tucson.

Old Pueblo Archaeology Center
2000   *Archaeological Test Excavations at AZ BB:9:24 (ASM) AZ BB:9:95 (ASM) near the Southwest Corner of River and Craycroft Roads, Pima County, Arizona*. Letter Report 2000-031. Old Pueblo Archaeology Center, Tucson.

Olsen, John W.
1978   A Study of Chinese Ceramics Excavated in Tucson. *The Kiva* 44:1–50.

1983   An Analysis of East Asian Coins Excavated in Tucson, Arizona. *Historical Archaeology* 17(2):41–55.

Olsen, Stanley
1974   The Domestic Animals of San Xavier del Bac. *The Kiva* 39:253–257.

Olson, Alan P.
1985   Archaeology at the Presidio of Tucson. *The Kiva* 50:251–270.

O'Mack, Scott, and Eric Eugene Klucas
2001   *San Xavier to San Agustín: An Overview of Cultural Resources for the Paseo de las Iglesias Feasibility Study, Pima County*. Draft. Technical Report 01-72. Statistical Research, Tucson.

O'Mack, Scott, and Charles R. Riggs
2001   *Archaeological Testing at AZ BB:9:356 (ASM) for the Pantano Wash Bank Protection Project, Pima County, Arizona*. Technical Report 01-51. Statistical Research, Tucson.

Opler, Morris E.
1937   An Outline of Chiricahua Apache Social Organization. In *Social Anthropology of North Amercian Tribes*, edited by Fred Eggan, pp. 171–239. University of Chicago Press, Chicago.

1941   *An Apache Life-Way: The Economic, Social, and Religious Institutions of the Chiricahua Indians*. University of Chicago Press, Chicago.

1942   *Myths and Tales of the Chiricahua Apache Indians*. Memoirs of the American Folklore Society 37. Menasha, Wisconsin.

1983   Chiricahua Apache. In *Southwest*, edited by Alfonso Ortiz, pp. 401–418. Handbook of North American Indians, vol. 10, William C. Sturtevant, general editor, Smithsonian Institution, Washington, D.C.

Orrell, F. L.
1998   Kentucky Camp and the Santa Rita Water and Mining Company. In *History of Mining in Arizona*, vol. 3, edited by J. Michael Canty, H. Mason Coggin, and Michael N. Greeley, pp. 113–132. Mining Foundation of the Southwest, Tucson.

Ortega Noriega, Sergio
1985a   El sistema de misiones jesuíticas: 1591–1699. In *Historia general de Sonora*, vol. 2, edited by Sergio Ortega Noriega and Ignacio del Río, pp.35–75. Gobierno del Estado de Sonora, Hermosillo.

1985b   Crecimiento y crisis del sistema misional: 1686–1767. In *Historia general de Sonora*, vol. 2, edited by Sergio Ortega Noriega and Ignacio del Río, pp. 111–150. Gobierno del Estado de Sonora, Hermosillo.

Painter, Muriel Thayer
1986   *With Good Heart: Yaqui Beliefs and Ceremonies in Pascua Village*. University of Arizona Press, Tucson.

Parkhurst, Janet H.
2001   *Binghampton Rural Historic Landscape, Pima County, Arizona.* National Register of Historic Places Registration Form. Prepared by Janet H. Strittmatter, Inc., Tucson.

Parkhurst, Janet H., Eric J. Kaldahl, James E. Ayres, and Allen Dart
2001   *Cultural Resources Survey and Historical Assessment for the River Road Expansion and Realignment between Campbell Avenue and Alvernon Way, and the Binghampton Public Park Development in Pima County, Arizona (Pima County W.O. 4TRRCA).* Draft. Technical Report No. 2001.005. Old Pueblo Archaeology Center, Tucson.

Pashley, E. F.
1966   Structure and Stratigraphy of the Central, Northern and Eastern Parts of the Tucson Basin, Pima County, Arizona. Unpublished Ph.D. Dissertation, University of Arizona, Tucson.

Pearthree, Marie Slezak, and Victor R. Baker
1987   *Channel Change along the Rillito Creek System of Southeastern Arizona 1941 through 1983.* Special Paper No. 6. Arizona Bureau of Geology and Mineral Technology, Geological Survey Branch, Tucson.

Perry, Richard M.
2000   *Archeological Survey of the Pantano Wash and Tanque Verde Creek for the Proposed Tanque Verde Creek, Craycroft Road to Sabino Canyon Road Bank Protection and Riparian Preserve Project.* U.S. Army Corps of Engineers, Los Angeles District, Los Angeles.

Peterson, Charles S.
1973   *Take Up Your Mission: Mormon Colonizing along the Little Colorado River, 1870–1900.* University of Arizona Press, Tucson.

Peterson, Thomas H., Jr.
1963   Fort Lowell, A.T., Army Post During the Apache Campaigns. *The Smoke Signal* 8:1–19. Tucson Corral of the Westerners.

Pfefferkorn, Ignaz
1989   *Sonora: A Description of the Province.* Translated and annotated by Theodore E. Treutlein. Reprinted. University of Arizona Press, Tucson. Originally published 1949, University of New Mexico Press, Albuquerque.

Pilles, Peter J., Jr.
1981   A Review of Yavapai Archaeology. In *The Protohistoric Period in the North American Southwest, A.D. 1450–1700*, edited by David R. Wilcox and W. Bruce Masse, pp. 163–182. Anthropological Research Papers No. 24. Arizona State University, Tempe.

Pima County
1922   Official relief map of Pima County including Santa Cruz County, Arizona. Compiled by the Pima County Highway Department. On file, Arizona Historical Society, Tucson.

1932   Map of Pima County including Santa Cruz County, Arizona. Compiled by the Pima County Highway Department. On file, Arizona Historical Society, Tucson.

1954   Aerial photograph DHQ-3N-99, 17 February. On file, Mapping and Records Division, Pima County Transportation Department, Tucson.

1958   Legal Rights of Way, Tucson District: Pima County Engineer. Map on file, Arizona Historical Society, Tucson.

1960   Legal Rights of Way, Tucson District: Pima County Engineer. Map on file, Arizona Historical Society, Tucson.

1961   Legal Rights of Way, Tucson District: Pima County Engineer. Map on file, Arizona Historical Society, Tucson.

Pima Land and Water Company
1888   Right of Way to Pima Land and Water Company. Report No. 1670. House of Representatives, 50th Congress, First Session. Washington, D.C. On file, Arizona Historical Society, Tucson.

Pinkley, Frank
1936   Repair and Restoration of Tumacacori, 1921. *Southwestern Monuments Special Report* 10:261–284. USDI National Park Service, Washington, D.C.

Polzer, Charles W.
1968   Legends of Lost Missions and Mines. *The Smoke Signal* 18:170–183.

1976   *Rules and Precepts of the Jesuit Missions of Northwestern New Spain.* University of Arizona Press, Tucson.

1998   *Kino: His Life, His Works, His Missions, His Monuments.* Jesuit Fathers of Southern Arizona, Tucson.

Polzer, Charles W., and Thomas E. Sheridan
1997   *The Californias and Sinaloa-Sonora, 1700–1765.* The Presidio and Militia on the Northern Frontier of New Spain, vol. 2, pt. 1. University of Arizona Press, Tucson.

Radding, Cynthia
1997   *Wandering Peoples: Colonialism, Ethnic Spaces, and Ecological Frontiers in Northwestern Mexico, 1700–1850.* Duke University Press, Durham, North Carolina.

Rapp, G., Jr., and J. A. Gifford
1982   Archaeological Geology. *American Scientist* 70:45–53.

Ravesloot, John C.
1987a   Chronological Relationships of Features. In *The Archaeology of the San Xavier Bridge Site (AZ BB:13:14), Tucson Basin, Southern Arizona,* edited by John C. Ravesloot, pp. 61–69. Archaeological Series No. 171. Cultural Resource Management Division, Arizona State Museum, Tucson.

1987b   Results of Excavations: Feature Descriptions. In *The Archaeology of the San Xavier Bridge Site (AZ BB:13:14), Tucson Basin, Southern Arizona,* edited by John C. Ravesloot, pp. 155–179. Archaeological Series No. 171. Cultural Resource Management Division, Arizona State Museum, University of Arizona, Tucson.

Ravesloot, John C. (editor)
1987c   *The Archaeology of the San Xavier Bridge Site (AZ BB:13:14), Tucson Basin, Southern Arizona.* Archaeological Series No. 171. Cultural Resource Management Division, Arizona State Museum, University of Arizona, Tucson.

Ravesloot, John C., and Stephanie M. Whittlesey
1987   Interpreting the Protohistoric Period in Southern Arizona. In *The Archaeology of the San Xavier Bridge Site (AZ BB:13:14), Tucson Basin, Southern Arizona,* pts. 1 and 2. Archaeological Series 171. Cultural Resource Management Division, Arizona State Museum, University of Arizona, Tucson.

Rea, Amadeo M.
1997   *At the Desert's Green Edge: An Ethnobotany of the Gila River Pima.* University of Arizona Press, Tucson.

1998   *Folk Mammalogy of the Northern Pimans.* University of Arizona Press, Tucson.

Reff, Daniel T.
1990   *Disease, Depopulation, and Culture Change in Northwestern New Spain, 1518–1764.* University of Utah Press, Salt Lake City.

1998   The Jesuit Mission Frontier in Comparative Perspective: The Reductions of the Río de la Plata and the Missions of Northwestern Mexico, 1588–1700. In *Contested Ground: Comparative Frontiers on the Northern and Southern Edges of the Spanish Frontier,* edited by Donna J. Guy and Thomas E. Sheridan, pp. 16–31. University of Arizona Press, Tucson.

Reid, Jefferson, and Stephanie Whittlesey
1997   *The Archaeology of Ancient Arizona.* University of Arizona Press, Tucson.

Renk, Thomas
1969   A Guide to Recording Structural Details of Historic Buildings. *Historical Archaeology* 3:34–48.

Riley, Carrol L.
1975   The Road to Hawikuh: Trade and Trade Routes to Zuñi-Cíbola during Late Prehistoric and Early Historic Times. *The Kiva* 41:137–159.

1976   *Sixteenth-Century Trade in the Greater Southwest.* Mesoamerican Studies No. 10. University Museum, Southern Illinois University, Carbondale.

1985   The Location of Chichilticalle. In *Southwestern Culture History: Collected Papers in Honor of Albert H. Schroeder,* edited by C. H. Lange, pp. 153–163. Papers of the Archaeological Society of New Mexico No. 10. Ancient City Press, Santa Fe.

1987 *The Frontier People: The Greater Southwest in the Protohistoric Period.* University of New Mexico Press, Albuquerque.

Rillito Irrigation Project
1909 *Preliminary Report of [the] Special Irrigation Committee on the Rillito Irrigation Project.* Pamphlet. Papers of George E. P. Smith, Ms. 280, box 11, folder 18. On file, Special Collections, University of Arizona Library, Tucson.

Rillito Race Track
1988 Birthplace of an Industry . . . Rillito Race Track (pamphlet). Ms. 1196, box 1, folder 3. On file, Arizona Historical Society, Tucson.

Robinson, William J.
1963 Excavations at San Xavier del Bac, 1958. *The Kiva* 29:35–57.

1976 Mission Guevavi: Excavations in the Convento. *The Kiva* 42:135–175.

Rogers, Malcolm J.
1939 *Early Lithic Industries of the Lower Basin of the Colorado River and Adjacent Desert Areas.* Museum Papers No. 3. San Diego Museum of Man, San Diego.

1958 San Dieguito Implements From the Terraces of the Rincon-Pantano and the Rillito Drainage System. *The Kiva* 24(1):1–23.

Rogers, W. Lane
1993 From Colonia Dublán to Binghampton: The Mormon Odyssey of Frederick, Nancy, and Amanda Williams. *Journal of Arizona History* 35(1).

Roskruge, George J.
1885 Specifications for road from Martinez Ranch to San Pedro River, May 1885. Manuscript 697, George J. Roskruge Papers, box 2, folder 27. On file, Arizona Historical Society, Tucson.

1893 *Official Map of Pima County, Arizona.* Pima County Board of Supervisors, Tucson.

Roth, Barbara
1992 Sedentary Agriculturalists or Mobile Hunter-Gatherers? Evidence on the Late Archaic Occupation of the Northern Tucson Basin. *The Kiva* 57:291–314.

1995 Late Archaic Occupation of the Upper Bajada. *The Kiva* 61:189–207.

Roubicek, Dennis
1969 The Historical Archaeology of the Jacobs Mansion, Tucson, Arizona. Unpublished Honors thesis, College of Liberal Arts, University of Arizona, Tucson.

Rowe, Robert A., and Laurie V. Slawson
1999 *A Cultural Resources Inventory and Environmental Assessment for the Tanque Verde Interceptor along the Southern Bank of Tanque Verde Creek in Tucson, Arizona.* Technical Report No. 99-02. Aztlan Archaeology, Tucson.

Ruiz Engineering Corporation
  1985   *Rillito Corridor Study.* Prepared by Ruiz Engineering Corporation in association with Harland Bartholomew and Associates, Wilbur Smith and Associates, EDAW, and Simons, Li and Associates, Tucson.

Russell, Frank
  1908   The Pima Indians. In *Twenty-Sixth Annual Report of the Bureau of American Ethnology to the Secretary of the Smithsonian Institution 1904–1905*, pp. 3–389. Bureau of American Ethnology, Smithsonian Institution, Washington, D.C.

Ruthrauff, J. Moss
  n.d.   Map of Rillito Irrigation District [ca. 1910s–1920s]. On file, Arizona Historical Society, Tucson.

Sayles, E. B.
  1941   Archaeology of the Cochise Culture. In *The Cochise Culture,* by E. B. Sayles and Ernst Antevs, pp. 1–30. Medallion Papers No. 29. Gila Pueblo, Globe, Arizona.

  1983   *The Cochise Cultural Sequence in Southeastern Arizona.* Anthropological Paper No. 42. University of Arizona Press, Tucson.

Sayles, E. B., and Ernst Antevs
  1941   *The Cochise Culture.* Medallion Papers No. 29. Gila Pueblo, Globe, Arizona.

  1995   Mogollon, Hohokam, and Ootam: Rethinking the Early Formative Period in Southern Arizona. *The Kiva* 60:465–480.

Schellie, Don
  1968   *Vast Domain of Blood: The Story of the Camp Grant Massacre.* Westernlore Press, Los Angeles.

Schiffer, Michael B.
  1987   *Formation Processes of the Archaeological Record.* University of New Mexico Press, Albuquerque.

Schillingberg, William B.
  1999   *Tombstone, A.T.: A History of Early Mining, Milling, and Mayhem.* Arthur H. Clark, Spokane, Washington.

Schoenwetter, J.
  1981   Prologue to a Contextual Archaeology. *Journal of Archaeological Science* 8:367–379.

School District No. 16
  1931   Protest to Annexation to Amphitheater. 10 June. Manuscript on file, Arizona Historical Society, Tucson.

Schroeder, Albert H.
  1974a   A Study of the Apache Indians, Part V: "Tonto" and Western Apaches. In *Apache Indians IV*, edited by D. A. Horr, pp. 327–645. Garland, New York.

1974b A Study of Yavapai History. In *Yavapai Indians*, by A. H. Schroeder and A. B. Thomas, pp. 23–354. Garland American Indian Ethnohistory Series, D. A. Horr, general editor. Garland, New York.

Schuetz-Miller, Mardith, and Bernard L. Fontana
1996 Mission Churches of Northern Sonora. In *The Pimería Alta: Missions and More,* edited by James E. Officer, Mardith Schuetz-Miller, and Bernard L. Fontana, pp. 61–95. Southwestern Mission Research Center, Tucson.

Seymour, Deni J.
1989 The Dynamics of Sobaipuri Settlement in the Eastern Pimeria Alta. *Journal of the Southwest* 31:205–222.

Seymour, Deni J., Robert P. Jones, Robin Stipe-Davis, Kerry Nichols, and Laura L. Paskus
1997 *Archaeological Survey of 1,755 Acres for Vail Valley Ranch Development, Pima County, Arizona.* Report No. 124. Lone Mountain Archaeological Service, Albuquerque.

Shenk, Lynette O.
1976 *San José de Tumacácori: An Archaeological Synthesis and Research Design.* Archaeological Series No. 94. Arizona State Museum, University of Arizona, Tucson.

Shenk, Lynette O., and George A. Teague
1975 *Excavations at the Tubac Presidio.* Archaeological Series No. 85. Arizona State Museum, University of Arizona, Tucson.

Sheridan, Thomas
1986 *Los Tucsonenses: The Mexican Community in Tucson, 1854–1941.* University of Arizona Press, Tucson.

1988 Kino's Unforeseen Legacy: The Material Consequences of Missionization. *The Smoke Signal* 49–50:151–167.

1992 The Limits of Power: The Political Ecology of the Spanish Empire in the Greater Southwest. *Antiquity* 66:153–171.

1995 *Arizona: A History.* University of Arizona Press, Tucson.

2000 Human Ecology of the Sonoran Desert. In *A Natural History of the Sonoran Desert,* edited by Steven J. Phillips and Patricia W. Comus, pp. 105–118. Arizona-Sonora Desert Museum Press, Tucson, and University of California Press, Berkeley.

Sheridan, Thomas E., Charles W. Polzer, Thomas H. Naylor, and Diana W. Hadley (editors)
1991 *The Franciscan Missions of Northern Mexico.* Garland, New York.

Sherman, James E., and Edward F. Ronstadt
1975 Wagon Making in Southern Arizona. *The Smoke Signal* 31:2–20.

Simpson, Kay, and Susan J. Wells

    1983   *Archaeological Survey in the Eastern Tucson Basin, Saguaro National Monument, Rincon Mountain Unit, Cactus Forest Area.* Publication in Anthropology 22(1). Western Archeological and Conservation Center, USDI National Park Service, Tucson.

    1984   *Archaeological Survey in the Eastern Tucson Basin, Saguaro National Monument, Rincon Mountain Unit, Tanque Verde Ridge, Rincon Creek, Mica Mountain Areas.* Publication in Anthropology 22(3). Western Archeological and Conservation Center, USDI National Park Service, Tucson.

Sires, Earl W., Jr.

    1987   Hohokam Architectural Variability and Site Structure During the Sedentary–Classic Transition. In *The Hohokam Village: Site Structure and Organization,* edited by David E. Doyel, pp. 171–182. Southwestern and Rocky Mountain Division, American Association for the Advancement of Science, Glenwood Springs, Colorado.

Slaughter, Mark C.

    1996   Architectural Features. In *Excavation of the Gibbon Springs Site, A Classic Period Village in the Northeastern Tucson Basin,* edited by Mark C. Slaughter and Heidi Roberts, pp. 69–140. Archaeological Report No. 94-87. SWCA, Tucson.

Slaughter, Mark C., Susan B. Bierer, and Linda M. Gregonis

    1995   *Archaeological Monitoring of Tree Holes at the Roy P. Drachman Agua Caliente Park: The Whiptail Site and Agua Caliente Ranch Site, Pima, County, Arizona.* Archaeological Report No. 95-46. SWCA, Tucson.

Slaughter, Mark C., Susan B. Bierer, and David A. Phillips, Jr.

    1993   *Archaeological Test Excavations at AZ BB:9:242 (ASM), The Sabino Springs Project, Pima County, Arizona.* Archaeological Report No. 93-89. SWCA, Tucson.

Slawson, Laurie V., David C. Hanna, Skip Miller, and Ronald P. Maldonado

    1987   *The Espinosa Site: An Example of Prehistoric and Historic Utilization of the Santa Cruz River.* Southwest Cultural Series No. 8. Cultural and Environmental Systems, Tucson.

Sliva, Jane

    1998   *Archaeological Survey of Four Water Main Alignments North of Glenn Street near Swan Road, Tucson, Arizona (DAI Project No. 98-120M).* Letter Report No. 98-155. Desert Archaeology, Tucson.

Smiley, Terah, Henry F. Dobyns, Bonnie Jones, and James T. Barter

    1953   *San José de Tucson, Its History and Archaeological Exploration.* Manuscript on file, Arizona State Museum Library, University of Arizona, Tucson.

Smith, Cornelius C., Jr.

    n.d.   *Tanque Verde: The Story of a Frontier Ranch, Tucson, Arizona.* Privately printed.

    1967   *William Sanders Oury: History-Maker of the Southwest.* University of Arizona Press, Tucson.

Smith, George E. P.

n.d.   The Work of the Irriga[tion] Eng[ineering] Department of the University of Arizona. Undated manuscript. Papers of George E. P. Smith, Ms. 280, box 10, folder 2. On file, Special Collections, University of Arizona Library, Tucson.

1907   *Cement Pipe for Small Irrigating Systems and Other Purposes.* University of Arizona Agricultural Experiment Station Bulletin No. 55. University of Arizona, Tucson.

1910   *Groundwater Supply and Irrigation in the Rillito Valley.* University of Arizona Agricultural Experiment Station Bulletin No. 64. University of Arizona, Tucson.

1911a   Report to Messrs. Chas. H. Bayless, R. D. Cole and F. W. Jordan on the underflow ditches near Fort Lowell. Unsigned manuscript, apparently by George E. P. Smith. AZ 563, Papers of Harold Christy Schwalen, Box 34, folder 21. On file, Special Collections, University of Arizona Library, Tucson.

1911b   Signed letter to Hon. W. H. Sawtelle, 21 October. AZ 563, Papers of Harold Christy Schwalen, Box 34, folder 21. On file, Special Collections, University of Arizona Library, Tucson.

1911c   Irrigation Investigations. In *Twenty-Second Annual Report*, pp. 566–572. University of Arizona Agricultural Experiment Station, Tucson.

1913   *Weirs for Irrigating Streams.* Rev. edition. Timely Hints for Farmers No. 57. University of Arizona Agricultural Experiment Station, Tucson.

1918   *Machine-Made Cement Pipe for Irrigation Systems and Other Purposes.* University of Arizona Agricultural Experiment Station Bulletin No. 64. University of Arizona, Tucson.

1933   *The Financial Rehabilitation of Irrigation and Drainage Districts.* University of Arizona Agricultural Experiment Station Bulletin No. 144. University of Arizona, Tucson.

1936   *Groundwater Law in Arizona and Neighboring States.* University of Arizona Agricultural Experiment Station Technical Bulletin No. 65. University of Arizona, Tucson.

1938   *The Physiography of Arizona Valleys and the Occurrence of Ground Water.* University of Arizona Agricultural Experiment Station Technical Bulletin No. 77. University of Arizona, Tucson.

1955   Publications. Tucson [no publisher]. On file, Special Collections, University of Arizona Library, Tucson.

1964   Underground Water Supplies for Tucson. Ms. 741, G. E. P. Smith Papers, 1880–1961. On file, Arizona Historical Society, Tucson.

1967   My Trips into the Cordon of Mountains Surrounding Tucson. Ms. 741, G. E. P. Smith Papers, 1880–1961. On file, Arizona Historical Society, Tucson.

Soil Survey Staff

    1994   *Keys to Soil Taxonomy* (6th edition). U.S. Department of Agriculture, Soil Conservation Service, Pocahontas Press, Blacksburg, Virginia.

Sonnichsen, C. L.

    1982   *Tucson: The Life and Times of an American City.* University of Oklahoma Press, Norman.

Southwestern Mission Research Center

    1986   *Tucson: A Short History.* Southwestern Mission Research Center, Tucson.

Spicer, Edward H.

    1940   *Pascua: A Yaqui Village in Arizona.* University of Chicago Press, Chicago.

    1954   *Potam: A Yaqui Village in Sonora.* Memoirs of the American Anthropological Association 77. Menasha, Wisconsin.

    1962   *Cycles of Conquest: The Impacts of Spain, Mexico, and the United States on the Indians of the Southwest, 1533–1960.* University of Arizona Press, Tucson.

    1980   *The Yaquis: A Cultural History.* University of Arizona Press, Tucson.

    1980   *Fort Lowell Historic District: "A Place in Time"—to Live In, to Visit, to Foster for the Future.* Fort Lowell Historic District Board, Tucson.

    1983   Yaqui. In *Southwest,* edited by Alfonso Ortiz, pp. 250–263. Handbook of North American Indians, vol. 10, William C. Sturtevant, general editor, Smithsonian Institution, Washington, D.C.

    n.d.   *Fort Lowell Community History Project.* Final Report to the Arizona Humanities Council. Electronic document, http://dizzy.library.arizona.edu/images/diverse/ftlowell/ftlowell.html, accessed April 10, 2002. Old Fort Lowell Neighborhood Web site.

Stein, J. K., and W. R. Farrand

    1985   Context and Geoarchaeology: An Introduction. In *Archaeological Sediments in Context,* edited by J. K. Stein and W. R. Farrand, pp. 1–3. Center for the Study of Early Man, University of Maine, Orono.

Stein, Pat H.

    1990   *Homesteading in Arizona, 1862–1940: A Guide to Studying, Evaluating, and Preserving Historic Homesteads.* Arizona State Historic Preservation Office, Phoenix.

    1993   Historical Resources of the Northern Tucson Basin. In *The Northern Tucson Basin Survey: Research Directions and Background Studies,* edited by John H. Madsen, Paul R. Fish, and Suzanne K. Fish, pp. 85–122. Archaeological Series No. 182. Arizona State Museum, Tucson.

    1994   *Historic Trails in Arizona from Coronado to 1940: A Component of the Arizona Historic Preservation Plan.* Report No. 94-72. SWCA Environmental Consultants, Flagstaff.

Stephen, David V. M.

1997   *Preliminary Report for Fort Lowell/Orlando Archaeological Survey.* Job. No. 97806. Submitted to The DeGrazia Company, Tucson. Professional Archaeological Services and Technologies (P.A.S.T.), Tucson.

1998   *Report for Presidio/Craycroft Road, NWC Archaeological Survey.* Job No. 980868. Submitted to Planners Ink Corporated, Tucson. Professional Archaeological Services and Technologies (P.A.S.T.), Tucson.

Sterner, Matthew A.

1996   *Schroeder's Well and the Davidson Flume: A Glimpse into Tucson's Mormon Culture.* Technical Report 96-5. Statistical Research, Tucson.

1999   Historical-Period Resources at Sunset Mesa Ruin. In *Investigations at Sunset Mesa Ruin: Archaeology at the Confluence of the Santa Cruz and Rillito Rivers, Tucson, Arizona*, edited by R. Ciolek-Torrello, E. K. Huber, and R. B. Neily, pp. 193–202. Technical Series 66. Statistical Research, Tucson.

Sterner, Matthew A., and Teresita Majewski

1998   *Homesteading and Ranching on Fort Huachuca's East Range: National Register of Historic Places Evaluations of the Slash Z Ranch Site (AZ EE:7:84 [ASM]) and Three Associated Sites (AZ EE:7:194 [ASM], AZ EE:7:196 [ASM], and AZ EE:7:201 [ASM]).* Technical Report 98-22. Statistical Research, Tucson.

Stolbrand, Vasa E.

1891   *Irrigation in Arizona.* University of Arizona Agricultural Experiment Station Bulletin No. 3. Tucson.

Stone, Lyle M.

1979   *Archaeological Research, Site Stabilization, and Interpretive Development Planning at Calabazas, an Historic Spanish Visita in Santa Cruz, County, Arizona.* Archaeological Research Services, Tempe.

Strittmatter, Janet H.

2000   *Architectural Evaluation of Historic Features of St. Philip's Church Plaza.* Report No. 00001. Janet H. Strittmatter, Inc., Tucson.

Sugnet, C. L., and J. Jefferson Reid (editors)

1994   *The Surface of Presidio Santa Cruz de Terrenate.* Bureau of Land Management, Tucson.

Swanson, Earl H., Jr.

1951   An Archaeological Survey of the Empire Valley. Unpublished Master's thesis, Department of Anthropology, University of Arizona, Tucson.

Swartz, Deborah L.

1991   *Archaeological Testing at the Romero Ruin.* Technical Report No. 91-2. Center for Desert Archaeology, Tucson.

1993   *Archaeological Testing at the Romero Ruin: Part 2.* Technical Report No. 93-8. Center for Desert Archaeology, Tucson.

Taylor, Bruce R.
1993   Oral history interview with Bruce R. Taylor, conducted by William H. Hale. On file, Arizona Historical Society, Tucson.

Teague, George A.
1980   *Reward Mine and Associated Sites: Historical Archeology on the Papago Reservation.* Publication in Anthropology No. 11. USDI National Park Service, Western Archeological and Conservation Center, Tucson.

Thiel, J. Homer
1993   *Archaeological Investigations of Tucson Block 94: The Boarding House Residents of the Hotel Catalina Site.* Technical Report No. 93-5. Center for Desert Archaeology, Tucson.

1995a   *Archaeological Testing along the A-Mountain Drainage System.* Technical Report No. 95-6. Center for Desert Archaeology, Tucson.

1995b   *Archaeological Testing on the Rio Nuevo South Property, Tucson, Arizona.* Technical Report No. 95-11. Center for Desert Archaeology, Tucson.

1995c   *Archaeological Testing of the Proposed Evo A. DeConcini Federal Building and United States Courthouse Property.* Technical Report No. 95-12. Center for Desert Archaeology, Tucson.

1995d   *Archaeological Test Excavations in Sunset Park, Tucson, Arizona.* Technical Report No. 95-15. Center for Desert Archaeology, Tucson.

1997   *Archaeological Survey of the Fort Lowell Alignment Extension Between Vista del Forte and Swan Road.* Letter Report No. 97-153. Desert Archaeology, Tucson.

1998a   *Uncovering Tucson's Past: Test Excavations in Search of the Presidio Wall.* Technical Report No. 98-1. Center for Desert Archaeology, Tucson.

1998b   In Search of El Presidio de Tucson. *Archaeology in Tucson* 12(3):1–4.

1998c   Uncovering the Story of Tucson's Chinese Gardeners. *Archaeology in Tucson* 12(2):1–5.

1998d   *Archaeological Testing Beneath the Duffield Addition to the Fish-Stevens-Duffield House, AZ BB:13:24 (ASM), Tucson, Arizona.* Technical Report 98-14. Center for Desert Archaeology, Tucson.

Thiel, J. Homer, and Danielle Desruisseaux
1993   *Archaeological Test Excavations for the Water Plant No. 1 Expansion, Historic Block 138, City of Tucson.* Technical Report No. 93-12. Center for Desert Archaeology, Tucson.

Thiel, J. Homer, Michael K. Faught, and James M. Bayman
1993   Archaeology in the Heart of Downtown Tucson. *Archaeology in Tucson* 7(3):1–5.

1995 *Beneath the Streets: Prehistoric, Spanish, and American Period Archaeology in Downtown Tucson.* Technical Report No. 94-11. Center for Desert Archaeology, Tucson.

Thrapp, Dan L.
1967 *The Conquest of Apacheria.* University of Oklahoma Press, Norman.

Tompkins, Charles Nichols
1997 *An Archaeological Assessment of a 5.6 Acre Parcel near the intersection of River Road and Craycroft Road, Tucson, Arizona.* Technical Report No. 97-04. Tierra Archaeological and Environmental Consultants, Tucson.

Tuck, Frank J.
1963 *History of Mining in Arizona.* 2nd rev. ed. State of Arizona Department of Mineral Resources, Phoenix.

Tucker, David B.
1997 *Data Recovery at Site AZ AA:12:311 (ASM) and Archaeological Monitoring for the Coventry Homes Pipeline Project.* Archaeological Report No. 97-177. SWCA, Tucson.

2000 *The Craycroft Road Survey: A Class III Cultural Resource Survey of Craycroft Road between River Road and Sunrise Drive, Tucson, Pima County, Arizona.* EEC Project No. A20050. SWCA, Tucson.

Tucson Citizen (TC) [Tucson]
1928 Pioneer Contractor Who Built Ft. Lowell Recalls Perils from the Apaches. 25 March.

1929 Rites for George H. Doe, Arizona Pioneer, at All Saints Church. 10 March.

1932 Vicksburg Hero Who Rode into Tucson 65 Years Ago Attends Memorial Services. 30 May.

1932 Civil War Hero and Builder of Old Arizona Forts Dies. 8 September.

Tucson City Directory
1940 Tucson City Directory. Arizona Directory Company, Tucson.

Tucson Magazine
1936 Catalina Foothills Estate. 9(1).

1938a Hacienda del Sol. 11(6).

1938b Verde Desert Ranch School. 11(6).

1939 Desert Ranch School of Arizona. 12(11).

Turner, Jeanne B.
n.d. The Old Chapel, an Introduction. In *Fieldnotes From a Neighborhood: A Portrait of the San Pedro Chapel.* Electronic document, http://dizzy.library.arizona.edu/images/diverse/ftlowell/ftlowell.html. Old Fort Lowell Neighborhood Web site.

Turner, Teresa

    1981   Of Ditches and Silos and Mormonees. Unpublished paper in the possession of the Old Fort Lowell Neighborhood Association, Tucson.

    1982a   *The People of Fort Lowell.* Fort Lowell Historic District Board, Tucson.

    1982b   *The People of Fort Lowell.* Rev. ed. Fort Lowell Historic District Board, Tucson.

    1990   *The People of Fort Lowell.* Rev. ed. Fort Lowell Historic District Board, Tucson.

Underhill, Ruth M.

    1938   *Singing for Power: The Song Magic of the Papago Indians of Southern Arizona.* University of California Press, Berkeley.

    1939   *The Social Organization of the Papago Indians.* Contributions to Anthropology No. 30. Columbia University, New York.

    1946   *Papago Indian Religion.* Contributions to Anthropology No. 33. Columbia University, New York.

Underhill, Ruth M., Donald M. Bahr, Baptisto Lopez, Jose Pancho, and David Lopez

    1979   *Rainhouse and Ocean: Speeches for the Papago Year.* University of Arizona Press, Tucson.

U.S. Geological Survey

    1905   Arizona (Pima County) Tucson Quadrangle. Map on file, Arizona Historical Society, Tucson.

Valley of the Moon Memorial Association

    1945   *The Valley of the Moon.* Handbill. Valley of the Moon Memorial Association. Ms. 828, box 1, folder 15. On file, Arizona Historical Society, Tucson.

Vanderpot, Rein, and Teresita Majewski

    1998   *The Forgotten Soldiers: Historical and Archaeological Investigations of the Apache Scouts at Fort Huachuca, Arizona.* Technical Series 71. Statistical Research, Tucson.

Vanderpot, Rein, Stephanie M. Whittlesey, and Susan A. Martin

    1993   *Archaeological Investigations at AZ AA:12:57/377: A Butterfield Stage Stop, the Ruelas Ranch, and a Hohokam Village (Los Morteros) near Point of the Mountain, Pima County, Arizona.* Technical Report 93-1. Statistical Research, Tucson.

Van Willigen, John

    1971   The Role of the Community Level Worker in Papago Indian Development. Unpublished Ph.D. dissertation, Department of Anthropology, University of Arizona, Tucson.

Villalobos, Ruth Bajza

    2002   Letter to James Garrison, Arizona State Historic Preservation Officer, regarding an archaeological survey for the Rillito River Ecosystem Restoration Project in Tucson, Arizona. 17 July. Los Angeles District, U.S. Army Corps of Engineers.

Vinik, Joanne Hamilton, and Salley Calkins Wegner
1984   National Register of Historic Places Inventory-Nomination Form, Rillito Racetrack Chute. On file, Arizona Historical Society, Tucson.

Wagoner, Jay J.
1952   *History of the Cattle Industry in Southern Arizona, 1540–1940.* University of Arizona Bulletin 23(2). Social Science Bulletin No. 20. University of Arizona, Tucson.

1970   *Arizona Territory, 1863–1912: A Political History.* University of Arizona Press, Tucson.

1975   *Early Arizona: Prehistory to Civil War.* University of Arizona Press, Tucson.

Walker, Henry P.
1973   Wagon Freighting in Arizona. *The Smoke Signal* 28:182–204.

Walker, Henry P., and Don Bufkin
1979   *Historical Atlas of Arizona.* University of Oklahoma Press, Norman.

Wallace, Henry D.
1995   *Archaeological Investigations at Los Morteros, a Prehistoric Settlement in the Northern Tucson Basin.* Anthropological Papers No. 17. Center for Desert Archaeology, Tucson.

1996   *Documentation of a Platform Mound Compound and Monitoring of the Excavation of a Septic System Leach Field within AZ BB:13:8, San Xavier District, Tohono O'odham Reservation.* Letter Report No. 96-128. Desert Archaeology, Tucson.

1998   *A Research Design for the Dove Mountain Project: The Archaeology and History of the Northern Tucson Basin.* Technical Report 98-9. Center for Desert Archaeology, Tucson.

2003   *Roots of Sedentism: Archaeological Excavations at Valencia Vieja, a Founding Village in the Tucson Basin of Southern Arizona.* Anthropological Papers No. 29. Center for Desert Archaeology, Tucson.

Wasley, William W.
1956   *History and Archaeology in Tucson.* Manuscript A-767. Manuscript on file, Arizona State Museum Archives, University of Arizona, Tucson.

Waters, Michael R.
1985   Late Quaternary Alluvial Stratigraphy of Whitewater Draw, Arizona: Implications for Regional Correlation of Fluvial Deposits in the American Southwest. *Geology* 13:705–708.

1987   Holocene Alluvial Geology and Geoarchaeology of AZ BB:13:14 and the San Xavier Reach of the Santa Cruz River, Arizona. In *The Archaeology of the San Xavier Bridge Site (AZ BB:13:14), Tucson Basin, Southern Arizona*, edited by John C. Ravesloot, pp. 39–60. Archaeological Series No. 171. Arizona State Museum, University of Arizona, Tucson.

1988a   Holocene Alluvial Geology and Geoarchaeology of the San Xavier Reach of the Santa Cruz River, Arizona. *Geological Society of America Bulletin* 100:479–491.

1988b   The Impact of Fluvial Processes and Landscape Evolution on Archaeological Sites and Settlement Patterns along the San Xavier Reach of the Santa Cruz River, Arizona. *Geoarchaeology* 3:205–219.

1992   *Principles of Geoarchaeology: A North American Perspective.* University of Arizona Press, Tucson.

Waugh, Rebecca J.
1995   Plainware Ceramics from the Midden at Presidio Santa Cruz de Terrenate, Arizona. Unpublished Master's thesis, Department of Anthropology, University of Arizona, Tucson.

Weaver, John
1947   The History of Fort Lowell. Unpublished Master's thesis, Department of Anthropology, University of Arizona.

Weber, David J.
1979   *New Spain's Far Northern Frontier: Essays on Spain in the American West.* University of New Mexico Press, Albuquerque.

1982   *The Mexican Frontier, 1821–1846: The American Southwest Under Mexico.* University of New Mexico Press, Albuquerque.

1988a   Turner, the Boltonians, and the Spanish Borderlands. In *Myth and the History of the Hispanic Southwest,* by D. J. Weber, pp. 33–54. University of New Mexico Press, Albuquerque.

1988b   John Francis Bannon and the Historiography of the Spanish Borderlands: Retrospect and Prospect. In *Myth and the History of the Hispanic Southwest,* by D. J. Weber, pp. 55–88. University of New Mexico Press, Albuquerque.

1988c   *Myth and the History of the Hispanic Southwest.* University of New Mexico Press, Albuquerque.

1991   Introduction. In *The Idea of Spanish Borderlands,* edited by D. J. Weber, pp. xiii–xxxviii. Garland, New York.

1992   *The Spanish Frontier in North America.* Yale University Press, New Haven, Connecticut.

Weed, Carol S.
1985   Letter from New World Research to Eva Folsom of Sun County Development. On file, Arizona State Museum, Tucson.

Wellman, Kevin D., and Mark C. Slaughter
2001   *Archaeological Investigations at Roy P. Drachman Agua Caliente Park: The Whiptail Site and Agua Caliente Ranch.* Cultural Resources Report No. 00-03. SWCA, Tucson.

Wells, Susan J., and Stacie A. Reutter
  1997   *Cultural Resources of the Tucson Mountain District, Saguaro National Park.* Publications in
          Anthropology No. 69. Western Archeological and Conservation Center, USDI National Park
          Service, Tucson.

West, Robert C.
  1993   *Sonora: Its Geographical Personality.* University of Texas Press, Austin.

Wetmore, Ralph A.
  n.d.   Biographical file. On file, Arizona Historical Society, Tucson.

Whalen, Norman M.
  1971   Cochise Culture Sites in the Central San Pedro Drainage, Arizona. Unpublished Ph.D.
          dissertation, Department of Anthropology, University of Arizona, Tucson.

Whittemore, Isaac T.
  1893   The Pima Indians, Their Manners and Customs. In *Among the Pimas; or the Mission to the
          Pima and Maricopa Indians,* edited by C. H. Cook, pp. 51–96. Printed for the Ladies' Union
          Mission School Association, Albany, New York.

Whittlesey, Stephanie M.
  1994   Three Centuries of Pottery in the Pimería Alta. Paper presented at the Prehistoric and
          Historic Archaeology of the Borderlands Symposium. Arizona Archaeological Council
          Spring Meeting, Tucson.

  1995   Mogollon, Hohokam, and Ootam: Rethinking the Early Formative Period in Southern
          Arizona. *The Kiva* 60:465–480.

  1997   Culture History: Prehistoric Narratives for Southern Arizona. In *Background and Research
          Design for Archaeological Resources*, by Carla R. Van West and Stephanie M. Whittlesey,
          pp. 45–80. Cultural Resource Management Plan for the Fairfield Canoa Ranch Property,
          vol. 1. Draft. Statistical Research, Tucson.

  1999   *Introduction and Results of Fieldwork.* Draft. Archaeological Investigations at the Julian
          Wash Site (AZ BB:13:17 ASM), Pima County, Arizona, vol. 1. Technical Report 99-27.
          Statistical Research, Tucson.

Whittlesey, Stephanie M., and Su Benaron
  1998   Yavapai and Western Apache Ethnohistory and Material Culture. In Overview, Synthesis,
          and Conclusions, edited by S. M. Whittlesey, R. Ciolek-Torrello, and J. H. Altschul, pp.
          143–183. Vanishing River: Landscapes and Lives of the Lower Verde Valley: The Lower
          Verde Archaeological Project. SRI Press, Tucson.

Whittlesey, Stephanie M., Richard S. Ciolek-Torello, and Matthew A. Sterner
  1994   *Southern Arizona the Last 12,000 Years: A Cultural-Historic Overview for the Western Army
          National Guard Aviation Training Site.* Technical Series 48. Statistical Research, Tucson.

Wilcox, David R., Thomas R. McGuire, and Charles Sternberg
  1981   *Snaketown Revisited.* Archaeological Series No. 155. Arizona State Museum, Tucson.

Williams, Jack S.

1986a   San Agustín del Tucsón: A Vanished Mission Community of the Pimería Alta. *The Smoke Signal* 47–48:112–128.

1986b   A Plan for Mission Visita of San Agustín del Tucson City Historic Park. Manuscript on file, Statistical Research, Tucson. Submitted to the City of Tucson.

1986c   The Presidio of Santa Cruz de Terrenate: A Forgotten Fortress of Southern Arizona. *The Smoke Signal* 47–48:129–148.

1988   Fortress Tucson: Architecture and the Art of War (1775–1856). *The Smoke Signal* 49–50:168–188.

1992   *Archaeological Investigations at the Captains' House at the Presidio of Tubac 1992.* Center for Spanish Colonial Archaeology, Mesa, Arizona.

Wilson, Eldred D.

1949   *History of Mining in Pima County, Arizona.* 5th rev. ed. Tucson Chamber of Commerce, Tucson.

1952   Arizona Gold Placers. In *Arizona Gold Placers and Placering,* 5th rev. ed., pp. 11–86. General Technology Series No. 45. Bulletin No. 160. Arizona Bureau of Mines, University of Arizona, Tucson.

Wilson, John P.

1995   The Mining Frontier. In *Tearing Up the Ground with Splendid Results: Historic Mining on the Coronado National Forest,* by Mary M. Farrell, William B. Gillespie, James A. Mc-Donald, Patricia M. Spoerl, and John P. Wilson, pp. 2–26. Heritage Resources Management Report No. 15. Southwestern Region, USDA Forest Service, Albuquerque.

Wood, Raymond W., and Donald Lee Johnson

1978   A Survey of Disturbance Processes in Archaeological Site Formation. In *Advances in Archaeological Method and Theory*, vol. 1, edited by Michael B. Schiffer, pp. 315–381. Academic Press, New York.

Wright, J. B.

1909   Plat of Rillito Park: Being a Subdivision of South ½ of Northeast ¼ and North ½ of Southeast ¼ of Section 23, Township 13 South, Range 13 East. Map on file, Arizona Historical Society, Tucson.

Xia, Jingfeng

2001   Foodways and Their Significance to Ethnic Integration: An Ethnoarchaeogical and Historical Archaeological Survey of the Chinese in Tucson. Unpublished Ph.D. dissertation, Department of Anthropology, University of Arizona, Tucson.

Yoder, Thomas D., Laural Myers, and Mark C. Slaughter

1996   *Archaeological Testing Report for the Proposed Juvenile Courts, Pima County, Arizona.* Archaeological Report No. 96-171. SWCA, Tucson.